D1126145

STUDIES IN THE
NEW TESTAMENT
I

STUDIES IN THE NEW TESTAMENT

BY

J. DUNCAN M. DERRETT

D.C.L. (Oxon.), LL.D., Ph.D. (Lond.), of Gray's Inn, Barrister;
Professor of Oriental Laws in the University of London

VOLUME ONE

GLIMPSES OF THE LEGAL AND SOCIAL PRESUPPOSITIONS OF THE AUTHORS

LEIDEN
E.J. BRILL
1977

By the Same Author

Law in the New Testament (Darton, Longman & Todd, London)
Jesus's Audience (Darton, Longman & Todd)

also

Religion, Law and the State in India (Faber & Faber, London)
Introduction to Legal Systems (edited) (Sweet & Maxwell, London)
Dharmaśāstra and Juridical Literature (Harrassowitz, Wiesbaden)
Bhāruci's Commentary on the Manusmṛti (Steiner, Wiesbaden)
Essays in Classical and Modern Hindu Law (Brill, Leiden)
and (translation)
R. Lingat, Classical Law of India (University of California Press)

ISBN 90 04 04928 2

Copyright 1977 by E.J. Brill, Leiden, Netherlands

PRINTED IN BELGIUM

Ἰδοὺ ὁ Νυμφίος ἔρχεται, ἐν τῷ μέσῳ τῆς νυκτός· καὶ μακάριος ὁ δοῦλος, ὃν εὑρήσει γρηγοροῦντα· ἀνάξιος δὲ πάλιν, ὃν εὑρήσει ῥᾳθυμοῦντα. Βλέπε οὖν, ψυχή μου, μὴ τῷ ὕπνῳ κατενεχθῇς, ἵνα μὴ τῷ θανάτῳ παραδοθῇς, καὶ τῆς βασιλείας ἔξω κλεισθῇς· ἀλλὰ ἀνάνηψον κράζουσα· Ἅγιος, Ἅγιος, Ἅγιος εἶ, ὁ Θεός, προστασίαις τῶν Ἀσωμάτων, σῶσον ἡμᾶς.

Ἀκολουθία τῆς Ἁγίας καὶ Μεγάλης Ἑβδομάδος [3] (1965), τῇ ἁγίᾳ καὶ μεγάλῃ δευτέρᾳ, ἐν τῷ ὄρθρῳ (p. 20).

TABLE OF CONTENTS
(with particulars of original locations)

PREFACE

When my *Law in the New Testament* appeared in 1970 I expected soon to see a companion volume follow it, which would include some conclusions to both. In expectation of that book several journals abstained from reviewing the first: perhaps with relief, since an adequate reviewer admittedly did not always present himself. This might well be the fate of a book written by one who has not been a pupil of the Scribes, and thus does not have an obvious home in the academic pigeon-loft. The continual flow of unexpected discoveries, each of which automatically imputes a corresponding oversight to the learned if it does not also impugn their methods, indeed arouses curiosity, but not without some dismay. This is a field in which anything which is disliked is open to be described as 'highly speculative', or 'hardly enlightening', whereas the familiar and oft-repeated, however ill-founded, will always excape the reviewer's censure.

My projected *Law and Midrash in the New Testament* has not materialised on account of forces which were beyond my control. In the meanwhile I gratefully take the opportunity of republishing, with a needed 'up-dating', with some important corrections also and indexes, a series of some thirty further articles, each demonstrating, in a compressed style, a technique.

It is time that some conclusions were outlined, to which there may be no hesitation in applying the mind. Whatever one thinks of technique, one wastes no time in appraising a man's conclusions. I shall be pronounced wrong in some quarters — one cannot please everyone. In a field where knowledge is out of the question, and nothing asserted, even by a person who is profoundly secure, can rise above conjecture, it is quite surprising that people know their own minds with just as much confidence as do their colleagues in, for example, my kind of world, wherein opinions may be verified.

My own motives, conscious and unconscious, have been ventilated at large in the preface-and-introduction to my *Jesus's Audience* (1973), which was written for young people. It introduced them to the idea that subjective considerations go far to determine nearly all of the results of even the most high-flying academic theological study, and must be seen to do so: there was room, therefore, for independent thought and research, even by those who, without such a warning, might otherwise have been discouraged by existing publications. One should never hesitate to rethink that very bizarre story, the 'history' of 'Jesus son of Joseph the building contractor said to have been domiciled at Nazareth', merely out of a suspicion that the story would somehow evaporate. If Jesus is to achieve anything he achieves it within the individual now, as he did then, and there is not the smallest evidence (rather the reverse) that that individual requires for that purpose any particular ignorance on the one hand, or any particular scholastic training on the other. The full-time academics do, however, owe it to the taxpayer to communicate as best they can whatsoever they have found out about the sources of information on this highly intricate subject, so subjectively framed, sources known to constitute the most difficult material extant, requiring the greatest number of mental resources and skills to expound. One may well enter with a just diffidence upon the subject of the New Testament, which has exhausted so many learned lives without hope of agreement, and has clothed the lofty walls of such spacious libraries. What would be inexcusable would be for one to refuse to enter, when he could do so, and to stop others from entering, whether upon the hypothesis that his own powers could never place him beside the names that have achieved greatness in the previous decades, or in the overt expectation that a youthful mind within reach of his voice or his pen could never outstrip both them and him.

The present work is in two volumes. The first embodies further evidence for the assertion that legal and social information illuminate parables and other *pericopai*. In other words technical background-information makes the passages concerned come to life, and enables us to discard the inadequate explanations hitherto swallowed perforce by persons less well guided. The second volume embodies the congruous but more provocative assertion that midrash, and literary devices in the nature of midrash, are illuminative of not only parables, but even actions of Jesus and accounts of his life (including the nativity). The slight overlapping and repetition in these studies is to be regreted in this volume, but it is the result of two factors, the slow moving away of the millennia-old mists, and the lack of tolerance on the part of editors for more than a bit of such researches at a time. Further at all but the earliest stages of my research the midrashic and the legal discoveries coincided and were found mutually supporting, though at different levels: therefore a perfect division between these two volumes is impossible, and overlapping occurs between them.

I did not, and do not set out when I commence a piece of research to achieve any particular object, except to clear a known doubt. I do not mind what the results suggest. Some astonishing things have come to light which I myself was much slower to accept than would appear from the printed page. My studies of the virgin birth and the resurrection (properly *anastasis*) are thought to be too shocking for conservative taste and cannot be published without a subvention and a fearless publisher. But when I set out on those two adventures in scholarship I had no idea what I should find. I should have thought that the results of both would be greatly in theologians' long term interests, but the estimate is long in finding support among the generation which supplies potential reviewers.

Unconcerned as I am about the results, I have never felt obliged to do as professional teachers and pastors must usually do, namely project an overarching or attractive thesis : hence I can tackle adjacent passages in isolation from each other, seeing where research takes me, unbothered by incongruity. The real inconsistencies of our material have, to some extent, been hidden from us by the scholars' tendency to iron them out. Ancient copyists of the gospels used to do this at the textual level; commentators and preachers must have done this from the first: the line of corrupters is of respectable age and shows no sign of dying out. There may, therefore, be merit in some activities which take place in scientific isolation, done by one with no axe to grind.

It seems that I may offer the following tentative conclusions, based upon what I published in my previous books and in the contents of these two volumes.

1. In his ministry Jesus behaved as a prophet, concentrating on preaching (described as 'teaching'), and healing. He regarded himself as God's agent, and, as nearly as might be, God's son. He knew by heart the sacred scripture, as well as some para-scriptural material now classified as apocryphal. He visualised his programme (for this is the appropriate word) as authorised, authenticated, 'blueprinted' by scripture, not because scripture embodied the race's traditions and idiom (as it did), but because it was the voice of God communicated from time to time to man. It was true.

2. Granted that scripture was true, it did not follow that everything there recorded was to be taken literally. Unlike ourselves, Jesus and his generation had no objection to an irrationally literal use of the text. Not only unhistorical and unintellectual but even childishly inappropriate uses of scripture came quite naturally to people who learnt the texts by heart (as is usual in the orient) at an age at which they were hardly

expected to understand it. No doubt an intelligent literal use of scripture
was never precluded, but that did not exclude other uses. Further, unlike
ourselves, they had no objection (quite the contrary) to puns.[1] Yet
scripture was basically exhortation, precept: everything that was written
was written for the race's profit (Rom. iv.23, xv.4). Therefore one *may*
scrutinise the context to see whether a precept, for example, is perpetually
enjoined upon one. The apocalyptic and the juridical elements in
scripture remained in tension (the former is considerably etiolated in
modern orthodox Jewry), and a teacher might choose his own balance
in expounding them: Jesus himself leaned heavily upon the apocalyptic.

3. The Jews had, as they still have, a fixation on that remarkable
man, Moses. To him are attributed all virtues, and all human qualities,
even if they seem inconsistent. The contradictory aspects of his
personality were not lost on his admirers, yet his miraculous experiences, including his end, were taken completely for granted. Jesus
allowed his followers to visualise him as a 'greater than Moses', with
all the metaphor and poetry that involved, for he would personally
'mediate' the new 'covenant' which was dimly outlined by those ultra-
poets, the prophets of long ago. In the land where 'as if' is only an
aspect of reality such metaphors and such poetry can operate as a
powerful and enduring force. One has only to draw attention to the
poetry of our own world (e.g. 'Man was born equal...') to recollect the
power of fantasy.

4. Not only Moses, but also Elijah and Joshua offered models for
Jesus, in his self-image as well as in the *persona* which he authorised
his students to project upon him. It is not that he was later visualised
as a prophet as a compensation for the 'failure' of his mission, or that
all kinds of ludicrous vanities were foisted upon his memory by an
idiotic following. He not only authorised this unique complex of

---

[1] For an egregious pun see Mk. xiv.6, the lexica on the various meanings of *tóv*,
and Qo. vii.1. For a tendentious adaptation of phrases out of context note that
Mt. x.30/Lk. xii.7 comes from Ps. xl.12, lxix.4 (Jesus's point is comical). The amazing
pun at 1 Cor. xi.10 has escaped professional exegetes to a man, though it is explained at
Mishnah, Naz. IX.5 (see Blackman, *Mishnayoth*, iii,324). The female Nazirite vows that
a razor shall not come near her head, i.e. no man's power comes over her head (cf. 1
Sam. i.11, etc.). She thus refuses what is called *môrâ* (Jastrow, *Dict.* 749) in both senses:
(i) razor, (ii) authority (*exousia*). One who keeps her hair trim at the hairdresser's, or
otherwise, acknowledges her husband's *exousia* by wearing a head-covering in public. If
she refuses that covering she might as well be shaved. The sharp-mindedness of this
kind of thinking is revolting to the slower, Western intellect, which even resents the
rediscovery of such puns. For one that is not a Nazirite must have either *exousia* or
the razor.

identifications during his lifetime amongst them, but utilised it to produce a unique effect in his followers. This was not an architypal Galilean holy-man. To the question of his sanity we are bound to come shortly. Meanwhile it is to his lifetime, and not to the earliest churches, that we must attribute the numerous sayings that project Jesus as a source of norms (even casuistic sayings!) which rivalled Moses by supplementing and relevantly correcting him. It is to his 'stage-management' that we must attribute acts like the borrowing of the ass, and the extraordinary episode of the so-called Cleansing of the Temple (not examined fully in these two volumes) in which he acted as Elijah, as the Prophet (so Mk. xi.28-33) and Judge who shall put all things right (cf. Mal. iv.5) inside that juridical enclave (cf. 1 Macc. iv.46). Not content with this vision St. John sees the particulars available in his source as proving that Jesus acted as Son of Man (see Ps. viii.4-8). The scripturally-certified functions were actually performed 'before the face of all people'.

5. The messianic age was visualised by Jesus and his students as immediately upon them. It is too gross to say that after the *anastasis* and 'ascension' they expected the Second Coming very soon, e.g. next month. We should not project our own naïvety upon them. There are difficulties of definition. Because the Messiah was popularly associated with nationalistic-apocalyptic programmes, with some vague and mutually incompatible aspects, Jesus, who preferred to refer to himself as 'Son of Man', was unprepared to accept the title Messiah. Yet he acted in some respects as the Messiah was expected to act: because (it seems) he applied to himself passages of scripture which, in a contemporary Jewish setting, were regarded as messianic. His programme would operate to some extent within Jewish myths and fantasies. It is remarkable that he was able to proceed upon a very extraordinary course, for which the only precedent was a mythical one (that of Isaac, the pioneer of resurrection), as if both the most material world around them and the tenor of scripture authenticated and identified his role and himself.

6. His actions, therefore, in healing and preaching, and finally offering himself as a sacrifice for his people, were the culmination of a period immediately prior to the messianic age as he understood it. His coming again was thus part of the idiom. He, the one and only Messiah, took his 'house' to the barrier separating them from the World to Come. It is usually thought that he explained this in crude temporal terms. My own conjecture is that he told them that that world would

come when they were perfectly ready for it, and he explained how they
not only could but must make themselves ready. One wonders whether
he indeed promised a return when he left his disciples (or rather they
left him) in the garden. The expectation of a Second Coming must be
traceable to a historical source since it is not a necessary conclusion
from any biblical study, Pharisaical, sectarian, or otherwise. The
anastasis was an earnest or pledge of it, but it must have had some basis
in Jesus's teaching at an earlier stage: and St. John obviously had no
doubt of this. It is not impossible to grasp how the witnesses of that
remarkable triumph over death should believe that the victor, no
longer requiring resurrection, would welcome them into a paradise
which both Jew and gentile could comprehend. Even if it is impossible
to deny that Jesus taught that the individual believer could be taken
into heaven at his death, without waiting for a general resurrection
(Mk. ix.1 par. as against Jn. vi.10,44,54 — this point of view is supported by Lk. xi.7-9) it is clear that the community of the living were
taught to live in anticipation of the Messiah's presiding over an eternal
banquet in the Hall, in whose Antechamber they were, for the time
being, standing.

7. The actions of Jesus, as described by all four gospels, and his
parables and many of his sayings, rely on the students' understanding
allusions to scripture, to haggadah and to halakah. The traces of those
allusions were not 'planted' where we find them by scholars more clever
than Jesus or than the disciples whom he taught to memorise his dicta
and to relate and interpret his actions. Our real difficulty is to recover
enough of the silent documentation of his sayings and doings, seeing
that the evangelists may neither have been entirely qualified nor correctly
briefed, or may have had to make excruciating choices in diction, any
one of which must deprive us of vital information. The translation of a
pun is the most obvious example. My attitude is correctly portrayed by
St. John in the episode of the Cleansing of the Temple referred to
above. St. John, studying a text like that of our Mark, knew that
Jesus's behaviour was intended to exhibit, in action, the authorised
representative of God *visiting suddenly* his temple. He also knew that
as a matter of history Jesus wanted his church to embody himself and
at the same time supersede the temple (the sacrificial atonement cults
were wearing out). He looked into Mark, and made Mark's words tell
him what it was all about. He was morally certain that Mark chose
his words with the intention of revealing, and not concealing, what
went on. And what Mark, and after him Matthew, signify in shorthand,

St. John has written out at large. This attitude is manifested by St. John, and I am happy to have had such a predecessor. A totally different approach would be content to assume that the doings of Jesus were those of an enthusiast of a political complexion, whose misguided followers turned him into a deity after he had suffered a merited punishment. His words were then twisted about by religious manipulators in order to give the impression that his questionable proceedings had authority from scripture. Bizarre as is the life and work of Jesus, this, to my mind, is much less credible.

It is true that in Jesus's capacity to compose units of teaching, in particular his parables, a power of allusion to scripture and power of *insinuation* is to be detected which testifies to a degree of intellectuality that can be galling to those who are not his equals (and who would those be?). But for the irritation this causes some academics I admit no responsibility.

8. I do not believe in the boundless prevarications and infinite inventiveness attributed in some quarters to that figment of imagination, the 'Early Church'. I do not doubt that the gospels and epistles reveal some traces of struggles between factions, each imperfectly wedded to the teaching of Jesus: and the rapid decay of the enterprise is testified to even in that highly tendentious document, Acts. I do not deny that there were moments when invention came to the aid of the evangelists, since in compiling their material they must make it as plain as possible what they had to offer by way of improvement upon what was available previously. Theologians of our day who have spent time, during their student days, mocking the wishful-thinking and corruption of the church, especially in the West, slide, all too easily, into assumptions about the dishonesty and ease of misrepresentation at work in the times and at the places where the evangelists wrote. But one must not let one's scepticism get out of hand: nor should one's instinctive dislike of aspects of Jesus's teaching (e.g. that regarding divorce) lead one through a labyrinth of artificial argumentation whereby one saddles every unwelcome piece of information upon incompetent and unfaithful stewards of Christ's mysteries. This is especially naïve. It is much better to tackle the story head-on.

9. Over all the activity of New Testament authors, especially in the earliest times of which we have knowledge, there reigned a responsible selection of fact from fiction, sober presentation as opposed to enthusiasm and romance. All is impregnated with a historical Jewishness, as contrasted with cosmopolitan religiosity. The mixed

Jewish-Hellenic civilization to which the New Testament belongs never
lost its contact with Moses, however critically it must assess that
forerunner of the second and last Redeemer. This is the point at which
to express my scepticism of another figment of imagination, 'Hellenistic
Judaism', which has sounded to me somewhat like 'rococo music'.
My impression, on the contrary, is that, apart from sects with different
theological and even social view-points, all Judaism of the time was
hellenistic, as was their coinage. The two civilizations, the Jewish which
was rooted in an archaic, Asian thought-world which has many
representatives today and which is not yielding to temptation to
conform to the West, and the Greek, which is the linal ancestor of
that West, were in an uneasy suspension and tension to which
Christians remain the heirs. There is much profit in singling out the
opposed elements (especially in the field of law), and the incom-
patibilities of the two cultures: but Palestinian Judaism and Alexandrian
Judaism were regarded by contemporaries and for long afterwards as
not merely contiguous, but continuous. It is wrong, therefore, to
imagine Jesus as operating in a hermetically sealed, fervid Hebrew
environment into which non-Palestinians could penetrate only at the
cost of some trauma. Diaspora Jews were delighted to receive lively
preachers from the Holy Land, who were no more foreign in Thessalonica
than would lecturers from London be in Toronto. Paul's unashamedly
Jewish arguments with the Corinthians, not to speak of the Romans,
have suffered greatly from the assumption that Moses was not quite at
home in those synagogues.

10. The earliest Christians believed that Jesus purified, but did not
set aside the faith of his fathers. He did not deny the validity, for
conscientious Jews, of the old covenant. It could not be set aside.
Jesus, as God's agent, offered a second, which could be accepted by
all men (we have no trace of his discussion of circumcision, though we
have valuable indications in his treatment of purity). The presuppositions of the entire scheme were Jewish, but they fitted on the one
hand the promises of Isaiah and Zechariah, and on the other hand the
social and political situation of Judaism on a world basis. Jesus figured
as the hinge between a scriptural promise and a socio-religious fulfilment.
The gospels vividly describe and reflect the bad terms on which some
sections of Palestinian Jewry stood towards Jesus personally, and one
can trace easily the deteriorating relationship between synagogue and
church even during the period of composition of the gospels. It did not
occur to anyone at that time that Jesus, in his opposition to those whom

St. John pleases to call 'the Jews', was in any sense disloyal to his race or its traditions. The sharpness of intellectual conflict soon produced dichotomies that went much further. But Jesus's own programme was a revivified Judaism with a world potential of which it had been starved by a lack of foresight. And the not infrequent, continual conversions of thinking Jews to Christianity even to this day testify to the fact that no amount of *odium theologicum* can conceal Jesus's being, in an entirely constructive sense, the 'end' of the Law.

11. On the basis already described, New Testament authors do not hesitate to use cosmopolitan images (e.g. adoption), supposing themselves in no danger whatever of being thought disloyal to Judaism, the parent culture. In Lk. xv we find explicit reference to emigration from Palestine, coupled with the theme of home-coming. In the same chapter we hear of a Saviour bearing a sheep on his shoulder: this at once makes any contemporary think of Hermes criophoros, and other (including semitic) deities which rescue from the underworld. St. Luke had not the least fear of the possible illegitimate extension of this idea, since Jesus used the image to recall the paschal lamb, which was so taken into the Temple or other place of slaughter, and (such was the order of ideas) to recall Moses, whose taking of a lost sheep on his shoulders when he was shepherd of Jethro led immediatly to the episode of the Bush, when Moses was commissioned (much against his will) to lead the children of Israel out of Egypt. And what if Christians, visualising their Saviour as the Good Shepherd, were to use that symbol as a sign of their hope that they would personally be rescued from hell? Though he did not specifically say so, he encouraged that very idea in the (at present) obscure Matt. xii.11-12.

12. But there are inconvenient facts to be faced. Jesus expected to be, even wished to be, crucified. His emotional draft upon his compatriots' loyalty required that experience. Was he optimistic in expecting Greek admirers to swallow the intricate intellectual groundwork of this otherwise bold programme? Could one who moved mainly amongst the very shrewd people which the Jews were be forgiven for being optimistic about the brainpower of foreigners? The mental tortures which St. Paul himself suffered, and projected upon his very mixed converts, could not be obviated. No Greek cult could offer the emotional pressure which Jesus was able to apply within that area and that period.

13. The question of Jesus's sanity has occupied me. Every martyr's balance is suspect. Jesus's effect on demonised people could be explained if his own mentality had a paranoid touch to it. The notion that

one should sacrifice oneself to redeem one's fellow men is, prima facie, paranoid. Even civilizations accepting animal sacrifices find the analogy difficult: for the stages when human sacrifices were usual has long since been forgotten, and even if it were not so, the idea would not fit the 'programme' at all, as we shall see. The eucharist in its earliest recoverable form is so amazingly un-Jewish and bizarre, so repugnant, that no one can doubt its historical authenticity. I have explained some aspects.[2] But granted that the students drink their teacher's blood *in symbolic form*, who, if not a lunatic, would suggest it?

The key to this may lie in his authority over his disciples. His behaviour won their adherence, if not (as a sane man must have been aware) their internal conviction. Could he really have visualised that, leaving aside some sort of conspiracy, a series of events, including his repugnant execution, followed by a hasty burial, followed by a revival under the most unfavourable circumstances for survival, could set into movement all the preparations, by teaching and by action, he had carefully made, each incapable of full effect without that consummation? Up till now I find no other solution, and it begs important questions. Jesus knew what he was about, and the evangelists seem to have taken this explanation seriously. The petty coincidences of Jesus's life were, they declare, intelligible in terms of the whole of it (Jesus was exposed, immediately after his birth, as a 'snack' for shepherds, the family to which he potentially belonged!), and in terms, coincidentally, of the Law, the Prophets and the Writings. Jesus's own compositions, in my view, authorised just that. It is not the case that God, by inscrutable foresight, provided for scriptural themes to be 'fulfilled' without Jesus's informed volition, or the training he gave his students.

It is of the essence of Jesus's teaching that each individual must keep himself pure as if he had already returned to the Garden of Eden (the Garden and the World to Come were one and the same), and any sane man must have known that, under temptation, even the most promising student would evince the Old Adam, not the New. Ethics are, after all, group experiences; individuals maintain their moral behaviour in relation to their neighbours, and especially their chosen companions. If one seriously propounds an exacting doctrine such as was never propounded before one may well take thought for the recovery of 'backsliders' and the strengthening of the community which potentially harbours them. The doctrine is of no value if one generation exhausts it.

[2] *Law in the New Testament*, 441.

St. John in the Farewell Discourse openly adverts to this aspect. Jesus was presumed to have occupied his mind with the perpetuation of his church. To secure the continuing welfare of the convert, and of second and subsequent generations of Christians, Christ himself must be present with them solemnly: they would have a perpetual point of reference in their formal meals, in their 'breaking of bread', and their eucharist. The example, headship, and doctrine of their founder would never utterly escape them. Only a proportion of mankind, from age to age, would be sincere in its submission to his extraordinary spell; but that would serve. And the perpetual motion would be fuelled by his remarkable manipulation of a historical event (his crucifixion) in conjunction with the then available theory of the second Redemption, with the then available symbol of the paschal lamb.

14. I take, therefore, a much more favourable view of the possibility of recovering the historical Jesus than was fashionable when I went in 1959 to Germany for my first piece of research in this field. My fondness for midrash, my reinvestigation of the role of the Law and the law, my identification of actuality in the darker places of the texts, taking us back to the semitic past which was previously visualised only as a linguistic experience, and that too extremely tenuously, are now answered (of course by coincidence) by studies of a character very different from that of those which appeared about 1959. Bold, even 'way-out' adventures into midrash appear without self-consciousness.[3] Midrash in various measures clarifies St. Matthew and St. Paul.[4] St. John is found to be an excellent Jewish lawyer.[5] In redaction-criticism what is sought now is not outdated hellenistic-magical propaganda but the Hebraic homeland: the communication of the message of Christ takes place in authentic strata, and these are more

[3] N.J. McEleney at *C.B.Q.* 38/2 (1976), 178-192, is an example. The very tentative tone of T.C.G. Thornton's 'Stephen's use of Isaiah lxvi.1', *J.T.S.* 25/2, 1974, 432-4, was probably unnecessary. W. Grimm's midrashic handling of Lk. xiii.31ff. at *N.T.* 15/2 (1973), 114-133, is good; and there is a general demand for R. Le Déaut's excellent exposition of the nature of Targum at *Bibl.* 52/4 (1971), 505-525. Law plays a beneficial role in S. Pancaro's reexamination of Jn. vii.51 at *Bibl.* 53/3 (1972), 340ff. The authoritative voice of J. Neusner ('First cleanse the inside', *N.T.S.* 22, 1976, 486-495) clarifies Lk. xi.38-41/Matt. xxiii.25-6 with the aid of Jewish law as found in Mishnah and Tosefta *Kelim*. I. Jacobs, 'The midrashic background for James ii.21-3', *N.T.S.* 22 (1976), 457-464, is a splendid example of the utility of recovering early Jewish exegesis if one wishes to 'anchor' a New Testament passage in its intellectual environment. At one blow masses of helpless conjecture are rendered obsolete.

[4] M. Goulder, *Midrash and Lection in Matthew* (London, 1974); A.T. Hanson, *Studies in Paul's Technique and Theology* (London, 1974).

[5] A.E. Harvey, *Jesus on Trial* (London, 1976).

and more carefully disentangled.[6] His sacrifice, and no sophisticated alien thing, touches, through those channels, section after section of believers to whom his egregious teaching is neither merely idealistic nor merely poetical.

15. I reject the comment of a older generation of scholar that Jesus could not possibly have alluded to scripture and haggadah, and to contemporary practices, in the ways I make him out to do. Their resentment (as I have said) of his cleverness was pathetic. Those scholars were plainly unaware of how Shakespeare, or for that matter any great poet, fills his work with allusion, and how the Jews themselves were constantly alluding, as Muslims still do in high style. Jesus spoke to the learned and to the simple, to the alert as well as to the stupid. Again, it is sometimes objected that I do not prove the date of the materials I am using. Since the objectors' selection of material and their attribution of a date to it is often guided by their predetermined conclusions, I need not go further than saying what I have said before on the subject, viz. that old traditional material can be presumed to hand on something very like what was in vogue in the material times. Larger insistence upon dating may prove unfortunate. The priority of Mark is now questioned, and the lateness of John: the status of Q is questioned, even its existence. In such a climate it is naïve to argue about the dates of material, especially of that of which one did not think oneself. To those who say they do not want to hear from me anything which I cannot positively prove, I reply that their own productions lie open to the same query; and I will superadd that I shall require them to prove many basic matters of life they, and others, take on trust. When they have done that we can proceed to look for further proofs in this highly conjectural field of scholarship. The proof of the pudding is in the eating: the proof of hypotheses is their efficacy. Do these studies illuminate the text? If they do, they proceed, by whatever methodology, upon a profitable path, and I am happy to count myself with those who proceed by trial and error, as in bio-chemistry and in rose-growing.

Attacks have been made upon my mode of transliteration, even by persons who explain that they use no single system themselves. Editors, as shown in this very volume, have had very various ideas on the subject, including editors who are dedicated semitists. I am not very concerned, since no one will come to me for orthographical lessons. *Nihil est simul inventum et perfectum.* And, by the same token, *perfecta eruditione nonnumquam dictum est ieiunius.*

---

[6] B. Olsson, *Structure and Meaning in the Fourth Gospel* (Lund, 1974).

A criticism of my method in *Law in the New Testament* will assuredly arise in this volume also. It is that I present the reader with a mass of information, without providing him with a simple and single clue to the exegesis of the passage. In all the popular works written for Western students it is taken for granted that however detailed the information which the writer (e.g. Jeremias) supplies, the *results* are simple, sharp, unambiguous. This means that it is axiomatic that a quantity of detail and allusion contained in the text must be neglected or ignored, and a number of scholars obtain 'originality' by the selection of different sharp, unambiguous exegeses; and the abandonment in turn of different treasures of detail. This is one of the results of a Western educated mind (which cannot endure the complex and convoluted) when applied to ancient oriental filigree products which, whatever else they are, are poetry. G.M. Hopkins can be interpreted on a single, banal level; but no reputable scholar so deals with him. Similarly the New Testament is in large part intended for those who have well-stocked minds, avid for cross-rhythms and paradoxical allusions. The scholar who would unravel all this must give his reader the benefit of what he has detected (*little* must he have detected, if aided by adepts at the 'one simple message'), in the hopes that the seeds sown by the Master will germinate in that soil in their own time. To turn Jesus into a straight-forward teller of simple tales, free from artistry of the kind I have demonstrated, would be to do violence to the material.

As for the future, I expect great strides to be made in the field of the miracles,[7] where the prophetic background, and its midrash, bear a special relation to the action performed, the exact nature of which has

---

[7] Seeing that writings on miracles can be vitiated by disingenuous manipulation and prevarication, a short, clear, and sincere projection of the basic form-critical techniques can only be valued. R.H. Fuller, *Interpreting the Miracles* (London, 1963) is my favourite work in this area. On the other hand I cannot accept the form-critical criteria, which are swallowed wholesale by some postgraduate students as their starting points in some regions. Originally those most attractive criteria were invented to do away with the necessity to believe in any miracle, and were a symptom of the 'liberal' theology which is now, especially since the Dead Sea Scrolls, relegated to history. The problems of the miracles cannot, indeed, be settled by rationalistic or 'background' research alone—and it is certain that the stories survived for their instant value in the congregations to whom they were sung—but further criteria for study of the individual episodes are required, and these must arise from pre-rabbinical, including sectarian Judaism, keeping in mind that the actual stories were heard, and were intended to be heard, by persons well versed in Hellenistic myth, religion, and romance. The Walking on the Water (which even now some scholars would remove by saying that Jesus walked *along* the water!) is about the presence of the messianic age (see Vol. II below).

not been established. It does not follow that what is depicted by
St. Mark as a miracle, e.g. the Feeding of the Five Thousand, is or was
merely symbolic. My own attitude to all the material, including the most
evidently concocted as teaching for the congregation (whether or not
the gospels were compiled to be lectionaries, which is very likely), is
that it has a factual origin apart from its potential as edification.

Another fruitful avenue of research will prove to be the division of the
gospels' text into breath-units, the 'lines' arranged for delivery to be
sung (I suppose) by boys of 12. Material which is to be projected
to an audience of hundreds (e.g. at the feast of the *Anastasis*) in the open
air must be divided by the author/compiler in units of 7 or 8 syllables,
and he can, by artfully combining and alternating longer and shorter
'lines' provide that the singer shall automatically emphasise the
important words, which are placed at the beginnings and (more often)
at the ends of the 'lines'. As far as I can see traditional material tends
to stand out, by metrical regularity, from redactional material; and
chronologically later composition, such as St. Luke's, tends to use a
longer syllabic line, with a penchant for 11-syllable, 13-syllable and
even 15-syllable units. These would be more practical for a singer who
could rely on a roof and walls. Some of the strange variants as between,
e.g. Matthew and Mark, could in part be explained by the evangelist's
preference for certain words at the ends of 'lines'. The importance
placed in the traditionally-received material varied also with the
emphasis on the midrashic content, especially the direct allusions to
scripture. Each evangelist may have evaluated the midrashic potential
of his material independently. Whatever was lost by the decisions I
referred to above must once have been made up by oral tradition in
sermons and otherwise.

Enough. Let the reader, free from any pressure to be convinced, use
the results, so far as they please him, for what he will: that is the
way in which theological research achieves its purpose.

J.D.M.D.

Acknowledgements

The source of each article is indicated in the Table of Contents.
The marginal asterisks indicate that in the Further Annotation additions
and corrections will be found *ad locum*.

My work in the past few years has been helped by the Rev. Canon
Cheslyn Jones, the Rev. Dr. Kenneth Noakes, Rabbi Dr. David Kamhi,

and Dr. L. Rosenwasser. I have received many a useful hint from the
Rev. A.E. Harvey. I cannot exaggerate my gratitude to all those who
are prepared to listen to an enthusiast and nudge him, occasionally,
into a more propitious angle of vision. Their patience is commendable
when his 'discoveries' do not support their own predilections. I owe
much to the patience of Mr. R. May (Oxford), whose encouragement
and instant attention to my queries has set me an example of how
to deal with others'. However, in works of theology more than in any
other line of scholarship known to me it is advisable for one's friends'
sake to point out that each man's opinions are very much his own
— and I accept no 'influence' from anybody.

The versatile and polymathic Professor Elémire Zolla (Rome) kindly
translated some articles of mine into Italian for *Conoscenza Religiosa*,
which he edits. In the Further Annotation I attempt to indicate,
briefly, the drift of the items. The references are of course not obscured
from the scholarly reader by the change of language, and that is what
he will value.

J.D.M.D.

LIST OF ABBREVIATIONS

The references to tractates of the *Mishnāh* or the Talmuds are simple abbreviations (*e.g.* Berakot is shown as Ber.) and the tractates can readily be located by reference to a table of contents or the spines of the volumes. Complete consistency was not possible in this present work since its parts were published separately.

b.	Babylonian Talmud
Bauer-Arndt-Gingrich	W. F. Arndt and F. W. Gingrich, *A Greek-English Lexicon of the New Testament* (1957)
Billerbeck	H. L. Strack and P. Billerbeck, *Kommentar zum Neuen Testament aus Talmud und Midrasch* (1924/1961)
Blackman	P. Blackman, *Mishnayoth* (1951-5)
Blass-Debrunner	F. Blass and A. Debrunner, *A Greek Grammar of the New Testament and other Early Christian Literature* (1961)
BSOAS	Bulletin of the School of Oriental and African Studies, London
BZ	Biblische Zeitschrift
CBQ	Catholic Biblical Quarterly
CD	Zadokite Document, otherwise Damascus Document, or Damascus Rule
Chavel	*The Commandments. Sefer Ha-Mitzvoth of Maimonides*, trans. C. B. Chavel (1967)
C.I.J.	*Corpus Inscriptionum Judaicarum*
Cod.	Justinian's *Codex* in the *Corpus Iuris*
C.P.J.	*Corpus Papyrorum Judaicorum*
CR	Community Rule, or Manual of Discipline
Danby	H. Danby, *The Mishnah* (1933)
Dig.	Justinian's *Digesta* (or Pandects) in the *Corpus Iuris*
DSW	The War Rule, or War Scroll
Dupont-Sommer	A. Dupont-Sommer, *Les Ecrits Esséniens découverts près de la Mer Morte*, 3rd edn (1968)
ET or *Exp.T.*	Expository Times
F. Gr. Hist.	J. Jacoby, *Die Fragmente der Griechischen Historiker* (1958)
H.T.R. or H.Th.R	Harvard Theological Review
Horowitz	G. Horowitz, *The Spirit of the Jewish Law* (1953)
HUCA	Hebrew Union College Annual
ICLQ	International and Comparative Law Quarterly
IEJ	Israel Exploration Journal
j.	Jerusalem Talmud
JBL	Journal of Biblical Literature
JE	Jewish Encyclopedia
JJP or *J.Jur.Pap.*	Journal of Juristic Papyrology
JJS	Journal of Jewish Studies
J.N.E.S.	Journal of Near Eastern Studies
Jos.	Flavius Josephus
JRL	B. Cohen, *Jewish and Roman Law* (1966)
JQR	Jewish Quarterly Review
JThS or *J.T.S.*	Journal of Theological Studies
Lohse	E. Lohse, *Die Texte aus Qumran* (1954)
LXX	The Septuagint

m	Mishnah
M.T.	The Masoretic Text or Maim., *Mishneh Torah* (= 'Code')
Maim.	Maimonides
Midr. R.	Midrash Rabbah
Moulton-Milligan	J.H. Moulton and G. Milligan, *The Vocabulary of the Greek New Testament* (1914-30)
NEB	New English Bible
NKZ	Neue kirchliche Zeitschrift
NT	Novum Testamentum
NTS	New Testament Studies
PG	Migne, *Patrologia*, Series Graeca
PL	Migne, *Patrologia*, Series Latina
Q	Scroll from Qumran, the preceding numeral referring to the Cave: 1 *QS = CR*
RB	Revue Biblique
RE	Pauly's *Real-Encyclopädie der classischen Altertumswissenschaft*
R.H.P.R.	Revue d'Histoire et Philosophie Religieuses
RIDA	Revue Internationale des Droits de l'Antiquité
SBE	Sacred Books of the East
Sonc.	I. Epstein, ed., *The Babylonian Talmud*, English translation (London, The Soncino Press) or the English translation of the *Midrash Rabbah* (various editors) published by the same Press
STh	Studia Theologica
T.L.Z.	Theologische Literaturzeitung
ThWzNT	*Theologisches Wörterbuch zum Neuen Testament* (1933/1957-) originally edited by G. Kittel. An English version is appearing in America.
TuU	Texte und Untersuchungen zur Geschichte der altchristlichen Literatur
TQ	Theologische Quartalschrift
Vermès	G. Vermès, *The Dead Sea Scrolls in English* (1966)
VT	Vetus Testamentum
y	*see* j
ZDMG	Zeitschrift der Deutsche Morgenländische Gesellschaft
ZKT	Zeitschrift für katholische Theologie
ZNW or *Z.N.T.W.*	Zeitschrift für die neutestamentliche Wissenschaft
ZRGG	Zeitschrift für Religions- und Geistesgeschichte
ZSS	Zeitschrift der Savigny-Stiftung für Rechtsgeschichte
ZVR	Zeitschrift für vergleichende Rechtswissenschaft

'TAKE THY BOND ... AND WRITE FIFTY'
(LUKE XVI. 6)
THE NATURE OF THE BOND

I DISCOVERED what went on at Luke xvi. 6–8, and explained the point of the parable by showing that, under oriental conditions, loans of comestibles were made subject to a much higher interest-rate than loans of money, and that, whatever the Law of God might say, the law that was enforced in Palestine in the time of Christ permitted usury to flourish under the cover of acknowledgements framed as these 'bonds' were framed.[1] This explanation has appealed to many,[2] but not all.[3] Reluctance has been felt to accept a simple theological proposition ('If such a man is approved when he acts righteously under such impulses, how much more . . .?'), when subtle anfractuosities give their authors more credit and a sense of achievement.[4] However that may be, I never found an actual acknowledgement which demonstrated the point I was making: I had to infer one out of rabbinical and Indian material. Now, to my chagrin, I find that actual specimens exist, subject to the special conditions of Egypt. St. Luke knew what his Hellenic hearers would understand by the terms he uses in these verses. The (to us) archaic formulation was precisely apt. We can now depict perfectly the effect these indications would have on a hearer who knew that Jews, lending to Jews, had an opportunity to break the Law. The numerals point to a dilemma of everyday life.

N. Lewis studied the phenomenon that interests us in an article of 1945, but he had no idea that Luke xvi. 1–9 was involved.[5] A splendid survey of the subject was made by P. W. Pestman (of Leiden) in 1971. He documents the topic exhaustively, but he, too, seems never to have heard of Luke xvi. 6–7, which is the best evidence he could have had

[1] *N.T.S.* vii (1961), pp. 198–219. The Indian particulars were given more fully at *Zeits. für vergl. Rechtsw.* lxv (1963), pp. 172–82. The material was republished with improvements at ch. 4 of my *Law in the New Testament* (London, 1970).

[2] e.g. G. B. Caird, *Saint Luke* (London, 1963), ad loc.; I. H. Marshall, *J.T.S.*, N.S. xix (1968), pp. 617–19; J. A. Fitzmyer, *Essays on the Semitic Background of the New Testament* (London, 1971), pp. 161–84. Cf. J. D. Crossen in *N.T.S.* xviii (1972), p. 293 n. 1.

[3] H. Drexler, *Z.N.W.* lviii (1967), pp. 286–8; J. D. Crossen, *J.B.L.* xc (1971), p. 464.

[4] One should understand the word ἀδικία in the light of this treatment, and that explained in the reference p. 440, n. 4 below.

[5] 'The meaning of σὺν ἡμιολίᾳ and kindred expressions in loan contracts' (*Tr. Proc. Am. Phil. Ass.* lxxvi (1945), pp. 126–39). For Grenfell and Hunt's revision of the interpretation of P. Teb. 110 and P. Amh. 147 at P. Oxy. 1040 see Lewis at pp. 130–1.

for the Hellenistic practice.[1] I need only quote some of his words, repeat his examples, and draw my own brief conclusions. 'In considering *the customary interest* on loans one has to differentiate between loans of money and loans of consumer goods such as grain, wine, salt, and such like.'[2] Demotic loans were drawn in the form of acknowledgement of debt, interest *not* being specified separately. Greek loans of *money* usually *do* state the amount of interest. 'With regard to *demotic and Greek loans in kind* the debtor used, particularly in the time of the Ptolemies, to pay a compensation of 50 per cent of the goods borrowed, as interest. This is a fixed amount regardless of the duration of the loan.' The phrase is τόκοι ἡμιόλιοι.

Looking at examples we recognize: (1) the acknowledgement of a duty to repay an amount which comprehends at once capital and interest; and (2) an assessment of interest at a half the capital, obviously as a convention, and without reference to the real value of the commodity loaned. Some examples illustrate both points, as does a demotic loan of wheat: P. dem. Turin Botti 13 (114/13 B.C.), 7 artabas lent, but the amount acknowledged *simpliciter* was 10½ artabas. Pestman says: 'A loan of money only brings in a total of 50 per cent interest after 25 months, but a loan of goods brings it in *immediately*.' Here is a loan of wine, where the 50 per cent is mentioned as such: ὁμολογῶ ἔχειν π[α]ρὰ σοῦ τοὺς τρῖς μετρητὰς τοῦ οἴνου σὺν ἡμιολίᾳ, οὓς καὶ ἀποδώ⟨σω⟩ σοι (P. L. Bat. XVII. 4 (2nd cent. B.C.)).

A demotic loan of wine (P. dem. Adler 4 (110/109 B.C.)) runs: 'You have with us 30 (keramies) of wine in the name of the wine you gave us, whilst their addition is included in them: we shall give them (back) to you.' P. dem. Cairo 30. 610 (66/5 B.C.) runs: 'You have given us 4 artabas of wheat as principal (and) interest; we shall give them (back) to you.' The same explicit adding of principal and interest is coupled with the adding of 50 per cent in P. dem. Rein. 3 (108/7 B.C.) which must be read with the interlocking P. gr. Rein. 20: 'You have with us 50 artabas of wheat on the grounds of a claim concerning principal (and) interest'— the Greek document refers to a principal of 33 1/3 artabas of wheat and τόκοι ἡμιόλιοι, an interest of 16 2/3 artabas, giving a total of 50 artabas. To return to Pestman: 'The debtor states that he has received a certain

---

[1] 'Loans bearing no interest?' (*J. Jur. Pap.* xvi–xvii (1971), pp. 7–29). For our purpose the essential fact is that Egypt, an ancient civilization, had rationalized all the grounds for charging high interest on loans of commodities and reduced them all to 50 per cent. This meant a higher rate for wheat than was reasonable, and a lower rate for oil and wine. India retained what were there regarded as 'righteous' rates, and Palestine will have been aware of them customarily, though they were inconsistent with the Hebrews' antipathy to 'increase'. Pestman had not seen *Z.V.R.* lxv (1963), pp. 172–82.   [2] At p. 1, § 2.

sum of money or a certain amount of goods while in actual fact he has received less because the interest has already been added.'[1] Absence of actual mention of interest (as in our parable) by no means implies that interest was not owed.[2] The well-known phrase ἄτοκος seems actually to have included loans on which interest or the so-called 50 per cent 'compensation' *was* charged![3] In ἄτοκος loans of goods the debtor pays 50 per cent as a fine if he fails to repay at the due date (often, perhaps, unrealistically proximate, as in our own mortgage deeds).

Thus, Luke's hearers knew at once that the debtors had signed acknowledgements including additional sums which were, whether called 'compensation' or 'interest', unquestionably exigible in the Hellenistic courts, and equally unquestionably contrary to the spirit (but perhaps not the letter) of the biblical prohibition of 'usury'. A better example could hardly have been chosen of the concept of ἀδικία, the distinction between the world of Satan, and the 'kingdom' in which God's will operates.

---

[1] At p. 14.   [2] At p. 15.   [3] At pp. 15–28, an exhaustive analysis.

Law in the New Testament:
Si scandalizaverit te manus tua abscinde illam (Mk.IX.42) and comparative legal history

*

In a previous issue of *Z.V.R.* I broached the question whether the Parable of the Unjust Steward could be solved with the use of ancient Indian material. The result was acceptable in many quarters (but not all), and has been supported within limits by a fresh examination of papyrological material from Egypt, the full significance of which had escaped historians of law until very recently ([1]). The use of Indian material to illuminate utterly obscure passages in Holy Scripture has struck a commentator in Germany as strange ([2]), and it is timely to attempt the solution to another problem — with, I trust, even more convincing results. The passages in issue are the following. For typographical reasons the Vulgate and English versions are used but the original Greek will be found most conveniently set out in the first case at Kurt Aland's *Synopsis Quattuor Evangeliorum*, § 168, and in the second *ibidem*, § 56.

Mk.ix.42-48

et quisquis scandalizaverit	Whoever causes one of these
unum ex his pusillis credentibus	little ones who believe in me

---

(1) DERRETT, *Z.V.R.* 65 (1963), 172-82; H. DREXLER, *Z.N.W.* 58 (1967), 286-8; E.J.H. SCHRAGE, in *Uit het Recht, Festschrift P.J. Verdam* (Deventer, 1971), 189-200; P.W. PESTMAN, '*Loans bearing no interest?*', *J.J.P.* 16-17 (1971), 7-29; DERRETT, *J.Th.St.*, N.S., 23/2 (1972), 438-40.

(2) H.-J. KLAUCK, *Wissenschaft und Weisheit*, 1972/1, 72.

*

*in me: bonum est ei magis si
circumdaretur mola asinaria
collo eius, et in mare mitteretur.*

to sin, it would be better for
him if a great millstone
were hung round his neck
and he were thrown into the
sea.

*et si scandalizaverit te manus
tua, abscinde illam: bonum est
tibi debilem introire in vitam
quam duas manus habentem ire
in gehennam, in ignem inextin-
guibilem.*

And if your hand causes you
to sin cut it off; it is better
for you to enter life maimed
than with two hands to go
to hell, to the unquenchable
fire.

*et si pes tuus te scandalizat
amputa illum: bonum est tibi
claudum introire in vitam aeter-
nam, quam duos pedes habentem
mitti in gehennam ignis inextin-
guibilis.*

And if your foot causes you
to sin, cut it off; it is better
for you to enter life lame
than with two feet to be
thrown into hell.

*Quod si oculus tuus scandalizat
te ejice eum: bonum est tibi lus-
cum introire in regnum Dei, quam
duos oculos habentem mitti in
gehennam ignis: ubi vermis eorum
non moritur, et ignis non extin-
guitur.*

And if your eye causes you
to sin pluck it out; it is
better for you to enter the
kingdom of God with one
eye then with two eyes to be
thrown into hell, where their
worm does not die, and the
fire is not quenched.
[cf. Isa.66.24.]

Mt.xviii.6-9

*Qui autem scandalizaverit unum
de pusillis istis, qui in me cre-
dunt, expedit ei ut suspendatur
mola asinaria in collo eius,
et demergatur in profundum maris.
Vae mundo a scandalis. Necesse est
enim ut veniant scandala: verum-
tamen vae homini illi, per quem
scandalum venit.*

But whoever causes one of
these little ones who believe
in me to sin, it would be
better for him to have a
great millstone fastened
round his neck and to be
drowned in the depth of the
sea. Woe to the world for
temptations to sin! For it is
necessary that temptations
should come, but woe to the

man by whom temptation comes!

Si autem manus tua, vel pes tuus scandalizat te: abscinde eum, et projice abs te: bonum tibi est ad vitam ingredi debilem, vel claudum quam duas manus, vel duos pedes habentem mitti in ignem aeternum. Et si oculus tuus scandalizat te, erue eum, et projice abs te: bonum tibi est cum uno oculo in vitam intrare, quam duos oculos habentem mitti in gehennam ignis.

And if your hand or your foot causes you to sin, cut it off and throw it from you; to is better for you to enter life maimed or lame than with two hands and two feet to be thrown into the eternal fire. And if your eye causes you to sin, pluck it out and throw it from you; it is better for you to enter life with one eye than with two eyes to be thrown into the hell of fire.

It will be observed that Lk. has not the sayings about hand, foot, or eye. He retains (at xvii.1-2) the saying that ' scandal' must come but woe to him through whom it comes, and the saying that a mill stone should be tied round his neck and he be thrown into the sea rather than that he should ' scandalize' (i.e. tempt into sin) one of ' these little ones'. The precise sources of Mt. and Lk. are not certain. That Mt was following and adapting Mk. seems clear; but whether the hand-foot-eye saying was in Q or M (Matthew's additional sources) is not clear; for Lk. (who also used Q) may have omitted it for reasons which we can only guess. It is clear that Mt., in introducing the words ' and throw it from you' is commenting upon Mk., explaining that what is meant is not maiming, but utterly rejecting the object in question. It is clear that when he syncopated the ' hand' saying and the ' foot' saying and made them one he understood that nothing was gained by treating the two separately (perhaps he was wrong in this, as we shall see). Mt.'s introduction of ' Woe to the world for temptations to sin...' is interesting. As it is in Lk we can be sure it was in Q and was therefore one of Jesus's sayings, presumably not available to Mk. (or rejected by him). Mt.'s placing it where it is seems to be explicable on the basis that he (or his hearers) could not understand or justify the abrupt transition in Mk. from the 'mill-stone' saying, which is about protection of the 'little ones', to the 'hand' saying. With the words from Q introduced between the two the wider context of 'scandal' is suggested, and the strangeness of the transition is less obvious. Since in the ancient world they were quite as alive to the value of context in interpretation as we are, the problem must have been as evident, even by Mt.'s time, as it is for us now. Most theologians are agreed that Mk. placed the 'hand-foot-eye' saying after the 'millstone' saying on no other ground than that the word 'scandalize' occurs in both. They infer that the origin of the arrangement in Mk. is not very intelligent, is mechanical, and unhelpful — and in so inferring they repeat a common feature of theologians, namely the insinuation that the authors of the Gospels were men of much more limited intelligence than scholars (and students) of today. My own experience by no means bears this out, as my *Law in the New Testament* (1970) testifies in many places. Thus if we can find from Asian sources, and other sources relevant to the subject-matter, a better reason for Mk.'s placing of his material we shall know something which ought to have been known to Matthew, and which, if known to him, would certainly have guided him in his reconstruction of the material so as to utilise both the Q tradition and Mk. And we may (if we are on the right track) be able to guess more plausibly why Luke left the 'hand-foot-eye' saying out. Before we investigate oriental laws on the subject we must turn attention to a passage in the Sermon on the Mount, where Mt. has adapted the 'hand-foot-eye' saying to a specific purpose, even at the cost of producing a doublet in his Gospel.

Mt.v.29-30

Quod si oculus tuus dexter scandalizat te, erue eum et projice abs te: expedit enim tibi ut pereat unum membrorum tuorum, quam totum corpus tuum mittatur in gehennam.

If your right eye causes you to sin, pluck it out and throw it away; it is better that you lose one of your members than that your whole body be thrown into hell.

Et si dextra manus tua scan-
dalizat te, abscinde eam, et
projice abs te: expedit enim
tibi ut pereat unum memborum
tuorum quam totum corpus
tuum eat in gehennam.

And if your right hand causes you to sin, cut it off and throw it away; it is better that you lose one of your members than that your whole body go into hell.

One of the most noticeable facts about the saying in this position is that it agrees with the Mt.xviii passage in having ' throw it away ', but differs in not treating ' eye ' and ' hand ' together, as with the ' hand and foot ' in the later passage. Moreover the wording is smoothed out and rationalised; ' member ' appears. Thus we have two stages of commentary present. Further, the context makes the meaning of the first half clear. Since the previous verse (*v.* 28) deals with ' looking at (or after) a woman lustfully ', and since the next verse (*v.* 31) deals with divorce, it is beyond doubt that Mt. here applies the idea to sexual contexts, with particular allusion to adultery and its sequence....

For very long it was thought that ' right hand ' must refer to sexual play. But I have attempted to show that this is inappropriate, since in the East the right hand is not used for sexual (or other ' defiled ') contacts ([3]). Even in Greece the left hand was used for lavatory purposes and children were taught to eat with the right hand ([4]). On the whole, however, the taboo on the left hand is an Asian phenomenon. Thus ' right hand ' refers to property transactions. Apart from Ps.xxvi.10 and Sir.4.31 there is a passage in Sirach which is extremely relevant (21.19): ' Instruction is (as it were) fetters on the feet of an unwise man, and as manacles on the right hand '. This is extremely clever since, though on the surface it contrasts with Sir.21.21 (' Instruction is to a prudent man as an ornament of gold, and as a bracelet upon his right arm. '), at a deeper level it reminds us that wisdom is needed to restrain our steps and to inhibit all that a right hand can too easily do! In the Sermon on the Mount

(3) DERRETT, *Law in the New Testament* (London, 1970). xlv-xlvi.
(4) Plutarch, de lib. educat., Moralia, p. 5A (éd. Paton, etc., i, 8).

the 'eye' refers to arousing of sexual appetite through the vision, and possibly winking, and 'right eye' must mean peeping, squinting through cracks, keyholes, and the like, not merely vision, but carefully applied vision, such as will excite sexual appetite and its untoward psychological and social effects. The 'right hand' therefore refers to bribes, presents, and other transactions through which women are induced or obtained as objects of sex-enjoyment. Furthermore, since divorce comes immediately, the right hand has its very familiar meaning of oath-taking ([5]), and alludes to the oaths of lovers swearing that they will divorce their wives, that they will marry a lady when her husband divorces her, and so forth.

In all these reconstructions ingenuity meets the question, ' Can you be sure that the audiences of Mk. or Mt. would at once have seen the point? Would they have understood? Would they not have been as puzzled as we are, and would they not have thought of something else? You have to prove not only that they thought as you explain, but that they would not, or not for long, have thought otherwise!' So we proceed to examine the law on the subject as a comparative legal historian may do.

But first let us take note of theologians' understanding of the 'hand-foot-eye' saying. Ancient doctors were of the view that Jesus referred to all favourites, persons or objects, who or which enticed one into sin. Origen's idea that even emasculation was justified if it was the only way to avoid the distractions of sex appetite, is nowhere approved. The words were taken as metaphorical from the first. No doubt rightly. But it was understood as a violent exaggeration, according to which what he meant was that nothing should be allowed to stand in the way of the search for the Kingdom of Heaven. Modern commentators choose different forms of words, but differ little in their understanding. It is an oriental exaggeration meaning no more than that no price is too high to pay for Heaven, no price too high for the avoidance of sin and its effects. At all cost one should avoid succumbing to temptation, since temptation itself is inevitable([6]).

(5) Gen. 14.22 ; Isa. 62.8 ; Dan. 12.7.
(6) For earlier views, Cornelius a Lapide, ad loc. Modern views: P.

Scholars have for long realised that Job xxxi lay behind the
passage, verses 1, 5, 7 (especially in the Septuagint version) being
particularly relevant; and they have drawn attention to Prov.
xxiii.1-2, 1 Cor.ix.27, and Col.iii.5. My own suggestion (in the
light of rediscovered midrashic technique) is that Jesus, as
correctly represented in Mk., took Job xxxi as his principal text,
with the highly relevant Prov.xxiii.1-2 as helping material
(whether he actually cited them or merely alluded to them is
immaterial in a civilization which prized and knew by heart
scriptural texts), and was aware of the order in which Job
refers to ' eye ' (v. 1), ' foot ' (v. 5), and ' hands ' (v. 7), and treated
them in reverse order; Job in v. 7 in any case presents the three
in the rational order of ' foot-eyes-hand '. Further speculation is
undesirable since we can never know for certain how the original
sermon (if it was one) was framed, and Prov.xxiii.1-2 (which
refers to Satan, and to the ' throat ', meaning ' belly ' in fact)
tackles all the members involved in temptation under one metaphor. At any rate when Mt. at v. 29-30 places ' eye ' before ' hand '
he may have acknowledged that Job's order was significant. The
relation to all this of Isa.lxvi.24 will be apparent later. In sum,
whether or not Jesus was making, or utilising, a midrash on Old
Testament texts, everyone is agreed that what he meant was
merely that one should so carefully avoid succumbing to temptation that one should resolutely avoid all such causes of temptation as would be likely to offer such a danger. And since (it is
thought) ancient audiences were mostly uneducated, and could
not abide abstract statements (which we very much prefer) not
one concrete illustration only was given, but (in case it was

GAECHTER, *Das Matthäus Evangelium* (Innsbruck, 1963) ad loc. ; T.W.
MANSON, *Sayings of Jesus* (London, 1949), 157; A. PLUMMER, *Exegetical
Commentary* (London, 1909), 81 (' highly figurative '), 250-1; D.E. NINE-
HEM, *Saint Mark* (London, 1963), 255. On the history of the text: R. BULT-
MANN, *Hist. Syn. Trad.* (Oxford, 1968), 86, 144, 148; NINEHAM, ubi cit.,
J.C. FENTON, *Saint Matthew* (London, 1963), 293; C.E.B. CRANFIELD, *St.
Mark* (Cambridge, 1963), 312; B.H. STREETER, *Four Gospels* (London,
1926), 265; W. SANDAY, ed., *Studies in the Syn. Prob.* (Oxford, 1911),
175-6, 192; W.L. KNOX, *Sources of the Syn. Gospels I* (Cambridge, 1953),
67 (' This teaching was compiled on the worst system of verbal association '). So V. TAYLOR, cit. inf., n. 22.

insufficient) the solemn three-fold illustration from bodily members was chosen. The saying looks rather different, however, when it is realised that loss of an eye or eyes was popularly known as a punishment for sexual misbehaviour; loss of a hand or hands was popularly known as a penalty for theft, fraud, forgery, and sedition; and loss of a foot or feet was popularly known as a penalty for robbery, persistent theft, and (in the case of servants, slaves, and dependants) flight, running away! The whole significance changes, when we realise that all those punishments were liberalisations, humanitarian modifications (*Milderungen*) of the quasi-ubiquitous punishment of death for adultery, theft, robbery, sedition, and repeated misdeeds of slaves, who were regarded as worthless. The public were aware that loss of an eye was better than a death-sentence; that loss of a hand or even both hands was better than death; and the same applied to loss of a foot or feet. Defiance of the earthly sovereign would normally lead to a death sentence; but as a matter of humanity the hands might be chopped off. Thus one regained life at the cost of one's hands. How much better it would be to have avoided the crime! Just as it is better to lose one's hand or hands than to be executed capitally, so it is better to avoid the crime and the loss of the hand.

Jesus thus relies on the popular knowledge that punishment, as it were, of the member that caused the sin or crime, could follow a discovery, apprehension and trial for the offence, and seeks to explain that one who wishes to enter into Eternal Life must be prepared to sacrifice that member which corresponds to the sin which, if not checked, would condemn one to an eternal death. The ratio of the customary penalty to which Jesus alludes is simply that when the intending offender begins to snatch, or to climb up, or looks where he has no business to look, he asks himself whether the profit will really be worth as much as the member that obtains it, should he be caught and punished. In secular life criminals rely on not being discovered, or, if discovered, on not being punished: but in religion it is axiomatic that even the most secret sins are punished, and the loss of the earthly member would be a cheap price to pay for avoiding otherworldly punishment. It may be asked whether this is morally sound? Perhaps it is more acceptable if it is translated into modern idiom in this way: 'Imprisonments and fines are the normal punishment for crime; crime is due to uncontrolled appetite; sins are punished infinitely more efficiently than crimes (which may or may not be detected); hence radical control of the appetite will exempt one from other-worldly punishment certainly, as it will exempt one from this-worldly punishment certainly. One may take a chance with this-worldly punishment, hoping not to be detected or convicted; one cannot take a chance with other-worldly punishment. Whatever the cost of uncontrolled appetite in this world, its cost in the other world is far greater, and more certain. Hence attend to the appetites — not to the punishment! Those that seek to control their appetites can leave punishments to look after themselves!' It might be argued that the Markan and Matthaean passages about amputation could as easily be referred to the practice of surgical amputation, well known in the   * ancient world, and actually used metaphorically by philosophers. Self-amputation of a gangrened member must have occurred, and its rarity would help the public to remember it. But the notion is ill-founded. The texts speak of 'scandal', which is a snare, trap, or stumbling-block. This is in fact the key idea behind the passage. And it refers unquestionably to sin, or crime (or both), to a moral condition, not a physical calamity. Thus the allusion is to punishment, not to surgery for physical cure. Now for the proofs.

Students of Jewish law will find no biblical or talmudic evidence that hands were amputated for crimes, except Deut.xxv.11-12, 'When men strive together one with another, and the wife of the one draweth near for to deliver her husband out of the hand of him that smiteth him, and putteth forth her hand and taketh him by the secrets; then thou shalt cut off her hand, thine eye shall have no pity.' The Jewish law, however, holds that this   * means merely that the man who has suffered this indignity is entitled to damages (pecuniary compensation) from her for the insult(7)! The reason for this lay in the Pharisees' proposition

(7) Mishnah, Baba Qamma VIII 1 and H. DANBY's note (*The Mishnah*) thereon. Maimonides, Code (Mishneh Torah), XI (Book of Torts), IV, 1, 9-10 (trans. KLEIN, New Haven, 1954, p. 161).

that 'Eye for an eye' means compensation for injury, and that no one has the right to insist upon *talio* [8]. The Pharisees' position on this is the Jewish law and has been accepted as such since A.D. 132 at the latest. It must have existed as a theory in the time of Jesus. But Sadducees and sectarians, let alone the general public, will not have been committed necessarily to the Pharisees' position, and the Mishnaic law which we now study did not represent all traditions actually alive in Palestine in the first century. Thus the biblical rule that this woman should lose her hand, founded, we need not doubt, upon an ancient ratio that the member that offends should be punished was relegated by the Pharisees to virtual insignificance, whereas other sections of the Jewish people may well have regarded it not only as an authority for amputating the hand of such a woman but also for amputations in other crimes. And we have evidence that amputation of a hand or hands was in use in the first century in Palestine.

Indeed Josephus, who lived through the First Roman War, speaks of this in several places. At *Vita*, § 177 he says, ' I further reminded Justus that, before I came from Jerusalem the Galilaeans had cut off his brother's hands on a charge of forging letters prior to the outbreak of hostilities... ' We notice *Galilee* (a significant area) and *forgery*. At *Vita*, §§ 170-3, and at *Bellum Judaicum* II.642-4 there appear two accounts of a very remarkable episode which occurred during Josephus' reduction of a serious revolt or sedition at Tiberias, a city for which he was at the time responsible. The accounts do not quite tally, but their extraordinary coincidence with the notion to which Jesus alludes will soon strike every reader. St. Mark's Gospel was available when Josephus wrote, but there is no evidence that he had read it.

Vita, §§ 170-3: Seeing the wretched plight to which they (the Tiberians) were reduced, the people now urged me to take measures against the author of the sedition, a rash and headstrong youth named Cleitus. Deeming it impious to put a compatriot to death, yet imperatively necessary to punish him, I ordered Levi, one of my bodyguard, to step forward and cut off one of his hands. The man, notwithstanding these orders, was afraid to advance alone into such a crowd, whereupon, wishing to screen

(8) See Maimonides cap. cit. For the Sadducees see discussion summarised at S. BELKIN, *Philo and the Oral Law* (Cambridge, 1940), 97, n. 23.

the soldier's cowardice from the Tiberians, I called up Cleitus and said: 'For such base ingratitude (*acharistos*) to me you deserve to lose both hands. Act as your own executioner, lest, if you refuse, a worse punishment befall you.' To his urgent request to spare him one hand I grudgingly consented; at which, to save himself the loss of both, he gladly drew his sword and struck off his left hand. His action brought the sedition to an end.

Bellum Judaicum II, §§ 642-3: 'Those who were left indicated, with loud cries, a certain Cleitus as the prime mover of the revolt, and urged the governor to vent his wrath upon him. Josephus, being determined to put no one to death, ordered one of his guards, named Levi, to go ashore and cut off Cleitus's hands. The soldier, afraid to venture alone into the midst of a host of enemies, refused to go. Cleitus, thereupon, seeing Josephus on the boat fuming with anger and prepared to leap out himself to chastise him, implored him from the beach to leave him one of his hands. The governor consenting to this, on condition that he cut off the other himself, Cleitus drew his sword with his right hand and severed the left from his body; such was his terror of Josephus.'

These accounts have their discrepancies *inter se* and with common sense, and they are not to be believed implicitly, singly or together: but no one will doubt but that the penalty of losing one or both hands for sedition was taken quite for granted ([8a]).

It had been known for centuries that the Egyptian native penalties for crimes were not the ubiquitous death-penalty used in so many jurisdictions (apart from the Jewish). Diodorus Siculus (*c.* 36 B.C.) evidences what must have been common knowledge. At I.78 he says of the Egyptians that they cut out the tongue of those that betrayed secrets to the enemy; that both hands were amputated for coining, making false weights, imitating seals, scribes making false entries or erasures, adducing false documents, 'to the end that the offender, being punished in respect of those members of his body that were the instruments of his wrongdoing, should himself keep until death his irreparable misfortune, and at the same time, by serving as a warning

(8a) Indeed, in the Ancient Near East it was an established penalty. A negligent surgeon; a fraudulent obliterator of a slave's brand-mark; and one who struck his father were all punished by Ḥammurabi with the loss of their hand: CḤ §§. 195, 218, 226. That murderers should be punished with amputation of hands and feet, irrespective of the death penalty, was known to the author of 2 Sam.iv.12.

example to others, should turn them from the commission of similar offences. ' For adultery with rape castration was the penalty, and where a woman committed adultery with her own consent her nose was cut off ([8b]).

Cutting off a hand for a crime in connection with property is evidenced from the time of Galba ([9]). Plutarch shows Sulla threatening Mithridates with the amputation of his right hand for murder (*Syl.* 23.7). The emperor Severus Alexander, a Syrian, cut the nerves of the hand of a man who produced a forged document, and banished him ([10]). The practice of cutting off hands for property crimes was, however, not characteristically Greek. It was known only in the special context of slaves who, once maimed in this way, were useless as workers, but valuable (in a large *familia*) as a warning to the others. Galen (A.D. 129-199) speaks, by the way ([11]), of a practice which must have been known to him from the Asian environment in which he was brought up. He speaks of what people do to runaway slaves: they burn, break or beat their legs; and if they steal they maim their hands, and if they are gluttons they injure their bellies; if they talk too much they injure their tongues, in sum they punish each one in the member in which the wicked actions are performed. This practice was well known to Maximus Tyrius (A.D. 125-185), himself a Palestinian, who says (VII.7) ([12]) that diseases of the soul should be cured by removing the bodily powers, just as a robber's hands, the eyes of an *akolastos,* and the belly of a glutton. He improves on the metaphor by saying that judgment

(8b) Diod. Sic., ed C.H. OLDFATHER (London/N.Y., 1933), I, 268/9.

(9) Servius Sulpicius Galba, a contemporary of Jesus: Suetonius, *Galba,* 9: *nam et numulario non ex fide versanti pecunias manus amputavit mensaeque eius affixit.*

(10) Aelius Lampridius, *Severus Alexander* xxviii (in *Scriptores Historiae Augustae*, ed. trans. MAGIE II, London/N.Y., 1924, p. 232). We see that the writer of a bad book was thought fit to lose his hand even in rabbinical circles: j.Šabb.XVI.15 c. 51.

(11) De Hippocratis et Platonis placitis VI (ad fin.) (*Opera*, ed. C.G. KÜHN, 1823, repr. 1965, vol. 5, p. 583). Galen is discussing the liver as the seat of hybris, and commending Homer for visualising the hybristic Tityus as suffering in his liver for his attempted rape of Leto.

(12) Ed. H. HOBEIN (Leipzig, 1910), pp. 85-6.

and restraint (of a penal kind) will come too late. It is clear
that he refers to such punishments as well known. It is not
possible to say whether he knew the Gospel passages or the letter
of St. Paul. Since Maximus was a pagan philosopher it is more
likely that, whether he knew them or not, he was more influenced
by common knowledge of such punishments existing by custom in
his own part of the world, and adapted this to the same question
that had occupied Jesus, namely the greater value of prophylactic
constraint upon the bodily members in proportion to attention
to the question of punishment when the damage has already
been done. Of special interest to us is the word *akolastos*. Such
are punished by loss of their eyes. Normally the word, as Stepha-
nus shows (*Thesaurus* I, 1831, 1235 A-B), can mean either sexual
excess or gluttony (since from the context ' undisciplined ' is
impossible); but the precise context with its own reference to   *
' glutton ' shows that sexual excess is the point. Thus adulterers
and other sexual offenders could be assumed to be capable of
being punished by loss of their eyes. The loss of one eye, like the
loss of the lady's nose [as in modern India where the punishment
of cutting off the nose, unknown to the Penal Code, is constantly
imposed by relatives in flagrant cases] will be a perfect prophylactic (one may interject) against amatory adventures!

That it was commonly believed that the eye should be punished
for adultery is proved by the legend of Zaleucus. Zaleucus, the
famous legislator of Locri, an ancient Greek colony in South
Italy, is believed to have lived about 650 B.C. ([13]). He is known to
have compiled one of the first, if not the first, code of written
laws in Greece, with great severity and with a penchant towards
talio. Heracleides Pontikus (*c.* 390-310 B.C.) reports as follows: ([14]) ' if anyone was caught... his eyes were torn out. The
son of Zaleucus was caught, and the Locrians were for dis-

---

(13) *Oxford Classical Dictionary*, 2nd edn. (Oxford, 1970), 1144. K. VON
FRITZ in PAULY-WISSOWA, *Real-Encyclopädie*², XVIII (1967), 2298-2301.
F.E. ADCOCK, '*Literary tradition and early Greek code-makers*', Cam-
*bridge Hist. J.*II/2 (1927), 95-109; M. MÜHL, *Die Gesetze des Zaleukos und
Charondas, Klio* 22 (1929), 105-124, 432-463.
(14) *De Politiis Graecorum*, 30.

charging him, but Z. would not permit it. He took out one of his own eyes and one of his son's '. The question is what word should occupy the space. In some manuscripts *klepton* ('stealing') is found and editions of Cragius and Koeler so print the text. Koeler comments ([15]) that Heracleides might well have more authentic information than other sources, to which we come. But C. Müller, at Fr. Hist. Graec. II (Paris, 1878), xxx, p. 221 prints *moichos* ('adulterer') since one manuscript omits the *klepton*; a gap obviously existed in the original, improperly filled by a scribe; and the evidence as a whole pointed to adultery being the offence. The other sources are Aelian and Valerius Maximus. Though Aelian is late, he uses old sources.

Claudius Aelianus, *Varia Historia* 13.24 (ed. Hercher, 1866, pp. 152-3): Zaleucus the legislator of the Locrians decreed that an adulterer when caught (in the act?) should have his eyes knocked out. Fate unexpectedly and against his anticipation brought him what he had least envisaged. His son was taken in adultery and was immediately about to suffer under the law his father had introduced. Rather than that what had once been enacted should be infringed, the author of the law endured the exchange of one of his own eyes for one of his son's, in order that the lad should not be utterly blinded.

Valerius Maximus, *Factorum et Dictorum Memorabilium* (ed. C. Kempf, 1888, pp. 301-2), VI.5, ext. 3: *Zaleucus urbe Locrensium a se saluberrimis atque utilissimis legibus munita, cum filius eius adulteri crimine damnatus secundum ius ab ipso constitutum utroque oculo carere deberet, ac tota ciuitas in honorem patris necessitatem poenae adulescentulo remitteret, aliquamdiu repugnauit. ad ultimum populi precibus euictus suo prius, deinde filii oculo eruto usum uidendi utrisque reliquit. ita debitum supplicii modum legi reddidit, aequitatis admirabili temperamento se inter misericordem patrem et iustum legislatorem partitus.*

Valerius Maximus was a contemporary of Jesus. His manner of compiling this work was such that we can sure more or less notorious examples were chosen, and, though embellished, the tales were in general in no need of authentication. We need not believe the legend. Legislators who fall victims to their own laws seem to be the stuff of legend. But we can take it as certain that in the time of Jesus it was understood that if punishment were to be inflicted on a person's member for the crime which, with

(15) G.D. KOELER (Halle, 1804), pp. 77-78.

the aid of that member, he had committed, an adulterer would lose his eyes or an eye. Job xxxi.1 proves that the Jews saw the eye as the offender when sexual lust was in question. About the hands we have had contemporary and local proof. The rest follows, without having recourse to any theory that Jesus, or St. Matthew, knew of Zaleucus. However, the story of Zaleucus proves that the public were aware of the idea. Further, the interpretation of Zaleucus's actual law (that adulterers should lose their eyes), on the basis that Z. and his compatriots believed that the eye was the cause of adultery, or rather its preceding amatory exchanges, is accepted by modern critics ([16]), and is not worthy of debate.

We may now turn to the customary law which eventually, accepted into Islamic law, provided the notorious rule of the Shari'a that thieves should lose a hand, and, for persistent theft, both hands, or a hand and a foot. The Koran says, at Sura V, verse 36,

> The reward of those who make war against God and His Apostle, and strive after violence in the earth, is only that they shall be slaughtered or crucified, or their hands cut off and their feet on alternate sides, or that they shall be banished from the land...

Again, Sura V, verse 41, says,

> The man thief and the woman thief, cut off the hands of both as a punishment, for that they have erred ; an example from God, for God is mighty, wise.

It is noticeable that the penalty of amputation is applied here to sedition and crimes of violence (e.g. robbery). A great deal of information is available on the subject from treatises of Islamic law ([17]). Most of the casuistry, of great interest in itself, is

---

(16) Antonius MATTHAEUS, *De Criminibus* (Amsterdam, 1661), p. 75: ... quod primi nuptas incestent oculi, maximumque illicitae libinidi irritamentum, ardentius aspexisse matronam. *unde sacra quoque pagina avertere nos oculos iubet, ne irretiantur a vanitate.* S. PUFENDORF, *De Iure Naturae et Gentium* VIII, iii.26 (edd. 1688, 1715, p. 828) ; trans. B. KENNETT, 4th edn., ed CAREW (London, 1729), 791 (unfortunately printing ' Seleucus ' for ' Saleucus ' = Zaleucus). MÜHL, cit. sup., 450-1. The ἡ ἐπιθυμία τῶν ὀφθαλμῶν at 1 Jn.ii.16 may well refer to sex, or to any appetite.

(17) Ibn Qudama (a Hanbali author), *al Mughni*, vol. 8, p. 259 (a refer-

obviously much later in date than our period. The consensus of
the jurists is that on the first occasion the thief's *right* hand is
amputated from the wrist; if he steals a second time then,
according to the minority his left hand will be amputated, but
according to the majority his left foot will be amputated from
the ankle. The majority base their rule upon Koran V.36, the
minority on V.41. What we need to know is that by the seventh
century in Arabia the amputation of a hand, or hands, or a hand
and a foot, was a *humane* punishment for theft and repeated
theft. This notorious rule has two aftermaths of greater interest.
When Islamic countries came under European rule the European
rulers found it impossible to sustain the ancient traditional
penalties. Gradually amputation ('mutilation'), and *talio*, were
abolished and other penalties substituted. In India the problem
caused a great deal of attention, since the Islamic law was the
criminal law for all Indians, including non-Muslims. We have
a contemporary account of such a 'hand and foot' operation in
detail ([18]). Secondly, the traditional Islamic rule has so much
'common sense' about it that Mr. Justice Cornelius (a non-
Muslim) of the Supreme Court of Pakistan actually recommended it for general introduction throughout the world when
he attended a Commonwealth Lawyers' Conference held in Aus-
tralia about five years ago. In Africa the rule is very much alive.
The memory has been sustained everywhere Islamic law has
penetrated. A military man informs me that the emperor Menelik
of Ethiopia, after he routed the Italians at Adowa in 1896 and
took many prisoners, amputated a hand and a foot from each
prisoner whom he did not kill, and some of these were to be seen
as privileged beggars until the Second World War. President
Bokassa of the Central African Republic announced on July 31st,

ence I owe to Dr D. HINCHCLIFFE) ; al Marghinani, *al Hidaya* (a Hanafi
work), trans C. HAMILTON, *The Hedaya* (London, 1791), II, 87-107; Ibn
Qasim al-Ghazzi, *Fath al-Qarib* (a Shafi'i work), X, iv; Khalil ibn Ishaq
al-Juni, *al Mukhtasar* (a Maliki work), II, xlv; al-Sharani, *Mizan al
shari'a* II, xliv. L. BERCHER, *Les délits et les peines de droit commun
prévus par le Coran* (Tunis, 1926).

(18) T.K. BANERJEE, *Background to Indian Criminal Law* (Bombay,
1963), 52-8 (the law), 292-3 (the operation: quoting *The Calcutta Chronicle*, Feb. 19, 1789).

1972 that he intended to bring in new penal sanctions, including public executions, against thieves. For the first apprehended theft one ear was to be cut off; for the second the other ear; for the third the *right* hand (*Le Monde,* Aug. 2, 1972) ([19]). The Libyan Republic which had been governed by the Italian Penal Code reintroduced, on Oct. 11th, 1972, the Islamic penalties of amputation of a hand and, for armed robbery, a foot also, since evidently the government were of the view that the customary (but long suspended) penalty was much closer to the minds of the public (*The Times,* Oct. 13, 1972, p. 11 - Col. Gaddafi).

We are now in a position to look further East. In pre-Islamic Iran (so Prof. Mary Boyce informs me) amputation for theft was known. In modern Tibet it is still practised, that is to say it was practised until China took Tibet and is evidenced amongst Tibetan refugees in Bhutan and elsewhere. Tibet may well have taken the practice from India, or both India and Tibet took it from a third source. Indian law of the ancient period is very explicit. All the Sanskrit texts quoted below may be found with excerpts from their commentaries and full textual apparatus in L.S. Joshi, *Dharmakośa, Vyavahāra-kāṇḍa* (Wai, 1941) I/3, pp. 1656-1767.

Manu 8.279.

    yena kenacid aṅgena hiṃsyāc cec chreṣṭam antyajaḥ |
    chettavyaṃ tat tad evāsya tan Manor anuśāsanam ||

'With whatever limb a man of low caste does an injury to a superior person, even that limb shall be cut off: that is the teaching of Manu.'

8.321. tathā dharima-meyānāṃ śatād abhyadhike vadhaḥ |
       suvarṇa-rajatādīnām uttamānāṃ ca vāsasām ||

'So shall corporal punishment be inflicted for stealing more than a hundred of articles sold by the weight, of gold, silver, etc., and very valuable clothes.'

8.322. pañcāśatas tv abhyadhike hasta-cchedanam iṣyate |
       śeṣe tv ekādaśa-guṇaṃ mūlyād daṇḍaṃ prakalpayet ||

'For more than fifty it is required that the hands shall be cut

(19) I am obliged to Dr. R. RATHBONE for the information.

off; but in other cases let him (i.e. the king) inflict a fine of eleven times the value. '

8.325. goṣu brāhmaṇa-saṃsthāsu chūrikāyās ca bhedane |
      pasūnāṃ haraṇe caiva sadyaḥ kāryo 'rdha-pādikaḥ ||

' For cows belonging to Brahmins, for piercing the nose (?) of a barren cow (?), and for stealing cattle (generally) he (the thief) should be made half-footed [it is not certain whether this means removing one foot, or amputating the toes of a foot or both feet]. '

Even more closely approximating to the Middle Eastern evidence is Vishṇu 5.48, which cannot possibly have been influenced (chronologically) by Islamic contacts with India:

      gajāśvoṣṭragoghātī tv ekakara-pādaḥ kāryaḥ |

' One who injures an elephant, a horse, a camel or a cow, must be made single-handed and single-footed. '

The text as printed by Ganganatha Jha, *Hindu Law in its Sources* I (1930), 408, differs from that printed with the commentary of Nandapaṇḍita (Adyar, 1964), I, 96, but the ' foot ' figures in each reading. Vishṇu 5.81 reads:

      suvarṇa-rajata-vastrānāṃ pañcāśatas tv abhyadhikam
      apaharan vikaraḥ ||

' One who steals gold, silver, or clothing beyond the value of 50 must be deprived of a hand. '

Likewise Vishṇu as reported in the Vivādaratnākara (p. 320) and Vivādacintāmaṇi (p. 136) and reprinted at Jha, ubi cit. p. 451 reads:

      go'śvoṣṭra-gajāpahāry eka-kara-pādikaḥ kāryaḥ |
      ajādyapahāry eka-karas ca |

' A thief of a cow, horse, camel, or elephant must be made one-handed and one-footed; and the thief of a goat, etc., must be made one-handed. '

Vyāsa, printed, from various sources, by Jha at p. 451 reads:

      aśva-hartā hasta-pādau kaṭim chitvā pramāpyate |
      paśu-hartus cārdha-pādam tīkṣṇa-sastreṇa kartayet ||

' One who steals a horse should have his hands, feet and loins cut off, and then killed. One who steals an animal should have half of his foot cut off with a sharp weapon. '

Yājñavalkya 2.274. utkṣepaka-granthi-bhedau kara-sandaṃśa-
    hīnakau |
    kāryau dvitīyāparādhe kara-pādaika-hīnakau ||

' The " lifter " and the " cut-purse " should have their thumb
and index-finger cut off; if the offence is repeated, one hand and
one foot should be cut off. '

Yājñavalkya 2.297. kūṭa-svarṇa-vyavahārī vimāṃsasya ca
    vikrayī |
    tryaṅga-hīnas tu kartavyo dāpyas cottama-sāhasam ||

' He who trades with counterfeit gold, and sells bad meat must
be made " wanting in three limbs " and shall be forced to pay
the fine called " highest violence ". '

Commentators on this verse, the reading of which is disputed
in what, for us, is the vital word, are found to say that the hand,
the nose and the ear are to be cut off; but the phrase bears an
interpretation which would cost the offender both hands and a
foot.

The unfortunate cutpurse figures in Manu 8.277 (he loses a
hand and a foot for a second conviction) and in Nārada as quoted
in the Vīvādaratnākara (p. 322) (see Jha, ubi cit., p. 453), where
an index finger and *toe* are cut off for the first offence, and the
remainder of the hand and foot are taken off for a second
offence. Death is the penalty for the third offence.

Not to belabour these Hindu references, it is clear that just as
the Koran proves that amputation of the hands, or a hand and a
foot were known in customary law in Arabia long before Islam
(a fact more or less corroborated from Egyptian and Hebrew
sources to which we have referred), so, long before the compila-
tion of the *smṛitis* in India (i.e. in the first to fourth/fifth centuries) the punishment of amputation for theft and other crimes
to do with property was common knowledge — what was open
to dispute was the order and stages at which these punishments
should be inflicted and what degree of humanity could be
invoked. The developed Islamic law shows the same features in
various stages of elaboration.

To return from the East to the Roman world again. Roman
law did not sanction amputation as a punishment for theft or

robbery. For robbery the penalty was crucifixion, and many of the states subsidiary to Rome found no more difficulty than did the Romans in using that, originally, Punic punishment in the same context. The would-be emperor, Avidius Cassius, who died in A.D. 175, inflicted hand-amputation on disobedient soldiers, including deserters [20]. Avidius was himself a Syrian, and was governor of Syria, whence a great many of his troops came. He was, to my mind, simply using a customary penalty of which the public had common knowledge. At last we may turn to the emperor Justinian (6th cent.) who, in his Novella 17.8 prescribed the amputation of a hand for frauds in the fiscal service, and in his Novella 42 for writing heretical books, in Novella 134.13 provides in general that the amputation of *both* hands should never take place, nor the amputation of both feet; and in particular he forbids the amputation of any part of the body for theft [21]. Where were these penalties previously in force? Obviously in the eastern parts of the empire.

Finally we may approach the passage in the Mishnah (Niddah, II.1) which is often consulted in order to throw light on our New Testament passages. It runs:

> kol ha-yad ha-marbah libdoq benashiym meshubachat,
> uba-anashiym tiqatsets.

'Every hand which frequently examines (the pudenda for symptoms, e.g. of menstruation) is, among women, praiseworthy; but among men, let it be cut off.'

The obvious explanation is that men have no occasion to examine their pudenda frequently with the hand, and no excuse so to do is sufficient, and a hand which does so should be cut off. It is alleged that Jesus had some such idea in mind at Mt. 5.30. Apart from the critical problem whether the actual form at Mt. 5.30

(20) *Scriptores Historiae Augustae*, MAGIE (London/N.Y., 1922), I, *Avidius Cassius* IV.5 (p. 238) also V.2 (pp. 240-2). In this environment rabbis were themselves acquainted with amputation as a punishment by governmental decree, as a saying of Abba b. Abba (c. 200-225), the father of Samuel, reveals.

(21) Jac. CUIACIUS, *Observationum* VII.13 gives many of our references on this subject.

does go back to Jesus (which is unlikely, as we have seen), no one would use the *right* hand for examining, or handling, the pudenda (whether amongst men or women), so that a verbal similarity is out of the question. However, did the rabbis to whom the Mishnah is due believe that a hand deserved to be cut off for sexual irregularity? Deut. XXV.12-13 seems their authority; and the exaggeration is said to be of the same type as that figuring in our New Testament texts. It is possible to explain the Mishnah in the same way as we have explained those texts. A hand which misbehaves in property law or by way of sedition is liable, in practice (whatever the book-law might say), to be cut off. Though sexual malpractices are generally a question for the Court of Heaven, the same principle would apply: rather cut off the (left) hand than engage in sexual malpractices. Both the Mishnaic and the New Testament passages utilise and allude to the customary penal law, of which the public were perfectly aware,   * though the contemporary jurists' law of every western country ignored it and it survived amongst the learned only as an antiquarian curiosity (hence Luke's omission of the passage?). This would seem to be further proof that Jesus was concerned, in his sermons, to reach his audience not at the level of dry, abstract academic thought, but rather in terms with which their daily experience made them familiar. This is indeed a parallel case to that of usury in the parable of the Unjust Steward. The rabbis' books know nothing of usury-law (it is forbidden), but custom knew much because it was practised.

May we now return to the theologians' belief that Mk.ix.43ff were placed after *v.* 42 for no more cogent reason than the fact that both pericopae possessed the word to 'scandalize'? Does our new information put the problem in a new light? I submit that it does. Jesus is speaking at *v.* 41 about cooperation with the disciples, and about the (other-worldly) reward for friendliness to those who belong to Christ. At *v.* 42 he speaks of the (other-worldly)punishment awaiting those that cause any of the 'faithful' to stumble, i.e. undermine their loyalty to Christ, procure their defection, and thus put an end to their effectiveness as 'casters out of demons'. That punishment is worse than having a millstone put round their necks and being thrown into the sea (presumably the Sea of Galilee?). The next following verses mean, as we have seen, that other-worldly punishment can be (and must be) avoided by rooting out the causes of being tempted, so far as these lie in oneself. Evidently Mk. wishes these verses to be taken (whatever their original context) in the sense of preparations, by the disciples, to do their function, and to continue doing it. In order to remain effective they must root out the means whereby their loyalty can be undermined. Fear of punishment was universally understood in the ancient world to be the most general means whereby people, whose loyalty was unstable and good behaviour undependable, could be attached with reasonable certainty to their leader for the time being. It is of interest that drowning in the sea was a means whereby people in Palestine punished folk with whom they were on terms of political enmity ([22]). Thus the whole passage from *v.* 42 onwards is speaking in terms of punishments actually known in Palestinian practice, in order to throw light on the great difficulty of remaining effectively loyal to the spiritual leadership of the Kingdom of Heaven.

Confirmation from Mk.ix.48-50.

Modern theologians are dissatisfied with the old attempts to make coherent sense of Mk.ix.42-50. In their view the passages were put together only because of similarity of vocabulary, and *v.* 49 is unintelligible. It is not surprising that they take this view of it since a similar view was held in the earlier stages of gospel transmission, during which the text was altered to accommodate glosses which are now universally excluded by textual scholars (the American 'Greek New Testament' assigns the

(22) Josephus Ant. XIV, § 450. V. TAYLOR, *Gospel acc. to St. Mark* (London, 1963), 410. The punishment is known from Roman sources also: Suetonius, *Augustus*, 67: *oncratis gravi pondere cervicibus praecipitavit in flumen.* Babylonian Talmud, Qidd. 29b is often cited (since C. SCHÖTT-GEN, *Horae Heb.* ad Mt. xviii.6) as illuminating the 'millstone'. But the passage (R. Johanan said " With a millstone round the neck one should study Torah "), whether pointed as a question or not, merely refers to possession of a wife as an actual or potential hindrance to Torah-study and has nothing to do with punishments!

category ' B ' of certainty to the printed reading πᾶς γὰρ πυρὶ ἁλισθήσεται which is Nestle's reading, adopted in Aland's *Synopsis*). Below I give the text which would agree with this modern critical reading.

Omnis enim igne salietur.	For every one will be salted with fire.
Bonum est sal: quod si sal insulsum fuerit: in quo illud condietis? Habete in uobis sal, et pacem habete inter uos.	Salt is good; but if the salt has lost its saltness, how will you season (or ' prepare ') it? Have salt (or ' you have salt ') in yourselves, and be at peace with one another.

I submit that there is a way of understanding these verses which completely confirms my reconstruction, and it retains an intellectual continuity and integrity in the whole passage.

The factual material is this. Amputations in the ancient world were cauterised with a red-hot iron or with caustic materials ([23]). When animals are castrated they are cauterised with the hot iron still, or they would bleed to death. A penal amputation would be treated with cauterisation, and the stump would be treated afterwards with caustic medicaments in which a kind of salt would figure, since salt was (as it remains) a treatment for surface wounds. For sealing the arteries and veins the hot iron, or some other application of fire was necessary. In Islamic law it is explained by many authors that the Koranic penalty of amputation cannot be carried out when there is danger to life, or when the cauterisation would be prejudiced, since the penalty is intended to save life, not to endanger it. The Islamic texts

---

(23) E. GURLT, *Geschichte der Chirurgie... Alterthum* (Berlin, 1898), III, 794; F.E. KIND, ' Kauterisation ', *Pauly-Wissowa, R.E.*, XXI (1921), 94-99; F. KUDLIEN, ' Kauterisation ', *Der Kleine Pauly*, III (1969), 172. I am obliged to Prof. Dr. F. KUDLIEN for these and other pieces of information. Hipp. IV.608; ' Das stärkste und beste Ätzmittel ist das Feuer ' (!) (Kind). On the subject, Preuss's references are abundant (*Biblische-talmudische Medizin*, Berlin, 1911, 573). See also *ibid.* 224, referring to Mishnah, Kerit.III.7; b.Ket.50b.

refer to 'fire', 'boiling oil', and other boiling fats for immediate cauterisation of the wound ([24]).

If surgical operations are properly performed the destroyed matter is sloughed off, and the wound heals. If surgery is not done properly gangrene sets in, and if gangrened matter is not removed immediately sepsis, under Eastern conditions, produces 'worms'. The ancient world was familiar with these worms, and they were not distinguished from the worms which infest, 'eat', corpses of humans and animals. It was a commonplace expression that the just shall, at the End of Days, see the unjust in a living hell, in which, paradoxically, fire never ends, and yet does not consume, or prevent, the worms of decay which consume the wicked as they are burnt in an unending fire. This is stated in so many words in Isa.lxvi.24, which Jesus quotes at Mk.ix.48, and upon which he immediately gives a midrash justifying his previous lively metaphor of spiritual, supersensory self-amputation or mutual amputation. The idea that the wicked suffer from *both* worms *and* fire, while they can still feel them, was popular: in pre-Christian authors the idea of Isaiah appears in Sirach vii.17, and Judith xvi.17, both perfect examples of popular thought and feeling. Irrespective of Jesus's quotation at Mk.ix. 48, though no doubt reinforced by it, post-Christian authors utilise the picture — 2 Clement vii.6, xvii.5; Petrusapokalypse * 25 (Dietrich, *Nekyia²*, 1913, 6, 200, 215) ([24a]).

Historical persons were 'eaten by worms' while still alive. Sulla bred *phtheires* (Plutarch, *Syll.* 36.3). Isaiah (in the LXX), and all the texts quoting or taking their inspiration from him, use the word *skolekes*. It was by *skolekes* that Herod the Great was eaten (Josephus, *Bell. Jud.* i.656; *Ant.* xvii.169); and, on the other side (chronologically) of the Jesus-story, Herod Agrippa I (Acts xii.23). Moreover, the condition (gratifying in wicked princes) was attributed to Antiochus Epiphanes (2 Macc.ix.9).

---

(24) *al Mughni*, vol. 8, p. 260; *al Hidaya* (HAMILTON), VIII.iv, p. 107; *Fath al-Qarib*, pp. 583-5 (VAN DEN BERG); *al Mukhtasar*, sec. 1980 ('fire': N. SEIGNETTE, 1911, p. 608); *Mizan al-shari'a* (N. PERRON, 1898, p. 501); *The Calcutta Chronicle* (n. 18 above).

(24a) On breeding worms see Exod.XVI.20. On the power of worms to hurt the dead: b.Šab.13b.

A good example of worms as a symptom of gangrene appears at Lucian's *Alex.* 59 (ed. Iacobitz, ii, 142).

Now salt, apart from being a popular medicament in one form or another, including materials (e.g. ashes) having some saline qualities, was notorious as a preservative for meat and fish. Salted meat and fish did not bread worms. By fire the amputated man was preserved ('salted') for further life; by spiritual fire the spiritually amputated man was preserved ('salted') for the Life to Come. Moreover, in purely practical terms, a community whose members must spiritually amputate themselves to avoid non-Christian sex relationships, for example, must have the affection and support of their friends to sustain them, and prevent their bleeding to death, or their being eaten by the worms of madness. Amputation, in the sense of severe self-discipline is only a practical possibility if the 'patient' is sustained by the love of the community. The community upholds him in his self-criticism, and supplies the medicines that will heal his wounds. Psychologically the teaching is obviously sound, for there is no one without experience that the reverse proposition is a hopeless failure. Meat cannot be preserved (or 'dressed') without good salt. Wounds cannot be healed without saline materials which retain, or have not lost, their saline component. The community must not be satisfied with the power to condemn, or to reprove, but must retain the power to heal. Then it will be at peace, for *shalom*, 'peace', means also 'health'. Jews used salt to draw out the blood from meat which was forbidden to them with the blood still in it; the capacity of salt to perform   * this function was limited, and it could not be used over and over again. A good supply of salt was essential, and salt as a medicament would suffer from the same limitation: it was expendible.

Thus Jesus's teaching was so clever that it defeated even early Christian exegetes (who added the glosses and spoiled their copies of the gospel), and almost certainly intensified by its acuteness Luke's reluctance to include a metaphor so little understood amongst Hellenes, to whom amputation was not a regular punishment for free men, and savoured of barbaric treatment of slaves (utterly incompatible with the outlook of the church).

Jesus taught not merely a paradox, and a double meaning with a double paradox, but a cross paradox as well: oriental intricacy at its most characteristic. I. Everyone will be preserved (*a*) in this world spiritually, (*b*) in the next world in hell, by a fire that is not a normal consuming fire, for it endures. II. Everyone will be preserved by a fire which will (A) consist with (paradoxically) and (B) prevent (*a*) the worm of (spiritual) decay and (*b*) the worm of hell, which is not a normal consuming worm. The salt which preserves actually amputated persons from superficial sepsis, and helps to avoid worms, will preserve them (in a meta-phorical amputation) for the Life to Come in which they will be preserved from *both* worms *and* fire.

Isa.lxvi.24 is the last verse of Isaiah. The blessed will see with their own sight the torments of the wicked which are an utter paradox, eternal worms and eternal fire. Jesus uses this not in a negative sense, as similar ideas are used by prophets, psalmist, and apocryphal writers, ancient and post-Christian alike, but *positively*. This is a characteristic of Jesus's teaching. ' Take Isa.lxvi.24 seriously, and preserve yourselves from the worm and the fire of hell by preserving yourselves from worm and fire in this world. ' We have not done with fire yet. In Jesus's world burning alive was a penalty for certain crimes even according to the Pharisees (25), and it certainly figures in the scriptures (26). Herod the Great burnt alive certain men whom he had con-demned for sedition (27). But applying the fire of cauterisation in a spiritual sense in this life many of Jesus's contemporaries would avoid the actual fire of real amputations and even burning alive. The real worm and the real fire of real injuries and real death can be avoided by spiritual amputation and spiritual treatment which will save the patient-victim from the eternal pains of hell. This throws a new light on St. Paul's words at 1 Cor.iii.15, v. 5 (which do not justify an auto da fé) !

(25) The subject is handled in detail by Hyman E. GOLDIN, *Hebrew Criminal Law and Procedure* (New York, Twayne, 1952), 34-35.

(26) Lev.xx.14 ; xxi.9. It is of interest that all the biblical and rabbinical crimes originally punished by burning alive were sex crimes (incest and adultery), which throws a special light on St. Paul's famous saying (1 Cor. vii.9), ' for it is better to marry than to burn '. Gen.xxxviii.24 ; Josh.vii.15.

(27) Josephus, *Ant.* xvii.167.

FURTHER ANNOTATION

Tit. A shorter treatment of this theme appeared in 'Salted with fire', *Theology*, 76, no. 637 (1973), 364-368, where some further particulars appear.

p. [11], n. 2. Whereas the relevance of India is powerfully testified to by Bishop N. C. Sargant at *Bangalore Theological Forum*, 4/2, 1972, 88-90, and the behaviour of Honi the Circle-drawer and even Hanina ben Dosa (for both see G. Vermes, *Jesus the Jew*, London, 1973, 69-74) betrays recognisable Indian influence.

p. [15], l. 21. *Midrash hagadol* on Exod. xx.4 shows that 'adultery' can be committed with the hand.

p. [15], l. 26. Or valour is alluded to: Plutarch, *Crassus*, xxxi-xxxii.

p. [16], n. 5. Targ. Pal. (Neofiti), Exod. xv.12.

p. [17], l. 19. Jewish piety watched the hands and feet: Midr. R., Gen. LXVII.3 (referring to 1 K. xiii.4, Prov. i.15f); See Is. lvi.2, lviii.13, lix. 7; Job xxxi.5, 7. Ibn Paquda, *Duties of the Heart* II, 321-3.

p. [18], l. 22. One's life might be saved by the loss of a member through which one had offended the party, in whose power it lay to apply the precaution: Cic., *de Offic.*, iii.11. A suicide's hand (Aesch., c. Ct. 244; Jos., *BJ* iii.378)!

p. [19], l. 16, b. Kerit. 15b; Semaḥot IV.28; j. Naz. VII.1.

p. [19], l. 32. Cf. Manu VIII.283!

p. [23], l. 15. Cf. Sir. iii.12-14 (the eye which incites).

p. [25], l. 3. Num. xv.39. Apocryphal literature (Sir. ix.5, Ps. Sal. xvi.7: the eye may offend as recipient and donor of impressions, Test. Rub. v. 3). CD II.16. Sifre on Num. XV.38 (§. 115). Pes. Rabb. 24; Midr. R., Lev. XXIII.12. Goulder, *Midrash and Lection* (1974), 259, 290. For *hypsēlophthalmos* see Didache iii.3. b. Soṭ. 8b (a blind man may complain of the want of aural pornography!). Moore, *Judaism*, ii, 268.

p. [25], l. 7. Dio Chrysostom (born *c.* A.D. 40), xxxiii.49.

p. [25], n. 16. See also Philostratus, *Vit. Ap.* VI.10 (214). Also p. [25], l. 3.

p. [26], l. 21. M. Fazlul Haq at 1974 Kerala Law Times, Journal, 49-51, argues for the reintroduction of the Islamic rule in view of Manu's precepts and Mt. v. 29-30. H. Chakraborti, 'Theft now and then', *Law Quarterly* (Calcutta), xi/1 (1974), 61-66.

p. [26], n. 18. Amputation was abolished as a penalty in 1791.

p. [27], l. 15. Amputation was much used in Nepal in 1826-43 as testified to by B.H. Hodgson (L. Adam, 'Criminal law and procedure in Nepal...', *Far Eastern Quarterly* 9 (1950), 146ff, 161-8).

p. [27], l. 17. Manu VIII.125 lists places suitable for punishment, including the two hands, both feet and the eyes. Hand and feet were cut off for false witness and mayhem: Megasthenes at Strabo XV.1.54 (Jacoby, FGrHist 715 F32, p. 635, ll. 12-14). Not merely a talionic penalty.

p. [29], l. 24. Deussen was of the view that Mahābhārata XII.168.34 should be compared with Mt v.29. See also Mahābhārata XII.24.2-27.

p. [29], l. 34. For the law in action in the Turkish empire see Uriel Heyd, *Studies in Old Ottoman Criminal Law* (Oxford, 1973), index, 'mutilation'. Hooker, *Int. Comp. L.Q.* xxii (1973), 494. S.M. Ikram, *Muslim Civilisation in India* (Calcutta, 1964). 235-6.

p. [30], l. 9. The government ordered amputation of the hand as a punishment: Abba b. Abba (*c.* A.D. 200-225) at b. Yeb. 105a. One who lost a hand or fingers was called *gîdēm*. R. Hûna' (end 3rd cent.) inflicted amputation for striking relying simply on Job xxxviii 15 (cf. xxxi.22): b. Sanh. 58b.

p. [31], l. 16. b. Sanh. 58b. j. Shab. XVI.15c. Philo, *Spec. Leg.* II.244, 247. b. Pes. 57a-b.

p. [32], n. 22. Keim calmly says (*Jesus of Nazara*, iv, 336 n. 3) 'it is said that penal drowning was practised only by the Syrians, Phoenicians, Greeks, and Romans (Dio. xvi.35; Suet. *Oct.* 67)' and he refers to the Jos. passage above. See also Dio Chrysostom xxxi.96. Chariton, *de Chaerea et Callirhoe* V. 5.

p. [34], l. 24. The generation which heard God at Mt. Sinai was never infested with worms or maggots: Midr. R., Deut. VII.11; *Midr. on Ps.*; Ps. 23, §4, etc. Worms had no dominion over Abraham, Isaac, Joseph, etc. (Ps. xvi.9): b.B.B. 17a. The blasphemer and slanderer are eaten alive by worms: ps. Philo, *L.B.A.* 58-9, 63-4. Ginzberg, *L.J.* iii.283, vi.213 n. 136. The rebellious Israelites in the Wilderness died of worms in their abdomens and tongues: Targ. Pal., Num. xiv.37.

p. [35], l. 27. b. Ber. 5a. Rav Papha (*d.* 375) at b. Nidd. 31a. P. Fiebig, *Jesu Bergpredigt* (1924), 21.

p. [36], l. 21. Cf. Maimonides, *Code*, XIV.I.xxiv, 4 (trans., p. 73) (based on b. Sanh. 46a).

p. [36], n. 27. 2 Macc. vii.4-5. The Gevat ha-Mivtar ossuaries included a skeleton of a man burnt to death over a griddle.

LAW IN THE NEW TESTAMENT:
THE PARABLE
OF THE UNJUST JUDGE

The parable of the Unjust Judge (Luke xviii. 1–8) is invariably explained in one way,[1] namely that the tale of the unscrupulous judge, who gives way out of weariness to the poor widow's plea, shows, by contrast, how much more readily God will hear the prayers of his elect! There are some minor differences of opinion as to the exact point of the parable, what it has to do with prayer in general, and to what degree it was originally bound up with any eschatological expectations. Assuming that eschatology was, from the first, an ingredient, and not an embellishment by the early church,[2] there is a difference of opinion as to what was really meant by ἐν τάχει.[3] If it was the church's gloss upon a simile of Jesus, it is still of great interest to try to recover exactly what was meant. There is some doubt what is meant by πίστιν, and even (though it is difficult to see why)[4] whether it *could* go back to Jesus.[5] It was remarked long ago that the words ὑπωπιάζῃ με have as many translations as there are versions.[6] But on the whole it is felt that the kernel of the story is

---

[1] A. Plummer, *Critical and Exegetical Commentary...S. Luke* (Edinburgh, 1901), p. 411 ff.; A Jülicher, *Die Gleichnisreden Jesu*, II (Tübingen, 1910), 276–90; D. Buzy, 'Le juge inique', *R.B.* xxxix (1930), 378–91; K. Bornhäuser, *Studien z. Sondergut des Lukas* (Gütersloh, 1934), pp. 161–70; B. T. D. Smith (below, p. 180 n. 2); W. Michaelis, *Das hochzeitliche Kleid* (Berlin, 1939), pp. 251–62; C. Spicq, 'La parabole de la Veuve obstinée et du Juge inerte, aux décisions impromptues', *R.B.* LXVIII (1961), 68–90; G. Delling, 'Das Gleichnis vom gottlosen Richter', *Z.N.T.W.* LIII (1962), 1–25; C. E. B. Cranfield, 'The parable of the Unjust Judge and the Eschatology of Luke–Acts', *Scot. J. Theol.* XVI (1963), 297–301; J. Jeremias, *Parables of Jesus* (London, 1963), pp. 48, 153–7; G. V. Jones, *The Art and Truth of the Parables* (London, 1964), pp. 86–7; W. Grundmann, *Das Evangelium nach Lukas* (Berlin, 1964), pp. 345–8; E. Linnemann, *Parables of Jesus* (London, 1966). I may be permitted to remark that the pericope has a surprising number of ambiguous words, and several contributions, especially those of Jeremias, Spicq, and Delling, go minutely into the linguistic and literary background without reaching convincing conclusions; whereas a knowledge of the cultural background places the primary meanings of those words beyond doubt. As in so many New Testament passages, however, a more secure knowledge of the *primary* meaning by no means excludes the scope or scopes which the evangelist may have permitted to the secondary meanings. Naturally we must commence with the primary meaning. [2] So Jülicher, Bultmann, and many recent critics.

[3] 'Suddenly': Bornhäuser, Spicq, Jeremias, Grundmann. 'Speedily': Jülicher, Deissmann, Delling, Linnemann, Cranfield. A. Feuillet in Davies and Daube, edd., *Background of the New Testament* (Dodd volume) (Cambridge, 1956), p. 278. N. Geldenhuys, *Commentary on the Gospel of Luke* (London, 1950), p. 448, amusingly equates ἐν τάχει with ἐπὶ χρόνον, implying that to an Asian speed implies 'after a long time'. I find it hard to disagree.

[4] Cf. A. Schlatter, *Der Glaube im Neuen Testament*, 5th edn (Stuttgart, 1963), pp. 158–9. Note Matt. viii. 10, Luke vii. 9, and cf. Luke xxii. 32 (Satan!).

[5] E. Grässer, *Das Problem der Parusieverzögerung in den synoptischen Evangelien...*, 2nd edn (Berlin, 1960), pp. 36–8.

[6] So Trench, *Notes* on the passage. The only approximately reliable translation (and I include Luther's amongst the modern versions) was that of the Rheims version (1582): 'lest at the last she come and defame me', Polus, *Synops.* IV (1669), col. 1070. Delitzch's trans. utilizes Job xix. 2.

so clear and obvious that a lack of sharpness in the details is not a serious loss.

In what follows I want to offer two contributions to a clearer understanding of the parable; first by showing what Jesus was talking about, assuming for the purposes of argument that no eschatology was involved. Then for a moment we can take up *vv.* 7–8 and see how well they may fit with that. If they fit well it does not prove that they were indeed Jesus's own application of his little parable, but the possibility that they were will be affected by the degree of intrinsic appropriateness of the idea. I believe there are ways, at once internal to the parable and external to it, by which we can check up upon the meaning; and something can be added to our comprehension of the authenticity of the much-doubted contextuality of *vv.* 2–5 and 7–8. Corroboration of my contention, regarding 'what Jesus was talking about' comes readily from the little parable of Reconciliation with the Adversary, which is splendidly drafted for my purpose, whether in the Lucan or the Matthaean version. It glories in the twin characteristics of being a lifelike picture, an impressive metaphor from people's actual behaviour, and a symbolic sermon at the same time. That is obvious from the very surface of that parable and will not be disputed, though the exact meaning of it (oddly enough) has eluded the church since the latter has been in predominantly gentile hands.

My second contribution is, on the surface, small enough. I explain what ὑπωπιάζη means. It is a well-known Asian expression which I have often used myself. It is in daily use from Smyrna to Singapore. Curiously it is not known in Africa or Europe, though Holland's long contact with Indonesia seems to have given the Dutch some awareness of it. Since we can be sure what was the expression the Judge used, we know the reason why he acted as he did, and we known why God will 'avenge' his elect. The behaviour of the Judge is parallel to that of God, and is not offered as a contrast with it. It was not by accident that Jesus did not use the words πόσῳ μᾶλλον here, as he did elsewhere.[1]

I trust there will be no feeling of disappointment. The little story does not have biblical allusions, except didactic ones. The feeling of the man in the street that the parable is unsatisfactory, in that it suggests that God can be pestered into action, is perfectly reasonable. The theologian who tells him that he is superficial[2] is less reasonable than he is. The truth of the matter is that the Jewish man in the street living in an environment which was not

---

[1] Luke xi. 13. A. Loisy, *Les évangiles synoptiques*, II (Ceffonds, 1908), 189, appropriately shows that Christ is to be the judge, not God, i.e. God judges through Christ (as at John viii. 16, 26, 50; xii. 47, 48). Regarding the Johannine paradox I would suggest that Christ, in the earthly ministry and in the second coming, plays opposing roles: he acts as man's advocate (and thus convicts unbelievers of sin), and later, when advocacy is over, he comes as judge. Yet the player of the two roles is one and the same person.

[2] K. H. Rengstorf, *Das Evangelium nach Lukas* (Göttingen, 1962), pp. 205–6. Professor Rengstorf is the only commentator to notice that at 8 *b* Jesus may well have referred to all 'comings', including his ministry on earth (cf. Luke xvii. 21; v. 24). Such ambiguities are in order.

ruled as a Jewish state would grasp the point at once. The widow pesters the judge, and she gets her investigation: the pious, the elect, pester their Judge, and they will get their Investigation. Too true! It may seem a pity that unlike the parable of the Samaritan, or the Prodigal Son, the story is not loaded with haggadic or midrashic insinuations. But the reference to the contrast between the Law of God and the law of Man is closely parallel to that in the parable of the Steward, and this is where the contact between those two parables lies, as has been dimly seen ever since the words τῆς ἀδικίας (i.e. of the world of Satan, the world in which the true Law does not run) was recognized as linking them.[1] It is to the contrast between those two laws that we first go.

TWO JURISDICTIONS IN A SINGLE LAND

It is odd that not a single discussion of this parable has pointed out who the actors are and what they are doing; nor what are the implications of their behaviour. A so-called parallel from the experiences of Tristram has figured in commentaries,[2] but all oblivious of the want of correspondence in the situations. Some elementary legal history was needed, and though Sherwin-White apparently knew the point, he stopped short of actually uttering it.[3] The point is simply this, that there were two sorts of legal jurisdiction in force concurrently. They were both *de jure* and *de facto* valid and efficacious. But the 'worse' one (as so often with 'worldly' things) had the best of it whenever, as could frequently be, there was a conflict between them. Compendiously, there were συναγωγαί on the one hand and there were ἐξουσίαι, viz. ἡγεμόνες and βασιλεῖς, on the other (Luke xii. 11; xxi. 12), and the latter were much more effective than the former. The widow and the Judge belong to one sphere: they are participating in the intriguing and absorbing drama of human litigation in its raw and unregenerate state, exactly as might gentiles anywhere. In the very same city there would be righteous folk bringing their complaints before righteous judges and, if the latter were not able to give them satisfaction, leaving their problem with God—which was the course of action which the Psalms recommended.[4]

In Palestine the customary courts amongst the Jews were run, or were sought to be run, on lines laid down by the Torah.[5] Where Pharisees were in

---

[1] F. Delitzch, *Zeits. f. d. gesammte lutherische Theologie u. Kirche*, xxxvii (1876), 601.

[2] Quoted in B. T. D. Smith, *The Parables of the Synoptic Gospels* (Cambridge, 1937), pp. 148–54. Summarized by Jeremias. The analogy would have been apposite if the woman had been appealing to an administrative (*mazālim*) judge over the head of a *kādi* who applied the Quranic law.

[3] A. N. Sherwin-White, *Roman Society and Roman Law in the New Testament* (Oxford, 1963), pp. 133–4.

[4] Ps. ix; xii; xxxiv. 15–19; xxxv; xxxvii. 7–13, 33; xxviii. 12–22; xxxix; xl. 13 ff.; xliii. 2; liv; lvi. 1, 4, 9–11; lxix. 4; xcix. 8. Ps. xxvii. 11–12 seems particularly relevant. Prayer is a kind of fight: Rom. xv. 30; Col. iv. 22. Note Ps. Sal. ii. 36 (referred to by Spicq); ὅτι χρηστὸς ὁ κύριος τοῖς ἐπικαλουμένοις αὐτὸν ἐν ὑπομονῇ... See p. 185 n. 3 below.

[5] A. Schalit, *König Herodes, Der Mann u. sein Werk* (Berlin, 1969), pp. 148, 223–32. His correction of Sugranyes De Franch at p. 233 n. 303 is important. H.-P. Chajes at *Rev. Études Juives*, xxxix (1899), 52 speaks of the Jewish judicial administration in a way that must have been true in large measure even before A.D. 70.

control we have, in the Mishnah, an approximation to what their rulings would have been, and how they would have been enforced. Where more enthusiastic circles were in power stricter rules would be enforced. Yet even there some limits would have been observed. There would have been areas in which complaints could not receive satisfaction. Many misdeeds, over which the unlucky or the orthodox might have reason to complain, must, according to the Torah, be left to God for him alone to punish. The customary courts were staffed by local notabilities. To be a single referee was a social as well as a political distinction.[1] Men renowned for piety would be approached to solve problems which a keen and impartial mind could solve.[2] Left to himself the Palestinian Jew would have expected the holy Law to be resorted to for the solution of any and every problem. But he had not been left to himself.

Since the Ptolemaic–Seleucid period a system had grown up alongside the customary system, which left the latter in full control in religious matters (including a good deal of criminal law, e.g. blasphemy), but superimposed upon it a jurisdiction which could be called 'police', or 'administration'. In the time of Herod the Great it is clear that royal administrators and royal judges existed, whose task it was to apply the royal ordinances. The king had no power to vary the Torah, but he evidently enacted measures of his own supplementary to it. It is clear that a contrast between the customary law and the law administered in the 'administrative' courts became endemic, and continued even when, after some time, a measure of Jewish self-government returned.[3] In any part of the Land of Israel the organs of the tetrarch and, still more, of the procurator, would be found assisting in the maintenance of law and order, facilitating the collection of the revenue, and applying the ordinances that came from the palace. We can see how it was very well from the state of Egypt. Egypt too had customary, village courts. But here bureaucracy was so highly developed that it was easier sometimes for a litigant to urge that the customary courts were not giving justice, and to invoke the aid of the στρατηγός, petitioning him to exercise his 'administrative' or 'police' justice. There were two types of courts in Egypt, the regular judiciary and the administrative officials, and far more is known of the doings of the latter.[4] This was because they could hear cases summarily, were not bound by any restrictions like a Rule of Law, and could execute a sentence in a way which few customary courts could do. The Jewish courts of three could not easily

---

[1] Job xxix. 11–17.

[2] See Luke xii. 14. The word μεριστής (with its double meaning) is a conscious improvement on Exod. ii. 24.

[3] M. Bloch, *Das Mosaïsch-Talmudische Polizeirecht* (Jahresbericht der Landes-Rabbinerschule in Budapest, 1878–9), pp. 10–14, is important. For the general position: L. Mitteis, *Reichsrecht u. Volksrecht*... (Leipzig, 1891), pp. 91 ff. For the Ptolemaic–Seleucid era, M. Hengel, *Judentum u. Hellenismus* (Tübingen, 1969), ch. 1. J. Felten, *Neutestamentliche Zeitgeschichte*, 1 (Regensburg, 1925), 315–17, is useful.

[4] H. J. Wolff, *Das Justizwesen der Ptolemäer* (Munich, 1962), a work of extraordinary value for our purposes. Greek courts greedily snatched at suits between Egyptians: *Pap. Tebt.* I. 5, 217–20.

force unwilling litigants, and certainly not Samaritan or gentile litigants, to observe their rules. Moreover they were strict in their taking of evidence, and those who were not well supplied with unimpeachable witnesses would have preferred a non-Torah court in which the false witness had not to fear the penalty laid down in the Jewish law.[1] The judges in the administrative courts might well have Jewish assessors, or assessors who could explain the customary law, and there is no reason why the judges themselves should not have been Jews. But their business was to keep the peace with an eye to political necessity, and to apply the ruler's orders, which consisted, we may be sure,[2] of a mass of instructions which no rabbi could construe, let alone apply.

The situation was paralleled in Muslim countries until very recent times. The sacred law was applied by *kādis* in the *shari'a* courts, but alongside them there were the 'administrative' courts, the so-called *mazālim* jurisdiction,[3] which could, and often did, cut across the religious courts' work, and which would, in the case of conflict, get the upper hand. A somewhat similar situation is known to this day in Cyprus, Israel, and South Asia, where one or more religious laws are administered under the aegis of a civil and secular power which can, and often has, set aside or ignored the decisions of the traditional and customary tribunals where these would conflict with governmental policy. The pious will not scruple to run to a secular court if they would gain an advantage thereby, and this is everywhere viewed with dismay as a cultural treachery, disloyalty.[4]

The parable of Reconciliation with the Adversary plays upon this tendency to run to a 'higher' (i.e. more efficacious, more summary) judge.

Matt. v. 25–6	Luke xii. 58–9
ἴσθι εὐνοῶν τῷ ἀντιδίκῳ σου ταχὺ ἕως ὅτου εἶ μετ' αὐτοῦ ἐν τῇ ὁδῷ· μή ποτέ σε παραδῷ ὁ ἀντίδικος τῷ κριτῇ καὶ ὁ κριτὴς τῷ ὑπηρέτῃ, καὶ εἰς φυλακὴν βληθήσῃ· ἀμὴν λέγω σοι, οὐ μὴ ἐξέλθῃς ἐκεῖθεν ἕως ἂν ἀποδῷς τὸν ἔσχατον κοδράντην.	τί δὲ καὶ ἀφ' ἑαυτῶν οὐ κρίνετε τὸ δίκαιον; ὡς γὰρ ὑπάγεις μετὰ τοῦ ἀντιδίκου σου ἐπ' ἄρχοντα, ἐν τῇ ὁδῷ δὸς ἐργασίαν ἀπηλλάχθαι ἀπ' αὐτοῦ, μή ποτε κατασύρῃ σε πρὸς τὸν κριτήν, καὶ ὁ κριτής σε παραδώσει τῷ πράκτορι, καὶ ὁ πράκτωρ σε βαλεῖ εἰς φυλακήν. λέγω σοι, οὐ μὴ ἐξέλθῃς ἐκεῖθεν ἕως καὶ τὸ ἔσχατον λεπτὸν ἀποδῷς.

We may paraphrase the meaning of the parable in this way:

Though out of anxiety for your financial security, out of righteous indignation, impatience, or even a desire for revenge, you are, with the best case in the world,

---

[1] Derrett, *Law in the New Testament* (London, 1970), ch. 7. Maimonides, *M.T.* xiv, v, iii, 10.

[2] M.-T. Lenger, *Corpus des Ordonnances des Ptolémées* (Brussels, 1964), illustrates the material adequately. A. Théodoridès, *R.I.D.A.* xiv (1967), pp. 107–52.

[3] E. Tyan, 'Judicial organisation', ch. 10 in M. Khadduri and H. J. Libesny, edd., *Law in the Middle East*, 1 (Washington, 1955). N. J. Coulson, *Conflicts and Tensions in Islamic Jurisprudence* (Chicago, 1969), ch. 4, esp. pp. 66 ff.

[4] Plato, *Rep.* 405 (trans. Jowett, 3rd edn, iii, 92). See p. 184 n. 2 below.

taking your defendant (the man who owes you something)[1] before a civil court (an official who will be sure to listen to your case and offer you your remedy when the defendant is unable to obtain a respite) ;[2] the true (as contrasted with the apparent) position is that it is *you* who must beg the defendant for a respite! Your cruelty to him, or at the very least your insistence upon an enforced remedy, has given him a case against you in the heavenly court. Before you have reached your court-house he has delated you to the true Judge. You may obtain a decree which he can work off in a year. But meanwhile you have been condemned to hell for eternity.

That this is the correct way of reading the text occurred to Dr G. B. Caird,[3] but so far he is alone in this, for almost everyone imagines that ἄρχοντα and κριτήν are the same person.[4] Jesus is relying on the habit of taking a case from one court to another. It is very natural that people should do this, and to make the point fully intelligible and verifiable I am bound to take illustrations from very recent history in India and from the not-so-remote history of England.

In Bombay the court of the religious leader of a Muslim sect had excommunicated a member of his sect for breaches of caste discipline. Such excommunications occurred rarely, and they were very unpopular because they were thought to be an abuse of the almost autocratic powers of the leader. A local statute purported to prohibit all excommunications and to make them offences. In reliance upon this statute the excommunicate dragged his erstwhile spiritual head from one civil court to another until he reached the Supreme Court of India, which (to the indignation of almost the entire public) held that excommunications cannot be prohibited (under the Constitution) if they are decreed in the interests of the religious integrity of the community.[5] India is a country in which a *modus vivendi* has been worked out as between the two jurisdictions, with the aid of concentrated attention from

---

[1] E. Lohmeyer, *Das Evangelium des Matthäus* (Göttingen, 1956), p. 124. εἰ μετ' αὐτοῦ is neutral, the meaning being carried by ἀντίδικος (= 'defendant' at P. Oxy. I. 37, Moulton and Milligan, *Vocabulary, ad v.*). But the word, meaning simply opponent in a law-suit or a dispute amounting to a law-suit, is ambiguous. The context shows that it must mean 'defendant' because the only person with an option is the plaintiff. The defendant having no option is not sinning in being brought before the earthly judge. ὑπάγεις suggests that the person addressed has the option, *ergo* he is the plaintiff. Mishnah B.B. x. 8 (Danby, 382), Derrett, *op. cit.* p. 34 n. 1.

[2] ἄρχων is any functionary, especially a Jewish customary 'ruler' as at Matt. ix. 18 (at Matt. xx. 25 Jesus explains how the non-Jewish 'rulers' lack the democratic ethos of the Jews!); Luke xviii. 18. At Luke xxiii. 13 the 'rulers' are the (as it were) native chiefs in contrast to the *real* ruler, Pilate himself. The word does not imply, as it would in a Hellenic context, that they were formally appointed under any constitutional authority.

[3] *Exp. T.* LXXVII (1966), 37. Also W. C. Allen, *Critical and Exegetical Commentary on the Gospel according to S. Matthew* (Edinburgh, 1912), pp. 49–51.

[4] P. Schanz, *Commentar über das Evangelium des heiligen Lucas* (Tübingen, 1883), p. 364; B. Weiss, *Die Evangelien des Markus u. Lukas* (Göttingen, 1901), p. 501; K. H. Rengstorf, *Das Evangelium nach Lukas* (1962), p. 167 (both are translated *Richter*). It is upon this misunderstanding that interpretations rest such as that of R. Bultmann, *History of the Synoptic Tradition* (trans. Marsh) (Oxford, 1968), p. 193. *Four* kinds of judicial authority are listed at Sir. xli. 18 (was this a parallel?).

[5] The celebrated case of Sardar Syedna Taher v. State of Bombay (A.I.R. 1962 S.C. 853) discussed in Derrett, *Religion, Law and the State in India* (London, 1968), pp. 473 ff. A pertinent example of the conflicts between custom and the State's foreign-based law is discussed by P. V. Kane, *History of Dharmaśāstra* II, 620. Other examples are given in Derrett, *op. cit.* pp. 287 nn., 358 n. 3.

constitutional lawyers. In first-century Palestine the problem was notorious,[1] but no solution, except that of utter righteousness (i.e. reliance upon God alone) had been proposed. In Britain up to the Reformation the ecclesiastical courts exercised jurisdiction in many spheres now regarded as civil (libel, slander, tithes, and secular rights connected with churches). But, like many an Indian caste now and many customary courts in first-century Palestine, the ecclesiastical courts had small and uncertain powers of coercion: unless action was taken irregularly or surreptitiously even an excellent case could come to nothing. Right up to the eighteenth century in England it was possible for a man guilty of defaming his neighbour to escape penalty altogether by going, as soon as the libellant (plaintiff) served the libel (or writ, as it were) upon him, to the common-law court and obtaining a writ of prohibition ordering the ecclesiastical judge to stop hearing the case. No *modus vivendi* was ever worked out satisfactorily in England. The illustration is apt enough since it shows how, even when the rights are clear to any impartial observer, the wrongdoer will go to any court which offers him a chance of a better outcome.

The Jewish Law is quite clear about this. Though judicial administration antedates the giving of the Torah (Exod. xviii. 21 ff.), no non-Torah rule has any force in conscience. The Torah itself forbids access to non-Jewish courts, even if they give decrees which coincide with what a righteous Jewish court would grant.[2] This is Mishnaic, Pharisaical law. The common people would be sorely tempted not to follow it, but to go to the procurator's officials, or the Hellenistic 'administrative' judge if thereby, appealing to some political or fiscal argument, they could have their opponent's rights frustrated or could force him to do what the customary law would have left alone, whether out of incompetence (because the remedy did not exist), or by choice (because it must be left to God). In the communities of strict sectarians access to any judges outside the community was out of the question, for the power of judgement resided in the community as a whole, the ultimate sanction being excommunication.[3] Jesus himself objected to litigation of all kinds. His recommendation is well known. The ultimate sanction he recognized was the personal boycott (if the community would not pronounce excommunication for any reason).[4] That the earliest church followed the Pharisaical or a stricter view, or that they were urged to do so, is plain from St Paul's teaching on the subject. The passage[5] has given rise to some doubts regarding words here and there, doubts which I would solve in the light of

[1] See Ps. Sal. xvii. 20: ...καὶ ὁ κριτὴς ἐν ἀπειθείᾳ... (this is our 'unjust' judge). For 'Satan's world' see Ps. ii. 3; Luke iv. 6; xxii. 3, 53; John xii. 31; 2 Cor. iv. 4; Rev. xii. 9.
[2] The authority is Lev. xxiv. 22. Mekilta on Exod. xxi. 1 (Lauterbach, III, 1–2). To volunteer testimony against a Jew in certain non-Jewish courts merited excommunication after A.D. 130: b. B.Ḳ. 113b.
[3] G. Vermes, *The Dead Sea Scrolls in English* (London, 1966), pp. 18–29. Excommunication at the hands of non-sectarians is referred to in Luke xxi. 12.
[4] Mat. xviii. 17 (σοί).   [5] 1 Cor. v. 12–vi. 9.

this article,[1] but it is plain to all that St Paul recommended the church at Corinth to submit all *unavoidable* litigation to the church as a body, including its spiritual head,[2] with the aid of delegates from its own general assembly, as it were. There could be no question of Christians litigating with other Christians before non-Christian (Hellenic) judges. Of course if the complaint was against a non-Christian other considerations might apply, but even there the Christian was under the biblical obligation to appeal to the conscience, to avoid force, and to leave the rest to God.[3]

The Jewish Law itself developed in an interesting way. It is obvious to everyone that Jews, including the pious, did not boycott gentile courts. Every effort was made to keep disputes internal to the community. The Bet Din everywhere attempted to apply effective sanctions and to bring about justice by appropriate means. But recourse to gentile courts was not in itself an offence worthy of excommunication. The attitude of the Mishnaic and Talmudic law to litigation is remarkably lenient. Unlike another Asian civilization which openly regarded litigation between relatives as blameworthy, and which attempted to render such suits impossible or impracticable,[4] the Talmudic law takes the view that where rights are infringed or remedies are available they should be put into effect. It is taken absolutely for granted that both parties want the holy Law applied to them and that the judge, so far from being one of the corps of Satan (τῆς ἀδικίας), will be one versed in holiness and qualified in sanctity as well as jurisprudence. Thus recourse to such a court could never be a sin. Yet, reasonably enough, the view gradually made itself felt (as Rabbi Dr H. J. Zimmels informs me) that the Torah itself contemplated solution of disputes by arbitration and compromise, and that it was better to give way here and there rather than to come before the court, even on a cast-iron case.[5] This is manifested quite late

---

[1] ἀδίκων, ἐξουθενημένων = non-Christian judges. ἐλάχιστος = worldly (cf. Luke xvi. 10). Take ἀνάξιοι in the sense of 'above' (cf. Lucian, *Fugit.*, c. 1; Soph., *Oed. Col.* 1446). Rom. xii. 19 is in point (cf. Deut. xxxii. 35, 41) and 2 Thess. i. 5–12 seems actually to be based on Luke xviii. 1–8. On κρίνω τὸ δίκαιον see A. Deissmann, *Light from the Ancient East* (London, 1927), p. 117.   [2] 1 Cor. v. 4.

[3] See above p. 180 n. 4. The model is described at 1 Pet. ii. 23. As plaintiff she should not have gone to law: Matt. xviii. 15–17 (based in part on Lev. xix. 17); as defendant she should have offered no opposition: Matt. v. 40. The just 'restores which he took not away': Ps. lxix. 4. This teaching improves upon Sir. x. 6: ἐπὶ παντὶ ἀδικήματι μὴ μηνιάσῃς τῷ πλησίον.

[4] The Hindu view. Nārada refers disputes between father and son to an *ex officio* jurisdiction called *prakirṇaka*. On husband and wife see L. Rocher in J. N. D. Anderson, ed., *Family Law in Asia and Africa* (London, 1968), at pp. 110–13. Those who give evidence in the cases which are forbidden by the holy law (but which are nevertheless heard under the State's current system of judicature) are subject to social penalties. And so is the son who litigates with his father (Yama and other authorities cited by Lakshmīdhara, *K. K. T.*, *Śrāddhak.* 83, 85, 89).

[5] B. Talmud, San. 6 b (Sonc. trans. 21). The Tosefta relates the opinion of R. Judah b. Karha (2nd cent.): Zech. viii. 16 exhorts litigants in money matters to achieve a compromise by arbitration. So Maimonides, *Mishneh Torah*, Hilkot Sanh. xxii. 4 (trans. Hershman, *Book of Judges*, New Haven, 1949, p. 66); Jacob b. Asher, *Turim* in Tur Ḥoshen Mishpaṭ xii, followed in Joseph Caro's *Shulḥan Aruch*. R. Jacob b. Asher saw a command to attempt compromises, before proceeding to execute judgement, in the letters of the word *ha-mishpaṭiym* at Exod. xxi. 1. For arbitration in Jewish law see Job ix. 33 (μεσίτης), and Isa. iii. 6 (cf. Isa. i. 23). B. Cohen, *Jewish and Roman Law*, ii (N.Y. 1966), 651–709.

in the story of Jewish law, but the seeds of it must have been old. I make this point because it is needful for the reader to realize that it was not by any means remarkable for a widow to do what she did, but that it was reprehensible of her to do it.

ESCHATOLOGY AND THE PARABLE

The Matthaean version of the parable of Reconciliation shows plainly that by his time that parable was taken symbolically. It is quite obvious that inherently it was so to be taken. In the Lucan version the helpless defendant himself hauls his confident plaintiff before the divine throne. Prayer (as at our *v.* 1) obtains a swift response. Matthew, contrasting the ideal behaviour of a plaintiff with the ideal behaviour of a defendant (Matt. v. 23–4), explains that it is Satan (the repeated ἀντίδικος) who will delate. By dragging your opponent to the court you give Satan an opportunity to inform against you. Just as the earthly judge you approach can exact a penalty from your opponent, so the Adversary will, on your opponent's behalf or otherwise, have a penalty exacted from you. There is a higher court. *Traditionally* God's court is an administrative court! The κριτής, who gives ἐκδίκησιν (vengeance, the technical term for administrative justice throughout the Hellenistic age as so many papyri testify),[1] often acts *ex officio* at the relation of a complainant. As the Mishnah says, he is the Judge, and the Accuser...[2] No Rule of Law applies in his court. In fact the notion of God as judge, with wrath, etc., goes back to a time when the Jewish law of evidence, procedure, and the like had not been developed. Thus the picture of God as judge was historically and ideologically parallel to the actual behaviour of Hellenistic administrative or police judges, who acted summarily, were not bound by rules of pleading and evidence,[3] and could send the plaintiff away as vexed as the defendant. God was viewed as a judge like the official of the fifth century B.C. whose letter we have, ordering his subordinate in Egypt to apprehend and punish certain malefactors without any question of a trial, let alone a fair one.[4] No one would suggest that God's trials are unfair: but they are not

[1] Theologians have not savoured the range of meanings, even though Delling (*Z.N.T.W.* LIII (1962), 8 n. 32) notices Preisigke's translation of ἐκδίκησις = punishment, which is an addition to the range noticed in Liddell–Scott–Jones and Moulton–Milligan. A. Schlatter (*Das Evangelium des Lukas*, Stuttgart, 1931, pp. 394–8) does cite Jos. *Ant.* VII. 294 and XVII. 242 for secular instances of 'vengeance'. F. Hauck, *Das Evangelium des Lukas* (Leipzig, 1934), pp. 219–20, takes the word to imply rather justice than vengeance. The strong final esoteric overtones of Sir. xxxv. 12–20, Wis. xii. 1–27, and the meaning 'sentence' at Sir. xlviii. 7 are relevant. Surely the word was chosen, by Luke, to convey at one and the same time the typical cry of the injured petitioner on the secular level (see R. Taubenschlag, *Law of Greco-Roman Egypt* (N.Y. 1944), p. 335 n. 65: πρὸς τὸ ἀκόλουθον γείνεσθαι καὶ τυχεῖν με τῆς δεούσης ἐγδικίας) with the Septuagintal meaning, 'avenge, take vengeance/punish' (59 times as against the 'visit/punish' meaning which appears 29 times). See especially Sir. v. 7; vii. 17; xxviii. 1.
[2] *Mishnah*, Avot IV. 22.   [3] Personal considerations figured: Matt. xxv. 32–41.
[4] G. R. Driver, *Aramaic Documents of the Fifth Century B.C.* (Oxford, 1954), p. 14. In ancient civilizations justice[1] = righteousness and justice[2] = exercise of royal administrative jurisdiction were often carefully distinguished. In India the dichotomy led to the development of two distinct sciences, each of which has its own scope, yet both must be studied by administrators: R. Lingat, *Les sources du droit dans le système traditionnel de l'Inde* (Paris/The Hague, 1967), pt. 2, ch. 3.

bound by procedure as earthly civil courts are—hence the concept of the spiritual delator, Satan.

Thus, to be brief, the widow, instead of resting content with what the community court could do for her (if anything) went to the administrative judge, trusting that he would sort out her case. This is the worldly pattern, a worldly widow and a worldly judge. Now 'widow' of course suggests Israel, just as 'judge' suggests God. There is a parallel. The judge can be induced   *
to take action, and the suggestion is that that form of inducement will help us to understand what will promote God's intervention. To that we return presently. Meanwhile, what connection could *vv.* 6–8 have with the story?

Those who cry day and night are the pious.[1] To them ἐκδίκησις, which means justice of the 'police' or 'administrative', as opposed to the civil and adversary type, is bound to come, because the Holy Spirit has repeatedly suggested as much.[2] And because they present themselves regularly in prayer there is no doubt but that they look to no one but God to grant their prayers. If we did not have the story to guide us we should interpret the texts in two ways: the ordinary folk would see God's hand in the ups and downs of life, evil punished in this life, or, if (as so often) this cannot be detected, then in some subsequent existence; the more sophisticated will see the final solution at the end of days, when all wrongs will be righted. And both these interpretations were current in Jewish thought, as is notorious. But as we have Jesus's little story we must see what it implies. Firstly the judge will take action, and hear her case. Ἐκδίκησόν με[3] means really 'take up my case'. He may well find that she is wholly or partially in the wrong. Women are often   *
so clear about their own probity that she may have overlooked the possibility that, in a wider view of her case, the adversary is better entitled to the property, or whatever it was she wanted to have from him. In any case she trusted that judge, whose business was *not* to apply the law of righteousness, to do justice. And there is no reason to suppose that, in the terms of his office, he will fail. *He himself will act as her advocate.*[4]

We are bound to pause over this idea. It is notorious that widows were forced into disputes, and needed advocates. The very situation of a widow, requiring to be paid a sum of money secured upon her deceased husband's estate,[5] places her at risk. Her own sons, and still more her step-sons (in a society with fairly easy divorces) would dispute the amount of her claim if not its validity. Granted that all parties adhered to the customary law, widows needed advocates, and Torah-lawyers used, on Jesus's own evidence (which

---

[1] Ps. vii. 11; lxxxvi. 3; lxxxviii. 1.
[2] Ps. xciv. 1; cxlix. 7; Nah. i. 2; Mic. v. 15; Isa. xxxv. 4; xlvii. 3; Jer. li. 36; Ezek. xxv. 14, 17.
[3] Cf. Job vi. 23; Ps. xciv; cxl. 12; cxlvi.
[4] Precisely as at Jer. l. 34 (M.T. = xxvii. 34 LXX); li. 36.
[5] *Mishnah,* tractate Ketubot. See e.g. Ket. iv. 12 (Danby, *The Mishnah,* p. 251).

has never been contradicted), to make quite good incomes out of them.[1] A
man noted for his piety would become an advocate for the poor and a trustee
for them. In Egypt it was almost unheard of for a widow to approach the
administrative judge direct: an advocate or representative was requisite.[2]
Of course a widow *could* go to the judge direct, but the implication would be
that she was so desperate that she did not care for the impropriety of a lady's
public belligerence. Constantly to show her face in a public place was in
itself a breach of etiquette that only the poorest could afford; and yet one who
had a case worth the judge's attention must have some assets. A personal
appearance thus implies a request that the judge will appoint an advocate
for her, or will act as her advocate himself. A civil court of three, or a full
sanhedrin, or even the righteous referee, dare not do anything of the kind:
for them the adversary system must be followed, subject to a judicial and
judicious exercise of shrewdness. But the police judge could indeed *suo motu*
take up any case and manage it in any way he pleased. I wish to emphasize
that the investigation of her case against the ἀντίδικος could not, even in the
most rough-and-ready milieu, have been carried on without investigation,
inquiry, report, and deliberation, in short an expenditure of administrative
time and energy, and, since it is presumed that neither party tells the truth
unless he must, mere declarations and protestations will achieve nothing.
Hence the widow wanted the judge to act actually or virtually as her advocate,
her avenger, literally or metaphorically, take it how you will.

This is a close parallel to the biblical notions of God's avenging Israel
against the 'heathen'. When the 'heathen' are seen as symbolic for the evil
inclination, Satan, which causes even the pious to stumble, it is clear that the
demand for justice can be interpreted as a demand for protection from evil
itself. The anger of God is directed against Israel as well as against the heathen.[3]
That life may be owed absolutely to the Advocate and Redeemer was known
since Job xxxiii. 23. Now it is time to turn to the passage which Jesus is
interpreting, and since we know a little about the circles in which the book
containing the passage was a favourite, we can even suggest a possible situation in which the parable might originally have been told. This is a little
presumptuous, but if it is taken as an illustration of the scope of meaning (and
not more) we are in safety.

It has been known for years that there was a close connection between
Sirach xxxv. 12–18 and this parable, but some have thought that the effect of
the similarity[4] was only to raise the doubt whether the early church, under

---

[1] Mark xii. 40; Luke xx. 47, to be studied in the light of Isa. i. 23. Note κρίμα. Luke's νομικός is
appropriate. *Midrash on Psalms*, Ps. 15, §5 (Braude, I, 192). I. Ziegler, *Königsgleichnisse*, pp. 98–9,
112 (on advocates).

[2] A widow needed an ἔκδικος (see Moulton and Milligan s.v.)! Wolff, *op. cit.* p. 135 and n. 42.
R. Taubenschlag, *op. cit.* para. 54. For others than widows see b. Shab. 32a = Sonc. trans. 146–7
(quoting Isa. xxxiii. 23). See Philo, *Spec. Leg.* IV. 179 (Colson, VIII, 118), commenting upon Deut. x.
17, 18 Israel is always an 'orphan'.   [3] H. Kleinknecht and others, *Wrath* (London, 1964), p. 123.

[4] H. Riesenfeld, in Blinzler–Kuss–Mussner, edd., *Fests. J. Schmid* (Regensburg, 1963), pp. 214–17.

threats of persecution, had turned the parable to eschatological uses for which Jesus himself had hardly authorized it. Many interpretations of the Greek, and even of the long-disputed μακροθυμεῖ ἐπ' αὐτοῖς could be given, but there is no point in entertaining any of them while we have before us what is almost certainly the text upon which Jesus was weaving his parable. In order to obtain this text all we have to do is to transfer into the Geniza text of the passage[1] the marginal readings in substitution for the textual readings, which are revisions in the nature of simplifications. The text of Sirach found at Masada, and so certified historically to be a book favoured by the Fighters for Jewish Freedom, corresponds to the Geniza fragments in exactly this way.[2] None of the changes is insignificant, but we can rely for our present purposes on two only. The problem about μακροθυμεῖ disappears. The original line which Jesus is closely paraphrasing has the ironical question in it literally: גם אדון לא יתמהמה וגבור מה יתאפק God will *not* delay (in satisfying the widow) until he has crushed the nations, etc. This is a promise not to tarry[3] until any eschatological final judgement. The one who will not wait is clearly called the 'strong one'[4] who will act as avenger. That the widow in Sirach is indeed Jesus's *dramatis persona* is proved by the extreme likelihood that the text he used showed her 'threshing out' her complaints, with a repetitive and almost rhythmic movement.[5]

The Unjust Judge goes into action, for a reason we now come to explore, and his activity from that moment admits no delay. Advocacy and execution —both are provided for the widow, who has demonstrated her willingness to sustain examination of her own rights and wrongs by her persistence. There is no question of his saying 'Yes, I imagine she may have quite a case. We can cope with that in the indefinite future. I can send her away with a good Asian promise to deal with it in due course!' Jesus gives his thoughts in order to show that the Asian actually contemplated activity, and that 'right early'.[6]

'...OTHERWISE SHE WILL BLACKEN MY FACE'

What stimulated that independent individual into activity? He found it was his function to 'take up her case', and it was inevitable that he should do so. What brought him to a realization of this? The answer is given in the best conceivable Greek translation of *tashᵉḥiyr pānay*, which is what he must have

---

[1] For the history, A. A. Di Lella, *The Hebrew Text of Sirach* (The Hague, 1966), p. 150. For the text of Sir. xxxv. 12–19 see I. Lévi, *The Hebrew Text of the Book of Ecclesiasticus* (Leiden, 1904), pp. 36–7; S. Schechter and C. Taylor, *The Wisdom of Ben Sira* (Cambridge, 1899), p. xli. H. P. Rüger, *Text und Textform im hebräischen Sirach* (1970, *B.Z.A.W.* 112) does not consider our passage.
[2] Y. Yadin, *The Ben Sira Scroll from Masada* (Jerusalem, 1965), esp. p. 7. For the technique of the LXX translator see the most revealing notes in J. A. Sanders, *The Psalms Scroll of Qumrân Cave 11* (Oxford, 1965), pp. 79 ff.   [3] Isa. xxvi. 20. Ps. xl. 17; lxx. 5; lxxi. 12; cxliii. 7.
[4] The Messiah (Isa. ix. 5) or God (Ps. xxiv. 8; Is. x. 21; Jer. xxxii. 18)?
[5] תחבט from חָבַט, which the reviser amended to the commonplace תרבה (multiplies), since the metaphor was too striking, and perhaps difficult.   [6] Hab. ii. 3.

thought. Unfortunately neither ὑπωπιάζειν nor its Latin equivalent (*sugillare*) has quite the appropriate meaning. 'Bruise', 'insult' is not the point. 'She will blacken my face!', a well-known expression throughout the Orient, is not unknown in Hebrew.[1] It is available in Arabic (where the overtones of final disgrace are drawn from the Quranic examples),[2] in Persian (where it is a commonplace),[3] in Turkish,[4] and in all languages of the Indian subcontinent, including those spoken by people of very dark skin.[5] 'He has blackened my face' means 'he has effectively slandered me, or has treated me in such a way that my prestige has fallen; he has, in effect, disgraced me'. 'My face has been blackened' means 'I have been disgraced'. This very ancient Asian idea goes back to a time when the words for the colours were few; the sallow skin turned ash-grey at the moment of realization of disgrace. To the European this is difficult to understand, since disgrace does not have the tragic and paralysing connotations it has in the East, where people in general will lose everything, even their lives, rather than lose their prestige, and where an enemy wishes nothing so much as that his enemy's prestige should suffer.

Now the widow could blacken the judge's face by spreading rumours about him, namely that he *could* not hear her case as he was obliged to her adversary. But it was not at all necessary that she should say anything to anyone (silent women may well have existed). The very fact that (as he actually says) she kept on coming[6] and annoying him proved that he was not performing his function, and raised the presumption that he was unable, or handicapped in some way; or even that her 'case' was a smokescreen to hide some quite different reason for frequenting his house and not being sent away. It would not be a correct objection that if he feared her slanders or wagging tongues (or winking eyes: Ps. xxxv. 19) he could not have been one who 'had no

---

[1] p. Hag. II, fol. 77 d. Jastrow, *Dict.* 1551. Cf. Lam. iv. 8; v. 10; Jer. viii. 21; and perhaps Job. xxx. 30. Also Joel ii. 6; Nah. ii. 10 (sc. like a burnt pot). Mr J. N. Postgate tells me that the contexts of the two known examples of faces 'becoming black' in Akkadian permit a translation 'be put to shame' without establishing it.

[2] Q. iii. 100 (Arberry, *Koran Interpreted* (1964), p. 59); xvi. 60 (p. 264) (and xliii. 15 (p. 506)); xxxix. 60 (p. 478); cf. xxxv. 25 (p. 447). *Iswadda wajhuhu*, 'he was put to shame'.

[3] *Rū-ye main siyāh shod*, 'I am disgraced'; *rū-yi siyāh*, 'shame'; *rū-yi sepīd* ('white face'), 'honour'; *āb-i rū* ('brightness of face'), 'unimpaired honour'.

[4] *Yüzüm kara oldu* ('my face has become black'), 'my prestige has been lowered', 'I am disgraced'; *Yüz karasi* ('blackness of face'), 'dishonour', 'disgrace'; *yüz aki/akhği* ('whiteness of face'), 'personal honour'. Prof. V. Ménage tells me that this is a calque from Persian.

[5] *Merā mūh kāla ho gāya* ('my face has become black'), 'my esteem has been lowered', 'I am degraded' (Hindi). *Avan mukam karuttadu* ('his face became black'), 'he felt insulted' (Tamil). In Dravidian languages (from which Burmese seems to have adopted the idiom) the face is envisaged as if smeared with charcoal or soot, a secondary development (*avan en mukattil kariyai pucivittān*, 'he made me ashamed', Tamil). The victim feels sudden shame at detection in crime, or acute disappointment (which, by coincidence, fits the eschatological context of the Quranic instances of darkened faces). Dravidian evidence is particularly significant, as the vast majority of speakers are of very dark complexion already. In Malay the same idiom exists. 'To make someone's face black' = 'to insult': see C. Skinner, ed., *Shair Perang Mengkasar* (The Hague, 1963), p. 284, a reference I owe to the kindness of Dr J. Knappert. Indian English: A. Ollivant, *Old For Ever* (London, 1923), pp. 256–7.

[6] Thus ἐρχομένη is correct after all, and ἐλθοῦσα (which many critics have suspected to have been better Greek) would have been wrong.

respect for man'. For what that description, which is by no means necessarily only a disadvantageous characteristic (it implies that he was impartial),[1] is intended to convey is that no one could put any pressure upon him. It was part of his prestige that no one could control his exercise of his discretion, but once it was rumoured that he was under obligation to the Adversary, or had somehow compromised himself with the widow, his reputation would be gone. A man who has no respect for men is in that enviable position because his prestige is uniquely high. Once his prestige is jeopardized people will disregard him or manipulate him, and he must fall to quite another category. And in any case no parable would contain an impossible character. No Asian fears anything more than loss of prestige. Thus the (apparently) weakest subject holds this power over the most independent ruler!

And this fits God perfectly, for he has made it plain that he has a reputation to lose.[2] For his name's sake[3] he will do justice to, and for, Israel.

The Fighters for Jewish Freedom could conceivably, in the persons of their predecessors of an older generation, have actually learnt (and not heeded) just such a commentary as this upon their favourite textbook. One must pray for God's help, and not play the coward (ἐγκακεῖν) (cf. Luke xxi. 36). The coward takes the law into his own hands. Real courage requires that we leave the problem with God.[4] If you doubt whether he has jurisdiction and capacity to execute his sentence you belong to Satan's corps, and not his.

ADDITIONAL NOTE ON ὑπωπιάζειν

A report on the subsequent history of this verb reveals how nearly suitable Luke's vocabulary was for this essentially Asian concept. The word was fully metaphorical by the fourth century. Macarius Magnes uses ὑπώπια in the sense of 'disgraces' (of sons that disgrace their fathers) at *Apocriticus* (1876), II. 19 (p. 35, l. 7) and in the sense of 'besmirchings' (suffered by public speakers) *ibid.* III. 12 (p. 83, l. 15). Nilus (d. 430) uses ὑπωπιάζεσθαι in the sense of 'to be put to shame' at *De vol. paup. ad Magnam*, xl (*PG* 79, 1017C), and ὑπώπια in the sense of 'reproaches', *ibid.* lxiv (1056C); while at *Narratio*, VI, § 87 (661D) the word appears in the sense of 'personal opprobrium': in all three cases Nilus connects the word with *conscience*, leading to shame. Plutarch, Luke's younger contemporary, used ὑπωπιάζειν in the sense of 'besmirch' (of the Moon as the victim of amateur lunographers) (*Mor.* II, 921; ed. Teub. 5, p. 407; a universally accepted conjecture), because it was literally most appropriate. We can see that Cicero's use of ὑπώπιον ('blot') at *Att.* I. 20. 5 was then a bold metaphor.

---

[1] Deut. i. 17; xvi. 19. Great attention should be paid to the principle at Lev. xix. 15, also Exod. xxiii. 3, which recurs in the Sirach passage with which we are concerned. Justice should not be tempered out of sympathy for the 'poor'. On the principle of not respecting persons see Prov. xxiv. 23; xxviii. 21; 2 Sam. xiv. 14; 2 Ch. xix. 7; Acts x. 34; Rom. ii. 11; Eph. vi. 9; Col. iii. 25; Jas. ii. 1;   *
1 Pet. i. 17. Wis. vi. 6–8 is most relevant to our parable.

[2] Exod. xxxii. 12; Deut. ix. 28; Ps. lxxiv. 22.

[3] Ezek. xxxvi. 21–3; xxxviii. 27; xxxix. 7; Ps. ix. 168; xxxi. 3; liv. 1; lxxix. 9; cix. 21; cxliii. 11;   *
Jer. xvi. 21; Mic. vi. 5; Lev. xix. 2; Midr. Rabbah Lev. xxiv. 1 = Sonc. trans. IV, 304.

[4] Ps. xxxvii. 5–6, 39–40.

FURTHER ANNOTATIONS

Tit. The parable has an exceptional number of biblical allusions (see below).

p. [178], n. 1. R. Deschryver, 'La parabole du juge malveillant (Lk 18.1-8)', *R.H.P.R.* 48 (1968), 355-66.

p. [179], n. 1. M. Hermaniuk, *La parabole évangélique* (Bruges, 1947), says (p. 246) that no one should see the judge as God nor the widow as the church.

p. [180], l. 9. *adikos* (1 Cor. vi.1) means 'inconsistent with the law of God'.

p. [180], n. 4. The misprinted references to Ps. should read xxxviii.12-22; lxix.3-4. Attention should have been drawn to Zeph. iii. 12-13 as possibly on this point, also 1 En. xlvii.1.2; Ep. Jer. vi.53. Is. xlix.25 and Ps. ciii.6 should be added, but Is. lxii.6-9 is most significant of all!

p. [182], l. 24. On agreement with the adversary it is of interest to refer to *Dikaiomata* (Pap. Hal. 1) (mid-3rd cent. B.C.) concerning Alexandrian city-laws, at ll.47, 54, 116, 119, 126. Both the *hypēretēs* and the *praktōr* are able to commit one to gaol. The pericope itself is well studied by R. Sugranyes at pp. 51ff., but without observing that the views of Theophylact and John Chysostom (see P. Schanz, *Comm. Matt.* 1879, 188) were much more correct than later writers. Development of the 'last farthing' is to be seen at Didache I.5. H. Braun, *Jesus*, 88-9.

p. [182], n. 3. Also H.A.R. Gibb, at Rosenthal, ed.. *Jud. and Christ.* III (1938), 162-3.

p. [182], n. 4. Z.W. Falk, *Introduction to Jewish Law of the Second Commonwealth* I (Leiden, 1972), 88 & n. 1 (referring to Mekilta on Mišpaṭîm [first lines]).

p. [185], n. 4. Note that at Sir. xix.17 we are warned to confront our neighbour before threatening him, and give time/room for the law of the highest to operate. *See* V. Tcherikover, *Hellenistic Civilization and the Jews* (1959), 304 (penchant for government courts).

p. [186], l. 17. Two points deserve emphasis. The *antidikos* (who figures in the parable of agreement with the adversary) is perfectly well known to scripture: Jer. xxvii.34 (LXX). *Ekdikēsis* is a powerful, and by no means uncommon word: Jer. v.9; Ps. xciv (xciii).1-3. The ideal judge must of course take up the cause of the widow: Jos., *Contra Ap.* II.27. But he need not act fairly: Job xxxiv.23-4! Sirach, so important for our purpose, uses *ekdikēsis* in the sense of punishment (xxiii.21) and of vengeance (xxv.14).

p. [187], l. 7. *Judgment* is of course a key word: Is xlix.25; xlii.4 (the latter being important as concerning the Servant/Messiah). Sir. xxi.5. Is.xxxiii.22. On the position of the widow, etc., see Fensham at *J.N.E.S.* 21 (1962), 120-39.

p. [187], l. 25. *ekdikēsis* can be vengeance upon someone: Is. lvii.16 LXX; Sir. xxiii.21, xxv.14.

p. [189], l. 10. On *speed* see Sir. xxi.5, Hab. ii.3 (b. Sanh. 97b, of Messiah). See Sir. iv.28. On the semi-canonical position of Sirach see A.A. Wider, *J.Q.R.* 61 (1970), 155.

p. [189], l. 19. That God should be prayed to for the deliverance (Jer. xxvii.34 LXX) of Jerusalem constantly is stated clearly at Is.lxii.7.

p. [189], at end of second paragraph add: There is a comical aspect which would have struck hearers of Luke. Who does not fear God or respect man? Hades, Pluto, Rhadamanthus and Egyptian gods of the dead! Widows were precisely the people to resort to magical practices. It is cheaper than hiring an advocate. A was tablet specifying the *antidikos* could be popped into a tomb and demonic forces would afflict the *defixus* (A. Audollent, *Defixionum Tabellae*, 1904, nos. 18, 22-35, 37, 93, 133). The 'just' needed such supernatural help (ibid., index, pp. 471-2; cf. no. 2), 8, 92 (*adikēmai, adikoumai, adikousi*). The gods of the underworld could put paid to a clever advocate's histrionics.

p. [189], n. 1. F. Vattioni, *Ecclesiastico* (Naples, 1968), 184-6.

p. [189], n. 3, 2 Esdr. iv.34: the exalted one *hastens* on behalf of many (i.e. relative to human impatience he is speedy).

p. [190], l. 12. The face goes pale with shame: Is. xxix.22. Cain's face was blackened: Midr. R. Gen. XXII.6 (Sonc. 184). Darkness over faces of those sinners who are sent away full of shame at the end of days: 1 En. lxii.10, lxiii.11. 4 Ezra vii.125-6.

p. [190], l. 22. J. Alexander Findlay, who was as sensible as he was prolific, is the only commentator (see *Jesus and his Parables*, London, 1950, 40) to catch the point. Using a Chinese parallel he points out that an official cannot afford to *lose face*.

p. [190], n. 1. *Midr. on Ps.*, Ps. 120 §5 (trans. Braude, II, 292); Syriac vers. of Sir. xxv.17 (Nestle, p. 548; Box and Oesterley at Charles, *A. & P.* I.276).

p. [190], n. 2. The Prophet said to a beggar, 'It is better to make your livelihood... than to come on the day of Resurrection with black marks on your face': *Mishkāt-al-Maṣābiḥ*, ch. 5, §.2 (trans. J. Robson, 1960-5, I, 392).

p. [191], n. 1. Ps. Sal. ii. 19 (18). 2 Bar. xliv.4. Charles, *A. & P.* II, 503.

p. [191], n. 3. *Midr. on Ps.*, Ps 44 §1. 2 Bar. v. 1 (Charles, *A. & P.* II, 483). A. Marmorstein, *The Doctrine of Merits in Old Rabbinical Literature* (London, 1920), 13-15.

Workers in the Vineyard: A Parable of Jesus

"... to give everyone according to his ways and according to the fruit of his doings." *Jer.* 32: 19.
"... who will render to every man according to his works." *Rom.* 2: 6.

IT IS a pleasure to treat of this parable as a contribution to a volume presented to one who has worked in the vineyard. And in a book dedicated by academics to a great academic one may surely discuss a topic dear to the English: equality, or inequality, of reward. Our parable has always been a puzzle, and imagination has liberally filled the gaps in factual knowledge.

Mt. 20: Ὁμοία γάρ ἐστιν ἡ βασιλεία τῶν οὐρανῶν ἀνθρώπῳ οἰκοδεσπότῃ ὅστις ἐξῆλθεν ἅμα πρωῒ μισθώσασθαι ἐργάτας εἰς τὸν ἀμπελῶνα αὐτοῦ· 2 συμφωνήσας δὲ μετὰ τῶν ἐργατῶν ἐκ δηναρίου τὴν ἡμέραν ἀπέστειλεν αὐτοὺς εἰς τὸν ἀμπελῶνα αὐτοῦ. 3 καὶ ἐξελθὼν περὶ τρίτην ὥραν εἶδεν ἄλλους ἑστῶτας ἐν τῇ ἀγορᾷ ἀργούς· 4 καὶ ἐκείνοις εἶπεν, Ὑπάγετε καὶ ὑμεῖς εἰς τὸν ἀμπελῶνα, καὶ ὃ ἐὰν ᾖ δίκαιον δώσω ὑμῖν. 5 οἱ δὲ ἀπῆλθον. πάλιν ἐξελθὼν περὶ ἕκτην καὶ ἐνάτην ὥραν ἐποίησεν ὡσαύτως. 6 περὶ δὲ τὴν ἑνδεκάτην ἐξελθὼν εὗρεν ἄλλους ἑστῶτας, καὶ λέγει αὐτοῖς, Τί ὧδε ἑστήκατε ὅλην τὴν ἡμέραν ἀργοί; 7 λέγουσιν αὐτῷ, Ὅτι οὐδεὶς ἡμᾶς ἐμισθώσατο. λέγει αὐτοῖς, Ὑπάγετε καὶ ὑμεῖς εἰς τὸν ἀμπελῶνα. 8 ὀψίας δὲ γενομένης λέγει ὁ κύριος τοῦ ἀμπελῶνος τῷ ἐπιτρόπῳ αὐτοῦ, Κάλεσον τοὺς ἐργάτας καὶ ἀπόδος αὐτοῖς τὸν μισθὸν ἀρξάμενος ἀπὸ τῶν ἐσχάτων ἕως τῶν πρώτων. 9 καὶ ἐλθόντες οἱ περὶ τὴν ἑνδεκάτην ὥραν ἔλαβον ἀνὰ δηνάριον. 10 καὶ ἐλθόντες οἱ πρῶτοι ἐνόμισαν ὅτι πλεῖον λήμψονται· καὶ ἔλαβον τὸ ἀνὰ δηνάριον καὶ αὐτοί. 11 λαβόντες δὲ ἐγόγγυζον κατὰ τοῦ οἰκοδεσπότου 12 λέγοντες, Οὗτοι οἱ ἔσχατοι μίαν ὥραν ἐποίησαν, καὶ ἴσους ἡμῖν αὐτοὺς ἐποίησας τοῖς βαστάσασι τὸ βάρος τῆς ἡμέρας καὶ τὸν καύσωνα. 13 ὁ δὲ ἀποκριθεὶς ἑνὶ αὐτῶν εἶπεν, Ἑταῖρε, οὐκ ἀδικῶ σε· οὐχὶ δηναρίου συνεφώνησάς μοι; 14 ἆρον τὸ σὸν καὶ ὕπαγε· θέλω δὲ τούτῳ τῷ ἐσχάτῳ δοῦναι ὡς καὶ σοί. 15 ἢ οὐκ ἔξεστίν μοι ὃ θέλω ποιῆσαι ἐν τοῖς ἐμοῖς; ἢ ὁ ὀφθαλμός σου πονηρός ἐστιν ὅτι ἐγὼ ἀγαθός εἰμι; 16 Οὕτως ἔσονται οἱ ἔσχατοι πρῶτοι καὶ οἱ πρῶτοι ἔσχατοι.

It is open to question whether *v.* 16 is part of the parable, and I am content to assume that it is not, though of course St. Matthew understood that it was.

THE BACKGROUND TO THE STUDY

This much discussed passage[1] may not have been available to St. Luke[2] but it is akin in workmanship to the parables of the Great Supper (*Lk.* 14: 15–24, *Mt.* 22: 1–14), the Good Samaritan (*Lk.* 10: 25–37), and the Prodigal Son (*Lk.* 15: 11–32: which, in one respect, this parable strongly resembles). There are parables in St. Matthew[3] which do not have midrashic allusions, double meanings, and insinuations as in the Lucan examples: but now we are again with that mind which taught by means of a simple, practical story, weaving together, at the same time, allusions to the Law, the Prophets, and the Wisdom literature. A reader may prefer to be told at the outset that this parable, apart from the allusion to the themes of the Vineyard (*Is.* 5: 1–7) and The Reward (*Is.* 40: 10), is a composite midrashic exegesis of *Gen.* 15: 1, *Deut.* 24: 14–15, *Is.* 62: 9–11, *Mal.* 2: 17, 3: 5, 11, 13–15, and *Prov.* 10: 22, 23: 17, 24: 1, 19. In Pharisaical terms a passage in Ecclesiastes becomes relevant (as we shall see), and a significant text is *Ps.* 99. My own choice for a single text, should we wish to call the parable a sermon, would be *Jer.* 31: 31–2, and the occasion might have been one for which that was part of the customary reading from the Prophets: but of course we cannot prove that there was a sermon, nor what was its occasion. One surmises that, in common with admirers of Wisdom literature, Jesus believed one could

---

[1] A. JÜLICHER, *Die Gleichnisreden Jesu* (Tübingen, 1910), Vol. II, pp. 459–71, attacked by A. NYGREN, *Agape and Eros* (London, 1937), pp. 61–4 (an erroneous treatment). See works cited at notes 4–5 below. R. C. TRENCH, *Notes on the Parables* (London, 1898), p. 168, followed by Plummer, says, "it is a parable which stands only second to that of the Unjust Steward in the number and wide divergence from one another of the explanations that have been proposed for it; and only second to that, if indeed second, in the difficulties which it presents". C. H. DODD, *Parables of the Kingdom* (London, 1961), pp. 91–2, saw the parable as illustrating "sheer generosity and compassion for the unemployed" paralleled by Jesus's concern for the outcasts. Hunter (below) takes the eleventh-hour men to be "undeserving sinners". T. W. MANSON (*Sayings of Jesus*, p. 220) followed by Hunter and J. A. FINDLAY, *Jesus and his Parables* (London, 1950) p. 52 points out that "there is no such thing as a twelfth part of the love of God". The correct answer is that there is no twelfth part of *zekhuth*. PREISKER at Kittel, *TWNT* IV (1942), p. 723, "the parable radically discards all thought of merit"(!). In my view O. MICHEL was right at *Z. Sys. Theol.* 9 (1932), pp. 47, 52. J. MOFFATT, *Grace in the New Testament* (N.Y., 1932), p. 78. A good treatment is to be found at A. T. CADOUX, *Parables of Jesus: their Art and Use* (London, [1930]), pp. 100–3. J. Arthur BAIRD, *The Justice of God in the Teaching of Jesus* (London, 1963), pp. 209–11 (the *eschaton*).
[2] On the source: W. C. ALLEN, "The book of sayings used by the editor of the first gospel", in W. SANDAY, ed., *Studies in the Synoptic Problem* (Oxford, 1911), pp. 270 ff.; B. H. STREETER, *The Four Gospels* (London, 1926), pp. 166, 279 (*g*). G. D. KILPATRICK, *The Origin of the Gospel according to St. Matthew* (Oxford, 1946), p. 88; W. L. KNOX, *The Sources of the Synoptic Gospels* (Cambridge, 1953), Vol. II, pp. 134–5. The origin of any material not in Mark or Q is uncertain, W. G. KÜMMEL finding it impossible to believe in an additional written source (*Introduction to the New Testament* (London, 1966) pp. 58, 60, 77–8).
[3] As that of the Unjust Judge (see below, n. 70). The parables studied in J. D. KINGSBURY, *The Parables of Jesus in Matthew 13* (London, 1969), exemplify both types.

teach spiritual truths effectively if one adopted a practical or even commercial form. The more intimately one referred to contemporary practice the better the lesson. The sense of humour is thus readily exercised, and greatly facilitates the spiritual communication. A vague parallel to our passage would be the pregnant advice of *Sir.* 33: 30–1 (servants are to be regarded as oneself), but Ben Sira himself intended (so it seems) to provide only the bare bones upon which little lectures or expositions could be founded.

Previous discussions of this parable have been inadequate,[4] and the books usually recommended to students jolt unhappily from a good and edifying point to falsity.[5] One regrets the failure of Oesterley, and more so of Edersheim, who was after all a Talmudist, though one can forgive N. Levison —a Palestinian Jew, he was not a student of the Talmudim.[6] Klausner recognised a relevant point (see below), but he has been ignored. What is incredible is that H. Heinemann, who wrote on the key to our parable in the 1949 issue of the *Journal of Jewish Studies* should in the very same volume write on the parable[7] without connecting the two.

The claim that the parable is contrary to actual behaviour is false. We should know by now that when one inveighs against a parable's quality, or asserts that details 'do not signify', he merely reveals his ignorance of the

---

[4] Early literature is listed by L. FONCK, *Die Parabeln des Herrn* (Innsbruck, 1902), Ch. 22. Other literature is summarised in Dom J. DUPONT's careful "Les ouvriers de la vigne", *Assemblées du Seigneur* 22 (1965), pp. 28–51, which shows how unsatisfactory exegesis has been. E.g. at p. 32: "Nous n'avons pas plus que [le paraboliste] à nous occuper encore des groupes intermédiaires, les ouvriers de la troisième, de la sixième et de la neuvième heure", which is false. Dupont's article at *Nouv. R. Théol.* 79 (1957), pp. 785–97, is often praised, except by Mouson (see below). J. C. FENTON, *The Gospel of St. Matthew* (London, 1963), p. 320 subscribes to the "idleness = laziness" theory. But he rightly connects τὸ βάρος at *v.* 12 with the Law, citing *Mt.* 11: 28 and *Acts* 15: 28. That ἐποίησαν = "worked" is shown at M. BLACK, *Aramaic Approach* . . ., 3rd edn. (Oxford, 1967), p. 302.

[5] J. JEREMIAS, *The Parables of Jesus* (London, 1963) pp. 33–8, 136–9. The notion that ἀρξάμενος ἀπό (as explained at pp. 35–6) implies only that the last comers are to be paid cannot be accepted. But the reference to 4 *Ezra* 5: 42 and *Rom.* 4: 4 is valuable. E. LINNE-MANN, *Parables of Jesus* (London, 1966), pp. 81–8, contends at p. 83 that it would be absurd to posit of a day labourer reliance upon his relationship with the employer where no wage was stipulated; *immo, peraccommodatum necnon perappositum!* At p. 85 she would replace "good" with "kind": this too does violence to the parable. She adds (p. 88) that the dawn-men must see the goodness of the eleventh-hour men, who had need of the owner's goodness —this goes beyond the parable, for they must acquiesce in the owner's judgment. J. MOUSON, "*Explicatur parabola de operariis in vineam missis*", *Collect. Mechl.*, n.s., 27 (1957), pp. 611–15, *minime explicat.*

[6] W. O. E. OESTERLEY, *The Gospel Parables in the Light of their Jewish Background* (London, 1936) pp. 100–11; A. EDERSHEIM, *Life and Times of Jesus the Messiah* (London, etc. 1906), Vol. II, pp. 415–21; N. LEVISON, *The Parables: their Background and Local Setting* (Edinburgh, 1926), pp. 196–203. Levison has the merit of seeing that "election" relates to fitness for the work. An admirer of the parable, C. G. MONTEFIORE, *Synoptic Gospels* (N.Y., 1968), Vol. II, p. 273, had no notion of the parallel between Jewish Law and the divine "mercy".

[7] *JJS* 1 (1949), pp. 85–9: ". . . this particular passage . . . is fully in line with contemporary Jewish conceptions both in form and in its main theme, viz: that man is assured of the reward due to him, though he should not crave for it and should acknowledge his absolute duty to work for the Kingdom of God".

subject-matter.[8] The paradoxes of parables, too, are amongst their beauties. Moreover, the so-called principle that parables cannot be allegorical, a post-Jülicher superstition, is untrue. I do not urge that we should look for correspondence (as, in this parable, it would be wrong to identify the dawn-men with Adam); nor is there a code wherewith the parable is to be deciphered. But resemblances to biblical precedents are to be given their weight.

Our parable is sometimes, and plausibly, taken as part of a literary unit, *Mt.* 19: 16–20: 16. 'The first shall be last and the last first', or *vice versa* (19: 30, 20: 16), and Peter's question about reward, in this view, dominates the context. Dodd, Jeremias, and others, may well sever the maxim from the parable, attributing its proximity to St. Matthew's editorship: but until the parable is understood such a decision is premature. Not that St. Matthew's motive is obscure; but that does not remove the possibility of there having been other implications in the original parable. The more common opinion is that Jesus is defending his ways against critics, and asserting against Pharisees the rights of the outcasts to enter into the Kingdom. What he indicates is, in my view, in one respect wider, but in another more specific. In common with others I proceed without reference to St. Matthew's context.

The Kingdom of Heaven is like a householder (i.e. a farmer, the typical employer of labour in Jewish law)[9] who goes out early, i.e. before dawn,[10] to hire workmen (*sekhirut po'alim*)[11] for his vineyard. The *po'el* ($\dot{\epsilon}\rho\gamma\acute{\alpha}\tau\eta\varsigma$) is the labourer. Since one of the titles or attributes of God is "he who pays the *sakhar*" (see *Ezek.* 29: 18–20, *Sir.* 51: 30; cf. *Heb.* 11: 6 and R. Eleazar at *mAb.* 2: 14), and since *sakhar* means pay, reward, and profit, we know that we are hearing a parable describing the "behaviour" of God, a commercial parable, and thus fun. After some bargaining he agreed with them at what may have been an inclusive rate (i.e. was he or was he not obliged to provide snacks, cf. *Bel et Drac.* 33?) of a denarius a day, and sent them (note how the initiative remains his) into his vineyard. Thenceforward this outlay will have formed the basis of his calculations. It is said that a denarius was the normal daily wage for an unskilled labourer.[12] Evidence is thin. In Talmudic times

*   *

---

[8] DERRETT, *Law in the New Testament* (London, 1970), Ch. 6, esp. pp. 153–5. Linnemann (*cit. sup.*, n. 5), amongst others, finds details irrelevant, but only because their function is not understood. Feuillet (cited below, n.100), rightly emphasises that the details heighten the picture (p. 314).

[9] οἰκοδεσπότης = *ba'al ha-bayit*. STRACK-BILLERBECK, *Kommentar zum Neuen Testament* (Munich, 1961), Vol. I, p. 830. S. KRAUSS, *Talm. Archäol.*, Vol. II, pp. 102, 252. The father in the parable of the Two Sons (below) is in exactly this position. I. ABRAHAMS, *Studies in Pharisaism and the Gospels* (Cambridge, 1917), Vol. I, pp. 100–1.

[10] ἅμα πρωΐ. See *Jer.* 25: 3, 35: 14: but there the point is a little different. Here God takes the initiative to supply grace whereby *zekhuth* may be earned. No merit is earned independently of God's grace. H. BRAUN, *Jesus* (Stuttgart 1969) pp. 70–1, 135–6.

[11] μισθώσασθαι implying hire and gain. *P. Lips.* 111, 11.

[12] J. KLAUSNER, *Jesus of Nazareth* (N.Y., 1959), p. 181. Billerbeck's references (I, 831) are not conclusive. Krauss (*T.A.* II, 105, n. 726) refers only to our passage (!), and to *Tob* 5: 14 (δραχμή). But Tobit is in any case an archaic or pseudo-archaic work, and

three denarii (or the equivalent) was a mediocre wage and four a good wage. I strongly suspect that a single denarius was consistent with the conditions when the parable was uttered, given an employers' market in labour, and thus hardly a good wage.

We cannot go on without economics, which are universal and notorious. There is the economic value of work, its social value, and the value of leisure. The price of work depends on the demand of the customer (the employer) and the supply of the commodity (the labour). Thus, whatever might be the local custom (which is significant in such matters), the employer's need is a factor. If he underpays he will be poorly served, if he can get labour at all; if he habitually pays more than the labour is worth to him he may go out of business. The price of work depends on the demand of the customer and the supply of the commodity; the same is true of the value of work to the employer. The demand for his product will fix an upper limit to the amount he may pay his workers. If there is a bumper crop the vineyard owner's price for his wine will come down, and wages will be depressed—but then employers are competing for labour, so that a collapse of wages is avoided. When the crop is unusual in quality the employer is in a favourable position: the demand for his product will be higher than competition for labour; thus he can pay a higher wage than his neighbours without going out of business. As against the employer's need for labour there is the worker's need for rest and recreation; and there is Asian psychology. This contains the element, known to the occidental only in children, adolescents and certain criminals, described as "indifference" or "insouciance", i.e. the intermittent abdication of the power and duty of decision-making, the refusal to accept life's challenge. That seems not to have arisen in our parable, but it is a factor likely to effect the market value of labour from time to time.

Because this is an ancient society another factor must be taken into account. The slow movement from a status economy (cf. the mediaeval manor) to a contract economy (with a free market in labour) leaves still a residual idea— in the ancient world much more than a notion—that the employee has a right to his employer's consideration. This right would protect him against the free operation of economic rules where these would otherwise impoverish him. Moreover residual beliefs in the status aspect of employment were suitably retained and expressed, because, unless such a conception regulated the effect of freely-contracted relationships, the combination of workers and employers to resist unrestrained competition would lead to inefficiency, the immigration of foreign labour, racial tension, and other inconveniences which

---

critics have failed to observe that T. promises the angel his expenses as well, i.e. the wage was 1 dr. net, *higher* than the wage in our parable. See F. C. GRANT, *Economic Background of the Gospels* (O.U.P., 1926), pp. 68–9. Trench thought it was a liberal day's pay (p. 177, n. 1) but this is unsupported. Note, by the way, how Tobit calls his "hired man" "brother".

would place far too high a price, in traditional social terms, upon the products of labour. The ancient *status* concept would thus come to the aid of the more modern *contract* concept of employment, and "mercy" ("righteousness") would, seemingly, mitigate "justice"!

To resume the tale, our employer went again to the market-place (*shuk*: corresponding to the area known in modern Turkey and Greece as the καφενεῖον) at the third hour (about 9 a.m.)[13] and found some others "hanging about",[14] and sent them off to the vineyard promising to give them "what is just" ὃ ἐὰν ᾖ δίκαιον. He went again at the sixth and ninth hours (i.e. noon and 3 p.m.) and did the same.[15] These men would have remained unemployed had he not hired them, as the reply which the next group give him reveals. The words "what is just" suggest a complex idea. At the first sight they suggest a proportionate day's wage, namely 0·5 den. for half a day. But, even though the rate of work was customary, and even though in Jewish law the labourer was bound to work honestly (customary pauses excepted) for his employer, the natural understanding of "what is just" is that he who produces more for his employer reasonably expects a higher wage. There was a further complication. The economic value of labour can fluctuate during the day, due to a change in the prospective demand[16] for it. The cheapest labour is found at dawn. At noon it will be dear. Competition for labour between employers in a hurry will then be at its height, if ever. By evening the demand has dropped to little, but whatever demand there is will be urgent and generous. Thus the sixth-hour men would expect to be paid more than would the dawn-men, even if the latter stopped work then and there. No doubt the difference would be little, say 0·1, but for very poor people every copper coin counts.[17]

Our employer went again at the eleventh hour (5 p.m.) and found others there. He enquired why they had been idle *all day*, and learnt that they had not been hired, whereupon he simply sent them into the vineyard.[18] The words καὶ ὑμεῖς, "you *too*", imply that he wanted them personally not to miss

---

[13] For the actual length of the (twelve-hour) working day in Palestine at harvest see G. DALMAN, *Arbeit und Sitte* (1928), Vol. I, pp. 43–4. Fonck (*op. cit.*) supplied similar particulars.

[14] ἑστῶτες is a word implying readiness for activity, in contrast to καθίσαντες which implies (in males) either unemployment or a "leisured" occupation. For standing in the market-place see MORIER, *Second Journey*, p. 265, cited by Trench. In answer to Joüon and Jeremias (p. 136) I say these men were *notionally* standing even if they had been *actually* sitting. On the subject DALMAN, *op. cit.*, Vol. IV, pp. 335 ff. is not informative.

[15] Promising "what is just". δίκαιον conjures up the Hebrew concept of *ẓedek, ẓedakah*, which implies liberality as well as justice! F. ROSENTHAL, "Sedaka, Charity", *HUCA* 23 (1950–1), pp. 411–30; R. MACH, *Der Zaddik* (Leiden, 1957). In the LXX *ẓadik, ẓedek* is frequently δίκαιος.

[16] *Sir.* 18: 26: ἀπὸ πρωΐθεν ἕως ἑσπέρας μεταβάλλει καιρός. . . .

[17] And employers could pay in copper coin if they chose: *bB.M.* 46a = Soncino trans. 294.

[18] The similar promise placed at *v.* 7 in the Textus Receptus (but not in the Vulgate) and in Tatian, *Diatessaron*, 29: 33 is recognised as a corruption due to a misunderstanding of the parable. Jülicher's idea (p. 461), that a promise of payment is omitted by accident, is erroneous.

something of value. We note that he did not hire them for a specific task, nor for a specific period. If he had done so he might have been liable to pay them a specific sum, and no more. It would have been quite a small sum, whatever the task. But we know that he wanted them to finish off his harvest for him, or at least to make a significant effort so to do. If charity had been his principal object he need not have gone so frequently. When it was getting late[19] he ordered his steward to pay off his workmen (to give them their "reward"), starting from the men whom he had engaged last. The eleventh-hour men were given a denarius. When those who were engaged at dawn came up they expected more than that. They did not want to diminish the late-comers' pay, but to enhance their own ($\pi\lambda\epsilon\hat{\iota}o\nu\alpha$ with Jülicher, not $\pi\lambda\epsilon\hat{\iota}o\nu$) on the sole basis that fellow labourers had done less than they had; and obviously the employer's profits from the labour—its value to him—must have become higher than it was when he bargained with them, hence a revision was called for (they thought, not unreasonably)? But they too were given a denarius. They complained,[20] which is behaviour almost expected from labourers (the traditional concept of *tar'ometh*, "grievance"), because they were treated on an equal basis with those who had done only an hour's work, whereas they had borne the brunt of the day. The employer explained that they had no ground for complaint. It was his wish to pay the last at the same rate: he was entitled to do what he wished with his own;[21] and surely they were not jealous[22] because he chose to be generous?

Criticisms of the parable include a doubt about the seemingly quixotic generosity of the employer.[23] Possibly tomorrow labour would be harder to

---

[19] $\dot{o}\psi\iota\alpha\varsigma$ $\delta\grave{\epsilon}$ $\gamma\epsilon\nu o\mu\acute{\epsilon}\nu\eta\varsigma$. Sunset was imminent, the moment when the employer's liability to pay began.

[20] $\dot{\epsilon}\gamma\acute{o}\gamma\gamma\upsilon\zeta o\nu$. One may grumble when one's right has been infringed, and also (as here) where it has not. The word $\kappa\alpha\acute{\upsilon}\sigma\omega\nu\alpha$ recalls the complaint of Jacob (*Gen.* 31:40). $\beta\acute{\alpha}\rho o\varsigma$ recalls the weight of the commandments (*Mt.* 23: 23).

[21] $o\dot{\upsilon}\kappa$ $\ddot{\epsilon}\xi\epsilon\sigma\tau\iota\nu$ $\mu o\iota$ $\ddot{o}$ $\theta\acute{\epsilon}\lambda\omega$ $\pi o\iota\hat{\eta}\sigma\alpha\iota$ $\dot{\epsilon}\nu$ $\tau o\hat{\iota}\varsigma$ $\dot{\epsilon}\mu o\hat{\iota}\varsigma$; Jeremias (p. 137) says this means "on my own estate", but that does not meet the sense. It is *with his assets* that he is independent; it is those that he gives away (shrewdly but philanthropically). Cf. *Rom.* 9: 20–23. The Vulgate, excepting some mss., omits the last three words, in error. An allusion to *Ex.* 33: 19 is probable.

[22] Jealousy is a vice: $\dot{o}\phi\theta\alpha\lambda\mu\grave{o}\varsigma$ $\pi o\nu\eta\rho\acute{o}\varsigma$ (= evil eye, blighting supposedly others' prosperity) at *Mk.* 7: 22. *mAb.* 2: 9 (Danby, 449). Cf. *Sir.* 35: 10 (32: 12) (*beṭuv 'ayin*). C. EDLUND, *Das Auge der Einfalt* (Copenhagen-Lund, 1952). Trench, pp. 169, 184 ff., adverts to the oddity of members of the Kingdom being envious—but in fact, as we shall see, they are *grumblers* (n. 20 above, n. 90 below) and would reject the allegation that they were envious. To query God's justice is not necessarily to forfeit his reward, as Malachi 2–3 shows.

[23] Almost universal. Levison, Oesterley, Jeremias (p. 37). For Feuillet see below, n. 100, citing Nygren to the same effect. I. K. MADSEN, *Die Parabeln der Evangelien* (Copenhagen/ Leipzig, 1936), pp. 80–8. Strongly J. SCHNIEWIND, *Das Evangelium nach Matthäus* (Göttingen, 1936/44), also Baird (*cit. sup.*). G. V. JONES, *Art and Truth of the Parables* (London, 1964), pp. 116–17 (the parable shocks). A. M. HUNTER, *Interpreting the Parables* (London, 1960), p. 52, called the parable one of the most beautiful and disconcerting of all the parables. G. BORNKAMM, *Jesus of Nazareth* (London, 1960), pp. 142–3 is most erroneous. H. LOCKYER, *All the Parables* (Grand Rapids, 1964), p. 220 says we must wait to the End for the explanation.

hire, for this employer and others.[24] When those who work longer are not paid more the quality of their work falls and the enterprise suffers alarmingly.[25] Should citizens of the Kingdom be quixotic in this way?[26] One wonders whether jealous people (whose "evil eye" might be thought to injure their more fortunate neighbours) really deserved their pay after all: true, their labour did not lose in value by reason of their subsequent attitude, but one wonders even so. The owner's phrase ἆρον τὸ σόν, however, defies complaint.[27] One wonders if the form of address, "Comrade", is not hypocritical.[28] Dupont puts it well: the employer's self-justification looks like pettifogger's sophistry.[29] Why did he go personally to the market? Is his conversation with the eleventh-hour men ironical? He insists on the dawn-men, and the others, having the chagrin of seeing that the eleventh-hour men are equated with them: the opposite arrangement would have avoided chagrin and even complaint. The attempt is made to rescue the parable from these criticisms by urging that God is merciful and just (cf. 4 *Ezra* [in N. E. B.] 8: 33–36), and that those who profit from his justice have no complaint if others benefit from his mercy. But this is unsound (for justice which is divorced from mercy is no part of justice-and-mercy), and the man in the street rejects it. It is usually thought that this parable teaches God's "behaviour" by a picture utterly unlike human behaviour: if this were true it would run contrary to almost every other parable. Parables do not teach *e contrario*, but rather *e fortiori*.

THE PARABLE AS A PRACTICAL TALE

On the contrary the story is as as lifelike as it is amusing. We need not dilate on the difficulties of owning and working a vineyard, since we are concerned with the harvest, the high point in the owner's and his regular

[24] A point made by E. FLOOD, *Parables of Jesus*, Living Parish Pamphlets (Ealing, 1970), p. 14 (he otherwise follows Linnemann).
[25] As explained by R. L. LANGWORTHY at *J. As. Af. Stud.* 1 (1966), pp. 100 ff., esp. p. 109.
[26] This is not the point: Jülicher, *op. cit.*, p. 466. Oesterley emphasises (a) that this parable depicts God's dealings with men but not men's dealings with each other; and (b) that it was an act of grace on the part of the employer to hire any men at all! Both notions are adrift in different measures. Flood, *op. cit.*, p. 15 rightly emphasises that the parable does not teach what kind of generosity Christians should have. C. L. MITTON, at *Ex. T.* 77 (1965–6), pp. 307–11 concentrates on the warning the parable offers to the spiritually ungenerous.
[27] *Law in the New Testament* gives the reference at p. 25.
[28] ἑταῖρε could be used ironically (see *Mt.* 22: 12, 26: 50), but always of a "comrade". Ammonius's definition (ἑταῖρος οὐ πάντως φίλος) does not cover the Hebrew *ḥaver*, which this represents. Rengstorf, *TWNT* II (1935, repr. 1960) p. 698. Jeremias, p. 137. Dupont, p. 35, n. 1. The allusion is really to the notional *ḥever* of all Jews.
[29] "Sa conduite est évidemment irréprochable si l'on envisage séparément la façon dont il traite les uns et les autres; elle ne prête à discussion qu'en raison de la simultanéité de ces traitements: aux uns la générosité du maître, aux autres la justice seulement. Séparer les deux cas pour les traiter à part, n'est ce pas rouerie d'avocat?"

workers' year. The moment is ripe in exactly the sense of *Mt.* 9: 37–8 (ὅπως ἐκβάλῃ ἐργάτας εἰς τὸν θερισμὸν αὐτοῦ). Dupont's objection, that if we visualise the harvest we deprive the owner of his generosity, is an example of reading theology into the parable instead of letting the parable teach us.[30] This is certainly the harvest. At the harvest (late August, early September) exactly the right time must be picked to gather the grapes, to pack and press them. If they are picked too soon there is not enough sugar in them, if they are left too late there is too much. If storms blow up haste must be made to get the harvest in. On a Friday the position can be critical, as the Sabbath rest may subject the grapes to too much sun. A model, highly prized patch producing grapes of some fame might well yield to a sufficient force in a single day. The employer, like a thrifty man, a good "householder", will take care not to engage more labour than is needed: but he can overestimate the worker's powers; and those he engages first may work, for all their good intentions, inefficiently. He must go out again, and he may be glad to do so if he can supply unemployed men with some work.

A Jewish hearer of our parable would recognise from the repeated trips to the market-place that the crop is expected to produce a high superior vintage, of great value: the grapes must be picked that day or failing that the next, unless, as I suspect, it is Friday and work could be resumed only on Sunday. What is a harvest for, but to be gathered (*Jn.* 4: 35)? It is rare for labour to be hired in the way he adopts (we shall see why), but it can, and will be done, if the value of the wine is expected to justify it.

It is normal for stewards to engage labour, but there were reasons why a master might hire personally. Stewards were known to hire labourers at one price, and pretend they had hired the men for more (pocketing the difference). It was possible[31] for the labourers to be in doubt whether to demand higher wages than the steward had indicated. But if the owner himself came they knew they could rely on his word. The second reason relates to the provision of Jewish law that a labourer must be paid at nightfall, unless he waives that right. In order to avoid the liability to pay at sun-down, employers might even engage each other's workers, or try other subterfuges.[32] The texts relating to payment on the day are of great interest and must be scrutinised carefully.[33]

---

[30] *Ubi cit.*, p. 31 ("explication désastreuse"!). Dupont's point was that a generous man would be (equally) generous to all. But it does not follow, as we shall see. Jeremias (p. 136) is quite right in seeing this as the harvest, and Linnemann wrong (p. 82) to recommend indifference to the question.

[31] *bB.M.* 46a=Sonc. trans. 294; 49a=Sonc. 292; 76a=Sonc. 438; 77a=Sonc. 444–5.

[32] *bB.M.* 111a=Sonc. 633.

[33] The biblical texts: *Lev.* 19: 13, *Dt.* 24: 14–15 and Targumim thereon. Note *we'elaw hu' nose' 'et-nafsho.* Philo, *De Virtutibus*, §88 (Colson, viii, 214). *Midr. R. Exod.* 31: 7= Sonc. 386. *mB.M.* 9: 11–12 (Danby, 363–4). *bB.M.* 110b–111a=Sonc. 634–6 (most illuminating). A man employed at the eleventh-hour must be presumed not to have waived his right to payment at the end of the day. A worker regards his wages as his life: *bB.M.* 111b–12a=Sonc. 639–40 (even if he is engaged to gather a single cluster of grapes).

The prophets tell us that withholding pay, though unrighteous, was not uncommon.[34] A worker's very life hangs on his wages (cf. *Job.* 7: 2).

The employer found the third-hour labourers, and other men *idle*. The word represents a technical term in Jewish law: *baṭel*, "void", "empty", "at a loose end", "unemployed". The Aramaic equivalent at *Ezra* 4: 24 means "ceased", "nugatory", "at a standstill". The word provided a Greek * neologism βαττο- (*or* βατολ-?) λογέω, "I utter empty, vain talk" (*Mt.* 6: 7).[35] Aramaic documents we possess from the early second century, employing formulae of much greater age, use BṬL with the meaning "without legal effect" (so *P. Mur.* 25.1,[7] 26.1[5]). The same sense of "empty", "of no legal effect", appears in the ancient Kol Nidre prayer of the Eve of the Day of Atonement, whose legalistic formulation as well as Aramaic vocabulary certify its age: vows are *beṭelin u-mevuṭalin* ("void and rendered of no effect"). To return to the parable, we do not need to note that the employer did not enquire whether anyone else had employed them that day: he, and our hypothetical Jewish hearer, could guess that no one had. In the case of the noon-men and ninth-hour men this is not immediately self-evident. The role of the steward[36] was normal: he had the prestige-worthy task of paying the men. The righteous employer pays the men before nightfall, so that they can go home comfortably, for a workman goes home in his own time, not his master's.[37] The instruction to pay in inverse order was reasonable. The eleventh-hour men will have been keen to get home, where their families will have remained, so that necessaries could be bought. The families of the dawn-, third-, and sixth-hour men may well have been with them in the vineyard, gleaning, and doing the less ardous work, especially the packing and pressing (the women will not have worked alongside the men). The eleventh-hour men did not have the advantage of this. But a much more cogent

---

Josephus, *Ant.* IV, viii, 38 (288) (Thackeray, iv, 614): οὐκ ἀποστερητέον ἀνδρὸς πένητος μισθόν, εἰδότας ὡς ἀντὶ γῆς καὶ τῶν ἄλλων κτημάτων ὁ θεὸς αὐτῷ τοῦτον εἴη παρεσχηκώς· ἀλλ' αὐθημερὸν ἐκτίνειν. . . .

[34] *Jer.* 22: 13; *Mal.* 3: 5, *Sir* 34: 22. *Job* 24: 6 (LXX), cf. 24: 10 (MT). *Jas.* 5: 4. Changing wages is a sin: *Gen.* 31: 7, 41–2.

[35] F. BUSSBY, *Ex.T.* 76 (1964–5), p. 26.

[36] On the ἐπιτρόπος (see Philo, *De plant.* 56, Colson, iii, 241; Josephus, *Bell. Jud.* II, 134, Thackeray, ii, 374) and exploitation of labourers see St. John Chrysostomos, *in Matth. com.* 61, MIGNE, *Patrol. Gr.* 58, § 614 (3). ἐπιτρόπος, *epitropos* or *apotropos*, figured in Jewish law as a steward, guardian or administrator, the implication of the use of this word instead of οἰκονόμος (*Lk.* 12: 42, 16: 1) being this, that the latter had a more general scope, the former a more limited one: but the legal rights and liabilities were similar (the words are linked at *Gal.* 4: 2). The *epitropos*, we are to understand, would have been paid a commission on the sales of the wine. For the word in guardianship law my study at *NT* 14 (1972), pp. 1–9, should be read subject to what is said by Z. W. FALK, "Zum fremden Einfluss auf das jüdische Recht", *RIDA* 18 (1971), pp. 11–23.

[37] *Midr. R. Gen* 72: 4 (on *Gen.* 30: 16). *bB.M.* 83b (unless there is a local custom to the contrary). Thus he may be paid actually at sunset. On the eve of the Sabbath payment must be concluded so promptly that the worker can be back home, light a lamp, and broil a fish before sunset.

reason was the desire to avoid haggling, which could have protracted the procedure until well into the night. Those who are hired without specified terms would naturally haggle about the value of their work. Even when there is a custom as to labour, people who are perfectly aware of it will complain about their treatment, well knowing that if, the next day, they are otherwise placed they will vigorously uphold the customary rate. The notion that the dawn-men were paid last because they grumbled is absurd:[38] they grumbled because when paid last they were not given a bonus.

The biblical and therefore rabbinical law also permit the worker in this situation to eat his fill of the grapes.[39] The average owner expects to lose between $1\frac{1}{2}\%$ and 3% of the value of his crop in this way.[40] When their families come with the workers they eat as much, and the small children cannot be stopped from doing so by any legal or customary device. When the time for a snack comes the families produce bread, and even salt, which restores appetites for the grapes (of which one otherwise soon tires), and is thought to be necessary since the workers in the heat of the day are sweating profusely.[41] It is conventional to disregard the loss thus caused to the owner. The sugar content, fluid, and minerals make the grapes a food during the day, valuable to the workers. Moreover the long discussion of this in the Talmud proves that the vineyard owners believed the loss in point of grapes *was* significant: the item is not to be pooh-poohed.[42] Now when the crop presages a high quality wine, every bunch counts. The workers do not appreciate the difference, but the vintage is related to the harvest, and what the owner loses in point of grapes he loses in point of sales.

The families benefited from the grapes, too, and the stipulated wage was exclusive of grapes. In the cases up to the ninth-hour men, the grapes would be worth about 0·03 den. The ninth- and eleventh-hour men would consume less, and we can imagine, for a rough calculation (as any contemporary hearer would), that they had about 0·02 worth of grapes. A preacher would at once think of the parallel between this and the Jewish concept of "fruit" now and "pay" at the end of the day.[43]

[38] Schniewind, *op. cit.*, p. 207. P. BONNARD, *L'Évangile selon Saint Matthieu* (Neuchâtel, 1963), p. 291.
[39] *Deut* 23: 24/25. *mB.M.* 7: 2–7 (Danby, 359–60), *bB.M.* 87a, 88b, 89a, 91b–92a = Sonc. 504–35. *mMeil.* 3: 6 (Danby, 578), *bMeil.* 13a = Sonc. 47, *bSanh.* 57a, *bHull.* 120a, *bNed.* 50b. He must not be gluttonous, for it would prejudice his further employment: *mB.M.* 7: 5, *bB.M.* 92a. Maimonides, *Book of Divine Commandments*, I, pos. comm. no. 201. Josephus, *Ant.* IV, viii. 21 (235) (Thackeray, iv, 589) allows even passersby to eat grapes on their way to the winepress.
[40] My information on conditions in Greek vineyards was obtained in Sept. 1970 from Nicholas Aslanis, an hereditary vineyard owner and manager in Samos.
[41] *bB.M.* 89b = Sonc. 515.
[42] *mMaas.* 2: 7–8 (Danby, 69). *bB.M.* 87b = Sonc. 504–7, 89a = 514. The worker can eat more than the value of his wages: *Sifre Deut.* 23, § 266 (BONSIRVEN, cited below n. 89, § 334 bis).
[43] *mPeah* 1: 1 (Danby, 10–11).

In modern Greece a vineyard-harvester can expect a daily wage of 150–180 drachmae. It is rare to hire labourers as late as 5 p.m. The proportionate wages would be 45 drachmae, but no employer would offer so little. He would give 80 drachmae, which is the least that could be offered for trudging out to the vineyard and back. In terms of *production* our eleventh-hour men would have been worth 0·083 den., but it is ridiculous to suppose that anyone would offer them such a sum. We now come to the Jewish concept of "unemployment pay", or wages *kepo'el baṭel*, which is the key to the parable. Klausner actually saw that this was so,[44] but no one has grasped the point.

WAGES KEPO'EL BAṬEL

Jewish employers and employees, like those in India to this day, were not related as exploiters and exploited, but as hypothetical "brothers", "comrades". They were not, perhaps, economic equals, but they could be social equals, because of the concept of "neighbourliness" between all Jews, sons of a common Father. Roles might be reversed at very short notice (*Sir.* 11: 21), which no one deplored (*Lk.* 1: 52–3), such was the insecurity of life. Important passages of scripture were interpreted as requiring (whereas in fact they illustrated) a practical recognition of the social reciprocity of the employer and employee.[45] For he who sows righteousness/charity earns himself a true profit (*Prov.* 11: 18).

If we had the Hebrew of the significant *Sir.* 33: 27–31 (ed. Vattioni, 30: 39 [31]) we should be happier about it, but at any rate the author warns the employer "if you have a servant, let him be as you are (cf. *Lev.* 19: 18), because you have him by virtue of blood-relationship (*lit.* "in blood") (cf. *Job* 31: 15); if you have a servant treat him like yourself (or as your brother) because you will need him like your own life (*Prov.* 11: 17) . . ." We are reminded of *Sir.* 7: 20–1, "Do not ill treat a servant that works faithfully, or a hired man who gives his life to you (cf. *Deut.* 24: 15). Let your soul love an intelligent servant (cf. *Lk.* 12: 37); do not cheat him of his freedom."

The specific concept, called for short *po'el baṭel*, is best explained by illustrations:

(1) If a skilled man is asked or morally bound to undertake an unskilled

---

[44] *Op. cit.*, p. 180 (ignored because Klausner gave no references?).
[45] *Eccles.* 5: 11 (12), *Ps.* 104: 22 f. Billerbeck, *op. cit.*, p. 830. See *bB.M.* 76a = Sonc. 439: *Prov.* 3: 27 (cf. *Rom.* 13: 7) applies: "Withhold not good from those entitled to it (i.e. the poor), when it is in the power of thy hand to give it."

task as a favour he is entitled at least to be paid as a *po'el baṭel*, i.e. on the basis that he should have a minimum honorarium.[46]

(2) A tradesman doing business on the basis of a half share in the profits must be paid a minimum wage.[47]

(3) If a skilled or unskilled man is employed to perform a certain task for a day with or without a stipulated wage and the work takes no more than half a day to perform he is entitled, if he cannot easily obtain other employment, to a wage for the remainder of the day which is not less than the pay of a *po'el baṭel*, i.e. he must not be deprived of a notional minimum remuneration.[48]

(4) If, without any fault on his part, a hired man's task falls through or is frustrated, so that he cannot work for the employer's profit nor can he obtain employment, he must be paid for that day as a *po'el baṭel*, i.e. the employer is liable to pay a minimum wage.[49] There was an exception when the worker was one who could not be presumed to welcome a hypothetical idleness or "rest": in such a case he has no notional wage as a *po'el baṭel*, and where others would be entitled to be paid at that rate he must have his daily wage, proportionately or wholly, according to its market value.[50]

(5) Thus, I submit, a skilled or unskilled man, employed for less than a day and so prevented from being idle the whole day, is entitled to be paid at least as a *po'el baṭel*, i.e. on the basis that an otherwise unemployed man would hire out his labour at that figure rather than remain at rest, or, to put it in other words, the pay he would theoretically accept to resile from a contract of employment upon which he had not yet commenced work, in order to remain idle.

Thus the wage of a *po'el baṭel* is a notional minimum wage, balancing the social and moral rights of the employer and employee. It fell to be paid, so it seems, whenever an employer took up *without a specified reward* a man who thereby forfeited a chance of alternative employment, or forwent the chance to spend the day idly. Every man's leisure has a value, and there is an inducement which is sufficient to make it "worth one's while" to work. When an employer hired a man at noon, a man who was entitled *proportionately* only to half a day's wage (subject to fluctuations in the value of

---

[46] *mBekh.* 4: 6 (Danby, 534), *bBekh.* 29a–b = Sonc. 185–6, cf. *tBekh.* 3: 9 (compensate the priest where he is made unclean while giving an opinion—he must be given food, drink, and perfumed oil (cf. *tTer.* 10: 10), and, if aged, transport, and pay as a labourer); *bB.M.* 31b = Sonc. 196 (payment for returning lost animals) (*mB,M.* 2: 9, Danby, 350). L. GOLDSCHMIDT, *Die Rechtswissenschaftliche Sektion* . . . (1907), Vol. I, p. 573. M. KATZ, *Protection of the Weak in the Talmud* (New York, 1925), p. 28.

[47] *mB.M.* 5: 4 (Danby, 356), *bB.M.* 68a–b = Sonc. 398. See the Mishnah as read in the pal. Talmud, and cf. *tB.M.* 4: 11.

[48] *bB.M.* 77a = Sonc. 444. Maimonides, *Mishneh Torah, Hilkhoth sekhiruth* 9: 7 (trans. J. J. Rabinowitz, 1949, 35–6).

[49] *bB.M.* 76b = Sonc. 441–2 (notice H. Freedman at n. 6). Maimonides, *Sekhiruth* 9: 4 (Rabinowitz, p. 33).

[50] See n. 48 above.

labour during the day), he knew he would barely get value for the man's work, for the rate is discretionary and negotiable, at the moment of payment if not before, and cannot be much, if at all, below the wage of unskilled labourers hiring themselves out by the day. When workers stand idle in the evening it is an employers' market, and day-wages are not much above subsistence. The *po'el baṭel* rate must thus have been 0·7 *at the least*. Because of the employer's urgency they might be worth 0·8 or more. Men hired at noon would receive more than their work was economically worth. The case of the eleventh-hour men was an extreme one. It is true they might, had he bargained with them, have accepted less than 0·7 (having enjoyed their leisure already) but he chose not to bargain and became liable at the standard rate. An employer *could* avoid this by bargaining, or, if this was felt to be unethical, by not employing labourers at all after the third hour. But his circumstances strongly recommended our owner to recognise the solidarity of Israel!

AN ERROR NOTED

The difference of opinion between J. H. Heinemann and some previous writers should be noticed.[51] Heinemann came to the correct conclusion that *po'el baṭel* was very well known. But he was wrong in supposing that R. Abaye's definition (*bB.M.* 31b) was unreliable, and that the rate was defined. It was negotiable. Heinemann found fault with S. Krauss,[52] an authority one hesitates to criticise, with S. W. Baron,[53] and with Jastrow's *Dictionary*. Heinemann does not notice the work by Herzog,[54] which must be taken seriously, nor that of Horowitz;[55] in their different ways those studies were fruit of keen legal minds applied to an institution so well known in Tannaitic times that no definition was then required.

Heinemann believed that *po'el baṭel* was a retainer, wet weather pay, a wage low relatively to the economic wage. All others explain it as pay which an unemployed man would accept rather than remain idle, or as the pay a man would accept in order to stop his normal work. Heinemann, not understanding the latter, rejected it, on the basis that no one pays a man to be idle, but Abaye's definition accords with the theory of the notional value of leisure.

[51] "The status of the labourer in Jewish law and society in the Talmudic period", *HUCA* 25 (1954), pp. 263–325, esp. 278–325. See also H. HEINEMANN, "Payment of a Po'el Baṭel", *JJS* 1 (1949), pp. 178–81.

[52] S. KRAUSS, *Talmudische Archäologie* (Lepzig, 1911), Vol. II, pp. 102, 251–2.

[53] Heinemann, *ubi cit.*, also BARON, *Social and Religious History of the Jews*, Vol. I, p. 412, n. 28. Baron did not accept Heinemann's idea.

[54] Chief Rabbi I. HERZOG, *The Main Institutions of Jewish Law* (1936/9), Vol. II, pp. 167–74.

[55] G. HOROWITZ, *The Spirit of Jewish Law* (N.Y., 1953), pp. 532–4.

It is obvious that in times of depression and unemployment the difference between *po'el baṭel* pay and unskilled wages will have narrowed. "What is a *po'el baṭel*? Abaye said, "Like a worker who is unemployed, as he is without his particular employment."[56] H. Freedman, with the assent of I. Epstein,[57] explained this as meaning "as much as the average man would demand for changing over from strenuous labour to work of a lighter nature". D. Farbstein,[58] whom Heinemann ignores, said "'Lohn eines arbeitlosen Arbeiter' versteht der Talmud wahrscheinlich die Minimalgrenze des Arbeitslohnes." All the material and attempts at a definition can be reconciled if we take the view that a worker had a notional minimum wage, fluctuating from time to time with the market in which he was hired. For that wage he would be prepared to give up an engagement upon which he had not actually commenced, in order to take a day's rest. His leisure would be worth more, on those terms, than the hire to which he had previously agreed. For much the same wage a man would give up a day's idleness. Whether the work offered was two hours or five the notional wage would be the same; but there would always be the hope that the employer might pitch the rate higher.

If our employer had engaged men at dawn and their work had finished at noon, he would have been obliged, if they had no alternative and he had no other task for them, to pay them "as unemployed labourers" for the rest of the day.[59] It was no one's fault that they could not get a day's work elsewhere. And if he offered them something below subsistence they would complain. ἄξιος γὰρ ὁ ἐργάτης τῆς τροφῆς αὐτοῦ (*Mt.* 10: 10). The concept of *po'el baṭel* was only one aspect of human relations from the Jewish standpoint. If a man injured another he was bound to compensate him, but amongst the heads of compensation is the item "loss of time", i.e. a minimum wage (literally "as if he were a watchman of cucumber beds"): see the Mishnah to this effect.[60]

When our employer considered the rights of his various workmen, and considered their contractual entitlement, together with their unequal enjoyment of the grapes and the operation of the law relating to *po'el baṭel*, he found that the social as well as the economic value of the labour worked out so nearly equal that, if he were to instruct the steward to pay the labourers in small change, e.g. 0·75 or 0·8 to the third-hour men, 0·7 or 0·8 to the sixth-hour men (*not* 0·5), 0·7 or 0·8 to the ninth-hour men—*not* 0·25,

---

[56] *kepo'el baṭel shel 'otah melakhah devaṭel minah* (*bB.M.* 68b). I strongly suspect that the law of *po'el baṭel* had a biblical basis for teaching purposes. The text I would favour is *Jer.* 22: 13, which implies exactly this. One must not employ one's *neighbour* gratis, even if he has not engaged himself to you for a specific hire! Hence a minimum remuneration/compensation/honorarium is obligatory.

[57] At the Soncino translation of *bB.M.* 68b = Sonc. 398.

[58] *Das Recht der unfreien und der freien Arbeiter nach jüdisch-talmudischem Recht* ... (Frankfurt, 1896), p. 54.

[59] See n. 48 above.

[60] *mB.K.* 8: 1 (Danby, 342), *bB.K.* 83b = Sonc. 473, 491.

and 0·7 or 0·8 to the eleventh-hour men—*not* 0·083, there would be so much haggling that most of the workers would not get home till very late. Moreover   *
his special harvest was either in or nearly so, thanks to the eleventh-hour men, and he felt philanthropic and optimistic (cf. *Tob.* 5: 15–16, 12: 1–5, 8–10). They should all have the same wage! The minute discrepancies would not affect the market, for he would not hire unskilled labour again that season, or if he did it would be for a very short period only.

That it was a reasonable thing to do, to pay unemployed labourers a whole day's wage, at the end of the day, when they had done only a single hour's work, is proved by a notable occurrence in the reign of Agrippa II, about 30 years after the crucifixion. The affair, properly noticed by Wetstenius *ad loc.*, has been ignored ever since. Josephus uses language which could not have been more apposite had he read our parable. The governing body of the Jews, which will have included a sanhedrin in which priests and levites participated,[61] encouraged Agrippa to rebuild the eastern cloisters of the Temple with the aid of some of the 18,000 or so unemployed in Jerusalem. The Temple treasurer and his associates must have acquiesced in the scheme in question (cf. 2 *Chron.* 29: 11–14) and they will have decided as a matter of Torah that no sacrilege would be committed by such payments from the sacred treasury: a decision consciously taken *bona fide* as trustees (*ve'emunah*: 2 *Kings* 12: 15 [16 M.T.], 22: 7). Partly as a matter of charity, partly in order to adorn the otherwise completed project of Herod's Temple, and partly, says Josephus, to save the accumulated treasure from being an attraction to the Romans or insurgents (they will have noted *Ezek.* 7: 22, and cf. 2 *Macc.* 5: 19–20!), a full day's wages were paid to every worker even if he had been able to contribute no more than one hour's work in the day.[62]

ANOTHER ERROR DISPOSED OF

The error was that of F. M. De Robertis in 1946.[63] He imagined that our parable was explained by certain provisions of Roman law regarding the rights of a freedman (*locatio conductio operarum*). Theo Mayer-Maly took this up in passing in 1956.[64] The error was snatched up, over-eagerly, by

---

[61] The meaning of δῆμος is vague: V. A. TCHERIKOVER, "Was Jerusalem a 'polis'?", *IEJ* 14 (1964), pp. 61–78.

[62] *Ant.* XX. 219–20 (Feldman ix, 504–6). βλέπων οὖν ὁ δῆμος ἀργήσαντας τοὺς τεχνίτας . . . μισθοφορίας ἐνδεεῖς ἐσομένους . . . εἰς τούτους ἀναλοῦν τοὺς θησαυροὺς βουλομένος· καὶ γὰρ εἰ μίαν τὶς ὥραν τῆς ἡμέρας εἰργάσαιτο, τὸν μισθὸν ὑπὲρ ταύτης εὐθέως ἐλάμβανεν. L. H. Feldman correctly adduces *Mt.* 20: 8! Fear of the Romans was justified (see *Ant.* 18: 60; *Bell. Jud.* 293). A saying of R. Akiba deserves some thought: *Ab. d. R. Nathan* 11 (trans. J. Goldin, 1955, p. 61): labourers building the Temple are privileged in the use of their wages.

[63] DE ROBERTIS, *I rapporti di lavoro nel diritto Romano* (Milan, 1946), pp. 141–6.

[64] T. MAYER-MALY, *Locatio Conductio* (Vienna, 1956), p. 124 (*Wiener rechtsgeschicht-liche Arbeiten* 4).

J. B. Bauer in an article[65] which has rightly been criticised by Dom J. Dupont.[66] Moreover Fr. Bauer misunderstood *mB.M.* 9: 11, which, as correctly explained by Maimonides,[67] does not reveal any such notion as that proposed. Indeed it proves the reverse, namely that hiring for stipulated tasks and periods was normal. When we look at the passages relied upon by De Robertis we find that they[68] say nothing to the point. The freedman might have been exploited by his "patron" and the "patron" was protected against inadequate performance by the freedman. Freedmen were presumed to hire their services by the day, but the status of a freedman was peculiar, as De Robertis later admits.[69] When De Robertis revised and republished his major contributions in 1963 he did not repeat what had previously been claimed, and instead cited our parable only as an example of labour continuing until nightfall.[70] Thus Mayer-Maly's and Bauer's support vanishes. It is unfortunate that a version of the error turns up in a valuable commentary on the New Testament.[71]

We are now clear that the employer was not quixotic, and that what he did was, though generous, only marginally so, and combined business sense with the behaviour of a man wishing to retain a good name in Israel. That is God's position as Jesus wishes to depict it. He had a good name to lose, and he can be counted upon not to lose it.[72] The interesting notion of Feuillet (1947) that the eleventh-hour men are the least favoured, in being the last hired, and therefore most fit for the divine bounty, is incorrect in substance and wrong in method (as so many theological treatments of this topic), since, contrary to his supposition, this parable too teaches the ways of God by noting the ways of men, and God makes contracts like a man.[73]

We are now ready to look into the midrashic overtones of the parable, not all of which can be set out verbatim, for want of space. All hearers would have realised that the employer meant, when he said ". . . because I am good", not that he thought himself generous, but that he was a good Israelite. He took the attitude depicted at *Job* 31: 13–15: solidarity with his servants was a mark of a true employer. And of course only the One is "good" (Mt. 19: 17).

---

[65] "Gnadenlohn oder Tageslohn (*Mt.* 20: 8–16)", *Biblica* 42 (1961), pp. 224–8.
[66] Dupont, *ubi cit.*, p. 34 n. 1.
[67] *Mishneh Torah Sekhiruth*, 9: 2 (trans., 40). Jeremias also thought *mB.M.* 9: 11–12 relevant: *Jerusalem zur Zeit Jesu*, 3rd edn. (Göttingen, 1962), p. 125, n. 3.
[68] *Dig.* 38.1.3.1, 38.1.15.1.
[69] Next note, p. 194, n. 58. à propos of *Dig.* 38.1.26.
[70] DE ROBERTIS, *Lavoro e lavoratori nel mondo Romano* (Bari, 1963), pp. 187, 194.
[71] A. E. HARVEY, *Companion to the [N. E. B.] New Testament* (Oxford/Cambridge, 1970), p. 80.
[72] DERRETT, "Law in the New Testament: the Parable of the Unjust Judge", *NTS* 17 (1971), pp. 178 ff. at p. 191. See also *Rom.* 9: 17 (referred to below).
[73] *Gen.* 15: 18 ff. T. H. GASTER, *Myth, Legend and Custom in the Old Testament* (N.Y., 1969), pp. 140–56.

CONCEPTS OF REWARD

As Morton Smith pointed out[74] there is no one Jewish concept of Reward, nor can we be sure that Jesus's teaching was unitary or simple.[75] This is not the place to go over the evidence, nor to correct in detail the biassed presentation of Billerbeck.[76] It is clear that Jesus believed that some rewards would be enjoyed in this life, and others in the world to come.[77] Rabbinical parables about rewards which take the form of stories about workpeople are numerous, and, for the most part, readily available in studies of the parables.[78] The question of equality, as is well known, also came up; and characteristically stories about grumbling workpeople figure here too.[79] A problem would occur to anyone who thought that reward should be measured according to results, i.e. labour. How can the world to come be enjoyed by people who have lived a long life successfully overcoming temptation to idleness and sin, and by people who die soon after they become sons of the commandments? The rabbinical answer is that all are rewarded equally, because the young, cut off in their youth, could complain that if God had not removed them they would have worked for him longer.[80] This is a midrash on *Eccles.* 5: 11 (12), "Sweet is the sleep of the labourer. . . ." Moreover, that people who live for different periods may have the same reward is proved by *Ps.* 99: 6: "Moses and Aaron among his priests and Samuel among them that call upon his name" (read with *v.* 7: "all of them kept the commandments (*hok*) which he

[74] *Tannaitic Parallels to the Gospels* (Philadelphia, 1951), pp. 49–71 (an elaborate treatment). G. F. MOORE, *Judaism* (Cambridge, Mass., 1958), Vol. II, Ch. 2.

[75] H. PREISKER in Kittel, *TWNT* IV (1942), s. v. μισθός, is of great value, but is biassed in favour of an hypothesis that Jesus did not conceive of merit as the key to reward. Our parable actually proves this wrong, though *sub modo*. See Bo REICKE, "The New Testament conception of reward", *Mélanges Goguel* (Neuchatel/Paris, 1950), pp. 195–206. *mAb.* 5: 19, *mPeah* 1: 1. Some part of hire is certainly in this world—e.g. children (*Ps.* 127: 3, *Prov.* 11: 18 LXX)! *Gen.* 30: 18.D. DAUBE, *Studies in Biblical Law* (Cambridge, 1947), pp. 18, 22. Our parable best illustrates the truth that Jesus was concerned less with the social effects of duty done, the collective significance of individual attitudes, than with the moral position of the individual. It is the prospect of personal merit which is the motivation upon which his teaching hangs, to which his parable is directed. So (a little exaggeratedly?) Henry J. CADBURY, *The Peril of Modernising Jesus* (New York, 1937), pp. 101–9.

[76] *Kommentar*, IV, exc. 20, pp. 484–500, devoted to our parable in the light of reward. H. Heinemann (*cit. sup.*) also deplores Billerbeck's treatment.

[77] In this life: *Mk.* 10: 29 f., *Lk.* 18: 29 f. (*Mt.* 19: 29 is equivocal).

[78] *Midr. R. Deut.* 6: 2=Sonc. 121–2; *Midr. R. Lev.* 24: 8=Sonc. 310. These passages have been known since at least as early as C. Schöttgen (n. 84 below). The funeral oration on R. Bun (he did more in a short life than many did in a long one) is familiar since the time of John Lightfoot (*Works*, London, 1823, XI, 254–5): *Mdir. R. Eccles.* 5:11 =Sonc. 150; *Midr. R.S.S.* 6: 2=Sonc. 258. Jeremias (pp. 138–9).

[79] The complaint of the Nazirite watchman at *Midr. R. Lev.* 24: 8 (*sup.*).

[80] *Tanḥuma* (Vienna, 1863), 110a, quoted by Billerbeck at *Komm.* I, 833 and IV, 1, pp. 498–9. Billerbeck's comment is unsound. Note that the Targum on *Eccles.* 5: 11 says that in the world to come he will have a sweet reward no matter how many years he has served God "with a whole heart". "Rich" means "rich in wisdom".

gave them"),[81] a text which shows that irrespective of age the faithful are treated as equals in God's sight, and that too irrespective of their period in world history.[82]

Moreover, those who labour till the evening, i.e. those who study and do good works till their death, are sure of their reward irrespective of the time at which they commence: or so, says R. Ze'era, who was fond of worker-parables, one could understand *Ps.* 104, especially *v.* 23, "man goeth forth unto his work and to his labour until the evening".[83]

There is a rare saying in Tanḥuma,[84] *'oseh le'aharonim bezekhuth ha-ri'shonim*, "he places the last in the stead of the first", *zekhut* ("stead") having the overtones of "privilege", "good standing", particularly by virtue of merit: i.e. God treats the last as as meritorious as the first. How do we know this? Because at *Gen.* 5: 1 we read "this is the book of the generations of Noah, Noah was a righteous man and perfect in his generations . . ."

Zekhuth is certainly the word here, because reward implies honour as much as money. Labourers' self-esteem is shaken when their efforts are disdained, even if the contract sum is paid to them. One "wrongs" a wage-earner not merely by depriving him of his due wage; you may "wrong" him if you treat him contemptuously, e.g. by making no distinction between him and someone less meritorious. To be praised, or to be promoted, has its psychological and social value (cf. the Honours List). What is so difficult to accept is that God will not esteem some "workers" higher than others when the former have laboured more valiantly. But we must understand that many squads of workers are needed (as with Solomon's Temple) before the task can be finished, and what matters is that the harvest shall be brought in, though the sower and the reaper worked at different stages (*Hos.* 12: 12, *Jn.* 4: 36), and it would be absurd for the sower and the ploughman, the harrower and the weeder, to complain at the harvester's sharing in the harvest celebrations (ἄλλοι κεκοπιάκασιν καὶ ὑμεῖς εἰς τὸν κόπον αὐτῶν εἰσεληλύθατε: *Jn.* 4: 38). Such metaphors are compelling, especially for the agriculturalist.

The word *zekhuth* means merit, and it is wholly in place in a study of this parable. In the long story of Jewish speculation on merit and reward the opinion emerged, which is accepted as the teaching of the rabbis, that one cannot acquire merit except by divine grace. True, the individual's merits are

---

[81] See last note. For an early ecclesiastical use of *Ps.* 99 see Justin, *Dial.* §§ 37, 64.

[82] *bR.H.* 25b=Sonc. 111 (citing *Ps.* 99: 6); *b.Taan.* 5b=Sonc. 17. *Midr. Ps.* 99 § 4 (trans. Braude, ii, 145).

[83] *bB.M.* 83b=Sonc. 477.

[84] Midrash Tanḥuma, ed. and trans. F. Singermann (Berlin, 1927), pp. 38–9 (R. 'Avuhu) was first noticed at C. Schöttgen, *Horae Hebraicae et Talmudicae* (Dresden/Leipzig, 1733) p. 165. (I am obliged to Mr. R. A. May for checking the reference for me.) Dr. B. S. Jackson drew my attention to *bMen.* 110b (the degree of merit depends on the motive, not the amount, of sacrifice).

important, but it would be disputed how far he could claim to rely upon them as if they were entirely his own. The ultimate view remains that but for God's initiative, which enables merit to be earned, the individual cannot rely upon merit. Still less could he rely upon the merits of the patriarchs (see 4 *Ezra* 7: [102]–45[115]), or upon solidarity between the faithful in general. It adequately represents this important and subtle teaching, to paint the picture of the labourer being given, without any claim by himself, the opportunity to earn a reward: and a twelfth of *zekhuth* is obviously absurd. A student of *zekhuth* might well comment that this works well, provided those who are permitted to earn merit are not equalised with those to whom grace abounds: God shows favour to the unworthy, helps and acquits them, and is this not unfair? No, says an old authority, *Ps.* 67: 6 assures us that his justice will be accepted: "Peoples give thanks to thee, O God, all of them give thanks to thee".[85] Moreover *zekhuth* is an unstable, fragile asset, and may waste away: those who have the covenant to rely upon are in any event secure.[86]

One may disagree with those who emphasise in connection with our parable the well-known Mishnaic principle that servants who work without reward (i.e. who work for their keep) are preferable to those who serve for reward.[87] It is a principle illustrated, incidentally, by the petition of the Prodigal Son (*Lk.* 15: 19). Our parable, however, does not possess the concept of work without reward. Some did better than they expected, but that was because they had the good fortune to be hired by an employer who was so placed that he could readily do his social duty, which was to be philanthropical. We are supported by *Rom.* 4: 4, which we need not enlarge upon here.

THE MIDRASHIC CONTENT OF THE PARABLE

The story of the vineyard recalls God's world, provided with a cultivator from the time of Adam (who originally worked for his keep). Noah was the

---

[85] *Midrash on Psalms* and *Yalḳuṭ* cited by A. MARMORSTEIN, *The Doctrine of Merits in Old Rabbinical Literature* (London, 1920), p. 14.

[86] S. SCHECHTER, *Some Aspects of Rabbinic Theology* (London, 1909), p. 179. The concept of the "failing"of *zekhuth* (i.e. theoretically the using up of treasure of merit of ancestors, of contemporaries, or of one's own acquisition, because of God's forbearance, but in fact the waning of the collective concept of the merit of the social unit), figures with references at pp. 176, 179. Yet in hyperbole the idea lives on. Apropos of this parable, one may obtain (it says) the world-to-come either on the basis of a covenant, or on the basis of the social value of merit-earning, but in either case the initiative comes from God, and in both cases the operative factor is his grace, since neither class of merit can be earned without grace.

[87] *mAb.* 1: 3 (Danby, 446). Moore, *op. cit.* II, 95. Maimonides, *Sekhirut* 10: 1–5. One who serves without wages has an identity of interest with his employer (see *Jn.* 4: 32, 34), like a servant under the "status" system of employment in the Golden Age.

next gardener. The key idea is exploitation of an estate in which human labour is essential. Man is, after all, a hireling (*Job* 7: 1, 14: 6).

Abraham was promised a great reward.[88] Though his covenant was unspecific, covenant he had. The Neofiti Targum (*Gen.* 9: 12, 15–16) tells us that the covenant was one "with all flesh". A repetition of the covenant to Isaac and Jacob did not vary the quality of the covenant (it was great, but still non-specific). The texts concerning Noah, and Abraham, generation by generation, make it plain that there was a concept of repeated hirings: *Gen.* 9: 12, 15, 17; 15: 13–21; 16: 4–14; *Ex.* 2: 25; *Lev.* 26: 42; *Deut.* 5; 2 *Kings* 13: 23. But Adam sinned, Noah's descendants occupied themselves with the tower of Babel, etc., the descendants of Jacob were involved in Egypt, and they had to be freed and given a new status and a new covenant. The covenant at Sinai had a specific reward, "profitable" to the children of Israel (the traditional interpretation of *Deut.* 1: 6). The episode of the Golden Calf revealed their natures. Nevertheless the "workers" began to put forth effort in pursuance of the covenant and so began to earn their hire. And yet the harvest was not in, the reward was not in their hands. Jeremiah, at 31: 31–2, takes up the idea of a new covenant, mentioned at *Lev.* 26: 9, 11–12. This new covenant, says Jeremiah, shall be more successful than the old, not written on paper (as it were) with explicit terms, but written on hearts (as it were) with equitable terms, a matter of good conscience. Sifra on *Lev.* 26: 9 explains that this means that those who have laboured for long without pay will be given a specially large reward in the world to come.[89] The interpretation of the Leviticus passage in the Targum Ps.-Jonathan shows how it was taken perhaps as early as the time of Jesus: "For I will turn from the wages of the Gentiles, to pay you in full the wages of your good works, and I will strengthen you, and multiply you, and establish my covenant with you." The word *strengthen* is interesting since it implies a payment or gift to a person suffering from want, and refreshed by it.

Furthermore, the concept of a "late" covenanting with God, on the basis that previous covenants had not come, as it were, to maturity, and that further covenant(s) were required, is found written out clearly in *Neh.* 9–10. The Jews, through the mouths of the Levites, admitted they were God's

---

[88] *Gen.* 15: 1: "Fear not, Abram, I am thy shield (*magen*), thy reward shall be exceeding great (*sekharekha harbeh me'od*)". It is interesting that up to the time of Irenaeus (*Adv. Haer.* iv. 36–7) and Origen (*Comm. in Mt.* 15: 32) the parable was interpreted with reference to the different generations of mankind and their dealings with God, but, as Fonck says, this is generally disregarded. Trench, *op. cit.*, p. 186, actually linked God's promise to Abraham with the denarius. Muslim applications of this parable are beyond our concern (Trench, p. 183).

[89] Sifra on *Lev.* 26: 9 (cf. *Targ. Ps. Jon., ibid.*): the employer (God) turns from the wages of the gentiles (in this world) and pays in full the wages of the Jews, strengthening them, multiplying them and establishing his covenant with them. BONSIRVEN, *Textes Rabbiniques* (Rome, 1955), § 215; BILLERBECK, *Komm.* IV, 493; and misunderstood in relation to our parable by Smith, *op. cit.*, p. 51.

servants, and servants in the land which God had given them to enjoy: and upon that basis entered into a faithful agreement to abide by the Law, etc. At *Neh.* 9: 32 we are told how the covenanting parties recognised God as one who *shomer ha-berit weha-ḥesed*, i.e. one who keeps to the terms of the (old) covenant (with Abraham, 9: 8) but is merciful, overlooking the poor per-formance of the other parties out of loving-kindness. The image of a repeated covenanting, necessitated by poor performance in earlier generations of "servants", is thus biblical, and there is no reason to doubt but that the behaviour of the Jews led by Nehemiah served as a model for any who wished to make a fresh start, enter into a new covenant, and commence, though late in the day (as it were), to earn the reward promised to Abraham. These several covenants raise the question: are they different agreements, the later superseding the earlier? If so, what of God's infallibility? Or are they not really *one* covenant, manifesting itself in repeated commands, dispositions (διαθῆκαι: *Rom.* 9: 4), *instructions* which the people receive, accept, acknowledge, on different occasions? This would appear to be more nearly correct.[90]

Thus the intermittent going to the market-place and hiring workers suggests the hiring of the human race, and the specific hiring of the children of Israel, while the payment of a single hire to all suggests that whatever the terms of the various covenants, those who began work and did not resile from it throughout the "day" will be paid equally, the kingdom will belong equally to all. The principle applies irrespective of the scope for labour; and the length of service, as well as its chronological position, are irrelevant. What is important is that the hirer's initiative is responded to. The bailiff or steward takes the place of the angels in a mythical representation of the Kingdom (cf. *Mt.* 16: 27, 22: 13). The grumbling of the dawn-men calls to mind the grumbling shown picturesquely in Malachi, where God expostulates with those who accuse him of unfairness,[91] and it calls to mind the fact that it is grumbling Man who is not just (*Ezek.* 18: 29, 33: 17). It also calls to mind the

[90] A. JAUBERT, *La notion d'alliance dans le Judaïsme* (Paris, 1963). C. ROETZEL at *Biblica* 51 (1970), pp. 377–90, would have been on stronger ground to understand διαθήκη as "(legal) disposition". An enlightening reappraisal of the whole concept of covenant in the Old Testament (with New Testament implications) is E. KUTSCH, *Verheissung und Gesetz* (Berlin and New York, 1973).

[91] *Mal.* 2: 4–5, 8: you have corrupted God's covenant with Levi (*Num.* 25: 12 f., *Deut.* 18: 1–8, 33: 8–11). Complaints: 2: 17, 3: 13–14. It is important to note that at 3: 15 the words *we'atah anaḥnu me'asherim zedim* ("and now we call the *proud* happy") were read by the LXX with *zarim* (as at *Deut.* 32: 16, *Jer*: 3: 13, 5: 19), "we call strangers, foreigners happy". I suggest that the eleventh-hour men seemed to the dawn men as elated and alien to themselves—they dissociated themselves from them, and attributed evil attitudes to them. Arguments as to God's fairness began with Abraham himself: *Gen.* 18: 25 (re Sodom), *Job.* 21: 7–15; *Ps.* 73: 2–3, 13; *Is.* 18: 3. Malachi figures in the New Testament at several places certainly and at others possibly: 1: 2–3 (*Rom.* 9: 13); 2: 10 (*1 Cor.* 8: 6); 3:1 (*Mt.* 11: 10, *Mk.* 1: 2, 76, 7: 27, *Jn.* 3: 28); 3: 2 (*Rev.* 4: 17); 3: 3 (*1 Pet.* 1: 7); 3: 7 (*Jas.* 4: 8); 4: 2 (*Lk.* 1: 78); 4: 5 (*Mt.* 11: 14); 4: 5–6 (*Mt.* 17: 10–11, *Mk.* 9: 11–12, *Lk.* 1: 17). Moreover *Mt.* 13: 24–30, 36–43, 44–5, 47–50 are based on *Mal.* 3: 7–4: 3.

behaviour of the children of Israel, whose sufferings in the desert were much increased by their grumblings.[92] They did not lose thereby the land of milk and honey, but their way thither was worsened by it. It calls to mind the attitude of Cain ("there is no good reward for righteousness").[93]

As for the concept of "idleness", it is wrong to suppose that activity is obligatory (Jülicher, p. 467), or that the men's unemployment must have been due to their oriental indifference (Meinertz, Jeremias). The word "idle" was needed to recall the *po'el baṭel* and all that that implied. But since *'avodah* means worship, especially in the case of those of whom Sirach says (38: 34) ἡ δέησις αὐτῶν (cf. *Lk.* 5: 33) ἐν ἐργασίᾳ τέχνης, the concept "idle" indicates absence of compromise with cults (*'avodah zarah* means heathenism) (see 1 *Kings* 19: 18). Naturally only those who are idle are fit for employment, but the Jewish labourer has the right to withdraw his labour: extending the idea to gentiles we know that they could give up their worship of idols, stars, and the like, and take refuge under the wings of the Presence. In sequence, they abandon idolatry and contemplate becoming proselytes. Before actually being proselytes they are "idle". Thus to be "idle" is a qualification for being employed at rates of pay which were socially acceptable. And it is consistent with life that the actual daily wage should turn out to be only slightly more, so that, following out the metaphor, all labourers who lend a hand at the harvest will enjoy the same wage, no matter whether born Jewish or gentile (see *Is.* 11: 10, 12).

When Abraham was offered his "great reward" (which was thought by many to be God himself)[94] Abraham was worried.[95] "Perhaps another will arise, to whom the promises to Noah would be made? Where would I stand then?" God promised Abraham a reward which is very great, in order to set his mind at rest: no subsequent promise will derogate from what has been promised to him. Both Noah and Abraham received their promises without any bargain, and by their righteousness they committed God to pay them the value of their work. Those, therefore, who obey God with no more specific promise than they had will neither diminish *their* rewards nor be disappointed in their own.

It was important that this should be taught, as a contrary opinion seems to have existed, if only in embryo, in Jesus's time. This was that Abraham, by whatever right, acquired, in that promise to him of a "great reward", not

---

[92] *Ex.* 16: 2, 7–12; 17: 2–7; *Num.* 14: 2, 27–37, 43–45; 16: 41–49. *Ps.* 106: 25. *1 Cor.* 10: 10 (ἐγόγγυσαν). *Heb.* 3: 9–19.

[93] *Targ. Ps. Jon. Gen.* 4: 8 (J. BOWKER, *The Targum and Rabbinic Literature*, Cambridge, 1969, pp. 132–3).

[94] Traditional interpretation of *Gen.* 15: 1 (M. M. KASHER, *Encyclopedia of Biblical Interpretation* N.Y., 1955, Vol. II, pp. 177–8), reflected in the Vulgate (not the LXX) and the English versions until the RSV.

[95] *Midr. R. Gen.* 44, §§ 4–5. *Midr. R.S.S.* 14, § 3 (Kasher, *op. cit.*, 173, § 2). Note how *magen* is taken as from *migen* (give), in the sense of free gift (Kasher, p. 175, n. 2).

merely what he himself and his descendants would earn, as it were, but the reward of all the ten generations before him, from Noah. *mAb.* 5: 2 says *wekibbel* [*'alaw*] *sekhar kullam*, "he acquired the reward (or hire) of them all".[96] Such a doctrine would throw doubt upon the validity of the promises to Noah and his generations, if it were conceivable that others, more worthy, would in fact supersede and exclude them. It seems far better to take each promise as valid in its own right, not excluding the validity of subsequent promises, none derogating from another, since all are needed at the end of the day.

One could compare the typical behaviour of a loving father, who (as Philo would put it) has partitioned his accumulations, or part of them, between his sons for them to work with, i.e. to invest, to speculate.[97] A commercial figure is once again used to make the point. Some, he says, invested wisely, and some fortunately: some on the other hand lost their investments and went downhill. He would, if he made no arrangements to the contrary, leave all his sons in the position of retaining at his death the capital he had apportioned between them. Some would be poorly off. A strictly just father would leave things as they were, a decision the successful ones might applaud. But a true Jewish father would use his parental authority,[98] demand an account from all his sons, and redistribute the capital, giving them equal shares, and so setting the formerly unsuccessful sons up again. He loved them all equally and was master of his own estate. Equality is equity and this is how God "behaves", irrespective of the individual's success. God "shows mercy on them on whom he will show mercy" and this is how his authority is used. With our parable cf. *Rom.* 9: 10–18. The notion that any that gather the grapes shall drink the wine in the presence of God when the Servant brings the Reward is of course biblical, stated in so many words at *Is.* 62: 9, 11. The remarkable frequency of reference to vines (including vineyards) and wine in the gospels can hardly be unrelated to this.

Furthermore a Tannaitic midrash shows that from the commandment to pay the worker's wage at nightfall we may know that God pays his reward "promptly" (i.e. in the "evening"), for the "behaviour" of God is disclosed by the rules he lays down for men.[99]

---

[96] Danby, 455; Blackman's *Mishnah*, IV, p. 526. This appears to me to be an instance of vicarious merit. Jesus's teaching on such merit appears at *Mt.* 15: 1–12 (see Derrett, "La Parabola delle vergini stolte", *Conoscenza Religiosa* 4 (1971), pp. 394–406).

[97] Philo, *De Virtut.* §§ 91–2 (Colson, viii, 217–19). Commenting upon *Lev.* 19: 10.

[98] Some fathers gave their sons separate accounts, and economies out of allowances were possible. Some sons had a *segulah* (*peculium*). *Sifre Deut.* 48; *yB.B* 9: 3 (17a). On the other hand barring evidence of advancement in these ways assets in the sons' hands were treated as the father's, especially when they ate at home. *mErub.* 6: 7, *bErub.* 72b–73a = Sonc. 505, 507; *bB.M.* 12b = Sonc. 69; *mB.B* 9: 3, *bB.B.* 52a = Sonc. 214. B. Cohen, *Jewish and Roman Law* (N.Y., 1966), Vol. I, pp. 196–7, 210–11, 215 n. 183, 222.

[99] *Midrash on Psalms*, 25 § 1; *Midr. R. Deut.* 11: 10.

THE MEANING OF THE PARABLE

God pays the reward promptly. To understand the subtleties of our parable we must be able to distinguish it from the metaphor of R. Ṭarfon (*ca.* A.D. 130), which is evidently based on the same association of ideas, but lacks the great allusion to God's concern that man should earn merit. R. Ṭarfon said (*mAb.* 2: 15), "The day is short and the task is great and the workers are sluggish and the hire is ample and the employer urges them on." The word I translate "urges them on" (*dohek*) gives the impression of an urgent, insistent, pressing, crowding importunity (cf. *Mt.* 11: 12; *Lk.* 16: 16). There is no doubt but that our employer, in going to the market-place, showed that as far as he was concerned there was a *deḥak*, an emergency. He actually urged the workers into the vineyard. But R. Ṭarfon continued (*ibid.*, 16), "It is not incumbent upon *you* that the work should be completed; and yet you do not have such freedom (*lit.* 'you are not a free man') that you can choose to be unemployed rather than do it (*lit.* to desist from it [*libbaṭel mimennah*], to cease, give yourself leave from it) . . . your taskmaster is faithful and shall pay you the hire for your labour (*sekhar pe'ulatekha*); and know that the righteous will receive their hire in the time to come." Jesus's parable, with apparently similar assumptions, goes into detail, refines the teaching.

God will indeed "reward every man according to his works" (*Job* 34: 11, *Ps.* 62: 12, *Prov.* 24: 12) but he will (on the pattern of the Torah) calculate (as it were) the reward according to the social as well as economic value of the work! There are at least two equally respectable ways of meriting that reward: in both of them God, as "employer", takes the initiative, but in both of them, though on different bases, he is bound to pay that reward. That is Jesus's midrash.

There are classes of faithful, some who work distinctly for reward, some who anticipate that God will reward them in some unknown way (*Sir.* 11: 21–28), and some who worship him trusting to his faithfulness to pay them according to reciprocity, a factor taken for granted in Asian life. These are psychological attitudes, and they could correspond to the different biblical covenants. The new covenant proclaimed by Jeremiah opened the door to a new concept of "employment" by God, and it left certain questions unanswered, namely who could take advantage of it, would it be worth their while, and how would they stand relative to those who had accepted the yoke of the earlier covenants?

Would the new covenant place those who accepted it upon an equal footing with the adherents of previous covenants, particularly that at Sinai?[100] Would not these latter be in a superior position, because prior? Those who had elaborately performed the covenant, the "righteous kings", sectarians, zealots, or others were presumably better placed than any who adhered to a less demanding covenant. Did the covenant with Abraham, "with all flesh", stand open, notwithstanding the covenant through Moses at Sinai? Could one by-pass the latter and submit to the former? Would the new covenant be like that with Abraham—presumably it would be the same in a new guise? Could a teaching which was *ex professo* not derived from that of Moses claim to be Jewish, and if not how could God be taken to have authorised it? One might even ask whether the Dead Sea sect's onerous and awful Covenant entitled its participants to supernatural privileges.

The parable seeks to tell that faithful adherents of *any* of the biblical *
covenants who had actually laboured in the vineyard will obtain their reward; and not inferior to them, in any respect, are those whom God has thought fit to call in "at the last hour", for his own purposes, for by holding themselves in readiness to be employed they are qualified to have the reward, though their actual contribution to the product is negligible. "Do not be afraid to accept that new covenant; and take no thought for the competing claims of those who have engaged themselves on other terms! All the terms had their own validities and will be honoured concurrently." The tax-gatherers and sinners had the option to become ultra-pious, and, after the necessary probation, could have reformed (cf. the dramatic conversions effected by the handsome R. Yoḥanan) and been reintegrated as disciples of the wise, i.e. Pharisees. There was nothing about the outcast condition which made it necessary to choose between damnation and the church; no more than was the church condemned to draw its membership only from the outcasts. The parable is about the validity of different theories of obtaining the world to come. It operated in Jesus's favour since it insinuated that his mission, in the guise of the new covenant, as a "light yoke" (*Mt.* 11: 30, cf. *Is.* 9: 4), placed no one at any disadvantage relative to the adherents of Mosaic observances.

The parable does not tell us whether Abraham received the promise entirely through faith; nor whether faith is equally meritorious with ob-servances (see *Rom.* 4: 5); nor that merit and reward are unrelated; nor that grace renders merit irrelevant; nor that "work" is obligatory and "reward" a secondary consideration; nor that God reserves absolute freedom to

---

[100] See A. FEUILLET, "Les ouvriers de la vigne et la théologie de l'alliance", *Rech. Sc. Rel.* 34 (1947), pp. 303–27, ". . . notre parabole est en somme une protestation contre une conception fausse de l'alliance" (p. 306). ". . . l'alliance religieuse n'est pas un pacte comme les autres, et c'est là l'idée fondamentale de notre parabole" (*ibid.*).

determine the identity and fate of the "elect";[101] nor that the Messiah will come even to the unworthy; nor whether last-minute repentance avails; nor whether circumcision is necessary to salvation; nor whether gentiles may obtain the world to come or on what terms; nor does it say that the church is superior to the synagogue (the reverse!); nor is it Jesus's own defence of his behaviour relative to the outcasts. I go so far as to contend that, *if* the passage had any connection with Peter's question, this, *if* it was the answer, will have assured Peter that he would do no worse, just as he would do no better, if he became, instead of Jesus's star pupil, a follower of the more genuine of the Pharisees' rabbis (*Mt.* 23: 1–2)!   *

St. Matthew, on the other hand, was conscious of the fears of Christians of the second generation, "Will not the apostles and actual followers of Jesus monopolise all the rewards which he promised them? Where do we fit into his scheme?" The answer is that the ministers and the faithful in general are not postponed, though their call is late. Though Jesus's promise did not reach them personally, they can rely on God's promises as the first generation of Christians did. Nor can any who have given up all imagine that they have earned on that account (so Mouson). It is in this sense that the first shall be last and the last first, as in a crown. All the workmen would sit down together, and the apostles would not begin dining until the last Christian arrived (*Heb.* 11: 39–40)! And since the end of the day, evening, is symbolic for the end of the phenomenal world, just as the harvest symbolises the

---

101 The Textus Receptus at *Mt.* 20: 16 adds the saying "for many are called but few are chosen". Whether or not the word "many" implies "all" (cf. 4 *Ezra.* 8: 3), many, but by no means all scholars agree (Feuillet, *cit. sup.*, at p. 319: his concept of exclusion at p. 321 is mistaken) that because the saying is read in only a proportion of the manuscripts it is a marginal gloss or editorial addition which is no part of St. Matthew's gospel. Yet we must guess how it came to be here. It occurs elsewhere in Matthew (22: 14) and study of the Great Supper has revealed what it means there (DERRETT, *Law in the New Testament*, Ch. 6). The question is how it could have been believed suitable at our present place (E. F. SUTCLIFFE, *Ir. Theol. Q.* 28 (1961), pp. 126–31, has an interesting short discussion). On the subject in general a careful treatment is that of I. DAUMOSER, *Berufung und Erwählung bei den Synoptikern* (Stuttgart, 1954). At *Mt.* 22: 14 the saying is paradoxical: "many are called" means that many are mustered (all hear the trumpet); "few are chosen" means that few are actually selected for the front line: but nevertheless all fighters will sit down together after the victory—those who refused or shirked the muster are missing. The "elect" are the privileged "front-line" corps. The saying probably antedates the parable of the Supper, which gives it an unexpected twist.

Our parable, by contrast, is about people *all* of whom serve, none being imposters. All have the same reward. In this parable (*pace* Feuillet) there are no "remnant", as are implied elsewhere—naturally the "remnant" coincides with the whole. In the parable of the Supper the guests (as described) signify the righteous poor, who further the enterprise of the host (i.e. the fight) with their prayers (cf. the Qumran War Scroll 11: 9–13; 13: 14; 14: 7). Thus they are entitled to enjoy the banquet prepared ostensibly for the élite, who, by unfortunate coincidence, all decline the invitation. In the parable of the Vineyard the takers of the reward include those who produce little, whose "merits" are insignificant: but they are needed for the harvest (i.e. the victory), and so they share as if they had been hired at dawn. So the gloss, if such it was, written into his manuscript by some student of scripture long ago was intelligent. It may not be part of St. Matthew's work, but it shows that the parable of the Supper was correctly understood at an early period. This is gratifying, proving the continuity, if only in this context, of Jewish teaching about that parable.

completion of the cycle (*Mic.* 7: 1–2), this image is true to the intention of the parable.

CONCLUSION

The eleventh-hour men were entitled to their minimum wage, and got something more, because they had not refused offers of employment during the other eleven hours, and they were not covetous, and in good faith eagerly relied upon the employer's urgency. Unemployed by man or mammon, they were fit for the owner's summons. To those that are hired their taskmaster, we now see, is said to pay not the wages of their labour (*mAb.* 6: 5, *ḳinyan torah*), but the wages of a labourer.

FURTHER ANNOTATIONS

p. [67], l. 21. 'Work' at Ps. civ.23 and Lev. xix.13 means 'reward'—the ideas are virtually inseparable. b.B.M.83b.

p. [73], l. 5. *argos* has been correctly identified by E. Stauffer in *Fest.* Fascher (Berlin, 1958), 94-102.

p. [79], l. 2. If I am right in suspecting that it was the eve of the Sabbath (the eve of the World to Come) this would be a real injury to them, in view of the preparations called for at that time.

p. [81], n. 78. So *Pearl* (14th cent.), ed. E.V. Gordon (1953), extracted by G.G. Coulton, *Medieval Panorama* (Cambridge, 1949), 201-2.

p. [81], n. 80. G. de Ru (1966) suggested that the story of R. Ze'era's eulogy on R. Bun was an application of Jesus's parable: it could be that both drew on a common idea.

p. [82], l. 21. A specialist in the fear aspect of psychology assures us that deprivation of expected reward is psychically equivalent to punishment.

p. [89], l. 13. The value of obedience (to God) does not relate to the actual reward as esteemed by the faithful: E. Jüngel, *Paulus und Jesus*[3] (Tübingen, 1967), 167. He rightly emphasises that the End is conceived of as near.

p. [90], l. 10. It is at this point that notice might be taken of Rom. ix.31-3: 'Israel pursued the Law which offered Righteousness (*sc.* as a prize) but failed to reach the standard (cf. Lampe, *Patr. Gk. Lex.* 922, *s.v.* III), because they did not rely on faith but on works (i.e. performance). They tripped over the "stone of stumbling" as scripture says...'. See C.E.B. Cranfield at *Fest.* Kümmel (1975), 39-40.

The Parable of the Two Sons

I am obliged to Professor George D. Kilpatrick for drawing my attention to this parable (Matt. 21: 28–32). He reminds me (in a letter of 22 Dec. 1970) of the puzzling story, and comments that a completely satisfactory explanation of the varying forms of the text has never been forthcoming. After an exhaustive study of the parable of the Workers in the Vineyard,[1] it occurred to me that I ought to be able to detect what the parable of the Two Sons taught, and this might throw light on the question of the text. My first problem was whether there *was* an original form at all: oriental texts often circulate in alternative forms, so that one can never be sure whether the author or his authorised representatives finally determined which text was correct. If that was the case here, and the confusions of the manuscripts are as provoking as they are tedious, my hope was vain. But Professor Kilpatrick, whose acquaintance with the Greek text and its manuscript traditions is as well known as his want of subservience to any fashionable theory about 'better' witnesses to the original, told me (in a letter of 6 Jan. 1971),' . . . the probabilities seem to be that one form of the text is from the evangelist and for some reason the other forms are deliberate changes'. I regard this as, for my present purposes, final.[2]

The nature of the case is such, that a tedious treatment is hardly avoidable. The labour of reading it can be mitigated by my assumption that the reader has a good edition before him, and that he can acquaint himself with the general position as to the evidence for the variants without my having to copy out the particulars for him. If this problem is to be solved at all it

---

[1] To be published in the Festschrift for David Daube edited by A. Watson and B. S. Jackson.

[2] J. R. Michaels, in 'The parable of the regretful son', *H. Th. R.* 61 (1968), 15-26, ∗ invents a new parable, ingeniously, but unconvincingly. He takes ἀπῆλθεν as 'went away' and μεταμεληθείς as 'being regretful'. On the textual problem he usefully refers to J. Schmid, 'Das textgeschichtliche Problem der Parabel von der zwei Söhnen', *Festschrift M. Meinertz* (Münster/W., 1951), 68-84.

must be on broad lines, and general principles of common sense, such as
need no pedantry to support them. The solution must come ultimately from
what the two main versions could conceivably mean. After studying vineyards and their midrashic significance, and the psychological position of
father-owners of vineyards, and those of elder and younger sons, I have
(unusual as it may seem) no hesitation whatever in pronouncing for one
version and rejecting the other. But I must attempt to account for the one
which is to be rejected, and I shall do so notwithstanding that the demonstration is bound to be tedious. Having disposed of this demonstration, the
meaning of the parable will be made plain, and I trust that in the graceless
task of dealing with the text of the parable I have earned the merit of throwing, by a side light, some illumination upon the attempt of Jesus to teach
his audience – an attempt which has been very nearly frustrated. I now print
the correct text:

28 Τί δὲ ὑμῖν δοκεῖ; ἄνθρωπος εἶχεν τέκνα δύο· προσελθὼν τῷ πρώτῳ
εἶπεν· Τέκνον, ὕπαγε σήμερον ἐργάζου ἐν τῷ ἀμπελῶνι. 29 ὁ δὲ ἀποκριθεὶς
εἶπεν· Ἐγὼ κύριε, καὶ οὐκ ἀπῆλθεν. 30 προσελθὼν δὲ τῷ δευτέρῳ εἶπεν
ὡσαύτως. ὁ δὲ ἀποκριθεὶς εἶπεν· Οὐ θέλω, ὕστερον δὲ μεταμεληθεὶς
ἀπῆλθεν. 31 τίς ἐκ τῶν δύο ἐποίησεν τὸ θέλημα τοῦ πατρός; λέγουσιν·
Ὁ ὕστερος. λέγει αὐτοῖς ὁ Ἰησοῦς· Ἀμὴν λέγω ὑμῖν ὅτι οἱ τελῶναι
καὶ αἱ πόρναι προάγουσιν ὑμᾶς εἰς τὴν βασιλείαν τοῦ Θεοῦ. 32 ἦλθεν
γὰρ Ἰωάννης πρὸς ὑμᾶς ἐν ὁδῷ δικαιοσύνης, καὶ οὐκ ἐπιστεύσατε αὐτῷ·
οἱ δὲ τελῶναι καὶ αἱ πόρναι ἐπίστευσαν αὐτῷ· ὑμεῖς δὲ ἰδόντες οὐδὲ μετεμελ-
ήθητε ὕστερον τοῦ πιστεῦσαι αὐτῷ.

The application by Jesus himself can be regarded as a dubious advantage,
throwing doubt on the authenticity of the text.[3] But, as we shall see, 'Taxgatherers and harlots...' makes very good sense. Since many commentators
have (erroneously) believed that Luke 7: 29–30 is a parallel to this parable,
I am bound to print that also for purposes of comparison.

[28...μείζων ἐν γεννητοῖς γυναικῶν Ἰωάνου οὐδείς ἐστιν...] 29 καὶ
πᾶς ὁ λαὸς ἀκούσας καὶ οἱ τελῶναι ἐδικαίωσαν τὸν Θεόν, βαπτισθέντες
τὸ βάπτισμα Ἰωάνου. οἱ δὲ Φαρισαῖοι καὶ οἱ νομικοὶ τὴν βουλὴν τοῦ
Θεοῦ ἠθέτησαν εἰς ἑαυτούς, μὴ βαπτισθέντες ὑπ' αὐτοῦ.

---

[3] Verse 32 is suspected as an old soteriological amplification, which ought to be
eliminated before study of the parable: J. Jeremias, *The Parables of Jesus* (London,
1963), 80–81; A. Jülicher, *Die Gleichnisreden Jesu* II (Tübingen, 1910), 382–383.

The textual problem

One manuscript tradition, weakly attested, ignores the fact that one son must have been elder and one younger. Although δευτέρος does not conclusively mean 'younger', it would mean that here unless the context cleared the ambiguity, which it does not. And the tradition referred to evades the difficulty. The Textus Receptus and the Vulgate, followed by Souter, show the elder son saying οὐ θέλω. This is abandoned by Westcott and Hort,[4] Nestle and most versions following his, with Jülicher's agreement. Consequently the Authorised Version, the RV, and the RSV, and for example W. Barclay follow the Textus Receptus, as also do the Hebrew translations by Delitzsch and by Ginzburg. They thus show the elder son first refusing to go and work in the vineyard and later changing his mind and going. But Moffatt, Schonfield, Phillips and the NEB take the opposite position, showing the elder consenting, but not actually going to work. The American *Greek New Testament* (2nd. edn., 1968), however, returns to the arrangement by the Textus Receptus, with all the consequential amendments this involves.

The chief factor assisting us to find the correct arrangement is psychological. The situation of the elder son in an archaic agricultural family is perfectly well known in Asia to this day. Though not all younger sons are alike, a typical younger-son behaviour can be predicated without difficulty. In the parable of the Prodigal Son it is the elder who is generally obedient, but fails the test ultimately; hence he would correspond to the one who first agrees and then fails to go. That parable is a masterpiece,[5] and the psychological position of the younger son is that of an instinctive rebel, who could well repent; hence the son who at first refuses, but later goes, should be the younger son. Further there would seem to be some parallel with the 'application', and if this is so the chief priests and elders must be parallel to the elder son, not the younger, to whom the taxgatherers could legitimately be likened; hence, since the latter are mentioned first, the behaviour of the younger son would fit them, and since it is said that they were at once converted, but the conversion was clearly at a later date than the laws (the Covenant) to which they were subject but which they had disobeyed (by their cultural treachery and moral impurity), it must be the younger son who first refused and later repented. Finally, there would have been a desire to see the elder as the nominally obedient – and not merely because of the agreement which that

---

[4] Jülicher, *ubi cit.* 374–381. B. F. Westcott and F. J. A. Hort, *The New Testament in the Original Greek. Introduction,* 2nd edn. (London, 1896), app., pp. 15–17, enter into the question inconclusively. See W. C. Allen, *International Critical Commentary*, Matthew, *ad loc.*

[5] Derrett, *Law in the New Testament* (London, 1970), ch. 5.

would give with the elder son in the parable of the Prodigal – because a Judaeo-Christian *haggadāh* on the covenants would fit that: the children of Israel (i.e. the 'synagogue') nominally accepted that covenant when offered to them, and sinned, whereas the gentiles, who refused that covenant when offered to them,[6] came in and obeyed after the new covenant had been preached to them by the church.

All reasons select the elder son as the one who says 'Yes, sir ' with true Asian politeness, but does not actually go. It is noticeable from the apocryphal addition found at Sir. 19:21 that instant obedience was prized,[7] perhaps even above substantial compliance,[8] and it is the elder son who is most likely to set an example of etiquette. Exactly the same view was taken by the so-called 'Western Text',[9] which understood ἐποίησεν τὸ θέλημα as if it were a translation of *shāmaʿ* ('he heard/obeyed'), evidence of D's contact with Asian notions. Thus Nestle was right.

We must consider why an early editorial hand 'corrected' the arrangement to produce the Textus Receptus. He might have imagined, as others (e.g. Jülicher, Jeremias) have since, that John the Baptist was analogous to the father, and that those who believed in him must be the outcasts who are mentioned first. He must have thought that the taxgatherers and (ex-)prostitutes in the 'application' were disobedient first and later repented, and that therefore they must correspond to a son who said 'No', but later changed his mind. So he altered the arrangement to make the refusing son the elder son. He forgot (or did he know?) that *relationship* alone is a formal acceptance of obedience, that working in the vineyard was a natural as well as economic obligation incumbent on the sons, and that both considerations apply equally to both sons. The son who is polite but fails to obey is a case of acceptance + acceptance + refusal; the other is a case of acceptance + refusal + repentance. Taxgatherers and prostitutes were also sons and daughters of the Covenant

---

6 *Pirqe dᵉ R. Eliezer*, par. 31. *Midrash on Psalms*, ps. lxviii, sec. 6. J. Bonsirven, *Le Judaisme palestinien*, I (Paris, 1935), 91. 2 Bar. xlvii. 40, li. 4 (?). F. Weber, *Jüdische Theologie²* (Leipzig, 1897), 57ff. Bab. Tal., Yoma 35b.

7 οἰκέτης λέγων τῷ δεσπότῃ 'ὡς ἀρέσκει οὐ ποιήσω', ἐὰν μετὰ ταῦτα ποιήσῃ παροργίζει τὸν τρέφοντα αὐτόν. The meaning, however, is not quite beyond doubt. It is reported by Box and Oesterley at R. Charles *Apocrypha and Pseudepigrapha* I, 383; also conveniently at F. Vattioni, *Ecclesiastico* (Naples, 1968), 98. We do not have the Hebrew of this verse, nor is it in the Syriac, which has a certain relationship to the lost Hebrew, and it is missing from the Vulgate.

8 J. A. Findlay, *Jesus and his Parables* (1950), 54.

9 Westcott and Hort, *ubi cit.*, show how the reading of D, etc., indicates that the nominally obedient (but really recusant) son is he who does the will of the father, but they could not see the point. It is taken up usefully by Guy, *Ex. T.* 51 (1939–40), 204–205. A. T. Cadoux, *Parables of Jesus* (London, [1930]), 117–118.

and thus were presumed to accept the command they later flouted, a command which was so evidently in their own interest. Thus the son who accepts and then refuses (or fails) is obviously the group of chief priests and elders; (as St Matthew understood it), but the reviser did not see it. If they are to agree, on his footing, with the *younger* son, a further discrepancy appears. They did not believe in the Baptist (Matt. 21: 25–26), and refused to be converted. Thus they would have appeared to accept the same command as the others and later flouted it; but whereas the younger son agreed (on this view) and later failed, these refused twice over. Thus we should be left with a pattern: acceptance + refusal + repentance = No + Yes; acceptance + refusal + refusal = Yes + No, which is wrong (it should be No + No).

There is, however, no intended parallelism between taxgatherers and the elder son on the one hand and chief priests and the younger son on the other. The taxgatherers are the object of the enquiry, and they are likened to that one of the sons who, politeness apart, ultimately did the father's bidding and so gained approval (as is implied). That this is the younger son is proved by the factor of prestige. *We* can live indifferent to respect: the Asian is disturbed by the thought that the prestige-holder should be humiliated. That the priestly hierarchy and social élite should walk behind taxgatherers and (ex-)prostitutes was a horrible and paradoxical prospect for them. This occurs when the younger precedes the elder (as in the parable of the Prodigal Son). Thus, the Textus Receptus being wrong, Nestle and others were right to adhere to other manuscripts.[10]

The further question whether *vv.* 31b–32 originally belonged to the parable is not clearly affected by the fact that Luke 7: 29–30 deals with a similar topic without the parable, since neither in vocabulary nor in ideas is the Lucan passage a parallel to our disputed parable, as Jülicher seems to have seen (p. 383). It is better to try to read the parable and its 'application' together.

The story and its meaning

The textual problem behind us, we return to the story. The father rises up early (cf. Jer. 25: 3; 35: 14) to give instructions for the day. The vineyard is the family's great asset, and it was to the advantage of all of them to work in it. The blistering heat in the summer was mitigated by the thought that the wine would be agreeable: no sweating in the sun, no wine. Jülicher's

---

[10] E. Riggenbach, 'Zur Exegese und Textkritik zweier Gleichnisse Jesu', *Festschrift A. Schlatter* (Stuttgart, 1922), 17–34. But note προάγουσιν is not temporal, but local!

notion, that only one son was needed, was baseless: but his conclusion, that it was the elder who failed to go, was correct. The father relies upon the relationship (τέκνον).[11] Though the vineyard was exclusively his, it was a heritage, and in asking sons to work in it he was by no means acting dicta-torially. The duty of obedience was backed up by financial considerations. It might have been another matter if he had ordered them to work in another man's vineyard. No precise instructions are given. Agriculturalists need none. The elder signified obedience by habit, politeness being second nature, but he used his discretion, as the father's would-be successor might well do. An elder son might well take more interest in form than substance, as the 'elder sons' of the world so often do. But in this case it looks as if he started by accepting the instructions and later followed his own inclinations.

The younger son had two men 'breathing down his neck', two people who might well beat him. He instinctively refused, in order to assert his independence, but later because of his relationship to the father and his need of his father's support more than his brother's (he might be jealous of the latter) he complied with the command. His independence was more formal than real. Both sons are really unpaid servants. It is the inheritance which softens hard moments for them. Their individual relationships to their father have been built up out of catenae of experiences, and not least of all their experiences of each other. Habitual deference preceded non-compliance; and frequent non-deference led to compliance: a paradox consistent with life.

Let us compare these sons with the Rechabites, whose fanatical obedience to their 'father' Jonadab could be used as a touchstone for obedience (Jer. 35). They appear to be models of traditional observance. They refused the delights of the earthly vineyard (35: 7,9). God in fact gave all the Jews better terms than the Rechabites wanted. They (the Jews) were entitled to exploit and cultivate the Land, as is plain from Dt. 6: 10–12; 8: 7–10; 9: 9–12 (cf. Num. 20:5), subject to the warning against 'fullness', being 'lifted up', and following the men of Sodom. Those who do their earthly father's will, like the Rechabites, may be models of obedience, but not, in the circumstances, obedience to God's will. If we contrast the Rechabites with the rest of the population we find, on the other hand, a contrast more favourable to the former. The Rechabites, like John the Baptist, were separatists and abstain-ers. They followed what was required of them, right or wrong. In fact it was wrong. The rest of the population, following their heavenly father's provision, exploited the vineyards, became 'lifted up', and ended by

---

[11] G. Delling, *Studien zum Neuen Testament und zum hellenistischen Judentum* (Gesam. Aufs. 1950-1968) (Göttingen, 1970), 270 ff.

being disobedient. The mechanical obedience, based on relationship alone, characteristic of the Rechabites, does have the effect of 'doing the father's will' in substance, and, who knows, in spirit also. For if the obedient son is in the wrong in his obedience, God will spare him, as a father spares an erring son (Mal. 3:17), 'the son who serves him'.

The parable teaches that it is actual performance which is to be approved, not lip-service (so Jülicher cites Matt. 7:21, rightly). The sons' obedience increases the income, and their father's table provides their reward. The description of John's 'coming in the way of righteousness' has led to divergent interpretations. 'In strict observance of the Law' seems to be incorrect, not only because there is no evidence that he did (he was too negative), but rather because the words imply John was not a rebel, nor an innovator, but in the tradition of those who demanded obedience to God's commandments. An alternative translation 'to show you the right way to live' indicates the effect of what is meant, but hardly the manner in which we arrive at it. It must be remembered that by obeying John's call the outcasts forfeited their right to an easy living. From being 'full' they suddenly became abstainers, and thereby objects of ridicule. The wages of corruption are always high. The blackmailers' attempts to earn an honest living will have commanded more approbation than success. What avenues there were for ex-prostitutes I do not know. The humiliation they would feel would be greater than any member of the élite would suffer who suddenly became pious.

Noting the consequences for the outcasts, the élite, far from copying their example, neglected the call. Had they obeyed it they would have lost their share in the profits of the vineyard (Is. 3:14) which they had not planted (Dt. 6:11-15), the vineyard in which they were hardly actual workers. Since no one works without some conception of reward, reward is certainly within this parable, though its presence is silent. Jesus is hinting that, having retained their share of the profits of this world they forfeited, by contrast, their share of the world-to-come.[12] The former outcasts, having lost this world, gained the world-to-come.[13] Meanwhile the outcasts and the élite are fellow-diners at their common father's table; and just as a real father allows his eldest son to continue to eat at his table even though he disobeys him,[14] so the élite under the impression that their disobedience has escaped detection, enjoy themselves. But the disposal of the inheritance appertains to the father.[15]

---

[12] Matt. 6:2,5,16.
[13] Mk. 8:34-7; Matt. 16:24-26.
[14] The chastisement of the firstborn: Ps. Sol. 13:8 (9), 18:4.
[15] Philo, *De Virtut.* par. 207 (Colson, viii, 290).

Might not the élite change their minds at the eleventh hour? Would they not then cease to be imposters? They might then join the outcasts in the world-to-come (Lk. 15:28). Working only one hour would not disentitle them to have as good a share as if they had worked alongside those whom they had despised in life. But we must beware of misapplying the parable of the Workers in the Vineyard.[16] The eleventh-hour men had not refused employment during the other eleven hours. The chief priests and elders had, on the contrary, acknowledged the call, and had then carried on in nominal obedience but actual independence of volition. Those that only pretend to serve will be shut out of the kingdom, as in the case of the Foolish Virgins (Matt. 25:1 ff.). They must thus rid themselves of their attitudes (μεταμεληθέντες), and go and stand in the marketplace, whereupon they may be engaged, and may thus be given an opportunity to earn enough merit to join in the feast with a quiet conscience.

Appended Note. If I am right in my explanation of the parable (which I see, *pace* Michaels, n. 2 above, as Jesus's genuine parable) it follows that the psychological raw material contained the following: (1) the high prestige of the elder son, (2) the low prestige of the younger son, (3) the greater pressure upon the younger son, (4) the financial interest of all parties that the work should be done, and (5) the essential obedience of the one who professedly rejects commands, asserting indifference or independence, but is the closer tied at heart for the very strength of his rejection. A most curious and unexpected illustration of this theme has been pointed out by J. Arthur Baird, *Audience Criticism and the Historical Jesus* (Philadelphia, Westminster Press, 1969), 42. The synoptic gospels consistently show the wider group of disciples (the prestige-less outer circle) as much more sympathetic to Jesus than the Twelve (the prestige-bearers from the point of view of the Church). Yet, notwithstanding this, the frequent opposition and recalcitrance shown within the 'home' by the Twelve by no means disqualified them from becoming, eventually, far better representatives of their leader's policies than the superficially admiring outer circle. This discovery gives an added dimension to our parable from the Church's standpoint. The position of the prestige-holders was not inherently hopeless. But the 'younger sons', i.e. those constantly hostile in their reactions, will ultimately turn out to show the fullest obedience. This could be an additional explanation for the textual confusion.

---

[16] R. C. Trench, *Notes on the Parables* (London, 1898), 179–180, elaborating on Greg. Naz., *Orat*.xl.20, is right. A previous contempt for the offer of 'work' can never be encouraged by a tender of full wages to one who condescends to hire his 'services' at the last minute. His quotation from Leo the Great (*De voç. omn. gent.* i. 17) is impressive: those that sweated were shown, and agreed, that the late-comers received a gift of grace, and not a reward for their labour as such.

FURTHER ANNOTATIONS

p. [109], n. 2. Note H. Merkel, *N.T.S.* 20 (1974), 254-61, whose objections to the genuineness of the parable, especially its concern with *doing* the will of God, I regard as far from proven.

p. [110], l. 7. I regret that I did not recollect that the story was intended to recall the celebrated jealousy of Esau against Jacob. The Greek word *egō* means 'yes' at Gen. xxvii.24 (LXX) (see Gen. xxvii.1 Targ. Pal.). The midrash goes, Esau said 'yes' but did not actually do what was needed, while the younger, Jacob, did what was wanted. It exercised the Jewish mind to justify Jacob (naturally) and to denigrate Esau, when it was obvious that Jacob obtained his birth-right by sharp practice and his father's blessing by fraud. Somehow the whitewashing of Jacob had finished long before Jesus's time, and it would be quite easy to show that the one who says 'yes' but actually does not do what his father (Isaac) really needed/wanted is inferior to the one who has to be prompted into satisfying him. The want of an *exact* parallel is *not* a reason for pushing aside this allusion, since in a competition between brothers (cf. the Prodigal Son parable) Esau is bound to be thought of.

p. [114], l. 12. If he gave the question of obedience much thought he will have remembered that in his culture fathers, however seriously they take obedience (Is. i.2), are reluctant to treat wayward elder sons harshly (Mal. iii.17, Ps. Sal. xiii.9-10).

p. [114], l. 24. B. Lohse, *Askese und Mönchtum...* (Munich/Vienna, 1968), 86.

p. [115], l. 16. In fact John set an example of how to live, because *although he was an ascetic* he occupied himself with people's dedication to a new (non-ascetic) life.

JUDAICA IN ST MARK

I

A DIFFICULTY HAS ARISEN in exegesis of the gospels. Allowing for variations, scholars figure in two main classes, the first largely introverted, the specialists, and the second "outsiders" who attempt to collaborate with them. The first, far the more numerous, comprises those who examine internally the New Testament, using Qumran and other intertestamental material, and Old Testament texts where they are cited or quoted in the New Testament, to enable the gospels to comment upon themselves and each other, employing in this procedure skills adequately described as "literary-historical". One may refer to these scholars as "the critics". Fashion gives great credence to "redaction-criticism", heir to "source-criticism" and "form-criticism". National traits tend to emerge, as is not surprising since subjective criteria are bound to operate in an estimate of what the evangelists were about, and national traits easily escape notice amongst their victims. In fact no one knows who the evangelists were or how they worked. Internal evidence alone leads to unending contradictions. Scepticism continues to play a role, and passages (such as one to which we come) which are not internally "corroborated" are more or less confidently dismissed as fabrications. The history, the archaeology of the New Testament is, at its most sensitive and useful point, at the mercy of skills that are principally literary and unashamedly academic. What is literary is of enormous value, but in no other field would it claim to exclude parallel sources of information.

The original authors or compilers had practical objects in mind, though our knowledge of them is dim. Occasional returns to the Middle Eastern (in certain distinctive respects *Asian*) background of the New Testament can produce unexpected results. Some of these findings are indeed, or appear to be, primarily literary, but they grow from an appreciation of intellectual habits in the environment. One acute point of difference between the "critics" and the Orientalists (my second class) is the validity of the latter's methods and intentions. To take a small example, the parable of the Unjust Steward contains some numerals.[1] The reasons are not known. No authentic testimony is available, "I, Jesus of Nazareth, intend to utter a parable to be known as 'the parable of the Unjust Steward', and numerals will figure in order to produce such-and-such an effect." Hence all reconstructions of the meaning must be conjectural. The "critics" take the view that all background particulars in parables produce dramatic effect, and are otherwise meaningless. In the realms where they received their education, no doubt, a spade was called a spade. My own reconstruction of that parable started[2] with the numerals, showing that they were intended to call the hearer's attention to the law of man, which allowed usury, as contrasted with the law of God, which did not. This destroyed the ingenious explanations given by theologians, namely that the parable of the Steward was to show how wicked behaviour offered a pattern to good Christians—they should be sly and smart in their search after righteousness. The pain and

---

[1] Lk. 16: 6–7.
[2] J. D. M. Derrett at *NTS*, VII, 1961, 198–219; idem, *Law in the New Testament*, London, 1970, ch. 4, pt. 1.

impatience aroused in some minds by my solution is now past history.[3] The methodological argument has gone further.

It is said to be impossible that cultural or historical materials *external* to the gospels can control, correct, or amend the exegeses offered by theologians based upon internal literary grounds. It seems to be a matter of faith in some quarters[4] that Jesus cannot, when he selected the vocabulary of his parables, have utilized words recalling Old Testament texts relating to the subject-matter, and it is "sheer impossibility" that the stages in his more elaborate parables were intended to recall to his contemporaries Biblical stories (e.g. the sale of Joseph) which were notorious, or texts (e.g. from the Psalms) which most Jewish boys knew by heart before the age of seven or eight. Similarly with the evangelists' dramatic tales. The cause of this reluctance could be that the "critics" are cultivated Western men, trained in the classics, who have never experienced personally a culture where all literature is oral, which has (apart from bills and conveyances) very little use for *prose*, and in which cultivated utterance employs complex allusion and paradox as a normal method of securing its primary aim, namely to be understood comprehensively and, nearly as important, to be remembered.

As between the two approaches, which are irreconcilable, the ultimate choice must be determined by results. Sometimes the cultural approach produces less smooth answers to the gospels' knotty problems; sometimes it removes difficulties around which theologians have built webs of hypothesis. The removal of such difficulties can be greeted with dismay, since the intellectual capital of a lifetime is thereby devalued. But time will show which method is sometimes essential, and sometimes preferable. Here I attempt to show how one massive problematical pericope (as the gospel "bits" are called) can be resolved astonishingly easily by recalling ancient Semitic modes of thought and utterance. Further I show how a simple and obvious facet of the Jewish mentality solves a question which stares the lay reader in the face but has been ignored by theologians. These last might not relish being disturbed in order to be told something rather banal: but it may not seem to everyone as banal as it might seem to them.

Semitica abound in Mark, in his crammed and knotty style, much less agreeable than the smoother and understandably more popular Matthew. Mark is usually believed to be the earliest gospel.[5] The method which appeals to me supports this, but until every single

[3] H. Drexler at *ZNW*, LVIII, 1967, 286–8; J. D. Crossen, *JBL*, XC, 1971, 464; J. D. M. Derrett, "Take thy bond ... and write fifty ...", *JThS*, N.S., XXIII, 2, 1972, 438–40.
[4] W. Selb at *Zeitschr. d. Savigny-Stiftung, Röm. Abteil.*, LXXXVIII, 1971, 549–50; C. Spicq at *Tijdschr. voor Rechtsgeschiedenis*, XXXIX, 1971, 603–5; J. Murphy-O'Connor at *RB*, 1971, 464–5; H. J. Klauck at *Wissenschaft und Weisheit*, 1972, 1, 72–3; P. H. Ballard at *JThS*, N.S., XXIII, 2, 1972, 344 n. 2(i); H. Merkel, "Recht im Neuen Testament", *Zeitschr. f. Religions- und Geistesgeschichte*, 1973, 266–9; J. Carmignac at *Revue de Qumran*, 1973, 275–7. An outlook favourable to the "Orientalists" is adopted by C. H. Cave, "The parables and the scriptures", *NTS*, XI, 1964–5, 374–87, and by J. Drury, "The Sower, the vineyard, and the place of allegory in the interpretation of Mark's parables," *JThS*, XXIV, 1973, 367–79.
[5] E. P. Sanders, *The tendencies of the synoptic tradition*, Cambridge, 1969; C. H. Talbert and E. V. McKnight, "Can the Griesbach hypothesis be falsified?", *JBL*, XCI, 1972, 338–68; Mgr. de Solages, *La composition des evangiles*, Leiden, 1973. A different view is taken tentatively by D. Wenham, "The synoptic problem revisited ...", *Tyndale Bulletin*, 1971, 4–38, and pressed, inconclusively, by R. L. Lindsey, *Hebrew translation of the Gospel of Mark*, Jerusalem, 1969; see also P. Vassiliadis, "Behind Mark: towards a written source", *NTS*, XX, 2, 1974, 155–60. The priority of Mark is assumed by M. D. Goulder, *Midrash and lection in Matthew*, London, 1974, but our Mark is a deutero-Mark according to D. L. Dungan, *The sayings of Jesus in the Churches of Paul*, Oxford, 1971.

pericope has been tested we cannot be sure. The present examples show the advantages of an *Orientalist's* approach. The same technique could be employed by others possessing similar skills, to at least as good an effect. On the assumption, then, that Mark is the first gospel available to us, we approach Mk. 2:23–8, the episode of the so-called plucking of the grain on the Sabbath, § 111 in Aland's *Synopsis*.[6]

Matthew 12: 1–8

'Εν ἐκείνῳ τῷ καιρῷ ἐπορεύθη ὁ 'Ιησοῦς τοῖς σάββασιν διὰ τῶν σπορίμων· οἱ δὲ μαθηταὶ αὐτοῦ ἐπείνασαν, καὶ ἤρξαντο τίλλειν στάχυας καὶ ἐσθίειν. ²οἱ δὲ Φαρισαῖοι ἰδόντες εἶπαν αὐτῷ· ἰδοὺ οἱ μαθηταί σου ποιοῦσιν ὃ οὐκ ἔξεστιν ποιεῖν ἐν σαββάτῳ. ³ὁ δὲ εἶπεν αὐτοῖς· οὐκ ἀνέγνωτε τί ἐποίησεν Δαυίδ, ὅτε ἐπείνασεν καὶ οἱ μετ' αὐτοῦ; ⁴πῶς εἰσῆλθεν εἰς τὸν οἶκον τοῦ θεοῦ καὶ τοὺς ἄρτους τῆς προθέσεως ἔφαγον, ὃ οὐκ ἐξὸν ἦν αὐτῷ φαγεῖν οὐδὲ τοῖς μετ' αὐτοῦ, εἰ μὴ τοῖς ἱερεῦσιν μόνοις; ⁵ἢ οὐκ ἀνέγνωτε ἐν τῷ νόμῳ ὅτι τοῖς σάββασιν οἱ ἱερεῖς ἐν τῷ ἱερῷ τὸ σάββατον βεβηλοῦσιν καὶ ἀναίτιοί εἰσιν; ⁶λέγω δὲ ὑμῖν ὅτι τοῦ ἱεροῦ μεῖζόν ἐστιν ὧδε. ⁷εἰ δὲ ἐγνώκειτε τί ἐστιν· ἔλεος θέλω καὶ οὐ θυσίαν, οὐκ ἂν κατεδικάσατε τοὺς ἀναιτίους. ⁸κύριος γάρ ἐστιν τοῦ σαββάτου ὁ υἱὸς τοῦ ἀνθρώπου.

Mark 2: 23–8

Καὶ ἐγένετο αὐτὸν ἐν τοῖς σάββασιν παραπορεύεσθαι διὰ τῶν σπορίμων, καὶ οἱ μαθηταὶ αὐτοῦ ἤρξαντο ὁδὸν ποιεῖν τίλλοντες τοὺς στάχυας. ²⁴καὶ οἱ Φαρισαῖοι ἔλεγον αὐτῷ· ἴδε τί ποιοῦσιν τοῖς σάββασιν ὃ οὐκ ἔξεστιν; ²⁵καὶ λέγει

αὐτοῖς· οὐδέποτε ἀνέγνωτε τί ἐποίησεν Δαυίδ, ὅτε χρείαν ἔσχεν καὶ ἐπείνασεν αὐτὸς καὶ οἱ μετ' αὐτοῦ; ²⁶πῶς εἰσῆλθεν εἰς τὸν οἶκον τοῦ θεοῦ ἐπὶ 'Αβιαθὰρ ἀρχιερέως καὶ τοὺς ἄρτους τῆς προθέσεως ἔφαγεν, οὓς οὐκ ἔξεστιν φαγεῖν εἰ μὴ τοὺς ἱερεῖς, καὶ ἔδωκεν καὶ τοῖς σὺν αὐτῷ οὖσιν; ²⁷καὶ ἔλεγεν αὐτοῖς· τὸ σάββατον διὰ τὸν ἄνθρωπον ἐγένετο, καὶ οὐχ ὁ ἄνθρωπος διὰ τὸ σάββατον· ²⁸ὥστε κύριός ἐστιν ὁ υἱὸς τοῦ ἀνθρώπου καὶ τοῦ σαββάτου.

Luke 6: 1–5

'Εγένετο δὲ ἐν σαββάτῳ διαπορεύεσθαι αὐτὸν διὰ σπορίμων, καὶ ἔτιλλον οἱ μαθηταὶ αὐτοῦ καὶ ἤσθιον τοὺς στάχυας ψώχοντες ταῖς χερσίν. ²τινὲς δὲ τῶν Φαρισαίων εἶπαν· τί ποιεῖτε ὃ οὐκ ἔξεστιν τοῖς σάββασιν; ³καὶ ἀποκριθεὶς πρὸς αὐτοὺς εἶπεν ὁ 'Ιησοῦς· οὐδὲ τοῦτο ἀνέγνωτε ὃ ἐποίησεν Δαυίδ, ὁπότε ἐπείνασεν αὐτὸς καὶ οἱ μετ' αὐτοῦ ὄντες; ⁴ὡς εἰσῆλθεν εἰς τὸν οἶκον τοῦ θεοῦ καὶ τοὺς ἄρτους τῆς προθέσεως λαβὼν ἔφαγεν καὶ ἔδωκεν τοῖς μετ' αὐτοῦ, οὓς οὐκ ἔξεστιν φαγεῖν εἰ μὴ μόνους τοὺς ἱερεῖς; ⁵καὶ ἔλεγεν αὐτοῖς· κύριός ἐστιν τοῦ σαββάτου ὁ υἱὸς τοῦ ἀνθρώπου.

St. Mark has many passages, including famous ones,[7] which do not figure in St. Matthew or St. Luke. It is a matter of conjecture whether the latter neglect them, or,

---

[6] K. Aland, *Synopsis quattuor Evangeliorum*, Stuttgart, 1964. Superseding the similar work of Huck-Lietzmann, this is indispensable to all serious students of the gospels.

[7] Three short reports and three short texts are special to Mark. The little children (10: 16), the parable of the seed (4: 26–7), names at 11: 21, 13: 3, also material at 5: 3–5, 7: 33–4, 8: 22–6, 9: 20–7, and especially "he expired" at 15: 37, 39 illustrate this.

since it is known that they base their works primarily on him, the alternative explanation might be that *our* Mark has received interpolations. The synoptic problem is one of such complexity and confusion[8] that internal evidence is inconclusive, except as to the inutility of further obfuscations. Our present passage has many words not in the parallel passages in Matthew and Luke. Verse 27 in particular embarrasses us by being absent there. Other discrepancies are Matthew's and Luke's insistence that the disciples *ate*, which Mark does not say; Mark alone mentions the name of the high-priest (and all critical commentators say this was an error), which is thought to have been omitted by Matthew and Luke to save Jesus's blushes; Matthew includes another argument, and it is not certain whether his version of Mark could not have included it. The climax saying at v. 28 is differently phrased in Mark. There are smaller discrepancies, and there is no proof that they are insignificant.

Critical discussions of the pericope[9] differ widely in their estimate of which is the nucleus of this story. Some think that v. 28 alone is a genuine Word of Jesus;[10] some that v. 27 is the original tradition, and the remainder was added to it.[11] Most are clear that the motivation behind the passage is the early Church's concern that its own neglect of the (Jewish) Sabbath[12] (irrespective of the status of Sunday, about which little is known for a really early date) should be authenticated not only by a precedent in the life of Jesus, but also one clinched by a striking saying. Many think that Matthew was anxious to exalt the

---

[8] See Mgr. de Solages, op. cit.; also R. Morgenthaler, *Statistische Synopse*, Zürich, Stuttgart, 1971.

[9] B. Weiss, *Die Evangelien des Markus und Lukas*, Göttingen, 1901, 40–2; idem, *Die Quelle des Lukasevangeliums*, Stuttgart, Berlin, 1907, 150; A. Schlatter, *Der Evangelist Matthäus*, Stuttgart, 1929, 392; E. Klostermann, *Das Markusevangelium*, 4th ed., Tübingen, 1950, 30–1; E. Hirsch, *Frühgeschichte des Evangeliums*, 2nd ed., Tübingen, 1951, 14–5; W. Beilner, *Christus und die Pharisäer*, Vienna, 1959, 25–31; E. Lohse, "Jesu Worte über den Sabbat", in W. Eltester, ed., *Judentum—Christentum—Kirche: Jeremias Festschrift*, Berlin, 1960, 79–89; F. W. Beare, "The Sabbath was made for man?", *JBL*, LXXIX, 1960, 130–6; K. H. Rengstorf, *Das Evangelium nach Lukas*, Göttingen, 1962, 81–2; R. Hummel, *Die Auseinandersetzung zwischen Kirche und Judentum im Matthäusevangelium*, Munich, 1963, 40–4; E. Lohse, "Die Sabbatkonflikte Jesu", in G. Kittel-G. Friedrich, ed., *Theologisches Wörterbuch zum Neuen Testament*, VII, 1964, 21–4; H. E. Tödt, *The Son of Man in the synoptic tradition*, London, 1965, 132; J. Bowman, *The Gospel of Mark*, Leiden, 1965, 116–8; E. Haenschen, *Der Weg Jesu*, Berlin, 1966, 118–23; M. D. Hooker, *The Son of Man in Mark*, London, 1967, 93–102; W. Grundmann, *Das Evangelium nach Matthäus*, Berlin, 1968, 320–2; idem, *Das Evangelium nach Markus*, Berlin, 1971, 67–71; E. Schweizer, *The good news according to Mark*, London, 1971, 70–3; A. J. Hultgren, "The formulation of the Sabbath pericope", *JBL*, XCI, 1972, 38–43; E. P. Sanders, "Priorités et dépendances dans la tradition synoptique", *Recherches des Sciences Religieuses*, 1972, 519–40 (the Lucan form may be the earliest!). In most treatments some attention is paid to *Mekilta* on Exod. 31: 13, "The Sabbath was delivered to you, not you to the Sabbath", a saying which, at first sight, resembles Mk. 2: 27. But, as Lohse points out, the intention there is merely to justify breaches of Sabbath restrictions in cases of danger to life, which cannot apply here. H. E. Tödt, op. cit., 130–2, finds a post-Easter commentary placing the title "Son of Man" into Jesus's mouth. E. Käsemann, *Essays on New Testament themes*, London, 1965, 101–2, says that the community was prepared to ascribe to its master what it was not courageous enough to claim for itself: it preferred to take refuge in a Christianized form of Judaism. A Duprez, "Deux affrontements au jour de Sabbat," *Assemb. Seign.*, XL, 1972, 43–53: the Jesus of Mark enunciates a scandalous universalism. M. Freimann, "Eine misverstandene Rede Jesu," *Monatschr. f. Gesch. u. Wissensch. d. Judentums*, LVIII, 1914, 281–9, supposes Jesus's words were early misrepresented, but otherwise has no useful contribution.

[10] Bultmann (see n. 16 below) regarded it as an open question whether v. 28 was original in Mark, or, from the start, an addition to v. 27; Dalman took v. 27 as interpolated; Beilner, op. cit.

[11] Hultgren, op. cit.; Beare, op. cit., took the story as original and vv. 27–8 as agglomerated to it. According to V. Taylor, *The Gospel according to St. Mark*, London, 1963, 214–20, v. 28 is a Christian comment. Haenschen, op. cit., 120, says vv. 25–6 were improperly introduced.

[12] H. Braun, *Jesus: Der Mann aus Nazareth und seine Zeit*, 2nd ed., Stuttgart, Berlin, 1969, 79 (the Church wished to limit his proposition to his Messianity [due to its early rejudaizing tendencies and re-casuistic development]), 82, see also 161–2; Hummel, op. cit.; Beare, op. cit. It is very generally believed that v. 28 is the débris of a proposition which originally stated that Man was superior to Ritual Law; an escalating Christology transformed it into its present state.

Messianic sovereignty of Jesus to the utmost,[13] and that v. 28 is not only a development of v. 27 but constitutes a subtle change of emphasis. All fail to explain the thread of ideas. The story of David does not figure as an adequate precedent for the behaviour of the disciples.[14] The addition of another argument by Matthew seems to emphasize Jesus's personal status above that of the Temple.[15] History is not looked for in this legend.[16] The earthly Jesus does not figure in this statuesque and obscure "conflict-debate". But the matter looks very different if we re-examine the vocabulary, and consider the Jewish law involved in the episode as it stands. The characteristic objection of the "critics" that one is wasting one's time looking into "cultural" or "background" explanations of a pericope which is legendary, unhistorical, and theologically fabricated, is to be met by the question whether the decisions as to the degree and purpose of the alleged fabrications have not been taken prematurely, when the story *as it stands* has not been understood. It is most unfortunate that August Wünsche's valuable article of 70 years ago should have escaped the attention of the learned, but the loss is mitigated by the fact that he, equally unfortunately, concentrated on the Matthaean version of the pericope.[17]

The verb παραπορεύεσθαι means "to by-pass".[18] The only purpose of "by-passing" on the Sabbath would be to avoid the quadrilateral Sabbath limits,[19] which stretched (and were often marked) 2,000 cubits (800 m.) from the outer edge of a village or town.[20] Once one has entered the Sabbath limits one cannot go out of them again,[21] and a traveller wishing

---

[13] Beare, 135; Hummel, 41. F. Hahn, *Christologische Hoheitstitel*, Göttingen, 1963, 43, claims that v. 27 was the original, here following Lohse, op. cit., 82. See also G. Friedrich at *Zeitschr. f. Theologie u. Kirche*, LIII, 1956, 289.

[14] Beare, 133–4 ("necessity knows no law"). So W. Bousset, *Kyrios Christos*, 1965, 41; Braun, op. cit., 82.

[15] An independent theme with its own history: Mt. 4: 5, 24: 1, 26: 61, 27: 40 (Mk. 15: 29); Jn. 2: 19–21, 7: 28; Acts 7: 48, 17: 24. Freimann, cit. sup. suggests plausibly that for μείζων we should read μεῖζον, which fits better with the Hosea passage.

[16] Beare emphasizes that both vv. 27 and 28 are inconceivable on the lips of any Jewish teacher. "Man" cannot be master of the Sabbath. The Church acknowledged Jesus as Messiah and this is one of the ways in which it showed it. Even the hunger looks fictitious. The anecdote was devised as a setting for the sayings. So R. Bultmann, *History of the synoptic tradition*, Oxford, 1968, 15–6, 47, 49. A possible refutation of these views, based on the Messiah's pre-existence of the world (let alone the Sabbath, cf. Jn. 8: 58), is noticed below, at n. 58.

[17] A. Wünsche, "Jesu Conflikt mit den Pharisäern wegen des Aehrenausraufens seiner Schüler," *Vierteljahrsschrift f. Bibelkunde*, I, 3, 1904, 281–306.

[18] It is used absolutely at Mk. 11: 20 (by-passing the city or the figtree?). It suggests "make a detour by". One by-passes, i.e. skirts a river (Exod. 2: 5 (LXX)), a group of people (Gen. 37: 27, Ruth 4: 1, Mk. 15: 29, Mt. 27: 39), a person (Lam. 1: 12), a place (Jer. 19: 8, 49: 16 (17)), a territory (Deut. 2: 4, 18), a city (Jos. 6: 7–8, 2: 15). It is the correct word for by-passing a ruined town or village which is, for the time being, impassable. The *furtiveness* of the movement as suggested at Mk. 9: 30 (Aland, § 164) is noteworthy. Klostermann, op. cit., takes σπόριμα as the object of the verb, i.e. they skirted the fields. In that case they would not have made a path in the same sense, and the Pharisees' complaint relates only to the plucking. Matthew and Luke could not understand παραπορεύεσθαι. It is quite possible that they understood the dispute to relate only to the limits upon Deut. 23: 25 placed by the Sabbath law, a by-no-means impossible supposition.

[19] Mishnah, Er. IV, 8, V, 8, Babylonian Talmud (hereafter, "b"), Er. 55a. The projections at the corners are called "wings". Explained neatly by Maimonides, *Mishneh Torah*, III ("Seasons"), I ("Sabbath"), 17,2; 18, 6–8 (for the English tr. see n. 22 below).

[20] Mishnah, Soṭ. V, 3, Er. IV, 3; Mt. 24: 20; Acts 1: 12; Damascus Document XI, 4–5 (XIII, 13–4); Jub. 50: 8, 12; Josephus, *Ant.*, XIII, 252. The legend of Elisha b. Abuyah (a first-century notable, a Sadducee?) (*Jewish Encyclopaedia*, V, 138–9) confirms the concern for the limits in the period. The Dead Sea material is not unanimous. 1,000 cubits is found in the Damascus Document (CDC X.21), but also 2,000 cubits (CDC XI.5–6; also in the War Scroll from Cave 1 at Qumran, 1QM VII. 6–7 [Yadin, *Scroll*, 290]). B. J. Malina, *Palestinian manna tradition*, Leiden, 1968, 52, refers to the Palestinian Targum on Exod. 16: 29 (2,000 cubits) as representing pre-Mishnaic *halakah*.

[21] The complex, but common-sense provisions are explained by Maimonides, op. cit., III, 1, 27, *passim*.

to move between two villages or hamlets, each of which is connected to a larger village or town by its own road, while nothing more than a footpath interconnects them both, must make his way across the fields. Footpaths were sown over and it was up to the public to make, and remake, the paths.[22] The difficulty about making one's way through a standing crop on the Sabbath was that it flattened furrows, which was forbidden.[23] It is not at all impossible that "by-passing" was also forbidden in strict circles, perhaps even Pharisaical circles of whom we no longer have knowledge.

What were the disciples doing? Townsmen may not give complete credence to a countryman, but their access to dictionaries is not inferior to his. τίλλειν does not mean "to pluck" except in the sense of plucking a hen or plucking out hair (its most common use).[24] It means to strip objects from their place of attachment, such as leaves from a stem, plants from the ground. It is a different operation from cutting, gathering, or snapping off. Since it was the *ears*, and not the stalks,[25] which they were treating in this way, the operation was not removing the ears from the stalk, but stripping the ears themselves. The precise action is described by Diodorus Siculus.[26] The ripe grains were detached from the ear by pressure of the thumbnail and the nails of the first and second finger. Perhaps both hands were used more or less simultaneously. People walking through long grass play with the heavy heads in this fashion and imagine they are doing no harm scattering the seed; it is an instinctive, childish act of which adults are not ashamed. Why did the disciples do this? Not because they were hungry. Mark suggests nothing of the kind. The idea that they had such a desire arose later from the "precedent" of David, which was professedly about eating bread. But there is also the prudent Jewish notion that sheer waste is wicked,[27] and that a valuable thing must be used or preserved, and it would have been difficult to believe that they ate none of the grains. Moreover it is extremely likely that they gave some to Jesus.[28] But the Pharisees' problem was with the trampling down of the stalks, with its consequent loss

---

[22] Mk. 4: 4; Mishnah, B. B. VI, 6 (see Drury at *JThS*, XXIV, 1973, 368–9).

[23] Maimonides, op. cit., 21, 1–3 (trans. S. Gandz and H. Klein, Yale Judaica Ser. 14, New Haven, 1961, 129–30). All operations analogous to agricultural operations were forbidden.

[24] See Liddell-Scott-Jones, *Greek-English Lexicon*, s.v.; also παρατίλλω (pull up, of weeds); ὑποτίλλω (pluck up, of vegetables). Note that Fr. Preisigke, *Wörterbuch der griechischen Papyrusurkunden*, II, 600, found τίλλω with the meanings "loosen" and "turn" as well as "pluck" and "strip".

[25] Mk. 4: 28.

[26] The ancient Britons first cut the ears and then stored them in the dry. As they ripened, ἐκ δὲ τούτων τοὺς παλαιοὺς στάχυς καθ᾿ ἡμέραν τίλλειν, καὶ κατεργαζομένους ἔχειν τὴν τροφήν: *Bibl. hist.* V, 21, 5. The translation by C. H. Oldfather in the Loeb Classical Library edition (III,154) is inaccurate; they did not "pick out" the heads, but stripped them. The true explanation was suggested to me by Mr. M. J. Atkinson. At Deut. 23: 25 (LXX) we have συλλέξεις ἐν ταῖς χερσίν σου στάχυς (neither the Masoretic Text nor the Targum of Onkelos confine the right to a hired labourer, but the Palestinian Targum does). Having "made a way" the disciples seem to have been allowed to satisfy their hunger in this way, if they were indeed hungry, which Mark does not tell us. B. Cohen, "The rabbinical law presupposed by Mt. xii.1 and Lk.vi.1", *Harvard Theological Review*, XXIII, 1930, 91–2, draws attention to b.B.M.87b, 92a (the law was not certain). For the Qumran version of the facility offered by Deut. 23: 25 see G. Vermes, *The Dead Sea scrolls*, London, 1966, 249.

[27] Deut. 20: 19; b.Qid.32a (Soncino trans., 156); B.Q.91b (Soncino trans., 529); Maimonides, op. cit., XIV, v, 6, 10.

[28] A. Büchler, "The ears of corn", *Expository Times*, XX, 1908–9, 278 (an article neglected despite the fame of its author). Büchler rightly says it is superfluous to read "Son of man" as "man" (as most do), but he did not realize why (see below). Ears of corn were brought to Elisha at 2 K. 4: 42, but the implications of the feeding-miracle which supervened *seem* to have no bearing on our story. Cf. 1 Sam. 10: 3–4; 2 K. 4: 42.

of grain to the owner; if the ears were ripe enough to eat, and the grain could be detached in that manner, the mere making of a path through the crop would cause many grains to be lost; animals or birds would have them. The action of the disciples stripping the ears was analogous to threshing, and therefore probably forbidden on the Sabbath in any case.[29] I feel confident that grain was *sown* by the action, which also was forbidden.

Mark uses the expression ἤρξαντο ὁδὸν ποιεῖν, literally "they began to make a way". It is obvious, and everyone has noticed, that this means that they made a path. But since this did not seem to link with the David-story, it has been suggested that this was one of Mark's alleged latinisms and so equalled *iter fecerunt*. ὁδὸν ποιεῖσθαι in fact has two meanings, "to make a way for oneself", and simply "to go". ὁδὸν ποιεῖν is amply evidenced in the sense, "build or make a path or road",[30] and I suggest that this is what it means here. The motive for making the way through the standing crop was to avoid Sabbath limits. They had mentally pitched their domicile in the village or hamlet whither they were going,[31] and they would be within 2,000 cubits of it by the time night fell on that evening. But the method they used with respect to treading down the furrows, as well as causing loss to the owner by their action analogous to threshing, was questionable on three separate counts. It was natural, since their teacher was responsible for their good conduct,[32] that he should be tactfully questioned about it.

The answer makes good sense once one knows the *haggadah* and the law evoked by the David story.[33] Briefly, David was a real (though unacknowledged) king,[34] and he was on campaign. He was, as Mark says, "in need".[35] He commandeered bread, which had become the priests' property immediately it was taken off the table upon which it had been placed the week before. The campaign, and the demand for the bread, and the receipt and eating of it took place on the Sabbath.[36] The actual High Priest, Ahimelech, and his family, suffered severely for giving in to the demand.[37] Only one escaped, and this was Ahimelech's son,

---

[29] Mishnah, Shab. VII, 2, X, 6; Dem. V, 10; b.Shab. 70b–71a (Soncino trans., 338), 95a–b (Soncino trans., 456–8). Maimonides, op. cit., III, ɪ, 8, 3 (but see 21, 14 [rubbing parched ears of grain, cf. Lk. 6: 1], trans., cit. sup., 133).

[30] It is exactly equivalent to ὁδοποιεῖν. Mk. 2: 23 has a variant reading in this form. Judg. 17: 8 is often cited to the contrary, but the man (17: 6–9) was one who did as he wished and may not have cared for paths! The normal use of ὁδὸν ποιεῖν is illustrated at Xenophon, *Anab.* IV, 8, 8, V, 1, 13, 14. Herod. VII, 42 is analogous with ποιεῖσθαι. See Diodorus, XX, 23, 5.

[31] See Maimonides, op. cit., III, ɪɪ, 7, 1–3 (trans., 245–7). The notes supplied in the translation provide the Talmudic references.

[32] The topic, and the episode, are dealt with by D. Daube, "Responsibilities of Master and Disciples in the gospels", *NTS*, XIX, 1, 1972, 1–15. Daube handled our passage at his *New Testament and Rabbinic Judaism*, London, 1956, 67–71.

[33] There are discrepancies between the Masoretic Text of 1 Sam. 21: 1–9, the LXX, and Jesus's summary. Even more varied *haggadah* may once have existed. Further midrashic material is referred to in n. 36 below.

[34] 1 Sam. 21: 11; Lk. 1: 31–2(!); Is. 9: 7; 2 Sam. 7: 8–29; Ps̄. 16: 8–11, 132: 11.

[35] See n. 55 below. I show now that *both* pericopes exemplify commandeering, in local idiom ἀγγαρία.

[36] Beare, 133 n. 10, says the midrash is "dredged up"; but he was unaware of the weight of it. Josephus, *Ant.* III, 255–7; Mishnah, Suk. V, 7 f.; Midrash Rabbah, Num. XXIII, 1; b.Men.95b (Soncino trans., 585); Yalqût, § 130 (ed. 1960, II, 727). A valuable article of B. Murmelstein has been ignored: "Jesu Gang durch die Saatfelder", *Angelos* III, 1928, 111–20. Rengstorf, op. cit., accepts the point, "some of the scribes regarded 1 Sam. 21. 2 ff. as happening on the Sabbath". Haenschen, op. cit., 120, summarily rejects it. Hummel, however, takes a more positive view of the midrash. The dispute was about the Sabbath, the circumstances of the showbread indicate a Sabbath event: why reject the utility of the midrash in the interests of a pre-determined exegesis?

[37] 1 Sam. 22: 11–9.

Abiathar.[38] He was of high-priestly status, naturally.[39] He was David's High Priest, the *first* to be High Priest at Jerusalem, and the *last* to have direct access to the divine will by means of the Urim and Thummim.[40] He was therefore peculiarly qualified to know what was ritually proper. He remained with David all his life, and there is no suggestion that he disapproved of David's behaviour. Why should this be? Because a king, even if another (improperly) occupies his throne, has regalian rights which lie loosely to the religious law. The word $\epsilon\pi\iota$ in $\epsilon\pi\iota\ '\!A\beta\iota\alpha\theta\grave{\alpha}\rho\ \grave{\alpha}\rho\chi\iota\epsilon\rho\acute{\epsilon}\omega\varsigma$ does not mean merely "in the time of Abiathar the High Priest", which has aroused the mirth of the instructed, but "in the presence of Abiathar, etc.", for $\epsilon\pi\iota$ with the genitive is well attested in this sense,[41] and Oriental texts do not abhor double meanings. It was not Ahimelech's actual giving of the bread which was significant; it was Abiathar's warranting, by his own adherence, the propriety of David's behaviour at that critical period. Though the ritual law appropriated not only the ownership, but also the enjoyment of the show-bread to the priests, David was able to set aside both considerations because of his *need*, his and his young men's actual hunger, and the fact that he was on campaign.

Now, says Mark, this was not the only answer. Jesus added another, which has never been explained. Verses 27–8 make an effective argument when it is realized that, thinking of David, Jesus prefers to quote David, who was, of course, the author of the Psalms.[42] Psalm 8, which is quoted in several places in the New Testament, and therefore formed part of the Christian missioner's portfolio of "useful texts",[43] must be consulted in the Hebrew but a translation of the relevant verses will do very well. Ps. 8: 4–6 runs (RV), "What is man that thou art mindful of him? And the son of man that thou visitest him? For thou hast made him but little lower than God, and crownest him with glory and honour. Thou madest him to have dominion over the works of thy hands; thou hast put all things under his feet. . . ." It is important to notice that a very small change in pointing of the original of "visitest" produces an excellent result. According to the well-known rabbinical technique called *'al tiqrey* we can read, for the Masoretic Text *tifqᵉdennu*, the form *tafqidennu*, which means "makest him an inspector, or officer". This fits Adam very well, to whom of course

---

[38] 1 Sam. 22: 20; Josephus, *Ant.* VI, 269. On Abiathar see White at Hastings' *Dictionary of the Bible* (1898), I, 6–7. The anomalous reference to Abiathar (instead of Ahimelech) is usually attributed to a slip of memory. But J. Bowker, more wisely, surmises something more subtle: *Jesus and the Pharisees*, Cambridge, 1973, 40. The Biblical discrepancy at 2 Sam. 8: 17, 1 Chr. 24: 6 could be a cause of confusion, but a rational explanation of the passage (such as Bowker looks for) seems more acceptable. Cf. the "wrong" addition of *hakohen* ("the Priest") to Jud. 20: 28 at b. Sheb. 35b. The *locus classicus* on evangelists' "mistakes" is "Zechariah the Son of Barachiah" (Matt. 23: 35), well on the way to explanation with the aid of Targ. Lam. 2.20 (M. McNamara, *New Testament and the Palestinian Targum to the Pentateuch*, Rome, 1966, 160–3).

[39] Josephus, *Ant.* VI, 262.

[40] 1 Sam. 23: 9, 30: 7; 2 Sam. 15: 24–36; b. Yoma 73b, Soṭ. 48b (Soncino trans., 258); Sanh. 16b, 95b (Soncino trans. 80, 643).

[41] Liddell-Scott-Jones, *Lexicon*, s.v., A2e. Blass-Debrunner-Funk, *Greek grammar of the New Testament*, Cambridge, Chicago, 1961, § 234. Mt. 28: 14 (cf. Mk. 13: 9, Acts 24: 19–20, 25: 9, 26: 2, 1 Cor. 6: 1, 6). Wetstenius, *H KAINH ΔIAΘHKH*, Amsterdam, 1751, 561 n. 26 (excellent).

[42] 11QPsᵃDav.Comp. Cf. J. A. Sanders, *Discoveries in the Judaean desert*, IV, Oxford, 1965, 91–3. Mk. 12: 36–7, Acts 2: 25.

[43] 1 Cor. 15: 27 (cf. Mt. 28: 18); Heb. 2: 6–8; F. Hahn, op. cit., 131–2. The first (and the only theologian) to recognize the relevance of Ps. 8: 4–6 (5–7 (LXX)) was K. Bornhäuser, "Zur Pericope vom Bruch des Sabbats", *Neue Kirchliche Zeitschr.*, XXXIII, 1922, 325–34. See also F. Delitzsch, *Biblical commentary on the Psalms*, I, London, 1887, 196–200 (Jesus's designation of himself as Son of Man leans upon this psalm no less than upon Dan. 7: 13); F. H. Borsch, *The Son of Man in myth and history*, London, 1967, 114 (see also 236, 322–3).

the psalm alludes, since he gave the animals (and, *haggadah* says, even God himself) their names. Now the plain sense of "son of man" is merely an elegant variation of Man. But if one assumed that David had in mind the apocalyptic figure known as Son of man,[44] whose sovereignty is an eternal sovereignty (in the LXX his *power* is a perpetual power), the parallelism resolves itself neatly: Adam remained in God's mind, notwithstanding the Fall, and a Son of Man, "Son of man", a second Adam as it were, is not only visited by God, i.e. subject to his inspection, but also made by him inspector over everything. So indeed the psalm says, "all things under his *feet*". Now it is usually believed that the gospels are not aware of the Second Adam metaphor, which is documented from Paul.[45] However, I have been able to prove that this is untrue, that the Adam theme is present in Mark, and, somewhat over-dramatically, in Luke.[46] If Mark was aware of the notion that the Son of man, i.e. Jesus himself, was identical with the Second Adam, all fits. The Son of man is a Messianic figure, and interchangeable with the Messiah if we are prepared to make the equation. The instances where "son of man" means a polite "I", and has no Messianic force,[47] do not diminish the Messianic force of occasions where "Son of man" is pointedly allusive. Here is a case, it would seem. The Son of man is made just a little lower than God,[48] and is "crowned". The Messiah is both Lord and King in rabbinic writings *passim*. The church acclaimed Jesus as Lord, and it was a cause of great grief in the traditional synagogues to which the first Christians belonged.[49]

To return to Mark 2: 27–8: Adam was created on the sixth day, and since the Sabbath was created on the seventh it is possible (though by no means conclusive) to argue that the Sabbath was for him. No doubt it is generally accepted that the Sabbath is a foretaste of the shadow of the World to Come, which will be all Sabbath, and for the righteous what is true for the Sabbath will be true for the world to come. It was arguable that the Second Adam would live in a perpetual Sabbath in his earthly ministry, but that takes us far from our argument. Now, granted that for Adam the Sabbath was created, and not *vice versa*, the Son of man, whom God has made "inspector", "crowned", with "dominion", i.e. as κύριος (*dominus*) over *all things*, with the created things listed ("all sheep and oxen . . .") *under his*

[44] Dan. 7: 13–4. The rabbinical interpretation of Ps. 8 (see Midrash on Psalms, Ps. 8, §§ 7–8) is Messianic. "Son of man" is equated with Isaac, "glory" refers to Moses, "to have dominion" with Joshua, and "under his feet" to David. All these figures are "types" of Jesus. b. Sanh. 38b (Soncino trans., 242) refers both "man" and "son of man" to Adam. "Little less than (a) God" implies Moses: b.R.H.21b (Soncino trans., 90); b. Ned. 38a (Soncino trans., 119).
[45] C. K. Barrett, *From first Adam to last. A study in Pauline theology*, London, 1962. F. Hahn, op. cit., does not consider the Adam-Christ typology as this lies outside his scheme. See also W. D. Davies, *Paul and rabbinic Judaism*, 2nd ed., London, 1955, 44.
[46] Mk. 1: 13, "he was with the animals" (cf. Gen. 2: 18 f.) (Davies, cit. sup., 42–3, is not convinced). Derrett, *Theology*, LXXIV, 1971, 566–71; *Heythrop Journal*, XIV, 3, 1973, 249–65; *Jesus's audience*, London 1973, 108. See A. Farrer, *Study in St. Mark*, Westminster, 1951, 233, 275–6.
[47] As at b. Sanh. 95b. G. Vermes emphasizes this meaning in his App. E to M. Black, *An Aramaic approach to the gospels and Acts*, 3rd ed., Oxford, 1967, and returns to this emphatically in his *Jesus the Jew*, London, 1973, 188–91. In his view Mk. 2: 28 would be an instance where *son of man* is unconnected with the Daniel saying (p. 180), which I now doubt. ἐξουσία (Dan. 7: 14) is also at Mk. 2: 10!
[48] LXX: "angels". A persistent *haggadah* interprets the psalm in terms of the angels' jealousy of (*i*) Adam, (*ii*) Moses, cf. Yalqûṭ, § 641. Historically "God" is the correct reading, and seems never to have been eclipsed.
[49] On 1 Cor. 12: 1–3 see W. C. van Unnik and C. W. H. Lampe's articles in B. Lindars and S. S. Smalley, edd., *Christ and the Spirit in the New Testament*, Cambridge, 1973. On the theme of royalty compare Mk. 15: 26 with Jn. 19: 21. Even Matthew includes a covert claim to royalty: Mt. 26: 55, cf. Jn. 8: 2, should be compared with Tosefta, Sanh. IV, 4 (only kings of the house of David may sit in the Temple courtyard).

feet, is "Lord" even on a Sabbath. The words κύριός ἐστιν ὁ υἱὸς τοῦ ἀνθρώπου καὶ τοῦ σαββάτου will not mean "The Son of man is Lord even of the Sabbath", which has no meaning whatever, and is sometimes retranslated "Lord *over* the Sabbath",[50] but, with the genitive as genitive of time,[51] and with κύριος as "Lord" in the absolute sense, as is attested in many good examples,[52] simply "Therefore the Son of man [meaning himself] is Lord [in the sense of absolute Master under God] even on the Sabbath day!" Such is the "perpetual" power/sovereignty at Dan. 7: 14.

And in what did his kingly right consist? To walk through standing corn on a campaign, as, at Jewish law, all kings may.[53] True, burial parties may do the same, but the relevance of that, in spite of one striking parallel,[54] is as yet tentative. We know that Jesus commandeered an ass on one occasion, because he *had need*.[55] This is a parallel. Did the disciples have any right to destroy the owner's grain? Yes, if thereby they smoothed their master's way, making plain the path of the Messiah. The heavy ears of grain are a great nuisance to walk through, when the seed was sown broadcast. The disciples were miming the actions of the servants of the Messiah,[56] irrespective of the actions seemly in students showing respect for their master.

Matthew wished to point out the sovereign position of Jesus, greater than the Temple, and the argument about the priests working on the Sabbath, which is unquestionably true,[57] only convinces if that is one's point of view. Luke was concerned with the aspect of divine compassion for suffering humanity, and the priority of acts of kindness over ritual precautions, a theme obviously present, though more literally, in Matthew. Both thought Jesus declared himself not merely "little lower than God" but virtually God, for it is *possible* to

---

[50] Haenschen, op. cit. The Christ of the New Testament is Lord over the Law: O. Betz, *What do we know about Jesus?*, London, 1968, 118.

[51] Blass-Debrunner-Funk, op. cit., § 186 (2): σαββάτου Mt. 24: 20D, τοῦ σαββάτου Lk.18: 12, τοῦ ἐνιαυτοῦ Heb. 9: 7, χειμῶνος Mt. 24: 20/Mk. 13: 18 (Thuc. 3, 104), ἡμέρας Rev. 21: 25, τῆς ἡμέρας Lk. 9: 37 (pap. 45), ἡμέρας καὶ νυκτός Mk. 5: 5, Lk. 18: 7 (Xen., *Anab.*, II, 6, 7), νυκτός Mt. 2: 14, etc., τῆς νυκτός Lk. 2: 8. ὄρθρου βαθέως Lk. 24: 1, ἡμερῶν *Homil. Clem.* 12.2.3, 3.6; 13.1.4.

[52] κύριος πάντων ὤν (Gal. 4: 1); πάντων κύριος (Acts 10: 36). See Acts 2: 36. κύριος = "master" at Josephus, *B.J.* I, 458, *Ant.* XIII, 300. ὁ κύριος = "owner" at Exod. 12: 28–9, 34: 22–8 (7), 15 (14); Jdg. 19: 22–3; Mk. 12: 9/Mt. 20: 8; "master or owner/boss" at Mt. 9: 38, 24: 42–50, 25: 18–21; "ruler/king" at Mt. 18: 25–34. See also Lk. 16: 3, 5, 8; 19: 33; Jn. 13: 16, etc. Most relevant of all is κύριος αὐτοῦ at Mk. 11: 3 (see G. D. Kilpatrick, *Jesus in the gospels and the early Church*, Drawbridge Memorial Lecture, 1971, London [Chr. Evid. Soc., 1971], 3–4, followed by Derrett at *NT*, XIII, 1971, 246 n. 2). In fact Mk. 11: 3 and 2: 23–8 constitute jointly evidence tending to refute the otherwise carefully-prepared conclusion of G. Vermes (*Jesus the Jew*, cit. sup., 103, and especially 143) that Jesus never accepted the dignity of "lord" nor arrogated to himself the title of Messianic king.

[53] Mishnah, Sanh. II, 4, B.B. VI, 7, b.B.B. 64b, 100b (Soncino trans., 259, 419); Palestinian Talmud, Sanh. II, 5 (20b) (M. Schwab, *Talmud de Jerusalem*, X, Paris, 1888, 249); Sifre Deut., § 161, commenting on Deut. 17: 19 (Ugolini, XV, p. dccxii; ed. 1769, p. 212). The wording of the formula, *pôres la'ᵃsôt lô derekh* agrees in part with ὁδὸν ποιεῖν. Maimonides, op. cit., XIV, v, 5, 3; Murmelstein, cit. sup., n. 36, p. 118.

[54] Semachot IV, 11, also editorial note at Soncino trans., b.B.B. 99b (p. 416); the Anointing at Bethany (Mk. 14: 3–9 and parallels) (Derrett, *Law in the New Testament*, ch. 12). The woman's expenditure of spices (below, n. 73) was justified in anticipation of Jesus's burial. R. H. Lightfoot, *History and interpretation in the gospels*, London, 1935, 222 n., pointed out that since "Son of man" occurs chiefly after Mk. 8: 27 ff., its occurrence at 2: 28 must point to the Passion!

[55] Mk. 11: 1–7 and parallels; χρείαν ἔχει (11: 3). See last citation at n. 52 above. What connexion has the hunger in Mk. 2: 25 with that at Mk. 11: 12 (A. Farrer, op. cit., 161)?

[56] Exod. 23: 20; Ps. 40: 3; Mal. 3: 1; Mt. 3: 3; Mk. 1: 3/Lk. 3: 4–5; Mt. 11: 10/Mk. 1: 2/Lk. 7: 27; Lk. 1: 76; Jn. 1: 23, 3: 28. Note Mk. 11: 8 and parallels (where Mark has special material).

[57] Num. 28: 9 f. (H. Strack-) P. Billerbeck, *Kommentar zum Neuen Testament*, I, Munich, 1961, 620; P. Gaechter, *Das Matthäus Evangelium*, Innsbruck, etc., 1963, 390 (well put).

understand "Lord of the Sabbath" as a divine title;[58] and so they went beyond Mark, writing a commentary upon a commentary. Mark is unquestionably prior here.

II

When we turn to the observance of the Sabbath by the friends of Jesus after the crucifixion (Aland, §§ 350, 352), we move from under a mound of "critical" discussion and rediscussion to relative silence. One would have thought that the crucifixion and resurrection would have provided an area for investigation more fully excavated than any other. One aspect of their observance of the Sabbath *has* been noticed, but since no systematic issue hung upon it, the matter has received minimal comment. Now Mark alone tells us that Joseph of Arimathaea *bought* a winding-sheet and placed the body of Jesus in the tomb. The stone was put to, and thereafter the two Maries saw *where he had been placed*. The question of Pilate, whether Jesus was known to have died *already*, is found only in Mark, and the versions of Matthew and Luke are manifest commentaries on the Marcan story. It would take us too far to explain each and every point. Mark describes Joseph as a "councillor" of good reputation. Luke retains the point that he was a councillor, which in fact links the story with a tomb-builder in Isaiah.[59] Matthew quite rightly says that Joseph was rich, because councillors were normally rich,[60] and because there is another important link with Isaiah thereby.[61] Luke says he was no party to the anti-Jesus proceedings, that he was a just man, and that he awaited the kingdom of God (Lk. 23: 50–1); Matthew, that he was a pupil of Jesus (Matt. 27: 57). Matthew could have had independent information, but if it is merely a commentary it looks like a guess. Mark's point, which Luke has built upon, was that Joseph was a pious man of an apocalyptic-Messianic persuasion: it is known that pious Jews would take great pains to see that crucified persons were buried before nightfall.[62] Mark does not say he was a disciple of Jesus: he was evidently an admirer of his with an intellectual, somewhat more remote attachment to him than actual disciples had. It was, perhaps, to make up for this want of intimacy that St. John has brought on the scene (Jn. 19: 38–9) an old disciple of Jesus's, so that the burial of Jesus is effected by a prestige-worthy couple, a covert disciple and a disciple of long standing whose conversations with Jesus St. John had already recorded. Our suspicions of the authenticity of John's story are increased by the fact that, combining gardens (and later the gardener, who is of course the second Adam!) (Jn. 19: 41, 20: 15) and spices (Jn. 19: 39–40), he has, with his usual irony, called up Cant. 6: 2), the beautiful text about "my beloved" (God or God's beloved according to the way of taking the text chosen for a poetical midrash) and his garden and the spices,

---

[58] Bornhäuser, ubi cit., 330 (cf. Jn. 5: 17, 18). "My Sabbaths": Exod. 16: 25, Isa. 56: 4, 58: 13; Ezek. 20: 12, 16, 20, and repeatedly. Matthew's and Luke's error had two supports: (*i*) anarthrous κύριος immediately suggests "God" (G. D. Kilpatrick, *Josef Schmid Festschrift*, Freiburg, 1971, 214–9); (*ii*) if we accept the rabbinic concept of the pre-existence of the Messiah, his presidency of the Messianic Banquet, and the nature of the Sabbath as prefiguration of the World to Come (which is all Sabbath: Is. 66: 23; Mishnah, Tam. VI, 4; Lampe, *Patristic lexicon*, Oxford, 1968, s.v., 1220, D2), the Messiah is obviously Lord in, and in respect of, the Sabbath.

[59] Is. 22: 15, 21.

[60] A βουλευτής is usually rich: Midrash Rabbah, Gen. LXXVI, 6 (D. Sperber at *Rev. Int. des Droits de l'Antiquité*, XIX, 1972, 31). On the ambivalences of Joseph see J. Schreiber, *Die Markus-passion* Hamburg, 1969, 58–60.

[61] Is. 53: 8 (Derrett, *Law in the New Testament*, 451–2).

[62] Josephus, *B.J.* IV, 317 (most precise and authoritative).

which is suitable for funeral sermons and is traditionally interpreted so as to speak of the sudden deaths of the righteous.[63] St. John's allusion (which no one has noticed) does not prove that there was no garden, nor that no Nicodemus took part in the burial. However, it is clear from Mark, and the others do not contradict him, that the burial proceedings were undertaken by Joseph, and by the women, independently and not by pre-arrangement. Yet both entered into purchases.

It is easy to believe that when Mark alone says Joseph bought the sheet, and he alone says the women bought the spices (Mk. 16: 1), the other evangelists might have felt it made no difference whether they begged, or borrowed them! The presence of Nicodemus is partly (I surmise) to answer questions in the minds of ancient readers of Mark, how the women came by the money. They could have collected it from rich devotees of Jesus. St. John felt, perhaps, that it would be easier, in the circumstances (to which we come), to suppose that a well-to-do male disciple should contribute embalming materials (to an enormous amount). Matthew merely tells us that the women were engaged in tomb-visiting, apparently according to the Jewish custom of visiting the (presumed) dead on the second and third day after burial.[64] Mark's picture is that the moment the Sabbath was over they bought the spices, i.e. absolutely at nightfall, so that they were able to go with them to the tomb as soon as it was light. Let us consider the timetable.

Joseph has Jesus taken down from the cross in order to deposit him in the tomb before sunset on Friday. To this end he buys a sheet (Matthew says it was a pure one: one wonders what alternative could have been considered?). During the Sabbath it is forbidden (Neh. 10: 30) to make purchases and sales, and even to consider transactions: there is an exception in favour of an act of charity and piety; one may make preparations for such a transaction, and make one's way even during the Sabbath so that the moment it is over one can make purchases for such purposes. There is no doubt but that the material for the embalming of a corpse can be bought the very minute the Sabbath ends.[65] On the other hand, since the lifting and turning of a corpse cannot be done on the Sabbath,[66] there is no excuse for purchasing or attempting to purchase a winding-sheet on that day; thus if a corpse is to be buried on a Friday, the sheet must be obtained in the nick of time, and this is what Mark says was done. The question of spices[67] arose, naturally, to honour the especially venerable dead, but that had to be postponed. St. John thought it made sense to involve more than one person in this, and yet he avoided mention of the Twelve: first because, evidently, his sources did not permit this, and secondly because he knew what the point of the story was (as we shall see).

Scholars have applied their minds to Joseph's (but not the women's) purchase for one purpose only. There is a dispute as to the date of the crucifixion. It is agreed that it took place

[63] Midrash Rabbah, Cant. VI, 2, 1 (Soncino trans., 206), also ibid., §§ 2–4; Midrash Rabbah, Gen. LXII, 2 (Soncino trans., 551–2); Yalqût, § 991. The garden is studied by B. Hemelsoet, "L'ensévelissement selon S. Jean", *Studies in John*, (Sevenster Volume), Leiden, 1970, 47 ff., at 55–6.

[64] Derrett, "La resurrezione di Gesù", *Conoscenza Religiosa*, 1973, 3, 306–14, citing, *inter alia*, Semachot VIII, 1; N. Brüll, "Die talmudischen Tractate über Trauer um Verstorbenen", *Jahrb. f. Jüd. Gesch. und Lit.*, 1874, 14, 51–2. Tomb-visiting on a Sabbath would in any case violate the rule against ostentatious mourning on that day: Semachot X, 15 (Judaea); b.M.Q.23b, cf. b.Shab. 12 a–b.

[65] Mishnah, Shab. XXIII, 4; Maimonides, op. cit., III, I, 24, 1–5 (especially the last); Tosefta, Shab. XVII, 3 (ed. Zuckermandel, 137, 14).

[66] Mishnah, Shab. XXIII, 5; Maimonides, op. cit., III, I, 25, 6.

[67] On the spices themselves see R. Sigismund, *Die Aromata in ihrer Bedeutung für Religion, Sitten, Gebräuche, Handel und Geographie des Altertums bis zu den ersten Jahrhunderten unserer Zeitrechnung*, Leipzig, 1884 (repr. 1974). For a general survey of such behaviour, see, e. g. E. Bendann, *Death customs*, London, 1930.

on a Friday, but which day was the Passover day? A superficial reading of Mark (Mk. 14: 12–4) strongly suggests that the Last Supper was eaten at the same time as Jews in Jerusalem ate the Passover meal, i.e. on Passover night. Thus the actual Passover had occurred before Jesus came before Pilate. The Johannine chronology, which greatly appeals to the majority of scholars, places the Last Supper on the night before the Passover, so that the disciples did not eat the Passover at all, Jesus was crucified approximately during the time paschal lambs were slaughtered, and the Last Supper was a Jesus-Passover, a new ritual intended, from the first, to supplement (we do not know whether also to supersede) the traditional Passover. There is no known method of solving this problem.[68] For those who, like Jeremias, argue strongly for the (superficial) Marcan chronology, it might seem a problem that Joseph was able to buy a winding-sheet, not on the day of preparation (Removal of Leaven), which was itself a holy day, but on the actual Passover day itself, which was subject to Sabbath laws as to purchases. My own view is that Mark was deliberately ambiguous for theological reasons (which St. John rejected). But that apart, Jeremias and others[69] are (in general) content that for the burial of the dead immediately before a Sabbath a purchase could be made even on a feast day. My own impression is of no comfort to them, namely that on a feast day one might *consider* transactions necessary for pious and charitable purposes, but not conclude them! That is the Mishnaic law, and it seems sensible. Hence Joseph's purchase, if he was a pious man (so that a purchase from a pagan would not have absolved him from impiety), fits very well if he bought the sheet not only on the Friday before nightfall, but on the Friday that was (at most) a day of preparation, a sacred day, but *not* the feast day itself.

We come at length to the point. In spite of a group of pericopes in the New Testament which proved that Jesus used a sovereign independence with regard to the Sabbath, and even encouraged his disciples to behave (in selected contexts, no doubt) as if it were a weekday, two independent witnesses of his teaching behaved, and expressed by their behaviour their beliefs, as if the strictest observance of the Sabbath rest was appropriate. To embalm a body that had been dead the best part of three days would not be an enviable task. The women waited till the first moment when they could, without profaning the Sabbath (in carrying the vessels and moving the stone or causing the stone to be moved), perform their self-chosen and melancholy duty.[70] Mark was a Jew and was writing primarily for Jews. My impression is that Jews, like most Asians whom I have known, view the passing of coin as a significant act. One avoids spending unless one is clear as to the purpose and propriety of the purchase. One might be more casual about borrowing and lending, though Talmudic

---

[68] J. Jeremias, *Die Abendmahlsworte Jesu*, 4th ed., Göttingen, 1967 (English trans., *Eucharistic words of Jesus*, London, 1964, cited below).

[69] Jeremias, op. cit., 76–7 (so previously at *JThS*, L, 1949, 5); G. Dalman, *Jesus-Jeshua*, London, 1929, 101–3; Billerbeck, op. cit., II, 815–34. The difficulty is raised in E. Lohmeyer, *Das Evangelium des Markus*, Göttingen, 1937, 350. See also Klostermann, *Markusevangelium*, 1950, 169; Grundmann, *Markus*, 1971, 318–9.

[70] διαγενομένου τοῦ σαββάτου (unacceptable to Matthew or Luke) seems to mean "on the outgoing of the Sabbath". The New Testament examples of the verb (which means "to pass, to continue on") imply that a period was over (Mk. 16: 1, Acts 25: 13, 27: 9). For the story see C. Masson, "L'ensévelissement de Jésus", *Rev. de Théologie et de Philosophie*, XXXI, 1943, 193–203; P. Gaechter, "Zum Begräbnis Jesu", *Zeitschr. f. Kath. Theologie*, LXXV, 1953, 220–5. D. S. Margoliouth, *Expository Times*, XXXVIII, 1926–7, 278–80 has been ignored: he denied the priority of Mark, but commented on the women's disbelief in resurrection.

law shows the utmost fussiness even there. Hence, in spite of the threefold prediction of the Resurrection, which, in Mark, is expressed with a verb implying physical resuscitation,[71] neither Joseph, whose intellectual appreciation of Jesus was obviously substantial or he would not have put himself to such pains and expense (the sheet will have been a fine one, and Pilate's officers will have wanted tips), nor the women who were always close to Jesus and had accompanied him in his wanderings[72] and knew all about his teaching and took a keen personal interest in him, had the slightest expectation of his Resurrection. They were not even in doubt. They paid good money for materials which were utterly inappropriate to any such possibility. St. John sees this point: he emphasizes (19: 40) that it was the custom to wind corpses in these long rectangular strips (in an action resembling swaddling a baby): this by no means encouraged revival. The spices were extremely costly and Jews are horrified at waste: this very point is made by the disciples in a closely analogous connexion![73]

Neither Joseph nor the women had the slightest suspicion that their burial preparations were inappropriate or unnecessary. And this is what Mark is saying with his verb ἀγοράζω, which no one has noticed—though it is altogether in keeping with the style and purpose of that gospel, with the biting sarcasm and irony with which the whole story is told.[74] The Old Israel was enthusiastic about "holy men" and had its indulgent moments in dealing with their idiosyncrasies. What happened when the women arrived at the tomb was no greater a shock to pagan hearers, or to Jewish hearers of Mark's gospel, than it was for the actual participants.

St. Mark's irony is not always easily disentangled, but a close look at the synoptic gospels' use of the verb "to buy" reveals pejorative implications: one should not buy at all in the context (e.g. Mk. 11: 15); or it is a questionable alternative (Lk. 14: 18–9, 17: 28); or is deplorable even if necessary (Lk. 22: 36); or it reveals a hopeless lack of comprehension of the true state of affairs (Matt. 25: 9)—the best example of the ironical use of "to buy" is Mk. 6: 36–7, which could conceivably look forward to our passage.

And so in the old texts, pored over, memorized, sifted interminably, century after century, there lie materials unexploited, unenjoyed. Jewish interest in Jesus has notably revived in recent times.[75] One testimony to the depth of that interest would be a closer application to the cultural material and the scriptural familiarity which are presupposed by the structure and vocabulary of the gospels.[76]

---

[71] Mk. 8: 31, 9: 31, 10: 34 (ἀναστήσεται); Mt. 16: 21, 17: 23, 20: 19 (ἐγερθήσεται—implying a miraculous revivification). Luke's vocabulary is mixed. Cf. Lk. 24: 7.

[72] Lk. 23: 55. Mk. 15: 40–1 can be taken as the explanation of the strange words at 16: 7.

[73] Mk. 14: 4/Mt. 26: 8! No one has connected Mk. 14: 4 with the funeral purchases. Money proves intention and sincerity: 1 Chr. 21: 22–25; 2 Sam. 24: 21, 24 (cf. Deut. 2: 4–7; cf. 26–30), and especially the curious Acts 21: 23–6.

[74] The concept of *buying* was known to be appropriate for the commencement of a cult: see 1 Chr. 21: 22–6. And for the ironical implications of the verb "to buy" here Mark's reader has been prepared by Mk. 6: 36: the point is that one must *not* go down to Egypt to buy corn, for that is how the first redemption itself became necessary! The same sarcastic point figures at Matt. 25: 9.

[75] The works by S. Ben Chorin and that by G. Vermes (cit. sup.) come to mind. A shift of research-concern from the *person* of Jesus to his community and his teaching would be welcome.

[76] Kilpatrick (cit. sup., n. 52, at p. 1) refers to neglect of linguistic evidence: "To elicit this body of evidence requires an investigation somewhat like archaeological excavations, but with a difference. We are concerned with words rather than with the physical remains of an ancient culture. We do not have to dig to find our words, but I suggest that we have to do something like digging to discover their significance for our problem and in the process may discover something like the stratification which is most important for the archaeologist when he wants to date his finds."

FURTHER ANNOTATION

p. [5], n. 9. It is noteworthy that, in a somewhat more conventional treatment of the pericope than mine, A. E. Harvey, *Jesus on Trial* (London, 1976) at pp. 68-72, indicates that the deliberately provocative behaviour of which the Pharisees complained was caused by nothing but the actual hunger of the disciples. They went a few hundred yards, he suggests, into the nearest cornfield. Unlike the position in John, the behaviour of Jesus relative to the Sabbath in the synoptics avoids all inexplicable direct attack on the Sabbath-laws. Robert Banks, whose *Jesus and the Law in the Synoptic Tradition* (Cambridge, 1975) makes a significant contribution towards an understanding of Jesus's attitude(s) towards the Torah, is of the view (pp. 113-15) that the Pharisees' objection related to the time at which the plucking and eating was done. Banks doubts whether the comparison between Jesus and David is substantiated, but insists that the passage emphasised Jesus's personal authority independently of his argumentation. In my view this is correct, but the Davidic parallel leads to the Son of Man theme, Ps. viii figuring largely in the Cleansing of the Temple episode. For bibliography on the story add: F. Gils, *R.B.* 69 (1962), 506-23.

p. [8], n. 29. Philo, *de vita Mosis* II.22 (referring to trees, but the point is general). j. Shab. VII.2 (Schwab, IV, 1881, 96).

p. [8], n. 34. See Is. xi.1-12; and cf. Mk. x.46-52.

p. [9], l. 8. A.D. Rogers, *J.T.S.* 2 (1951), 44-5.

p. [9], l. 9. For *epi* with the gen. meaning 'in the presence of' see B. Latyschev, *Ins. Ant. Or. Sept. Ponti Euxini Gr. et Lat.* II (1890), 52. The Hebrew equivalent (*lifnê*) naturally means 'with the authority of' (so b. Ber. 28*b*, bottom)!

p. [9], l. 19. See H.-J. Kraus, *Psalmen* I (Neukirchen-Vluyn, 1972) *ad loc.* S. Spiegel, *Last Trial* (1967), 117 n. connects Isaac with Ps. viii (a man worthy to be like God).

p. [9], n. 39. *archiereis* customarily included members of high-priestly families: e.g. Jos., *B.J.* vi.114 (Schürer, *Hist. Jew. People* II/1 [1885], 203-6).

p. [9], n. 43. B. Lindars, *New Testament Apologetic* (London, 1961), 50, 168, 186.

p. [11], n. 53. b.B.Q.60b; Midr. R., Ruth V.1.

p. [12], l. 2. The difficult word *deuteroprōtō* in Lk. vi.1 suggests a misunderstanding as to the disciples' misdeed, as if they were offending by eating new corn before the waving ceremony (Lev. xxiii.10-11). Subject to a really ingenious solution, or a chance find of a clue, this appears to be a corruption of Luke's text at some really early stage. The correct explanation for the corn-field episode had been lost, and some guesswork was afoot to make out where they went wrong.

A propos of p. [11], n. 57, and in further confirmation of the usefulness of Jewish law in the understanding of the gospels, we must note the conjecture of E. Levine, 'The Sabbath controversy according to Matthew', *N.T.S.* 22 (1976), 480-3. It had been suggested before that Jesus and his disciples might have been in trouble because it was *not* the '*omer* which they were reaping. No one took much notice of this recherché suggestion. Now Levine draws attention to the undoubted fact that, although the priests' sacrifical acts overrode the Sabbath, and such an allusion would not be *untrue*, it is known that the allegation would be irrelevant (as far as one could see) to the situation of Jesus's students, who were neither priests nor occupied in the Temple! To get Matthew, 'expert in the Law', out of this difficulty Levine says, 'he is referring to a precisely analogous practice which, like the disciples' action itself, involves the plucking of grain on the Sabbath. Specifically, he is referring to the widely contested and rigorously defended Pharisaic practice of reaping the first sheaves (i.e. '*omer*) offering'. The explanation is most probably correct. Pharisees, but not Sadducees, insisted on the reaping even if it must fall in a Sabbath—thus 'reaping' on a Sabbath *can* be justified on grounds of the Temple or, *a fortiori*, something greater than the Temple. Had this figured in St. Mark it would have been striking enough. Unlike Levine, I do not believe that St. Matthew had a better account of the actual controversy before him, for Matthew's motives, like his sources, were various. But if, as seems to be the case, his hearers would be reminded of a controversy of an arcane kind by so bare and skimping and tangential an allusion, this tells us a great deal about Matthew's church and its knowledge—and incidentally goes as far as ever I could wish to support my own thesis about these documents.

*   # La resurrezione di Gesù

« Non daranno retta neppure ad uno che
sia risorto dai morti » (Lc. 16, 31).
« Signore, già puzza, perché sono quattro
giorni che è là » (Gio. 11, 39).

Gli studi sulla resurrezione di Gesú hanno progredito note-
volmente negli ultimi anni e i contributi dei singoli evangelisti
alla storia sono stati identificati. Tutti gli studi moderni [1], almeno
nelle facoltà teologiche protestanti, dànno per scontato che la resurrezione di Gesú non si possa comprovare. Si può provare piut-
tosto la fede di san Pietro e c'è chi ritiene che la storia non
possa risalire piú in là della testimonianza di sconosciuti intorno
al fatto che san Pietro credeva ancor vivo, per ciò che lo riguar-
dava, il Signore [2]. Il problema della resurrezione è di una tale
complessità, date le difficoltà che incontriamo nella lettura delle
nostre fonti, che sarà meglio esaminarne particolarmente i vari
aspetti, e ci restringiamo ora a una domanda mai fatta seriamente
finora [3].

Ma prima di farla, non possiamo rimuovere certi timori. La
mia esperienza mi dice che l'idea che Gesú tornò in vita naturalmente (non soprannaturalmente) è accolta senza entusiasmo. Si
dà per dimostrato che, se tornò in vita dentro alla tomba, la fede

cristiana resterebbe scossa. Almeno uno studioso ha dimostrato, a parer mio giustamente, che la Chiesa primitiva non riteneva affatto essenziale alla fede la resurrezione fisica, e in particolare la modalità della resurrezione; fino a san Luca la resurrezione non era neanche considerata meritevole di essere celebrata. In altre parole, la fede non dipendeva dalla resurrezione del corpo reale di Gesú, bensí dal suo insegnamento e dai suoi miracoli, autenticati da lui nella passione, cioè nella storia della redenzione. La sua ricomparsa dopo tre giorni ebbe un certo effetto su san Pietro, e sicuramente anche su altri, e senza di essa il Credo della Chiesa sarebbe stato formulato in altra maniera; ma la resurrezione da sola non sarebbe valsa a fondare una nuova religione in assenza degli eventi anteriori.

Non c'è mistero piú celebrato della resurrezione, né problema piú degno dell'investigatore meglio attrezzato. Eppure non è l'unica reviviscenza dopo morte nel Nuovo Testamento. Facciamo l'elenco:

(1) la figlia di Giairo (Mc. 5, 22-43 e passi paralleli);
(2) il figlio della vedova a Naim (Lc. 7, 11-17);
(3) Lazzaro (Gio. 11,1-12,1);
(4) molti santi che entrarono in Gerusalemme (Mt. 27, 52-3).

C'è il caso di Gesú stesso, la cui natura ci è sconosciuta. Ma sappiamo che si presenta la locuzione « quattro giorni » (Gio. 11, 39) e che spesso ricorre « il terzo dí » (Mt. 16,21; 17,23; 20,19; *27,64*; Mc. 9,31; Lc. 9,22; 13,32; 18,33; 24,7; 24,21 e 46). Il passo in corsivo è il piú interessante della lista. Compare in una parte del Vangelo di san Matteo compilata chiaramente per venire incontro all'obiezione che non esisteva un testimone indipendente il quale certificasse che la tomba era vuota; ma proprio qui « il terzo giorno » è posto (e suppongo non ironicamente) sulle labbra degli avversari. Il celebre passo di san Paolo (I Cor. 15,4) « egli risorse il terzo dí secondo le Scritture » ci induce a domandarci non solo che cosa volesse dire il terzo dí e a quali Scritture si accenni.

Affrontiamo prima la domanda piú semplice. Non c'è ragione di nutrire il minimo dubbio sulle scritture accennate [4]. Si tratta di Osea 6,2; Giona 2,1 (Giona fu, sin da una fase precoce associato al « terzo dí »: Mt. 12,39-41; Lc. 11,29-39; Mt. 16,4; forse che fu usato Q e anche un'altra fonte?); e infine Gen. 42, 18. Si cita al riguardo anche Gen. 22,4. Giuseppe rimase nel fosso tre giorni e tre notti [5]. Questo ci conduce a un quesito affine. Gli ebrei erano convinti che dopo tre dí i morti entrano in una nuova fase della vita. Lo spirito non ascende se non dopo tre giorni dalla morte⁶. Rimane accanto alla tomba. Per altri 27 dí resta in qualche rapporto con la vecchia dimora. Dopo tre dí il volto del morto si appanna. La terra comincia a riprendersi ciò che aveva donato. Il giudizio dell'anima ha inizio dopo il terzo dí. Anima e corpo soffrono insieme il giudizio. A trenta giorni dalla morte l'anima sale al cielo e il corpo marcisce fino al risveglio (Is. 26,19). Queste credenze si connettono, come vedremo, alle pratiche funerarie e al lutto. Il lutto pieno durava trenta giorni. Un periodo piú breve di lutto stretto durava soltanto sette dí. I pagani facevano cerimonie sulla tomba il terzo e il trentesimo dí, oltre ad altri giorni. Non è strano che gli Ebrei visitassero anch'essi le tombe e che ci fosse bisogno di porli in guardia dall'imitare i pagani, i quali recavano doni ai morti. I pagani notoriamente celebravano feste funebri cui si riteneva partecipassero i morti, il trentesimo dí, sulla tomba medesima.

L'interesse per il terzo dí è chiaro. Se l'uomo va salvato dalla morte, non si deve aspettare oltre il terzo dí (incluso il giorno del decesso). Risorgere il quarto giorno è davvero un miracolo.

Il caso di Lazzaro necessita un esame molto stringente che esula dal nostro proposito⁷. Ma è strano che nessun commentatore (per quanto io sappia) abbia additato all'anomalia che avrebbe colpito qualunque ascoltatore ebreo o greco di Gio. 11,39, che cioè il risorto risorgesse contro ogni aspettativa concepibile. Quale aspettativa? Di solito si sa che gli Ebrei usavano visitare i sepolcri il giorno dopo il seppellimento, e anche l'indomani, il terzo dí⁸. Tutte queste visite si facevano alla luce del giorno (cosí come il seppellimento stesso). Il bisogno di visitare la tomba era semplice e ovvio. Tutti i morti si seppellivano il giorno della morte, spesso a poche ore dal decesso e se questo avveniva poco dopo l'inizio del Sabato, come nel caso di Gesú, la sepoltura era indecorosamente accelerata, tanto che il morto poteva essere adagiato nella tomba entro un'ora. Il caso piú famoso di seppellimento precipitoso è quello di Anania e Saffira⁹. Se non conoscessimo le costumanze ebraiche riterremo straordinariamente ridicolo il procedimento (Atti 5,6 e 10). Gli studiosi ebraici concordano nel ritenere che il passo rifletta genuinamente i costumi dell'epoca.

Il seppellimento precipitoso di Gesú è parte della santa Torah. È basato curiosamente su Deut. 21,33, che riguarda in modo spiccato la storia di Gesú¹⁰. La Torah esige un seppellimento affrettato e ancora nel XIII secolo gli Ebrei si opposero con forza all'ordine delle autorità d'allora, che nessun cadavere si seppellisse prima di 72 ore dalla morte. Vedremo perché una tal legge fu promulgata. Mosè Mendelsohn riuscí a convincere gli Ebrei che la nuova norma, la quale in certo modo coincideva con la costumanza universale della visita alle tombe, si adattava alla To-rah [11]. Ma in Oriente, dove queste leggi europee non avevano vigore, gli Ebrei ostinatamente seppellivano i loro morti lo stesso giorno (salvo dovessero viaggiare fino ad un cimitero distante) e, si dice, avvenivano di conseguenza degli incidenti. Quali incidenti? Nel Mediterraneo orientale il clima fa decomporre rapidamente i cadaveri. Inoltre nel caso degli Ebrei la presenza di una salma in un edificio infetta di impurità da contatto con un cadavere molte cose e persone che vi si accostino o che rimangano sotto lo stesso tetto [12]. Il seppellimento immediato o precipitoso era la soluzione di certe difficoltà pratiche. Ma essendo risaputo che la diagnosi della morte è soggetta ad errore [13], ed essendoci una leggenda secondo la quale qualcuno era ritornato in vita dopo essere stato sepolto ed era quindi rivissuto tanto da fondare una famiglia [14], la tomba non era sigillata che dopo tre giorni, ed il corpo si ispezionava due volte per accertare che non fosse in vita. Se il corpo era immobile da tre dí, sicuramente era morto. È una presunzione ebraica che quando una cosa è accaduta tre volte, si può prendere per certa o ricorrente [15].

Il bisogno di visitare le tombe non è esclusivamente ebraico né ristretto al mondo antico. Un autore occidentale del secolo XVI commenta le diagnosi di morte sbagliate [16]: si dava il caso di morti che ritornavano in vita a dispetto di tutti i metodi scientifici di diagnosi del decesso: lo specchio alla bocca e al naso, il bacile d'acqua sul petto (!) e altri mezzi per sentire il polso e il battito cardiaco. Anche in tedesco questa è chiamata *Scheintod*, morte apparente. Ci sono casi di reviviscenze in tombe chiuse (allorquando esse si aprivano per accogliere un'altra salma si vedeva che la vittima pareva essersi mossa, a prova del suo ritorno in vita) [17]. Casi di reviviscenza dopo un annegamento, perfino dopo 40 ore, sono noti [18]. È sicuro che certe persone rivivono dopo il piú scrupoloso accertamento della loro morte. C'è uno stato di catalessi nel quale il movimento del sangue si rallenta tanto e il respiro si attenua al punto che diventano inappurabili. Questi casi avvengono di continuo e i giornali ne riferiscono [19]. Di solito la pratica moderna di rimuovere la salma in un obitorio dove la temperatura è tenuta bassa, fa sí che, se un morto accertatamente tale rivive, riceve un tal trauma dall'ambiente che, salvo cure intense, la morte reale sopravviene ben presto. Ci sono esempi di sopravvivenza al di là della soglia della morte clinica [20]. La rianimazione di cuori che si sono fermati è un luogo comune della chirurgia moderna. Nelle primitive condizioni del mondo antico, specie in una società che imponeva l'immediata sepoltura, la possibilità che una persona ancora vivente fosse dichiarata morta, e portata a seppellire, non era delle più remote. Ecco perché legislatori vollero che trascorressero 72 ore prima che i morti fossero portati a seppellire o a cremare[21]. Era questa una prescrizione di Platone, e i motivi che la giustificano e che egli espone, appaiano evidenti[22].

Queste regole erano rafforzate nell'antichità da due fattori. Esisteva il mito di persone ritornate dall'aldilà dopo periodi relativamente lunghi di assenza di vita. Uno di questi miti fu usato da Platone nel suo « mito di Er », alla fine della *Repubblica*[23]. Nessuno avrebbe ascoltato questa lunga storia di ciò che Er vide tra i morti e delle lezioni che egli trasse osservando il contegno delle anime durante le loro avventure dopo la morte, se non avesse saputo che la sopravvivenza d'una persona apparentemente morta era ben possibile. Era un fatto storicamente certo che taluni erano rivissuti dopo la morte. Plinio, il raccoglitore di notizie, ne dà la lista[24]. Alcuni ritornarono in vita sulla pira funeraria per lo stimolo del calore, e almeno uno restò bruciato vivo[25]. Plinio fornisce nomi e condizioni e distingue fra un'informazione storica, una fantasia e un prodigio[26]. Altri ragguagli sono del primo secolo della nostra era, ed ebbero vasta risonanza[27]. Nelle terre abitate dagli Ebrei si visitavano le tombe il secondo e il terzo dí; e la gente sapeva perché lo faceva: nel caso che i defunti fossero tornati in vita.

Alla luce di questo fatto possiamo riesaminare certi vecchi racconti finora ritenuti fiabeschi. La capacità di accertare se una persona portata a seppellire fosse morta davvero o solo apparentemente, era considerata appannaggio di medici esperti o di chiaroveggenti. Si dice che un caso del genere fosse stato accertato da Asclepiade, e il racconto, con tutta la sua rettorica, non esce mai dai limiti del credibile[28]. Apollonio di Tiana risuscitò una giovane non senza parole segrete (!), e il modo come Filostrato ci narra l'evento, dà l'impressione che si trattasse di una meraviglia ma non d'un miracolo nel senso che violasse le leggi naturali[29]. Né l'una né l'altra storia si basa su Lc. 7,11-17, e una comparazione del vocabolario e dei motivi fa ritenere poco credibile che Mc. 5,22-43 faccia da sfondo alle parole dei decantatori pagani.

D'altronde pare che non sussista alcun motivo per dubitare che la figlia di Giairo (che san Marco non dichiara sicuramente morta)[30] ed il giovane di Naim fossero risuscitati per effetto dell'intervento di Gesú e la meraviglia non era minore per il fatto che l'azione era, si ha motivo di credere, entro e non al di fuori della natura [31].

Sembra che fra gli Ebrei fossero le donne a visitare le tombe. Esse avevano una minore importanza sociale e la loro reiterata contaminazione per essere passate fra le tombe e per aver passato la mano su pietre tombali sarebbe stato uno scotto abbastanza esiguo per una debita vigilanza; i maschi preferivano evitare questa triste incombenza; sono le donne che si lamentano drammaticamente (Gio. 11,31) e la visita ai sepolcri era di loro pertinenza. L'imbalsamazione avveniva al momento della sepoltura [32], ma, dovendosi posporre, mi domando se si sarebbe incominciata addirittura a 36 ore dal seppellimento. Il corpo non avrebbe consentito simili cure dopo tanto tempo. Perciò bisogna indagare attentamente (Mc. 16,1). La presenza delle donne al sepolcro e il fatto che esse si aspettassero che qualcun altro rimuovesse la pietra per loro sono comprensibili. Che la prima Chiesa avesse voluto una prova piú valida della testimonianza di donne (*Mishnah Shev* IV 1) è altrettanto comprensibile. Che la notizia della tomba vuota, che esse portarono ai discepoli, spingesse uno di questi ad accorrere per accertarsene, è del tutto credibile. Chi sente di una tomba vuota pensa subito o che il morto è tornato in vita (se il periodo di tre giorni non è trascorso) o che il corpo è stato rubato. La prima possibilità era insperabile, date le ferite del morto; il secondo sospetto rimaneva l'unico plausibile. Chiunque ammetterà che le lesioni della crocifissione erano cosí gravi da rendere la reviviscenza piú improbabile che in qualsiasi altro caso di ferita naturale [33], e ciò vale anche se sospettiamo che la ferita di lancia potesse non essere storicamente vera. Che qualcuno cosí gravemente colpito potesse rivivere è altamente improbabile. Comunque qui spicca un fatto mai finora spiegato, cioè che Gesú rese l'ultimo sospiro ad un momento che tutti gli astanti considerarono inaspettatamente prematuro [34] anche a tener conto degli aspri maltrattamenti che gli erano stati inflitti avanti la crocifissione. Divenne un'affermazione teologica che Gesú potesse dare la vita per riassumerla (Gio. 10,15-18).

Se passiamo in rassegna i casi storicamente noti di persone ritenute morte che sono rivissute ed hanno potuto tornarsene a casa, e sono casi rarissimi, non ne troviamo uno in cui i morti avessero da rivelare qualcosa di significativo intorno all'altro mondo, o impartissero un insegnamento o fondassero un movimento o compissero qualcosa di straordinario. A Lazzaro si sarebbe pensato che ci si sarebbe dovuti rivolgere per guida o informazione: non ci vien detto delle sue esperienze successive alla resurrezione

salvo che le autorità ritennero pericolosa la sua stessa esistenza
(se dobbiamo prestar fede a san Giovanni)[35]. Il mito di Er ci
narra cose che sarebbero ben strane se mai un tale « ritorno »
accadesse. Sta di fatto che coloro i quali rivissero dopo la morte
o non sopravvissero a lungo o furono banali dopo come prima
della risurrezione.

Non si dà il caso della reviviscenza di una persona che abbia
subìto un'orribile tortura e morte per affrontare l'inimmaginabile
dolore d'un ritorno in vita e che con le ferite ancora fresche abbia
ripreso un programma di riforma spirituale e sociale altamente
speculativo, a prova della quale si era offerto in olocausto.

Chi risuscita i morti se non Dio? Quale altra causa era accettabile per un caso come quello proposto dai Vangeli? Esistono parecchi quesiti, come quello su ciò che eventualmente accad-
de del corpo di Gesú, dato il suo gran prezzo. Dobbiamo aspettare
che albeggi l'aurora perché la soluzione di questo mistero si pro-
fili.

1 S. H. Hooke *The Resurrection of Christ as History and Experience*
London 1967; C. F. D. Moule (a cura di), *The Significance of the Message
of the Resurrection for Faith in Jesus Christ*, London 1968; W. Marxsen,
The Resurrection of Jesus of Nazareth, London 1970; C. F. Evans, *Res-
urrection and the New Testament*, London 1970; H. Grass, *Ostergeschichte
und Österberichte*, Göttingen 1970; R. A. Edwards, *The Sign of Jonah*,
London 1971; G. Kegel, *Auferstehung Jesu: Auferstehung der Toten*,
Gütersloh 1970. K. Bornhaüser, *The Death and Resurrection of Jesus
Christ* (1947 circa, stampato però a Bangalore, 1958) è di un'epoca ante-
riore.
2 Marxsen op. cit., p. 96; B. van Iersel, *The Resurrection of Jesus.
Information or Interpretation?*, in « Concilium » 60 (1970), pp. 54-67 (solo
la fede e la speranza dànno accesso alla resurrezione di Gesù).
3 Marxsen, op. cit., p. 21, taccia *l'esperienza* e la conoscenza *scientifica*
di non essere applicabile nell'indagine storica. « La nostra esperienza non
è una fonte d'informazione da cui si possa attingere per decidere come
vada intesa la parola " risorto " ».
4 Midrash Rabbah, Gen. 56, 1, 41, 7; Midrash Rabbah, Deut. 7, 6 (trad.
Soncino, 137; riferito alla resurrezione dei morti). I morti torneranno in
vita tre giorni dopo il giudizio: Midrash Rabbah, Ester 9, 2 (trad. Soncino, 112).
5 Talmud Bab., Shab. 22 a, Hag. 2 a, Test. Zeb. 4 (Charles, *Apocrypha
and Pseudoepigrapha*, II, p. 329). M. M. Kasher, *Encycl. of Biblical Interpretation*, New York 1962, vol. V, p. 24.
6 Midrash Jonah. Jellinek, *Bet ha-Midrash*, I, pp. 96-105. A Wünsche,
Aus Israels Lehrhallen, II, Leipzig 1907, p. 53 (Giona è l'anima degli
uomini); p. 55 (su « tre giorni e tre notti »). Queste idee riflettono:
hibhût ha-qebber (Leon Modena, *History of the Rites... of the Present Jews*,
London 1650, p. 243). Cfr. Talm. Bab., Shab. 151b; Midrash Rabbah, Gen.
100b. Anche i pagani notarono che la dissoluzione incomincia il terzo dì:
F. Cumont, *Lux perpetua*, Paris 1949, pp. 36-37. La *haggadah* ebraica ritiene

che Giona fosse la reincarnazione del figlio della vedova di Sarepta, che è anche considerato il « Messia figlio di Giuseppe ». Il tema di Giona-Messia è troppo complesso perché si possa trattare qui.

7 *Semachot* (Lutto) VIII 1 (fine III sec.). Trattato di D. Zlotnick, *The Tractate « Mourning »* (New Haven-London 1966), p. 11-12, 135 (con rinvii alla letteratura precedente). Il testo corretto sembra che sia « per tre dì », la ragione per cui critici recenti hanno letto « trenta dì » è dovuta al fatto che trenta dì è il periodo di lutto, e il costume pagano che dava un'importanza speciale al trentesimo giorno (cfr. nota 6) era in certa misura imitato dagli Ebrei. N. Brüll *Die talmudischen Tractate über Trauer um Verstorbene*, in « *Jahrb. für Jüd. Geschichte u. Literatur* » 1874, pp. 14, 51-52. Brüll cita espressamente il caso di Gesù. Per la cura nel prevenire le omissioni nell'accertamento della reviviscenza (c'era una casistica in merito), cfr. altresì Sem. VIII, Tosefta, Shab. II 10, Talm. Bab. Shab. 32a. Perles, *Die Leichenfeierlickeiten im nachbibl. Judenthum*, in « MGWJ » 10 (1861), p. 345 ss. S. Klein, *Tod u. Begräbnis in Palästina zum Zeit der Tannaiten*, Berlin 1908. (Cfr. « REJ » 60, 1910, pp. 110-113). F. I. Grundt, *Die Trauergebraüche der hebräer*, Leipzig, 1968, p. 22. S. Lieberman, *Some Aspects of After Life in Early Rabbinic Literature*, in H. A. *Wolfson Jub. Vol.*, Gerusalemme 1965, sezione inglese II, p. 495 ss. (cfr. nota 32).

9 Derrett in « Downside Review » 296 (1971), pp. 225-232.

10 Derrett, *Law in the New Testament*, London 1970, p. 454.

11 K. Kohler, in *Jewish Encycl.* III (1925), p. 434. Benché il Targum interpreti il testo ebraico di Num. 16, 29 come riferentesi al decreto emanato contro Korah e i suoi, non è impossibile riferire il testo masoretico (e i Settanta) alla pratica di ispezionare i morti. Un rabbino di Firenze nel 1798 diede disposizione nel suo testamento che non dovesse essere sepolto prima della scadenza di due giorni (Perles, op. cit., p. 353, nota 14).

12 *Mishnah*, Ahalot. Maimonide, Codice X 1.

13 A. C. Celsus, *De medicina* II 6, 13-16. Celso era contemporaneo ma più anziano di Gesù.

14 Sem. VIII 1 (cfr. 8).

15 Rinvii in *Law in The New Testament* cit., p. 300, nota 3.

16 Petrus Forestus, *Observationum et Curationum Medicinalium*, XVII, obs. 9, Francofurti 1634, 112: *qui non statim sepeliendi XXVII obs. 27.*

17 Forestus, op. cit., XVII, obs. 9: *locum mutavere, atque ita miserrime mortuae inventae sunt.*

18 Ivi (48 ore). La sepoltura di Gesù durò al massimo 36 ore e la sua reviviscenza, quale ne fosse la modalità, avrebbe potuto prodursi assai prima. Se nella tomba filtrava abbastanza aria da consentire ad una persona inattiva di viverci, non c'era alcuna scusa per sollevare la pietra (opera vietata di sabato) fino al tramonto del sabato. Poté emergere dalla tomba in un'ora qualsiasi del sabato sera. Ci si può domandare: « Come risorse dunque *il terzo dì*? », dato il principio rabbinico ben noto (riferito al lutto) che « parte d'una giornata si considera come giornata intera ».

19 « The Times », 14 aprile 1972 (Ruth Young, di 36 anni, rivisse il 13 aprile, morì il 14-15 aprile). « Statesman » (India), 29 luglio 1972 (fatto accaduto a Chirayinkill vicino a Trivandrum il 24 luglio 1972).

20 La storia di Ernest Priest riferita nel « Daily Mail », 7 ottobre 1972, p. 15. La storia dell'uomo inghiottito da una balena e poi riemerso vivo è riferita da Hastings, *Dictionary of the Bible*, II 750b (episodio del 1891, raccontato dalla « Neue Luth. Kirchenzeitung » 1895, p. 303 ss.).

21 Forestus, ibidem, obs. 9: *septuaginta propterea et duas horas antequam*

humentur decrevere: paria quoque intervalla debent iis, qui animo deliquere sine manifesta causa. È di notevole interesse che Rabbi (R. Judah I, c. 190 d. C.) proibì che i morti fossero sepolti prima di tre giorni dalla morte. Tuttavia i più erano tumulati il primo giorno. *Mishnah*, Sanh. VI 5. Talm. Jer., Hor III 48a. Sul funerale affrettato prima del sabato, vd. Talm. Bab., Shab. 94b, Ket. 20b.

22   *Leggi*, II 12, 531 (= XXII 958-9). Dato che occorre distinguere fra il coma e la morte, il terzo dì è un intervallo adeguato.

23   La storia di Platone (*Rep.* X 614B) si riferisce a una sospensione dell'animazione (trad. di Giuseppe Fraccaroli 1932, p. 433): «che tempo già fu, morì in battaglia, e come si levano i cadaveri dopo dieci giorni già putrefatti, fu tolto su intatto, e, portato a casa per fargli il funerale, il duodecimo giorno, quando era già sulla pira, tornò a vita, e risorto raccontò quello che laggiuso aveva visto». Er era un orientale: Clem. Aless. *Strom.* V 710 (cfr. Lc. 3, 25). Il mito di Er dovette essere noto all'autore di Lc. 16, 31. Vd. Plutarco, *Moral.* 740B. Valerio Massimo, I, VIII, ext. 1.

24   Plinio, *Nat. Hist.* VII 173-9. M. Valerio Messala Rufo (c. 103-27/26 a. C.) era evidentemente un uomo serio e fedegno (*Pauly* III 1243, n. 10) Anche il racconto di Varrone è probabilmente degno di credito.

25   *Aviola consularis in rogo revixit; similis causa in L. Lamio praetorio viro traditur.*

26   *... nisi quod naturae opera, non prodigia, consectamur.* Alla fine della storia di Gabieno, che certo non morì realmente se non dopo la sua profezia.

27   Valerio Massimo, *Factorum et dictorum memorabilium* I, VIII (*de miraculis*) 12, Proclo (410-85 d.C.), *in remp.* II (ed. Kroll 1901, 113-116, 122). Cleonimo fu portato a seppellire il terzo dì e rivisse (p. 114). Eusebio, *Hist. Eccles.* III 39, 25 (ed. Dindorf, IV 134). Si può di qui trapassare in un culto, cfr. V. MacDermot, *The Cult of the Seer in the Ancient Middle East*, London 1971, pp. 126, 217 (non tiene conto di riviviscenze naturali).

28   Apuleio, *Florida* XIX. Le obbiezioni degli eredi danno un tocco comicorealistico. Celso riferisce il caso di Asclepiade, medico famoso del I secolo, suo contemporaneo. Il medico Antigono domanda (in Luciano, *Philops.* 26) che cosa ci sia di straordinario nella riviviscenza, affermando di aver assistito un uomo rivissuto dopo essere stato sepolto per venti giorni. L'equilibrio lucianeo fra verità e scherzo è celebre.

29   Filostrato, *Vita di Apollonio Tianeo* IV 45. Brevemente citato da R. Bultmann (*History of the Synoptic Tradition*, trad. ingl., pp. 233-234).

30   οὐχ ἀπέθανεν ἀλλὰ καθεύδει (Mc. 5, 39c). Nota in Mc. 5, 23a ἐσχάτως ἔχει, e l'evidentemente errato ἀπέθνησκεν (cfr. Lc. 8, 49b). Cfr. il realistico δοθῆναι αὐτῇ φαγεῖν (Mc. 5, 43b) e il meno soddisfacente Gio 11, 44c il notevole ἔχετέ τι βρώσιμον ἐνθάδε; (Lc. 24, 41b soltanto).

31   L'azione di Gesù è (1) quella attribuita al Messia in Aggadat Shir, VII 44 (L. Ginzberg, *Legends of the Jews*, IV, Philadelphia 1933, p. 234; VI, p. 340), (2) una riproduzione degli atti di Elia (I Re, 17, 20) e di Eliseo (II Re, 4, 34-5) riferiti in Ebr. 11, 35 come resurrezione, ma nel testo masoretico, entrambe le volte, indicati come riviviscenze. W. L. Knox, *Some Hellenistic Elements in Primitive Christianity*, London 1944, p. 20, nota 1, chiama l'episodio un tipico *kerigma* in via di sviluppo.

32   Gio., 19, 39-40 forse riflette un dubbio sulla realtà letterale di Mc. 16, 1.

33   Dei crocifissi furono fatti scendere dopo un certo intervallo; uno visse, altri spirarono nonostante le cure mediche: Josephus, *Vita*, 420-21.

34   Mc. 15, 44.

35   Gio. 12, 9-11.

FURTHER ANNOTATIONS

Tit. Entitled 'The resurrection of Jesus' the article contains material concerning several connected matters. A short study is made of instances of resurrection or revival from death or apparent death as these appear in the New Testament. It cannot be taken that the authors were unaware of the possibilities of comparison with the case of Jesus himself. The comparisons are illuminating. The case of Lazarus stands apart from the rest (but how often the gospel of St. John calls for such a comment!). Generally it would be true to say that revivals as known in the New Testament do not suggest immortality, though, in the popular mind, they would have a bearing upon it. On the other hand the miracle-worker whose 'trick' it was to recognise persons wrongly diagnosed as dead was no stranger to the life of the time, nor to legend.

It is very much to the point that (i) revivals after clinical death occurred in the ancient world and (ii) they were known to occur and were celebrated: Pliny made a list of them known to himself, and his veracity has not been impugned. Furthermore, I find that the theme of revival in the cold tomb such as figures very prominently in Chariton's novel (*Scheintod* is one of the commonplaces of the form, it occurs again in Xenophon Ephesius) implies *the fitness of the idea for entertainment/amusement*. Prof. B.P. Reardon of Bangor kindly informs me that Papanikolaou's *Chariton-Studien*, which places Chariton in the mid-1st cent. B.C., could be misleading, and he himself prefers a dating of A.D. 25-75. See Giangrande at *J.H.S.* 1974, 197. But even if we assume that Chariton was well known only after A.D. 30, there remains the fact that most of his themes were in existence before him and taken over by him. It is unlikely that he invented Callirhoe's experience, but even if he did, his work proves the entertainment-value of the idea. No author of *c*. 70-100 could be unaware of this!

The concept of revival from death, coupled with subsequent metempsychosis, is very ancient, and extremely widely known before, during, and after the time of Christ: see the instance of Euphorbos/Pythagoras (references in *Der Kleine Pauly* II, 432).

A very famous example of revival from death is the Bhowal Sannyasi case: the facts are conclusively accepted by the Privy Council in *Srimati Bibhabati* v. *Ramendra Narayan* (1946) Law Reports 73 Indian Appeals 246, 249-50, 260-1 (see also 1942, 47 Calcutta W. Notes, 13, 26-7). That the ancient world was well aware of such possibilities is proved by the question whether a testator's will is rendered void by his resurrection (reference to commentaries on Justinian, Dig. 24.3.31 in Julius Clarus, *Sent.* III. *Test.* qu. 86: *de raro contingentibus*). Modern discussion arises from the question of organ-transplants: doctors cannot diagnose death perfectly in all cases. A friend of mine relates how he drove his mother in his car, found her to be dead, covered her up, and when she had been in the mortuary for a while she revived. A recent newspaper article by a physician relates, "... there are sources of error. Overdoses of drugs and severe cold can depress brain stem function to give the appearance of death. For that reason old people may sometimes appear dead when they are actually hypothermic, and it is an explanation of why a young woman who was found on a beach and given up for dead came to life when she 'warmed-up' in the mortuary". The legal problem, which is no joke, is probably best answered pragmatically by saying *non videtur mortuus qui tam citò resuscitatus est* (gloss on Dig. I.3.4, ed. Lyons

1627, I, col. 34; cf. Dig. I.3.6, referred to at Dig. 5.4.3). I suspect that research into the operation of the thalamus gland will reveal the two-way movement sustaining, or, as the case may be, depressing signs of life.

In the present article I emphasise the Jewish custom of tomb-visiting, which was professedly based on the possibility of premature burial.

The point of the article is that, knowing that a romantic revival was likely to be ridiculed, and that persons who actually revived were no better than they had been previously, the evangelists must have 'watched their step' a great deal more carefully than we usually assume, and were constrained much more (for all their deviations) to relate their material to a factual reminiscence than is usually supposed. The reader is then referred back to the second part of the immediately previous chapter.

KOPBAN, O EΣTIN ΔΩPON

It is said that Jesus' comments (Matt. xv. 4–6, Mark vii. 9–13) are unfair, or incompetently reported.[2] It is desirable to clarify the practice and the law to which he referred.

There were two kinds of vows in which the word *ḳorbān* (properly, gifted) or its euphemistic substitutes like *ḳonām*[3] figured. In the first the votary (*middar*) dedicated to God some property of his. He could dedicate future assets, but he could not dedicate something which he did not own or would never own.[4] The second type of vow was a vow of abstinence; the votary vowed to abstain from what would otherwise become his property: he said that the designated asset would be to him *as if it were* dedicated to God, and so hypothetically the property of the Temple.[5] In the second case the practical meaning is simply 'I repudiate it. It is extremely repugnant to me.'

---

[2] G. W. Buchanan, 'Some vow and oath formulas in the New Testament', *H.T.R.* LVIII (1965), 319–26, is ingenious but misleading. He refers to Belkin (below). J. H. A. Hart, 'Corban', *J.Q.R.* XIX (1907), 615–50, is unsatisfactory. C. G. Montefiore, *Synoptic Gospels* (London, 1909), I, 164–6, relies on post-Tannaitic usage. J. Mann, 'Oaths and vows in the synoptic Gospels', *Am. J. Theol.* XXI (1917), 260–74. S. Belkin, *Philo and the Oral Law* (Cambridge, Mass., 1940), 162, reporting the view of A. Wünsche, *Neue Beiträge*, p. 13. J. Klausner, *Jesus of Nazareth* (trans. Danby, 1925), p. 306. S. Leibermann, *Greek in the Jewish Palestine* (New York, 1942), pp. 129–32. G. M. Lamsa, *Gospel Light...from Aramaic and Unchanged Eastern Customs* (Philadelphia, 1939), p. 186 (interesting, but out of focus).

[3] Mishnah, *Ned.* I, 2; b. Shev. 20*b* = Soncino translation, p. 106.

[4] Mishnah, *Ned.* II, 5, III, 2; b. Ned. 42*a* = Sonc. 135; b. Shev. 25*a* = Sonc. 131. Mishnah, *B.Ḳ.* IX, 10 is a neglected passage. But it appeared in J. Bonsirven's index: see his *Textes Rabbiniques* (Rome, 1955), § 1645.

[5] Montefiore and Mann deceived T. W. Manson (*Teaching of Jesus*, 316 ff.) amongst others. A real dedication was envisaged. Unless the property were redeemed it could not be enjoyed without 'trespass'.

The ancient oaths called *ḳorbān*[1] fall into this category, because the form of imprecation was that, if the testimony was not true, a benefit was forsworn which the witness might otherwise lawfully have had from wife or child. Plainly this was a Jewish euphemistical manner of calling God to witness, with a characteristic allusion to property.

After the Temple fell a change took place. Previously there must have been machinery (not necessarily efficient machinery) whereby genuine vows were received periodically.[2] The Temple treasury, being in the nature of a trust, cannot have been indifferent to vows of money or money's worth, and rumours would have been followed up closely. After the fall of the Temple some of the charitable aspects of its work remained. In expectation of its being rebuilt people kept safely property they had vowed to its use.[3] When it at length became obvious that the Temple would not be rebuilt the first type of vow gradually became a fossilized residue of what for long had been a real feature of Jewish legal and social life. Pharisees never ceased to take it seriously, as Mishnah tractate *Neḏariym* proves.

The social aspect obviously lies at the root of Jesus' comment. Ancient, like contemporary, oriental societies were built upon reciprocal bonds between husband and wife, parent and child, brother and brother.[4] Tensions built up, and explosions occurred. A means was found whereby one could control the demands of relatives, friends, and associates.[5] Injunctions against molestation could not, after all, be obtained at law. Superstitious sanctions were appropriate. 'I will have nothing more to do with you' took the form of such solemn refusals to give, or to take. Food, drink, residence, and sexual intercourse figure in this, because they are the elements of social belonging.

Evidence about the use and development of the second category of vow, that of abstinence, must be put to one side. We are concerned only with the first type. *A* (the *middar*) said to *B* (the victim, called *muddar*), 'Whatever you might otherwise have benefited (i.e. received as a benefit) from me is *ḳorbān*'. Thereupon, while the Temple still stood, he became liable to pay the value of what the *muddar* might otherwise have had to the treasury.[6]

Let us suppose that a *muddar* sues his *middar* for maintenance. The court, unwilling to encourage light vows (especially those taken in a fit of bad

*

---

[1] Josephus, *c. Ap.* I, 166 f. (Niese), Loeb edn., I, 228–30. Discussed at Ned. III, 4 = Sonc. 267. Belkin, p. 158.
[2] Cf. the rule relating to vows of 'valuation'. Mishnah, *Avot*, v, 6 explained by Maimonides, *Code*, VI, III, iii, 14 (trans. Klein, 181). For busybodiness cf. Mishnah, *M. Sheni* v, 8 (Danby, p. 81); *Sheḳ.* I, 1–3. Vows of valuation were a category of *ḳorbān* as Josephus says, *Ant.* IV, iv, 4 (= 72–3. Loeb edn., IV, 511). On Philo's relation to the Torah here see E. R. Goodenough, *Jurisprudence of the Jewish Courts in Egypt* (New Haven, 1929, repr. 1969), pp. 45–6.
[3] See p. 367 n. 9 below. J. M. Allegro, *Treasure of the Copper Scroll* (London, 1960), pp. 53, 148 n. 109 (cf. M. R. Lehmann at *Revue de Qumran* 17, vol. v (1964), 102–4).
[4] Blackmail by use of the formula is illustrated at b. Ned. 27a = Sonc. 69.
[5] Philo's analysis is just: *De Leg. Spec.* II, 16–17. He does not contemplate the annulment of vows. Belkin, 159–60, 165 (does he represent Philo correctly?).
[6] Mishnah, *Ned.* IV, 9; *Arak., passim.*

temper), will insist that the amount which would otherwise have been decreed in the plaintiff's favour must be paid to the Temple. Such suits could not be brought by any persons other than those entitled to maintenance,[1] and the wife[2] and parents[3] are the obvious examples. But the suit would turn out to be infructuous. The *middar* might conceivably be flogged to remind him of his duty:[4] but if he were provoked even this is uncertain. Meanwhile the vow must be paid, as biblical law directs.[5]

Could such vows be annulled? Priests were authorized to annul vows provided God were satisfied in some other way.[6] Some priests might have thought rash vows hard on the unfortunate wives or parents, and might have found a way out of their difficulty—but no evidence of this has survived. The Pharisees, as is known, held that oaths and vows could be annulled by a sage or a court of three.[7] In their view, provided the *middar* came or was brought before them, he could be persuaded that the vow conflicted with his duty under the biblical law to maintain dependants.[8] If he agreed, the vow could be annulled, and the *muddar* could consume the property in question without committing a sin. This system was not universally accepted in Jesus' time, and where it was available there was no question of compulsory release from a vow, which in fact is an absurdity. The Mishnah clearly shows that all vows of dedication inhibited the *middar* as well as the *muddar* from enjoying the property.[9] The *middar*, by expressing his uncharitable intention, excluded everyone from enjoying the property, including himself. The *middar* could not be forced to abjure.[10]

---

[1] Cf. the report of Origen, below.   [2] b. Ket. 70a = Sonc. 434.   [3] See below, p. 368 n. 1

[4] See p. 365 n. 5 above. The view of the sect of the Dead Sea cannot be ascertained. *DR* (= *CR*) xvi, 14–15 (Charles, *Ap. and Pseud.* ii, 834; xx, 11–12) is disputed. Millar Burrows, *Dead Sea Scrolls* (London, 1956), p. 364 avoids the difficulty. Gaster (*Scriptures*, p. 94) has 'polluted food'; Lohse (*Die Texte aus Qumran*, p. 101) has 'Speise (seines) Mu(ndes)'; while Dupont-Sommer (*Les Écrits Esséniens*, 3rd edn. p. 178) and Vermes (*The Dead Sea Scrolls in English*, pp. 109–10) have 'food of his house'. The last attracts, because Mic. vii. 2 ('Each hunts his brother with a net/votive-offering (*ḥrm*)') is appropriate in view of the pun at Mishnah, *Ned.* ii, 5 (which has been missed: but see Liebermann, p. 128). J. A. Fitzmyer, *N.T.S.* vii (1961), 297 ff., at p. 323.

[5] Deut. xxiii. 21, 24; Ps. l. 14, lxxvi. 11; Eccles. v. 4–5; Ecclus. xviii. 22.

[6] So Philo. A. Büchler, *Die Priester und der Cultus in letzten Jahrzehnten des jerusalemischen Tempels* (Vienna, 1895), p. 93 (Jesus was aiming at the priests?).

[7] Belkin, pp. 164 ff. The doctrine was old, if not pre-Pharisaical.

[8] Mishnah, *Ned.* ix, 1 (vows generally). Discreditable vows reflect on the *middar's* parents (Danby, p. 275; Freedman, Sonc. trans. p. 204). *Ibid.* ix, 4 (a valid pattern); b. Ned. 64a = Sonc. p. 205.

[9] Mishnah, *Ket.* vii, 1 (Danby, p. 254): unless an agent is used, where the wife is the *muddar*, the relationship must end—no annulment is contemplated! b. Ket. 70a = Sonc. p. 434 raises Jesus' point (but with reference to the wife, so that it was overlooked). b. Ned. 35a = Sonc. p. 106. *Ned.* vii, 9 (Danby, pp. 273–4). At *B.Ḳ.* ix, 10 (Danby, p. 345) a father disinherits his son, and rights accrue therefrom to third parties. Cf. *Arak.* vi, 3 (Danby, p. 549): one may vow everything and this may well render one's wife and child destitute (but not oneself!). Maimonides, vi, ii, xi, 1–5 (trans. Klein, pp. 101–2); *ibid.* iii, iii, 15 (trans. pp. 181–2). Pending an annulment no use could be made of the property; b. Shab. 127b (Montefiore and H. Loewe, *Rabbinic Anthology*, § 1280). Ned. 35a = Sonc. p. 106: in one view a *ḳonam* loaf cannot be consumed without trespass and a need for redemption (at a period when the title of the Temple could not have been created).

[10] Philo cited at p. 368 n. 1 below. Belkin, p. 165 (antisocial vows might be annulled at the *middar's* application). T. Walker, *The Teaching of Jesus and the Jewish Teaching of his Age* (London, 1923), p. 277, was deceived by Montefiore and R. T. Herford (*ibi cit.*).

Jesus was right. The vow, impeding a claim by a dependant parent, rendered ineffective, nullified *pro tanto*, the biblical obligation to maintain.

'Honour' implies *inter alia* 'maintain when he/she is indigent';[1] 'curse' implies 'abuse', or any diminution of honour.[2] The son has lost his balance, and his vow, ostensibly religious, is unquestionably 'abuse' of the parent. The commandment to pay vows is manipulated to an unrighteous end. Jesus contends that in such a conflict between commandments his rabbinical contemporaries should hold the vow void *ab initio*.[3] The answer commonly made in the Pharisees' defence, that they allowed the annulling of vows, and even encouraged them (cf. the *kol nidre* prayer for the Eve of the Day of Atonement),[4] is not valid because, as the Pharisees admit,[5] the angry or impatient *middar* cannot be forced to recant.

Some miscellaneous points deserve mention before we close this account of *korbān*. The inscription upon the ossuary found in the Kedron Valley[6] should be translated 'All that a man may utilize from the contents of this ossuary is an offering to God from him who is within it'. With profound respect I hesitate to follow even so respectable an authority as Dr Falk,[7] and decline to insert 'like' before 'an offering'. The formula seems not to have been an attempt to make grave-robbers hesitate,[8] but a warning to the pious that utilization of anything ever found there would bring sin, the purpose of the inscription being the same as that of the initial 'ḳ' which, we are told, was put on vessels to warn that their contents had been dedicated.[9] It seems likely that at the time of the interment it was impractical to realize the value of the objects alluded to and pay it to the treasury, or (and here we guess) that the objects were designed to be an offering from the deceased at the resurrection.

Mishnah, *Nᵉdariym*, v, 6 is often referred to.[10] Since it illustrates the outlook of which Jesus complains, and has been misunderstood, it should be repeated and explained.

There was a man in Bet Ḥoron whose father had been forbidden to use his son's property. When the son prepared his own son's marriage, he said to a comrade that he wanted to transfer to him the premises and the meal, in order that his father could come and participate. The comrade answered that if the property was now his he dedicated it to Heaven! The *middar* protested. He had not transferred

---

[1] Derrett, *Law in the New Testament* (London, forthcoming), pp. 109–11.
[2] *Ibid.* pp. 453–4.
[3] Belkin, pp. 161, 168.
[4] *Jewish Encyclopedia, sub v.*
[5] Mishnah, *Avot*, IV, 18 (Danby, p. 455). Manson, *Teaching of Jesus*, p. 318 (Klausner corrected).
[6] J. T. Milik, *Studi Biblici Franciscani, Liber Annuus* (Jerusalem) VII (1956/7), 232–9 (not seen); *Rev. Bibl.* LXV (1958), 409; J. A. Fitzmyer, *J.B.L.* LXXVIII (1959), 60–5.
[7] 'Notes and observations on Talmudic vows', *H.T.R.* LIX (1966), 311–12.
[8] Superstitious sanctions do not affect them. On the *Diatagma Kaisaros*, J. Irmscher, *Z.N.W.* XLII (1949), 172–84; S. Agourides, *Theol.* (Athens), XXIII (1952), 122–31.
[9] Mishnah, *M. Sheni* IV, 10–11 (Danby, p. 80). *Ḳorbān* = a dedicated object, naturally.
[10] *H.T.R.* LIX (1966) at p. 310.

his property to let it be dedicated. The friend replied, 'You gave me your property only in order that you and your father might eat and drink and be reconciled, while I should be culpable.'[1]

He would be culpable because the vow, even though it was obviously regretted, excluded all persons from ownership of whatever the father might profit from. The overriding demands of peace did not annul that simple fact. And the friend would not connive at an irregularity. The repercussions are just as interesting. The rabbis decreed that thereafter a tacit condition should be read into such colourable donations: the *donee* should not vow them—not that the original vows were null, or could be compulsorily annulled. Yet a *middar might* construe his own act with the strictest possible interpretation, and so circumvent it by ingenious hairsplitting.[2] Or he could use an agent, who was not bound by the vow, it seems.[3] Agents were evidently not always trustworthy, so that the hairsplitting of which the rabbis were evidently proud proves my point: the vow stood. Jesus' outlook, that the vow was void, was much more convenient, and juridically no less respectable.

Origen did some research into what was, by this time, a dark subject (*Hom. in Matth.* xi, 9–10: *PG.* xiii, 929–32). His Jewish informant said that as far as he knew the ḳorbān system was used to put pressure on debtors or parents, by making the first debtors to God instead of the *middariym*, and the second paupers, dependent on the charity-collections instead of their own
* issue directly. The account is garbled, but it consists with what has been explained above.

---

[1] Blackman, *Mishnayoth, Nashim,* iii, 236–7 (Danby, p. 271). Philo states that when it is dedicated it is the property of Heaven: *Hypothetica, ap.* Euseb., *Praep. Evang.* viii, 7 (Loeb edn. ix, 425). Vows of the maintenance of wife and children or servants prevent the *middar* from supporting them until God is propitiated and the votary absolved. The redemption of ḳorbān objects was still discussed as late as b. Yev. 88a = Sonc. pp. 597–8. Belkin, pp. 159, 166.

[2] b. Yev. 71a = Sonc. p. 480. Mishnah, *Ned.* viii, 7.

[3] Mishnah, *Ket.* vii, 1 also *Ned.* iv, 7 (Sonc. p. 137; Danby, pp. 270–1, *q.v.*). b. Ket. 70b = Sonc. pp. 437–8. Compulsory annulment was out of the question.

FURTHER ANNOTATIONS

J.A. Fitzmyer's article (p. [367] n. 6 below) at *J.B.L.* 78 (1959), 60-5 is reprinted at his *Essays in the Semitic Background of the New Testament* (London, 1971), 93-100. It is useful, without going into legal niceties, which latter I regard as novel and essential to unravelling Christ's words.

p. [364], n. 5. But no twofold, fourfold, or fivefold restitution was required in respect of *Heqdēš*. This additional fact about the law of that juridical enclave, the Temple, needs to be borne in mind in reference to Jesus's Cleansing thereof. The sages held that there was no trespass-offering for *ḳônamôt*. The view is certainly illustrated that there could be a trespass if a man said 'this loaf is sacred' and *either* he *or* his neighbour ate it. If he said 'this loaf is to me sacred' *he* would trespass but not his neighbour (b. Shev. 22a, Sonc. trans. 116-17). The ultimate view (against R. Meir) is that he trespasses but his neighbour does not. Where he says 'it is sacred' it can be redeemed.

p. [365], l. 27. Of the greatest importance is a passage of Philo which had escaped my notice: *Hypoth.* VII.3-5 (Colson's trans., ix,424-5). A man could certainly deprive his wife of support by this means. Colson's comment is comical, at p. 539.

p. [367], l. 1. It had escaped me that Jesus's words are a slight adaptation of what is said at Prov. xxviii.24, 'He who robs (probably in the sense of *oppress* as in the Bible and the Dead Sea Scrolls: see B.S. Jackson, *Theft in Early Jewish Law* [Oxford, 1972], 29) (the LXX correctly gloss, 'rejects'!) father and mother and says "it is no sin" is a comrade of a destroyer'. To take 'curse' as implying *deprivation* was so obvious to the ancient Jew that Aquila translated *'āloh* at Hos, iv.2 by *arnēsis* and Symmachus by *omnuōn kai arnoumenos*! On the episode see Jackson, *op. cit.*, 24. There can be no doubt but that Jesus alludes to this piece of wisdom literature as if it were (for his pupils) *halakah*.

p. [367], l. 22-3. Galileans, afraid gentiles or Samaritans would defile dedicated objects due to reach the Temple at Jerusalem, used to prepare them in cleanness and keep them till Elijah returns: b. Ḥag. 25a (trans. Streane, 134-5).

p. [367], n. 8. See A.D. Nock, 'Tomb violations and pontifical law', *Essays* II (1972), ch. 31.

p. [368], l. 22. The poor of good family are said to have received support in secret from a chamber of the Temple (Mishnah, Sheq. V.6) (tradition of late 2nd. cent.): had these 'poor' no sons of their own?

'EATING UP THE HOUSES OF WIDOWS': JESUS'S COMMENT ON LAWYERS?

I did not deal with Mark xii 40 par. in my *Law in the New Testament* (London, 1970), and it should be dealt with. STRACK-BILLERBECK did not deal with it even superficially [1]), and C. G. MONTEFIORE made no attempt to explain the passage [2]). I believe D. DAUBE did not deal with it, and M. GERTNER has dealt with it only in passing [3]). J. KLAUSNER has referred to it with a reference to an interpretation by R. Eliezer of the phrase "plague of the Pharisees" (Mishnah, Soṭāh III. 4), but has otherwise left it unexplained [4]). Old JOHN LIGHTFOOT has something to say on the point (on Matt. xxiii 14 T.R.), but his comment reflects a misunderstanding of the passage, now almost universal. C. SCHÖTTGEN anticipated KLAUSNER with his reference to R. Eliezer's dictum (see below), but otherwise contributed nothing, besides quotations illustrating lengthened and shortened prayers [5]). And WETSTEIN followed him discreetly [6]).

It is not surprising that theologians have not been any better informed. A random list of names reveals that the meaning of Mark xii 40 is as good as lost: C. E. B. CRANFIELD; V. TAYLOR   * (whose treatment resembles NINEHAM's, below); A. E. J. RAWLINSON (honestly, he says "It is not known in what precise way the

---

[1]) P. BILLERBECK at STRACK-BILLERBECK, *Kommentar zum Neuen Testament aus Talmud und Midrasch*, I (Munich, 1924/1961), 33.

[2]) *Synoptic Gospels* I (1909), 294.

[3]) "The terms *pharisaioi, gazarenoi, hupokritai* . . .", *B.S.O.A.S.* 26, pt. 2 (1963), at p. 247 n. 9.

[4]) *Jesus of Nazareth* (New York, 1959), 214 n. 70. Either KLAUSNER, or more probably his translator, misunderstood the passage in question, as if the wicked adviser urged the orphans to compel the widow to maintain them: whereas normally the title to the estate would be in the orphans, not the widow. C. E. MONTEFIORE and H. LOEWE, *Rabbinic Anthology* (Cleveland, New York, Philadelphia, 1960), 487 quote, without amplifying, G. F. MOORE, *Judaism* (Cambridge, Mass., 1958) II, 194.

[5]) *Horae Hebraicae et Talmudicae* (Dresden and Leipzig, 1733), 199-200.

[6]) *Novum Testamentum Graecum* I (Amsterdam, 1751), 482-3.

scribes could be said to *devour widows' houses*".); H. B. SWETE (who actually saw the R. Eliezer dictum without recognising what it signified). D. E. NINEHAM [1]) presents what must be a common understanding of the passage:

"... this may be a self-contained saying with no special reference to the scribes. However, St. Mark is probably right in taking it to refer to them, in which case the point may be that they took large sums from credulous old women as a reward for the prolonged prayer which they professed to make on their behalf. If, however, we take the two parts of the charge in *v.* 40 separately, the second will be another reference to ostentatious and hypocritical exhibitions of piety, while, as to the first, religious leaders in every age have been known to make undue use of their influence over wealthy women in the cause of religious institutions (cf. JOSEPHUS, *Antiquities* xvii, 2, 4 and see ABRAHAMS, *Studies in Pharisaism and the Gospels*, 1, ch. 10). We have, however, no reason to think that this or any other form of 'devouring widows' houses' was common among the scribes, and in general the passage must be regarded as altogether too sweeping and unqualified in its attack on the scribes as a class."

As a matter of fact the meaning of Mark xii 40 (adopted almost without variation in Matt. xxiii 14 T.R. [2]) and Luke xx 47) is plain to the Jewish lawyer, and it is a lawyer's duty to explain it. I should add that I myself long thought that it was a condemnation of lawyers—which it is not—and that theologians omitted to point this out because of the courtesy that one profession owes to another (on the "glass houses" principle)! Had it been a condemnation of lawyers this would not necessarily have been strange: lawyers of all nations indulge in self-depreciatory irony, and their want of reluctance to take a fee is no more remarkable than a dentist's reluctance to take out a bad tooth.

Mark xii 40: οἱ κατέσθιοντες τὰς οἰκίας τῶν χηρῶν καὶ προφάσει μακρὰ προσευχόμενοι. οὗτοι λήμψονται περισσότερον κρίμα.

The word κατεσθίω is a technical term, though, as WETSTEIN showed, it was quite apposite even in classical Greek. οἰκία naturally means "property", but implies immoveable and moveable property indifferently. πρόφασις is something of a problem, in that literally

---

[1]) *The Gospel of St Mark* (London, 1963), 333-334. Vicarious prayer is not well authenticated in Jewish practice.

[2]) In view of G. D. KILPATRICK's animadversions on the subject no one can dismiss any verse of the Textus Receptus, nor any reading in it, out of hand, merely because it does not figure in "better" manuscripts.

it *could* mean "pretext" or "[by way of] deception". κρίμα means either "judgment" or "punishment", and the context shows that it implies divine punishment.

The state of facts to which the saying refers was this. Property had very frequently to be entrusted to trustees, and these, as a class, went by the name ἐπίτροπος, figuring in Mishnaic Hebrew as *apat*ᵉ*ropos*, and otherwise as *epit*ᵉ*ropos*, *apot*ᵉ*ropos*. There were two subdivisions of *epit*ᵉ*ropos*. The first, and privileged, were those appointed by the owner (or previous owner) of the estate (as at Gal. iv 2). It is with these that we are especially concerned now. The second class, less free in their conduct of affairs, were those appointed by courts. The courts were, as often as not, courts of three, or of a selected arbiter of outstanding reputation, since the institution of appointment of *epit*ᵉ*ropos* was an institution of Jewish customary law. The circumstances in which an *epit*ᵉ*ropos* was most frequently appointed were (a) when a husband left instructions that his young or incompetent widow should be cared for by a guardian and committed his estate after his death to that guardian, with instructions as to what was to be done (e.g. if she was to marry again), and (b) when a parent, male or female, left instructions that his or her minor children should be cared for by a particular guardian, and committed his estate to that guardian for the minors' benefit. The Hebrew term for the status is *apat*ᵉ*rop*ᵉ*sūt, epit*ᵉ*rop*ᵉ*sūt*, "guardianship". The *epit*ᵉ*ropos* was a guardian, custodian, manager, and trustee, all in one.

An *epit*ᵉ*ropos* had a remuneration depending upon the will of the former owner, or the practice of the court. In all cases he could claim his expenses (ἀναλώματα). The expenses of decently representing the minors or the widow in business on their behalf would be included [1]. Agents claim expenses, and the *epit*ᵉ*ropos* was a kind of agent. No doubt the best way to remunerate any administrator or guardian is to allow him a percentage of the income of the estate. That something like this was compatible with Jewish law, and may well have been practised in the first century, is clear from the mediaeval Jewish law on the subject [2]. We know from Jesus's own comments on stewards, who are agents very close indeed in status and rights to the adminstrators or guardians of the properties of

---

[1] See the passage from b. Giṭṭ. 52b quoted below.

[2] G. HOROWITZ, *The Spirit of Jewish Law* (New York, 1953), 424.

minors or incompetent persons [1]), that improper exploitation of the estate of the legal owner was a common thing.

The *epit^eropos* was suspect, at any time, if he seemed to be flourishing at the expense of the estate. In other words he paid himself his expenses at a lavish rate. The technical Jewish expressions are "he ate and drank and spent", "he covered and clothed himself" [2]). Jesus's parables use this kind of vocabulary: the wicked servant/ steward eats and drinks with the drunken [3]). There is nothing wrong in a guardian's eating at the expense of the minors when he visits them to superintend their affairs, or when he travels to the town to defend their cause in litigation (he should be very sparing in instituting litigation except in defence of their rights) [4]), but if one hears of him that he "eats and drinks" the meaning is that he gets fat at their expense. The same applies to guardians of the estates of widows.

This kind of bad behaviour is well within the terms of Isaiah i 23 and x 2, where the Greek translation of the unique word *shal^emoniym* at i 23, ἀνταπόδομα correctly gives the impression of compensation (Vulg. *retributiones*), i.e. the right to reimburse themselves (liberally) at the estate's expense when accounts will not be scrutinised carefully. How it could be said that the estates of widows are "spoiled" will appear from what I am going to say presently.

Since administrators and guardians were required very frequently, and since they were naturally suspect of dishonesty (the temptation being acute, cf. the situation of Vestrymen in eighteenth and nineteenth century England) the Jewish law was careful to keep them under control. But in all ancient Asian societies the basic proposition was that if you were to have the services of a skilled man you must pay for them at his own valuation. The responsibility rested upon him to value his services modestly and appropriately. No one would be appointed as *epit^eropos* unless he had a reputation for

[1]) HOROWITZ, cited above, gives, at pp. 422-430, a very full view of the institution.

[2]) See below for the phrases used.

[3]) Matt. xxiv. 49. The vocabulary of Luke xvi. 1-2 is relevant. The overtones of Matt. xxiv. 38 are now more apparent. See also 1 Enoch cii 9 (R. H. CHARLES, *Apocrypha and Pseudepigrapha*, Oxford 1913/1968, II, 274).

[4]) The *baraita* at b. Giṭṭ. 52a puts it as strongly as forbidding him to commence suits on their behalf, but this could not be taken literally, or it would menace the institution of guardianship itself.

piety, for fear of Heaven, since God alone knows whether fish in
water drink, or whether administrators indulge in peculation. If a
man is appointed by the court the court may remove him on suspicion alone. It may also submit him to an oath that he has not
robbed the estate. But it will be extremely reluctant to do this,
because if it is done often no one will accept guardianship or administration of an estate. If, on the other hand, the former owner,
father, or husband, appointed a chosen person by will or disposition
inter vivos, the court will not remove him except for proved dishonesty, nor will it in any case submit him to an oath.

Thus, since people were always on the look-out for suitable
trustees or administrators, there had to be a supply of "trustworthy" people who were known to fear Heaven. A suitable way of
advertising one's fitness to take an oath, if called upon, or fitness
to be excused an oath in any event, was public knowledge that one
was often in the presence of God, calling upon him for blessings, in
particular for release from the wiles of the evil one! That long
prayers were a sign of piety was a notion which even Christians
could not eradicate (Martyrdom of Polycarp vii 2-3). Thus it makes
perfect sense that men skilled in legal matters, adept in managing
affairs in and out of the courts that functioned in Palestine, should
take great care to be seen at prayer, since to be appointed *epit^eropos*
in a number of estates brought in, at the least, a certain income
(provided they were not too poor nor too few in number, and
especially if the estates were disputed and difficult to manage so
that care and time had to be expended), and what was as good as
income, namely the prestige of being trusted to look after the
helpless. In the ancient world, as in modern Asia, prestige was not
merely as good as money—it was better.

The sarcastic dictum of R. Eliezer relates to lawyers' oppor-
tunities of interfering, and so gaining means of claiming expenses.
The circumstances were interesting, though not precisely relevant [1].
The family concerned consisted of orphans and a widow, probably
their step-mother. There was no *epit^eropos* appointed. It seems that
they complained that she was wasting the estate with excessive
maintenance claims. They were told what to do. "You could pretend
to sell the estate. She will then be forced to demand her *ketubah*
(dower), and you can then pay this to her. Thereafter she will be

---

[1] Jerusalemite Talmud on Mishnah Soṭāh III. 4, j. Soṭ. f. 20a, translated
by M. Schwab, *Le Talmud de Jérusalem*, VII (Paris, 1885) 262-3.

able to claim no maintenance from you, and you can give up the plan of selling." They did this, and the trick worked. The widow complained. But, since all parties acted within their rights, nothing could be done about it. A perfectly righteous rabbi might well be tempted to offer to be appointed *epiteropos*, and might put through a fictitious sale on the orphans' behalf, naming one of his friends as ostensible purchaser: and in these ways it would be possible to slide from mere cleverness into fraud. There were dangers inherent in being a "man of business" according to the pattern established in the schools of the rabbis as we find them in the Talmuds themselves.

To return to our immediate subject, let us notice some passages of Jewish law directly bearing upon it. The vocabulary will attract attention. The Babylonian Talmud, Gittin 52b, contains the following:

"Amram the dyer was the *apoteropos* of orphans. Relatives came to R. Nahman and complained that he was clothing and covering himself from their assets. He said, 'It is to command respect (*lit.* that his words should be heard)'. 'He eats and drinks out of their money, as he is not a man of means.' 'Perhaps he came upon a valuable "find"'? 'He is spoiling the assets'. He said, 'Bring evidence that he is spoiling them and I shall remove him'. For R. Huna our colleague said in the name of Rab: If a guardian spoils the orphans' property we remove him. For it has been stated: 'If an *apoteropos* spoils the property, R. Huna says in the name of Rab that we remove him, while the school of R. Shilah say that we do not remove him'. The law is that we remove him".

Further discussion on the same page shows that doubts long remained as to the propriety of submitting to an oath an *epiteropos* who was appointed by the owner or former owner of the estate. It emerges that in all cases where the *epiteropos* undertook the task on a fiduciary basis and without remuneration, it was improper to submit him to an oath. The reason could have been stated thus: the man would undertake the onerous responsibility in this way, "if I undertake this it must be on the basis of trust, therefore I shall not be submitted to the indignity of having to take an oath that I have not defrauded the beneficiaries of the trust".

Maimonides, in his *Mishneh Torah* XIII, V, 10. 6-7, explains the position [1]).

---

[1]) I have preferred to follow the translation of A. BLOCH and H. KLEIN, *Maimonides' Laws of Inheritance* (London, 1950) rather than the less literal

6. If the testator has given instructions and said that the minor's share is to be given to the minor to do what he likes with it, he may do so. Similarly, if the testator appoints as trustee for the children a child, a woman, or a slave, he may do so. But the court must not appoint as trustees either a woman, or a slave, or a child or an ignoramus [i.e. a non-Pharisee]—who is presumed to be suspect of committing sins—but must search for a trustworthy person, an honourable man who knows how to turn things to the orphans' advantage and can plead their claims, and is sufficiently capable in worldly affairs to take care of property and make a profit with it. It should then appoint him trustee over the minors, whether he is a non-relative or whether he is a kinsman of the minor, except that if he is a kinsman he must not take over landed property.

7. If the court appoints a trustee and hears that he is eating and drinking and spending more than he is considered to be able to afford, it ought to be suspicious that he may possibly be eating some of the orphans' property, and it must remove him and appoint someone else. If, however, the orphans' father appointed him it should not remove him for he may possibly have found some "find". But if witnesses come and testify that he is causing a loss to the orphans' property the court should remove him. The sages have already decided that they should impose an oath on him, seeing that he is causing a loss. The same applies to a trustee whom the orphans' father appointed when he was of good repute, upright and anxious to fulfil the commandments, but has since become a glutton and a drunkard, and is walking in suspicious paths or is unrestrained in the use of vows and in matters within the "dust" (i.e. scintilla) of theft. The court has a duty to remove him and make him take an oath, and to appoint an honest trustee for the orphans. All these matters are at the discretion of the judge, for each individual court is the father of orphans.

Conclusion

The word προφάσει does not mean "excuse", or "pretext", and the suggestion is *not* that they induce rich widows to make presents to them (as at Jos., *Ant*. XVIII, 81-84: but notice that "expenses" figure there too), but that the motive for their long prayers (which they have an option to make) was to have the opportunity for "eating up" the widows' estates. It is well known that πρόφασις has two meanings, one a true reason or occasion, and the other a false pretext. Most translations and paraphrases of our passage assume that it is the latter, when it is actually the former. It would not make sense to suppose that men made long prayers in order to persuade widows to make gifts to them, and at the same time to say that they are "eating up" the "widows' houses", when that phrase belongs to the sphere, not of parasites in that sense, but of trustees

and more polished translation of J. J. Rabinowitz, *Book of Civil Laws*, Yale Judaica Series, II (New Haven, 1949). But I have introduced a few alterations of a marginal character.

and guardians, who were constantly suspect of misappropriation of others' property, and who obtained the facility to misappropriate it only through their public reputation for piety. Thus we must translate:

"... those that 'eat away' the estates of widows, and, with such an end in view, indulge in lengthy prayers: they shall suffer a heavier sentence".

The "sentence" is appropriate enough. Those who are suspect of exploiting the estate of which they are trustees, and still more those who are proved to have misappropriated the property of the beneficiaries of their trust, are liable to be removed from their trusteeship. This can be applied to mankind at large (cf. the parable of the Wicked Vinedressers). In the case of the would-be pious (not necessarily scribes only) a human court can remove them and order them to make restoration and, we may presume, an added proportion of the amount stolen would have to be paid—though this is not certainly established as juridical practice in this connection. But it was a sufficient penalty to remove the man. Once removed from his position of $epit^eropos$ in regard to one estate he would never thereafter be appointed to another! But there is a higher court, Jesus indicates, in which they will receive more condign punishment. It is not sufficient to make a parade of piety when the fruits of ostensible righteousness, namely responsibility and trust, are in fact abused.

Much the same point of view is actually expressed in a text which circulated in Hebrew, and possibly even in Greek, before St. Mark's gospel was composed. The *Assumption of Moses*, which CHARLES dated between A.D. 7 and 30, is to be attributed, says EISSFELDT, to not long after 4 B.C.[1]). DUPONT-SOMMER is of the view that the book was written in Essene circles (i.e. those connected with the Dead Sea sect), and EISSFELDT does not contradict this [2]). The author is speaking of "impious" men of professed piety and fastidiousness who are "devourers of the goods of the poor(?) saying that they do so on the ground of their justice, but to destroy them ..." (vii 6-7). Approximately the same attitude, the same criticism appears in the *Psalms of Solomon*, which is usually dated 63-30 B.C. There, apart from accusations of trouble-making and

---

[1]) O. EISSFELDT, *The Old Testament* (Oxford, Blackwell, 1966), 624.
[2]) A. DUPONT-SOMMER, *Les écrits Esséniens découverts près de la mer morte* (Paris, 1968), 308. For EISSFELDT, see last n.

adultery, a clear reference is made to unrighteous dealings with the property of orphans (iv 11-13), indeed in such a manner as to suggest that the suspicion was commonplace. R. H. CHARLES was aware of the relationship this had to Mk xii 40 ¹), but the point seems to have escaped notice (perhaps because CHARLES' masterpiece was never provided with a scriptural index).

¹) *Apocrypha and Pseudepigrapha* (cited above), II, 419, n. to vii 6.

FURTHER ANNOTATIONS

p. [1], l. 18. J. Jeremias, *New Testament Theology* (London, 1971), 146, says that scribes exploit their knowledge of the law to take advantage of the helpless.

p. [2], l. 23. It would be as well to look into the scribes' long robes, which is done by K. H. Rengstorf at *Abraham unser Vater. Festschrift Otto Michel* (1963), 383.

p. [3], l. 6. On the *epitropos* and Mishnah, Gitt. V. 4, see an article by Z. W. Falk at *R.I.D.A.* 18 (1971), 11-23.

p. [4], l. 17. We see from the Targum of Is. x.2 that it is the *goods* of widows which. are the object of attack.

p. [4], l. 23: Is. x.2 suggests judges appointing their friends as administrators for widows.

p. [5], l. 1. Abu Yusuf is reported to have said, 'To enter upon executorship for the first time is a mistake, for the second a fraud, and for the third a theft'.

p. [5], l. 6. No accounts may be required in charity matters from the charity officials or in Temple property matters from the treasurers: b. B.B. 9a.

p. [5], l. 22. An actual example of a blind man reciting prayers (Salve Regina) to cheat people, e.g. woman, of money is provided by the anonymous author of Lazarillo de Tormes (1554) (see D. Rowland's translation, 1568/9, 1586, available in J. B. Trend, *Spanish Short Stories of the Sixteenth Century*. Oxford, 1928, 6, 8). But though the blind man had learnt a great deal he was not a scholar, a scribe.

p. [8], l. 6. Objection has been taken to my 'with such an end in view'. *Prophasei*, preceded by *kai* is indeed a problem. The possible meaning 'openly', 'with a good style' (see Lampe's *Patristic Greek Lexicon*) is far too late and hardly meets the case. Perhaps 'with an ulterior motive' expresses the meaning better. *Prophasei* is a conventional antithesis to *phusei*. It can hardly mean 'as an excuse for eating' because even the longest prayers would hardly entitle one to an extra meal. It implies advertisement. They were professional trustees and they advertised their probity. They had time to. We may take note that at Phil. i.18 *prophasei* is opposed to *alētheia*: both *prophasin* and *prophasei* are in fact used to mean 'as a pretence'. They pretend to be pious, and in order to keep up this reputation they indulge in long prayers. An excellent example of *prophasei* meaning 'under cover of...' occurs in Aeschines *c. Timarch*, 40. The youth wanted a very different sort of life, for which he was well enough qualified, but he had to pretend to be a student or apprentice. The Jewish law will not allow workmen to prolong religious observances and prayers during the working day, for this *could* serve as a means of cheating the employer of his profits: they would thus be suspect of praying *prophasei*, 'motivatedly' (not with the purpose the action itself suggested).

It has crossed my mind that conceivably the trustees, unable to obtain justice for their clients in the ordinary course, especially in state courts, would devote their professional time to long prayers to Yahweh, the one who provides *ekdikēsis* for widows against their *antidikoi* (see above, p. 41). 'Your case is hopeless: only a miracle can save it and you from ruin!' A reputedly holy person modestly admitted that he was no prophet nor son of a prophet, but when he prayed fluently he knew his prayer (for recovery from sickness, etc.) would be answered (Vermes, *op. cit.*, 75). Since the prayers of our heroes would be motivated by claims for time spent, and not by pity for the widow who could afford the same, they would indeed be prayers said *prophasei*. I leave this intriguing conjecture, which has an aroma of the authentic, for the scholar to consider.

La parabola delle vergini stolte

La debolezza della teologia moderna si mostra nella sua incertezza intorno ai fatti dei Vangeli. Coloro che lavorano sullo sfondo ebraico (come J. Jeremias e W. D. Davies) non sono liberi da preoccupazioni teologiche e i laici che trattano, ad esempio, il processo di Gesú spesso ignorano le implicazioni teologiche dei ragguagli evangelici. Esistono parecchi fatti nel testo che tuttora aspettano di essere scoperti e sviscerati. Un caso che colpisce e che illustra questo stato di cose è l'esegesi contemporanea, o meglio i tentativi esegetici intorno alla parabola delle vergini o delle dieci fanciulle (Mt. xxv 1-12).

Una ricerca come la presente deve dar conto dei suoi fini. Chi scrive parte da un'opinione teologica, ma ritiene vana la teologia qualora i testi fondamentali non siano compresi nel loro contesto giudaico del I secolo. Ci dobbiamo trasferire in una strada, o nella casa o accanto al lago dove Gesú insegnava e cosí forse capiremo che cosa stesse dicendo. Nel caso di questa parabola, anzitutto bisogna tentar di capire la controversia cui la parabola risponde. Sappiamo che san Matteo la usò con un fine in mente, ma questo non ci deve impedire di capirla come fu concepita, a parte l'uso che l'evangelista ne fece. Certo dobbiamo domandarci se la alterò o complicò. Subito ci appare che xxv 13 non ne fa parte e che fu aggiunta o da san Matteo o dalla sua fonte. Ci sono altre parole nella parabola che debbono essere analizzate (si vedano in seguito le note) per stabilire se sono necessarie alla storia oppure se sono aggiunte allegorizzanti. Tanto per anticipare le conclusioni, si scoprirà che la parabola non ha tratti superflui anche se il suo vocabolario fu modificato quanto bastava per sottolineare le allusioni. Per il credente e lo storico delle religioni essa torna in vita una volta che si sia ricuperato il suo contesto intellettuale, il cosiddetto *Sitz im Leben*.

Seguirò lo schema messo a frutto in *Law in the New Testament* (1970) e nei saggi successivi sulle parabole, dando in primo luogo un ragguaglio della storia quale racconto di fatti, di natura secolare. Quindi esaminerò i significati midrascici, cioè le allusioni e le interpretazioni scritturali, dirette e indirette, celate nella parabola e alla fine enuncerò il suo significato quale mi appare. Spero che nessuno si offenda per il contenuto di questa ultima parte e non dedurrà esclusivamente da essa che debbano essere errati i miei argomenti e la mia ricostruzione.

Le vergini come attrici di un piccolo dramma

Mai come in questo caso è necessario stampare il testo quale dovette essere cantato nella chiesa giudeo-cristiana per la quale san Matteo scriveva. L'incantamento, la solennità serafica della parabola risuona tremendamente impressionante, bene in linea con la sua situazione, in questa parte escatologica del Vangelo. Una volta ristampato, il testo ci dice da solo quali sono le parole importanti. In ogni riga la prima parola (salvo articolo o preposizione) è importante, come anche l'ultima, salvo un possessivo enclitico (*sua loro*) che è un ebraismo e forse si pronunciava senza sottolineare (tuttavia le righe 5, 8 e 14 paiono ribadire il fatto che le torce appartenevano a chi le reggeva). L'ultima parola d'ogni riga è accentuata (con questa riserva) nell'ondeggiare della voce, terminando in un tono piú o meno alto a seconda del contesto. Basta una modesta conoscenza del greco per capire che san Matteo avrebbe potuto esprimere il contenuto con parole diverse o con le stesse parole disposte in diversi ordini. Se scelse a questo modo (o se cosí scelse la sua fonte), vuol dire che dobbiamo annotare con somma cura quelle accentuazioni. E dobbiamo fingere di non aver mai udito prima questa parabola, e di non conoscerne la fine allorché ne ascoltiamo l'inizio.

τότε ὁμοιωθήσεται ἡ βασιλεία τῶν οὐρανῶν

δέκα παρθένοις, αἵτινες λαβοῦσαι τὰς λαμπάδας ἑαυτῶν
ἐξῆλθον εἰς ὑπάντησιν τοῦ νυμφίου.
πέντε δὲ ἐξ αὐτῶν ἦσαν μωραὶ καὶ πέντε φρόνιμοι.
αἱ γὰρ μωραὶ λαβοῦσαι τὰς λαμπάδας αὐτῶν
οὐκ ἔλαβον μεθ᾽ ἑαυτῶν ἔλαιον.
αἱ δὲ φρόνιμοι ἔλαβον ἔλαιον
ἐν τοῖς ἀγγείοις μετὰ τῶν λαμπάδων ἑαυτῶν.
χρονίζοντος δὲ τοῦ νυμφίου
ἐνύσταξαν πᾶσαι καὶ ἐκάθευδον.
μέσης δὲ νυκτὸς κραυγὴ γέγονεν,
Ἰδοὺ ὁ νυμφίος, ἐξέρχεσθε εἰς ἀπάντησιν αὐτοῦ.
τότε ἠγέρθησαν πᾶσαι αἱ παρθένοι ἐκεῖναι
καὶ ἐκόσμησαν τὰς λαμπάδας ἑαυτῶν.
αἱ δὲ μωραὶ ταῖς φρονίμοις εἶπαν,
Δότε ἡμῖν ἐκ τοῦ ἐλαίου ὑμῶν,
ὅτι αἱ λαμπάδες ἡμῶν σβέννυνται.
ἀπεκρίθησαν δὲ αἱ φρόνιμοι λέγουσαι,
Μήποτε οὐκ ἀρκέσῃ ἡμῖν καὶ ὑμῖν·
πορεύεσθε μᾶλλον πρὸς τοὺς πωλοῦντας
καὶ ἀγοράσατε ἑαυταῖς.
ἀπερχομένων δὲ αὐτῶν ἀγοράσαι
ἦλθεν ὁ νυμφίος, καὶ αἱ ἕτοιμοι εἰσῆλθον
μετ᾽ αὐτοῦ εἰς τοὺς γάμους καὶ ἐκλείσθη ἡ θύρα.
ὕστερον δὲ ἔρχονται καὶ αἱ λοιπαὶ [παρθένοι] λέγουσαι,
Κύριε κύριε, ἄνοιξον ἡμῖν.
ὁ δὲ ἀποκριθεὶς εἶπεν
Ἀμὴν λέγω ὑμῖν οὐκ οἶδα ὑμᾶς.

Strana storia. Le fanciulline, di circa 12 anni, fanno una cosa
molto comune. Lo sposo è un giovane ordinario o un ragazzo di
18-20 anni. L'estinguersi delle lampade è una faccenda molto comune. Le fanciulle stolte ci rimisero ben poco. L'avvenimento era
una cosa di tutti i giorni. Proprio mercé il contrasto fra le circostanze ordinarie e la lezione spirituale il maestro nostro Signore
crea un'impressione orribile, cara allo *humour* acidulo degli Ebrei.
È esattamente come il finale della parabola dell'abito nuziale: l'im-
postore fu buttato fuori [1]. Ne risulta una strana storia, con implicazioni orribili. Ecco i fatti. Dieci fanciulle presero le lampade
che tenevano sicuramente per tali occasioni e uscirono ad accogliere uno (non « lo ») sposo. Cosa abbastanza consueta per delle
fanciulle. Un numero illimitato non sarebbe gradito, e il costume
avrà ridotto la brigata ad un gruppetto che potesse allinearsi sui
due lati del corteo nuziale, illuminandolo e accogliendolo con mo-
stre di gioia. Dieci è un numero adatto per una tale brigata. L'uti-

lità in senso stretto di una tale accoglienza era, per lo sposo
e il suo seguito, trascurabile e il servigio prestato, di nessun conto,
era tuttavia consuetudinario. Le fanciulle erano solite appostarsi
al limite del villaggio dello sposo, forse al riparo del muro, met-
tendo una vedetta, magari un fratellino, col proposito di unirsi
al corteo dello sposo con la sua sposa [2]; con i suoi amici e alcuni
amici della sposa, recandosi poi tutti insieme nella casa dello sposo, preparata per la festa, forse intrecciavano una piccola danza [3],
benché non sia certo che tale fosse l'usanza, ricevevano doni di
dolciumi e quindi se ne tornavano a casa, dove le si aspettava
fino a ore tarde. Credo sia certo che le fanciulline erano dello
stesso villaggio dello sposo e che non erano, in quanto tali, invi-
tate alla festa. Ma, avendo prestato un servizio allo sposo accogliendolo con le lampade, avevano diritto ad una mancia, un pic-
colo compenso. Venivano a prendersi i dolcetti.
    Delle dieci fanciulline, cinque erano stolte ed è il loro com-
portamento che dovrebbe interessarci. Le altre cinque erano intel-
ligenti, prudenti [4]. Le stolte si ricordarono delle lampade ma scor-
darono di portarsi ciò che era necessario per compiere il servizio,
l'olio, mentre le prudenti presero vasetti d'olio insieme alle lampade. Lo sposo mise molto ad arrivare, forse perché indugiò a
lungo con la sposa nella casa del suocero (in certe regioni il ma-
trimonio si consumava lí e non a casa dello sposo) [5], e forse perché c'erano parecchi affari da concludere fra i suoi rappresen-
tanti e i tutori della sposa, in rapporto alla dote e altri provve-
dimenti [6]. Non si sapeva quando il corteo sarebbe arrivato. I suoi
componenti avrebbero potuto essere costretti a nascondersi dai
briganti. Poiché i cortei nuziali incominciavano di notte, non c'e-
ra niente di strano che lo sposo giungesse a mezzanotte [7]. Le fanciulle fecero la cosa piú sensata, si assopirono. Furono destate
di soprassalto: « Ecco lo sposo. Andategli incontro ». Sarà stato
ancora a un miglio di distanza o piú, l'avranno segnalato le torce
ondeggianti. Tutte le fanciulle si levarono, approntarono le lampade, immergendole nei vasi d'olio o versando l'olio su di esse,
e naturalmente le stolte non seppero accendere le loro. Gli stop-
pini sono molto assorbenti [8] e se due sono intinti l'uno dopo l'altro, non basterà l'olio. Le fanciulle stolte, da par loro, chiesero
dell'olio dicendo: « Le nostre lampade sono spente » (o quasi
spente), ma le prudenti rifiutarono, dicendo che temevano non
ci fosse abbastanza olio per entrambi, invitandole ad andare da
« chi vende », cioè da chiunque a quell'ora di notte avesse del-
l'olio in avanzo e fosse disposto a venderlo. Poteva benissimo dar-
si che qualcuno fosse disposto a lasciarsi svegliare a bussi sulla
porta a quell'ora di notte, per un certo prezzo (Is. XXIV 2;

Ez. vii 12-13). E le fanciulle avevano i soldi. Ma quando il corteo arrivò esse erano in giro a tentare, forse senza fortuna, di procurarsi l'olio. Cosí quelle che erano pronte entrarono con lui alla festa e la porta fu chiusa. Dopo un po' vennero le prime e chiesero d'entrare: « Signore, signore, aprici, facci entrare ». Ma lo sposo, l'ospite, frugale interessato a tener lontani i parassiti e i profittatori, grida loro che non le conosce. « Davvero non so chi siate », risponde. La storia non fornisce la finale, e artisticamente ci guadagna. Immaginiamo le stolte che tornano a casa dicendo « che avaraccio! » invece di dare la colpa a loro stesse.

La domanda che subito si affaccia è: perché le stolte non si portarono dietro l'olio? Non ci è data risposta. Dobbiamo sospettare che non ci tenessero alla festa? No di certo.

E allora perché trascurarono di portar l'olio? La risposta piú semplice è forse la giusta. Speravano di ottenere i dolciumi alla festa per sé e perciò non conveniva loro chiedere dell'olio in casa. Le madri avrebbero potuto rifiutarlo. Né potevano andarlo a chiedere in casa dello sposo, perché cosí sarebbe stato estinto il loro diritto di partecipare, che dipendeva dal servizio prestato. Avevano, fra tutte, un po' di soldi, avrebbero potuto comprarsi l'olio per via, andando a raggiungere le altre, però, al momento in cui avrebbero dovuto provvedervi furono negligenti, immaginandosi che le altre che si sarebbero presentate avrebbero avuto dell'olio anche per loro. Forse ogni fanciullina immaginò che il suo fabbisogno d'olio sarebbe stato trascurabile, come gli invitati al Gran Pranzo nessuno dei quali credette che sarebbe stata notata la sua assenza, col risultato che non arrivò nessuno. Nel nostro caso, metà della brigata risultò sprovvista. Non che le fanciulle stolte non volessero eseguire il servizio. Non che fossero ipocrite. Dopo tutto, le lampade se le erano portate. Ma una lampada non serve a niente senza l'olio e questo credevano di ottenere da altri. La loro colpa fu di negligenza, non seppero connettere il desiderio (dei dolciumi) allo sforzo necessario (la provvista d'olio). Erano necessari e le lampade e l'olio. L'uno senza le altre non servivano a niente.

Ma c'è un altro aspetto del racconto. Il corteo nuziale, dal villaggio della sposa alla casa dello sposo, è scortato da torce e da gente carica d'olio e di vino [9]. I fiaschi sgocciolano a mano a mano che il corteo procede, perché vino e olio sono segni di prosperità e fertilità. Ogni sposalizio anche fra gente ordinaria è una ripetizione del dramma cosmico della fertilità e della produzione, della ierogamia che nel mondo antico simboleggiava la compartecipazione del divino al terrestre (l'olio è una materia magica) [10]. Perciò le fanciulle che volevano partecipare al corteo matrimoniale avrebbero dovuto provvedersi di fiaschi d'olio, anche se dentro c'erano poche gocce. Senza le fiasche dovevano sapere d'essere inadatte sul piano simbolico a unirsi al corteo. Ma speravano che sarebbero state provviste di tutto le loro amiche e che questo sarebbe stato sufficiente anche per loro.

Interpretazioni teologiche della parabola

La bibliografia abbondantissima mostra opinioni disparate. Per alcuni è importante il ritardo dello sposo [12]. Si pensa che la storia si imperni sull'idea che lo sposo dovrà per forza tardare. Per altri essa s'incentra sul dramma escatologico [13]. La vita va vissuta in uno stato di costante preparazione, come se s'avvicinasse la fine del mondo. San Matteo è vicino a questa interpretazione. Certuni ritengono che la parabola non riguardi la parusia, il secondo avvento del Signore, bensí la sapienza spirituale che si camuffa come saggezza mondana, nello stile della letteratura sapienziale. I piú credono che la parabola riguardi la parusia [14]: il Cristo verrà a prendersi la sposa, la chiesa, rappresentata dalle vergini e alcune di queste saranno non solo respinte ma maledette. La venuta dello sposo, in tale prospettiva, indica la certezza del giudizio finale e del Banchetto messianico.

Altri ancora la chiamano una parabola di crisi: bisogna imparare a rispondere senza indugio alla chiamata di Gesú (Lettera ai Romani XIII 11) o è troppo tardi.

Nessuna di queste interpretazioni spiega la parabola ed esse sono tutte manchevoli perché trattano parecchi particolari come fossero superflui.

La parabola nel suo contesto midrascico

Quando s'interpreta una parabola bisogna individuare i temi, cosa non sempre chiara a partire dalle sue parole, perché nel tradurre e parafrasare l'Antico Testamento, e nella trasmissione attraverso la quale il Vangelo ci è giunto, molte frasi diverse sono state usate per significare una stessa idea, talché le corrispondenze verbali sono talvolta accidentalmente lacunose.

I temi della parabola si dividono in due categorie, la primaria e la secondaria; le secondarie esistono in vista della spiegazione delle primarie, ma sono esse stesse dotate di senso.

I temi primari sono: 1) il rapporto fra il servizio e il compenso (ad esempio, i lavoratori della vigna), di natura non aritmetica bensí psicologica; 2) il bisogno di luce per onorare chi va onorato; 3) l'attributo della giustizia a chi presta un servizio. Temi secondari sono: 4) l'equilibrio numerico fra prudenti e stolte; 5) il ritardo dello sposo, cioè l'imprevedibilità della prova; 6) l'impossibilità di comprare olio (o la grande difficoltà di comprarlo a quell'ora); 7) la capacità di pagare l'olio, da parte delle stolte, solo che esso si fosse potuto ottenere; 8) la festa e la chiusura dell'uscio.

Il pensiero ebraico vuole che chi rende un servizio abbia diritto ad un compenso anche se non era certa la sussistenza d'un contratto e d'una consuetudine che ne imponesse l'esecuzione o il compenso. *Do ut des.*

La luce simboleggiava la gioia, la festa e l'olio che la nutriva simboleggiavano la pingue prosperità, il profumo e ogni diletto. Una vampa di luce era naturale ad una festa nuziale [15]. Si onora una persona cui vada tributato onore accogliendola con fiaccole. Un salmo ci dice che gli adoratori vanno ad accogliere il Messia, o almeno, cosí s'interpreta [16], e l'accoglienza, di notte, si farebbe con fiaccole. Uno sposo è una tipica persona cui vanno tributate onoranze. Usava coronarlo [17]. Le « figlie di Gerusalemme » debbono uscire ad accogliere Salomone alla sua incoronazione e (o) il dí delle nozze [18]. Ogni bambina in attesa di festeggiare il novello sposo ripeteva un'azione simile a quella con cui si accolse Salomone, il quale, dicono i rabbini, rappresenta il Messia [19].

Ma la vampa di luce, le lampade [20], l'olio, i vasi per l'olio, gli smoccolatoi e altri strumenti per l'illuminazione sono altamente simbolici nella Bibbia. Le fanciulle non rappresentano soltanto « le figlie di Gerusalemme » ma anche i sacerdoti. L'antico testamento ribadisce che il grande candelabro, che rappresenta la Presenza, e che illuminava lo spazio dove Dio stesso accondiscendeva a lasciar pensare di dimorare, e che da allora sempre sarebbe stato nel luogo dove avrebbe dovuto trovarsi l'immagine d'una divinità pagana come segno d'affiliazione culturale, doveva essere accudito in tutti i suoi particolari ed in ogni sua parte [21].

Perché i sacerdoti cosí significavano che, mentre il mondo dorme, per Colui che non si assopisce [22] si svolgono funzioni impeccabili. L'idea di tenere accesa una lampada per onorare chi va onorato è talmente diffusa ed evidente da non aver bisogno di trattazione. La Presenza è significata dalla lampada, ma questa dev'essere accesa e ben fornita d'olio.

S'è visto: le fanciulle stolte non portarono olio nei loro vasi e cosí contravvennero al costume simbolico dei cortei nuziali. Ma la mancanza dei vasi era simbolica anche in un senso midrascico. Perché Eliseo è cosí preoccupato per i recipienti d'olio in 2 Re IV 1-7? Vi si mostra che, se il recipiente è vuoto o quasi (come nel caso delle vergini prudenti), un'abbondanza di fede (come nel caso di Eliseo e della vedova) farà moltiplicare l'olio fintanto che ci sarà un recipiente per riceverlo, cioè la fede della beneficiaria del miracolo ha da essere piena e allora tutte le circostanze le saranno favorevoli, in altre parole la vita si conforma alle esigenze di lei. La storia di Eliseo è una parabola oltre che un mito. Coloro che non portano neanche i recipienti non possono neanche approfittare dell'olio altrui; la vedova ebbe tanta fede da prendere in prestito tanti recipienti, a costo di farsi deridere dai vicini. Come risultato, ella ne ebbe di piú del necessario e lo poté vendere e soddisfare i suoi bisogni.

Se le fanciulle fossero state attente e sincere (è un'idea da sviluppare), il loro olio sarebbe bastato, quale che fosse per essere il tempo d'attesa. Coloro che acquistano l'olio dalla vedova si possono interpretare come gli infedeli, che approfittano della fede dei fedeli, approfittando della loro fortuna e dei loro meriti.

S'è detto. Il servizio vuole un compenso. Ma dovrà essere esclusivamente un servizio personale? Questa è una difficoltà: certe società antiche, ancora tribali, stentano a credere che un compenso possa spettare ad un individuo; coloro che vivono ancora oggi in una vasta famiglia danno per scontato che il guadagno d'un membro vada goduto dall'intero gruppo. È un'idea che si estende facilmente al campo religioso. Il diritto ad un compenso si chiama « merito ». Ci si domanda quale merito consenta di rivendicare il mondo a venire. Dio compensa, ma su quale base? Questo è argomento di altre parabole, specie quella degli operai della vigna. Al tempo di Gesú tre specie di meriti erano fra le aspirazioni e dei pii e del volgo: 1. quello individuale; 2. quello di gruppo; 3. quello degli antenati o dei patriarchi o dei propri figli innocenti. Che si potesse acquistar merito mercé il sacrificio degli innocenti le cui sofferenze (specie la morte prematura) redimono i loro coevi, è un'idea sulla quale Gesú fondò, pare, il suo sacrificio, secondo la spiegazione data da san Paolo [23]. Coloro che a Lui sono uniti condividono il Suo merito. Questa è la dottrina del sacrificio vicariante, che ha basi ebraiche, si ritrova nell'induismo ed è una concezione orientale in genere.

L'idea del merito vicario conforta quanti non sono capaci di acquistare meriti da soli, ma può essere un motivo d'inerzia, di balordaggine e di manchevolezza morale. Perciò il concetto fu continuamente dibattuto nel giudaismo postcristiano e par chiaro che la polemica dovette incominciare fin dal tempo di Gesú [24]. La questione ha basi bibliche ed è stata oggetto di monografie interessanti ed illuminanti. San Giovanni spiega che ai suoi tempi si credeva al peccato vicario [25], anche se la questione era, in sede biblica, controversa. Per farsi un'idea dell'ebraismo normativo occorre partire dal principio che il merito individuale era il piú sicuro [26], ma in contesti poetici e nei discorsi esagerati, l'antica concezione, le cui radici affondano nella solidarietà tribale, riemerge. Non possiamo essere certi che la maggioranza degli Ebrei al tempo di Gesú avesse scartato l'arcaica idea che, se non si riusciva a mostrare il proprio merito personale (ottenuto per esempio col digiuno, la preghiera, la carità e altri atti d'ubbidienza a Dio, come l'esatto adempimento dei precetti), almeno si poteva fare affidamento sul merito dei propri confratelli o dei patriarchi, come Abramo, Isacco e Giacobbe, o perfino su quello dei propri figliolini innocenti.

Coloro che sperano di compiacere qualcuno affidandosi alle risorse dei compagni, come queste fanciulle, si assumono un rischio; il merito dei compagni può non bastare a tutti. Coloro ai quali non basti il merito dei compagni corrono disperati da coloro che ne abbiano in eccedenza, come i patriarchi, sperando di ottenerne, in grazia della consanguineità, una partecipazione. Ma anche se è vero che si può partecipare al merito di coloro che ne traboccano, che ne hanno un tesoro, bisogna essere sicuri che proprio all'istante sia possibile una partecipazione. Anche se si è pronti a una qualche transazione per ottenerlo da coloro che lo detengono, essi possono essere appena appena destati dal sonno e incapaci di rendere partecipi per tempo di ciò che hanno.

Ed ora osserviamo i temi secondari. Non c'è ragione di credere che i bisognosi di merito saranno in numero maggiore di coloro che ne avranno a sufficienza: i numeri si pareggiano. Il ritardo dello sposo non deve significare che si deve agognare invano il Regno, né che il servizio debba durare all'infinito; esso mira a indicare che c'è sempre tempo di rivedere la propria pretesa d'essere meritevoli. Inoltre il paragone delle fanciulle ai sacerdoti è accentuato dall'idea che le prudenti hanno fornito il lume, completo di tutto, per dare il benvenuto alla Presenza, che è ben desta e in movimento, mentre la gente minuta sta dormendo [27]. L'olio è difficile a trovare a mezzanotte, e costerebbe il doppio in un tale frangente. Questo significa che, qualunque merito si rivendichi in base al rapporto coi patriarchi, esso si può riscuotere soltanto nelle « ore d'ufficio », cioè quando debiti e crediti si possono annotare sui registri. Quando le fanciulle si destano siamo alla risurrezione. Il Giudizio incombe, la festa attende le meritevoli. I registri sono chiusi. È troppo tardi.

I patriarchi stessi sono giudicati ed il loro merito non è piú attribuibile ad altri. Le fanciulle avrebbero potuto comprare dell'olio soltanto se ci fosse stato qualcuno a venderlo. Questo è detto molto chiaramente, in modo che la truce parabola non riguarda le persone sfortunate o impedite. Sono chiusi fuori coloro che potendo non fecero. La festa è il Banchetto messianico, e gli esclusi sono gl'indegni. Lo sposo è il Messia, che è anche l'ultimo giudice. Va da sé che solo Iddio è lo sposo di Israele, e Israele fu destato, come vuole la leggenda ebraica, per incontrare lo sposo sul Sinai [78]. È un errore credere che Gesú non pensasse a se stesso come Dio e perciò non potesse essere l'autore dell'immagine dello sposo [29], la quale non si esaurisce nel mito della ierogamia, né nel quadro del Sinai; essa illustra altresí il fatto che l'individuo il quale invoca la grazia (nel caso nostro, i dolcetti vagheggiati dalle fanciulle) non è soltanto uno dei partecipanti alla sacra unione ma anche una specie di servo, il cui ruolo è in funzione di quello d'un superiore. Le fanciulle sperano in una mancia, questo le mette in rapporto col superiore. L'individuo ha rapporto coll'Era messianica come chi spera di avere quanto merito basti per entrarvi.

Il significato della parabola

Poiché il Giudizio finale è miticamente legato all'Era messianica, e questa si può rappresentare come lo sposo (Dio) che finalmente giunge a godere la sposa nel suo Regno [30], e poiché questo impone il secondo avvento di Gesú, che simboleggia tanto nella parusia quanto col suo primo ministero l'arrivo del Regno, la parabola non è escatologica. I riferimenti al sonno e al risveglio (cfr. Mt. XXVII 52) additano chiaramente alla risurrezione dei morti, dopo la quale nessun merito è piú acquisibile. La parabola non concerne la prontezza nell'accogliere il Signore al Suo secondo avvento se non nella misura in cui insegna che per entrare al banchetto bisogna acquistare dei meriti personalmente, e cosí si esige un'attenzione alla situazione individuale. Né è una parabola della crisi nel senso che l'ascoltatore sia chiamato a prendere subito una decisione intorno alla sua condizione, anche se questo non va escluso. È un'insegnamento che mira a inculcare una dottrina teologica.

La parabola insegna che il merito vicario è falso. Non si può fare affidamento sul merito dei propri contemporanei, per meritevoli che essi siano. Anche se ci si può affidare alle promesse fatte ad Abramo, ed ai meriti di Abramo, questo non basta a sciogliere dalla distretta di una morte senza meriti personali. Il merito collettivo postumo è un concetto assurdo. Il mondo a venire non sarà di chi dica: « Sono figlio d'Abramo », questo non basta per entrare nel Regno [31].

Poiché la parabola parla di servigi personali resi ad uno sposo, non getta luce sul problema se Gesú stesso credesse che il suo sacrificio generasse un merito disponibile per il credente. Per commentare questo punto si sarebbe dovuto narrare una storia su uno che visse meritoriamente ed i cui parenti o amici ottennero, in virtú di quei suoi meriti, qualcosa da un terzo.

Ignoro se una tal parabola fu mai narrata da Gesú, non ho incontrato questa idea. Ciò non toglie che essa potesse esserci.

1   Derrett, *Law in the New Testament*, London 1970, pp. 142-143.
2   I testi che danno le dibattute parole καὶ τῆς νυμφῆς non sono errati quanto al significato (le fanciulle non rappresentano collettivamente la chiesa), ma l'aggiunta delle quattro sillabe darebbe una riga di 19 sillabe, che in questo testo sarebbe unica. La sposa è certamente con lo sposo; non è al centro della vicenda, essendo l'escatologia un tema minore.
3   Cosí Jeremias.
4   Le vergini erano scelte come allusioni midrasciche al Salmo XLV 14-15. Cfr. Efes. I 8; Lc. XV 8; Mt. VII 24 (cfr. VII 26), X 16, XXIV 45; I Cor. I 25, 27; III 18, IV 10. Bertram in Kittel, TWNT IV (1942), pp. 837 e 838-842. Si noti Dan. XII 3. Non posso recare riferimenti in proposito, ma le cinque prudenti suggeriscono la mano destra e le cinque stolte la sinistra (Mt. VI 3). Le due mani sono necessarie per ἀπάντησις.
5   In Galilea, come la storia della nascita di Gesù (attentamente analizzata) suggerisce. Cfr. anche Giudici XIV 10; Tobia VIII 19 (cfr. XI 19).
6   Jeremias.
7   Cosí, erratamente, Grässer (*infra* n. 12, a p. 122). *Contra*: Jeremias.
8   La parola λαμπάς indica una torcia (cfr. Bauer-Arndt-Gingrich, *Greek-English Lexicon of the New Testament*, 1957), e suggerisce l'idea di qualsiasi lampada o lume. Il significato primario è spiegato da Jeremias ZNW 56 (1965), pp. 196-181 (a emendamento di ciò che scrisse in *Parables*).
9   Perles, *Jüd. Hochz.*, p. 17. S. Krauss, *Talmud*, « Archaeol. » II 39, trattato *Semachot* VIII.
10 S. Daiches, *Babylonian Oil Magic in the Talmud and in the Later Jewish Literature*, London 1913.
11 Un buon sommario in W. Grundmann, *Das Evangelium nach Matthäus*, Berlin 1968, pp. 514-519. F. C. Burkitt è utile in JTS 30 (1928-29), pp. 267-70. Egli addita un errore in C. G. Montefiore, *Synoptic Gospels*, vol. II, p. 316. La sua citazione di I Macc. IX, 31-42 è opportuna. Goudge replica in JTS 30, pp. 399-401, ma è tanto supercilioso quanto errato. Egli collega l'olio allo Spirito Santo (cfr. Targum su Zacc. IV 1-6), il che è interessante ma non persuasivo. Cfr. anche Jeremias ZNW 56, pp. 196-201. F. A. Strobel, NT 2 (1958), pp. 99-227, ha considerato la parabola in rapporto alla Pasqua. J. Massinberd Ford, NT 9 (1967), pp. 107-123 disapprova, ritiene che le fanciulle siano studiosi (cosa improbabile), che l'olio sia buone azioni (non è improprio, ma olio significa merito) e che la para-

bola sia un midraš sul Cantico dei Cantici (v 1-5 oppure 2-4). Il suo rife-
rimento a Taanit IV 8 è esatto. M. Meinertz, *Synoptische Studien*, in
Fests. A. *Wikenhauser* (München 1954), pp. 94-106. A. Jülicher, *Die
Gleichnisreden Jesu* II (Tübingen 1910), pp. 448-451; J. Jeremias, *The Para-
bles of Jesus*, London 1963, pp. 51, 171-3; E. Linnemann, *Parables of Jesus*,
London 1966, cap. 11.

12 E. Grässer, *Das Problem der Parusieverzögerung*, Berlin 1960, pp. 119.
A parer suo è un'allegoria sulla venuta del figlio dell'Uomo. G. Bornkamm, *
Die Verzögerung der Parusie, in *In memoriam E. Lohmeyer*, Stuttgart
1951, pp. 116-126 (la parabola è un detto del Cristo risorto). Del medesimo
Endeerwartung und Kirche im Matthäusevangelium, in *Background of the
N. T. and Its Eschatology*, Cambridge 1956, p. 231. *Contra*: Meinertz, op.
cit., p. 104.

13 W. G. Kümmel, *Promise and Fulfilment*, London 1957, pp. 55-58.
Cfr. anche N. Levison, *The Parables: Their Background and Local Setting*,
Edinburgh 1926, cap. 27.

14 Così Bornkamm. Anche W. O. E. Oesterley, *The Gospel Parables in
the Light of their Jewish Background*, London 1936, pp. 131-142. G. V.
Jones, *Art and Truth of the Parables*, London 1964, pp. 216-217 (questa
parabola va generalizzata).

15 Jeremias, fr. 4 Ezr. x 1-2.

16 Salmo CXXXII 16-18 (la parabola ne sarebbe un midraš). Midraš Rabbah, Gen. LVI 2. Sul Salmo XLV cfr. Midraš Rabbah, Esodo LII 1. Nota:
Esodo XIX 17: « E Mosè trasse il popolo dal campo per incontrare (LXX:
συνάντησιν) Dio »; e Mekilta sul passo.

17 Talmud babilonese (da ora in poi b.). Git. 7a.

18 Cant. III 11 (la nostra parabola ne sarebbe un midraš). Rabbinicamente
il verso allude a due eventi (avventi), Dio che dà la Legge per mezzo di
Mosè sul Sinai, e la discesa della Presenza sul Tempio. *Mišnah Taanit* IV 8
(Danby, *Mishnah* 201); *Sifre* su Lev. IX 21 (Bonsirven, *Textes rabbiniques*,
39, p. 175); Midraš Rabbah, Es. LII 5; ibidem, Num. II 25, XII 8;
Lam. XXXIII. Pesikta Rabbati v 11 (trad. Braude I 113).

19 Yalkut, cit. da A. Edersheim, *Life and Times of Jesus the Messiah*,
vol. II, p. 722.

20 Cfr. n. 8.

21 Es. XXX 7 (rif. XXVII 20-21), XXXV 13-15, XXXIX 37-8, Num. IV 9, 16
(e Targum Onkelos sul passo). Midraš Rabbah, Num. XX IV, 15. « Dio
non ha bisogno di lumi, ma Israele ha bisogno di merito »: Num. VIII 2,
interpretaz. in Tanchuma B. IV, p. 46, e Midraš Rabbah, Num. XV 2.
Marmorstein (infra), 16. Midraš Rabbah, Lev. XXXI 1, 10, 11. Nell'ultima
citazione R. Chanin dice che la lampada del Tempio indica la lampada del
Messia. Tenere accesa quella rende degni di vedere questa. Midraš Rabbah,
Es. XXXIII 4; XXXVI 1. Cfr. Is. LX 1.

22 Salmo CXXI 3-4;. Is. v 27. La lampada significa la Presenza: C. Shab.
22b, Men. 86 C. Non c'è funzione dalla sera al mattino, salvo la lampada
nel Tempio: C. Men. 89a, Yoma 15a.

23 Derrett, op. cit., p. 418 ss.

24 La base biblica è Es. XXXII 13. Il concetto è pienamente sviluppato in
Mišnah, Avot v 18. (Danby, *Mishnah* 458) *quod lege*. Per le discussioni
che ne nascono cfr. S. Schechter, *Some Aspects of Rabbinic Theology*,
London 1909, pp. 170-198; A. Marmorstein, *The Doctrine of Merits in
Old Rabbinical Literature*, London 1920; R. Travers Herford, *The Pharisees*,
London 1924, pp. 133-135; R. A. Stewart, *Rabbinic Theology*, London
1961, pp. 127-133 (cfr. anche R. Loewe, ibidem, p. VIII). Il punto di vista
di G. F. Moore, *Judaism*, vol. I, Cambridge (Mass.) 1958, pp. 538-545 è

abbastanza particolare, perché egli deduce che l'ebreo fa appello a Dio che lo salvi « causa i meriti dei padri », un'interpretazione di *zekut avot* che sarà corretta per quel che concerne il merito degli avi (in termini biblici) ma non spiega gli altri generi di merito vicario.

25   Gio. IX 2-3.

26   L'idea che il merito vicario potesse venir meno fu espressa fin da Hillel, *Mišnah*, Avot I 4 (Danby, *Mishnah* 447). Per tutta la questione Tosefta, Eduyot II 9; Avotde R. Nathan 55b; b. Shab. 55a (cfr. Shab. 89b, Sanh 81a, 104a, Ber. 10b); Ger. Sanh. 27d; Midraš Rabbah, Lev. XXXIX 6. Schechter, op. cit., p. 176. Midraš sui Salmi (CXXI 3). Sifre su Deut. par. 329.

27   C'è motivo di domandarsi se ἐνύσταξαν sia superfluo. La sua funzione midrascica è ovvia. Ma l'assenza dello sposo ed il suo ritardo sono parte integrante della storia. *Sonno* vale a ricordare la morte e la risurrezione, perciò due verbi sono appropriati. Esse trascurarono il loro dovere (cosí, con enfasi, Salmo XVI I, 4) e lo scontano dopo morte (due idee, due verbi). Cosí: è necessario μέσης? È simbolo (cfr. Lc. XI 5; Marco XIII 35) della notte fonda (non della mezzanotte), quando il fedele non deve scordare il suo Signore (Salmo CXIX 62, Atti XVI 25). σβέννυνται è un'altra parola simbolica (Prov. XIII 9), ma essenziale al racconto. τοὺς πωλοῦντας (invece di ἐλαιοπώλην, ἐλαιοκάπηλον) è simbolico ma anche del tutto ragionevole e necessario. Κύριε è *mar* (aram.), non è simbolico. ἀμήν è ti-
* pico dello stile personale di Gesù. Κραυγή potrebbe essere un termine escatologico (Grässer, op. cit., 123) ma sarebbe tutt'al più un abbellimento simbologico. L'approccio di A. H. McNeile (su san Matteo) e di A. T. Cadoux (*The Parables of Jesus: Their Art and Use*, London 1930, p. 71) non è accettabile.

28   Pirke de R. Eliezer XLI. Strack-Billerbeck, *Kommentar zum N. T.*, vol. I, pp. 969-970. Midraš Rabbah, Cant. I, 12. J. M. Ford, op. cit., p. 109.

29   Jeremias, *Parables* cit.

30   Es. XXIV II cosí interpretato in b. Ber. 17a. Is. LXII 1-5 ha particolare rilevanza (lampada-giustizia-corona-matrimonio-sposo-giubilo).

31   Mt. III 9.

FURTHER ANNOTATIONS

For this parable see Meinertz at the *Wikenhauser Festschrift* (1953), 94 ff. On waking servants, a connected theme, see P. Joüon at *Rec. S. Rel.* 30 (1940), 365. The present article explains the various meanings of 'oil', especially in relation to marriages. It draws attention to the pejorative implications of 'sellers'. I contend that our parable is, inter alia, a midrash on Ps cxxxii.16-18 and Cant. iii.11; and take note of Is. lxii.1-5! But the major emphasis is on the teaching of the parable, which is that there is no such thing as vicarious merit, at any rate after you are dead, and possibly under any circumstances. I omitted to notice the extremely important passage in 4 Ezra vii.102-115 (dated A.D. 96 and after) (see the N:E.B. version). This passage is a polemic against the conception of vicarious merit. Jerome was angry about this work (Hieron, *con. Vigilantium* [opp. ed. Vallersius, II, col. 392, 393]). We note however that at viii.20-33 the author admits an alternative proposition, namely that the pious may pray for mercy to be shown to sinners precisely because the merits of the righteous are of no avail to those who have no treasury of merit. 2 Bar. lxxxv.12-13 is likewise pessimistic on the subject. The Dead Sea scrolls agree that there will be no vicarious merit at the end of the Age (CD IV.10-12, Dupont-Sommer, 143). See also Const. Apost. II, 14. The opposite notion that the merits of the patriarchs will prevail in the messianic era is stated at Midr. R. Gen. LXX.8 (Sonc. 642). On the merits of the patriarchs see also *Midr. on Ps*, Ps. 106.44.

It is of interest that it was said that Elijah used to take even his own lamps and his own wicks from place to place so as not to trouble people: Midr. R., S.S. II.5.3 (Sonc. 110), a saying of R. Judah b. R. Ilai. K.P. Donfried, *J.B.L.* 93 (1974), 415-28, sees the 'oil' as good deeds (sup., xiin).

p. [405], n. 12. Bornkamm's article now appears in his *Gesammelte Aufsätze*, II, 46-55.
p. [405], n. 13. Donfried sees it as a summary of Matthaean theology.
p. [406], n. 27. I take note of the original and interesting proposition of A.E. Harvey, *Jesus on Trial* (cit. sup.), 23 n. 7, that *kraugē*, connected with *krazein*, really means 'testimony': since witnesses were expected to shout excitedly (to show their certainty). Thus the choice of word heightens the allusion to the coming of the kingdom.

Concluding comments: a defect in this article is that it does not emphasise as it should that the major fault of the foolish virgins was that they did not rely wholly on the grace of the 'lord'. Had they done so it is extremely likely that he would not, for very shame, have excluded them on the mere ground that they went to sleep and were generally insouciant—provided they did not attempt to obtain entry by fraud. We are required to observe this undersense in the parable. I submit that it is possible to argue that the parable is the source of the notion that *dipsychia* (uncommittedness) (see O.J.F. Seitz, *J.B.L.* 66, 1947, 211-19) is worse than positive absence of merit. The idea seems to belong to Hellenistic Christianity (Jas. i.6-8, iv.6-10), but nothing prevents our detecting the counterpart in Jesus's intention here. Those that 'nod off', and compound their unfounded expectation that they could 'get by' with others' 'oil' with an actual inattention to the needs of the hero (once again hinting at the Lord himself) will take part in the 'waking-up' and will be detected as wanting in devotion, a concept familiar enough to the Asian world. They cannot expect reciprocity. In a society based on *status*, not *contract*, even a slight service, with devotion, will win reciprocation.

The teme, 'the door was shut', can be taken simply as elegant embellishment, dramatic emphasis. The technique followed in *Law in the New Testament* and in these volumes is to look for the allusion. It was found by Goulder (*Midrash and Lection*, 192, 228). The door was shut on Noah too (and the saved): the Targ. Pal. on Gen. vii.16 alone mentions the door. According to Q Jesus certainly preached on the crisis when Noah went into the ark (Matt. xxiv.38/Lk. xvii.27).

LAW IN THE NEW TESTAMENT:
THE SYRO-PHOENICIAN WOMAN AND THE CENTURION OF CAPERNAUM

Synoptic studies have not explained these episodes. We must trace out what parts go back to Mark or Q, but we should also know why each evangelist made of them what he did. The meaning of each nucleus must be understood first, before the literary and theological quests are embarked upon. The deficiencies in existing studies are soon apparent [1]). No one has realised, for example, that the Centurion reminded St. Luke of Jethro, proselyte and maker

---

[1]) W. GRUNDMANN, *Das Evangelium nach Markus*, 2nd. edn. (Berlin, 1959), 152-5; *Das Evangelium nach Matthäus* (Berlin, 1968), 249-54, 375. K. H. RENGSTORF, *Das Evangelium nach Lukas*, 5th edn. (Göttingen, 1949), 42-5 E. KLOSTERMANN, *Das Markusevangelium*, 4th edn. (Tübingen, 1950), 71-2. E. LOHMEYER, *Das Evangelium des Markus* (Göttingen, 1963), 145-8. E. SCHWEIZER, *The Good News according to Mark* (London, 1971) 137, 151-3. V. TAYLOR, *The Gospel according to St. Mark* (London, 1963), 347-51. R. BULTMANN, *History of the Synoptic Tradition* (Oxford, 1968), 38-9. P. GAECHTER, *Das Matthäus-Evangelium* (Innsbruck, 1963), 501-4, 265-9. H. J. HELD in G. BORNKAMM, G. BARTH, H. J. HELD, *Tradition and Interpretation in Matthew* (London, S. C. M., 1963), 165 ff., 193-200. T. A. BURKILL, 'The historical development of the story of the Syrophoenician woman', *N.T.* 9 (1967), 161-177; 'The Syrophoenician woman, the congruence of Mk. 7.24-31', *Z.N.W.* 57 (1966), 23-37; L. WALLACH, ed., *The Classical Tradition . . . H. Caplan* (N.Y., 1966), 329-344 ('Mark 6:31-8:26: the context of the story of the Syrophoenician woman') (Valuable articles, but extremely sceptical). JOACHIM JEREMIAS, *Jesus' Promise to the Nations* (London, 1958), 12-71 (the leading study: see later editions of the German original); *New Testament Theology* I (London, 1971), 163-4. H. VAN DER LOOS, *The Miracles of Jesus* (Leiden, 1965), 328-333, 411-414, 530-550. E. HAENCHEN, 'Johanneischen Probleme', *Z.Th.K.* 56 (1959), 20, 23-8. B. FLAMMER, 'Die Syrophoenizerin', *Theol. Quartals.* 148 (1968), 463-478. J. KLAUSNER, *Jesus of Nazareth* (N.Y., 1959), 294-5. The 'Son of David' and the Canaanite woman are dealt with by J. M. GIBBS at *N.T.S.* 10 (1963-4), 446 f.f, at 458-9. S. SANDMEL is of the view that St Mark made a mistake to allow the Syro-Phoenician woman to say 'the tolerant thing' instead of Jesus (in R. BATEY, ed., *New Testament Issues*, London, 1970, 54). But the whole point of these passages is the coming of Jesus to a variously-prepared and unprepared gentile world, and the irony of the woman's quotation of scripture was lost on Sandmel.

of proselytes —Jethro who came to Moses and said, 'Don't trouble
yourself so much. Place yourself between the people and God (cf.
Deut. v 27) and delegate authority which you have from him to
πεντηκόνταρχοι and ἑκατόνταρχοι (Exod. xviii 13-27, MT, Pal. Targ.,
LXX)'. He was reminded also of Naaman. Furthermore we must
ask whether there was an historical episode behind each, from which
reminiscence [1]) might supply such summaries. Or are they products
of the church's legal problems, a discussion of Apartheid (Burkill)?
C. G. MONTEFIORE found the conversation with the woman 'quite
incredible'. Could Jesus have done, or pretended to do, 'absent
healing' (a main point the two 'gentile' passages have in common)? [2])
The absent healing of the 'Far off' (gentiles as well as repentant
Israelites), and by word of mouth alone, seems to have been promised in Is. lvii 19 [3]). Or is it the case that an abstract generalisation
is to be drawn from each case, crystallised in the dialogue? [4])

THE SYRO-PHOENICIAN WOMAN

(Mk. vii 24-30, Mt. xv 21-8).

It is usually thought (though not by EDERSHEIM) that Jesus, disappointed in his own flock, was rude to her to test her faith (or
allowed her to overhear a tart remark to his disciples)! St. Matthew,
here for once enlarging upon Mark, writes for a community beg-
inning to be out of touch with oral tradition: clues have to be
written out in full. He developed Mark's succinct, tantalising

---

[1]) JOHANNES JEREMIAS, *Der apostolische Ursprung der vier Evangelien*
(Leipzig, 1932), 125, would have Mk. vii 28 a literal report of the woman's
speech.

[2]) It is possible to exaggerate (as Bultmann) does, the similarity between
the episodes: their special value lies in the difference. Jeremias, *Promise*, 35
emphasises that these are the only cases where Jesus deals with the gentiles
(possibly the Gadarene demoniac is another). A synoptic study of the texts
appears at F. W. BEARE, *The Earliest Records of Jesus* (Oxford, 1962), 74-5,
132. A reconstruction of Q on the Centurion appears at A. HARNACK, *The
Sayings of Jesus* (London, 1908), 74-7, 131-2. The story of the woman is dismissed as anti-Jewish polemic by A. LOISY, *Origins of the New Testament*
(London, 1950), 86 (original edn., 1936, p. 92).

[3]) Cf. b. (= Bab. Talmud.) Ber. 34 b (R. Johsua b. Levi.).

[4]) DIBELIUS, LOHMEYER, and BULTMANN take the dialogue, the nucleus
of each passage, as more important then the healing. Bultmann, 390. T. W.
MANSON, *The Teaching of Jesus* (Cambridge, 1963), 30-1; *The Sayings of
Jesus* (London, 1949), 62-6. V. TAYLOR, *The Formation of the Gospel Tra-
dition* (London, 1953), 76 (were they once pronouncement-stories?). R. H.
LIGHTFOOT, *History and Interpretation in the Gospels* (London, 1935), 114.

writing. We might not have gone his way in every case (perhaps we should not emphasise the disciples' pessimism: Mt. xv 23 recalls xv 33; cf. Lk. ix 54) [1]). But he also wrote for a community that could take much for granted. Did it require to be told that faithful gentiles had a right to admission, as has been suggested? [2]) Our own study must concentrate on Mark, noting the rich allusiveness of his vocabulary: οἰκία = a self-contained, exclusive domain as illustrated at iii 25 (cf. 20), developed by Matthew at xv 24—εἰς τὸν οἶκον αὐτῆς at vii 30 implying the abstract sphere of paganism; while the unnecessary word κλίνην at that verse not only witnesses the healing (βεβλημένον, lying abandoned by the demon) but recalls 1 K. xvii 19-22.   *

Such rediscoveries cause resentment in some minds. We must remember that the earliest Christians had a verbal knowledge of the Old Testament not common now; their tastes and their abilities differed widely from ours. When the plain story holds incongruities (such as Jesus' pronouncement about the 'puppies') or dissonances (such as the Centurion's manner of showing what 'power' he is *under*) we should expect a midrashic explanation, whereas others would excise words as interpolations or suspect a mistranslation from a hypothetical Aramaic original. By Midrash I mean, in this context, the interaction of Old Testament text and first-century event, so that the former seems to be illustrated or revivified by the latter, and the former explains and illuminates the latter: the duty of the evangelist is not merely to tell a tale, but also to develop its contextuality with the Hebrew bible. To him Jesus's life was a representation of familiar Old Testament narratives [3]).

The setting of the story of the woman seems to be an appendage [4]). 'Tyre' may be stimulated by the identification of the woman as Syro-Phoenician [5]) in the nucleus of the tradition. Such women

---

[1]) P. BONNARD, *L'Évangile selon Saint Matthieu* (Neuchatel, 1963), 232 n. 1, continues the common view that they urged Jesus to satisfy her, which fits well with his comment, if it is a reply; but the contrary view is that they took the then conventional view, with which he partly agreed.

[2]) Held's suggestion.

[3]) B. LINDARS appositely, 'Elijah, Elisha and the Gospel Miracles', in C. F. D. MOULE, ed., *Miracles* (London, 1964), 61-80.

[4]) The result of all synoptic studies of the episode.

[5]) The usual explanation, 'Syro-' to distinguish her from 'Lybo-' (Justin, *dial.* 78; Strabo XVII.19) does not convince. C. G. MONTEFIORE, *The Synoptic Gospels* (London, 1909), I, 177; II, 656. P. WERNLE, *Sources of our Knowledge of the Life of Jesus* (London, 1907), 123. Naaman was a *Syrian*.

must have been known in Jewish districts; but Mark wishes to show
the Messiah visiting Tyre, for the daughter of Tyre would sue for the
Lord's favour (Ps. xlv 12; cf. Ps. lxxxvii 4). In the Old Testament
Tyre is proud and inimical to the Israelites ¹); but mention of Tyre
automatically recalls Sidon (Is. xxii; Jer. xlvii 4; Jl. iii 4-8; Zech.
ix 2). Matthew shows the woman coming from both regions, regions he understood to be typically wicked: xi 21-2. The crux in
Mk. vii 24 cannot be solved conclusively, since, irrespective of
geography, the woman is a Sidonian (v. *infra*). Jesus' alleged approach ²) to the borderlands with Tyre is enough to make the
contact between the God of the Hebrews and the nations long
threatened with punishment. Jesus's vision of eschatological punishment included joy, cosmic concomitants, obverse and reverse of
the same coin. Joachim Jeremias says ³) that vengeance is removed
—probably too optimistic, this opinion rightly places vengeance in
a wider perspective. Gentiles share in resurrection (Mt. xi 22 = Lk.
x 14) and ἐκδίκησις at Lk. xviii 7 is double edged! ⁴).

Jesus attempted to remain hidden, like Elijah, from God, whom
no one escapes ⁵). A Syriac version recognises the woman as a widow
(because of the Ṣarefat episode) ⁶). She appeals to Jesus, dramatised
by Matthew as 'crying after' him (an action referred to in Psalms) ⁷).
She cleaved to the righteous, an obligation of those that cleave
to God ⁸). Let the demon, demon of death (suicidal?—cf. Mk. ix
22) ⁹) be cast out of her daughter! Matthew sees her as asking
for help for *herself*, biblically as well as psychologically apposite (ψ.
cxvii; Is. i 9). Esther's protest is hidden in her words (iv 17): but
it is Matthew that uses the Esther vocabulary. 'Let the children be

---

¹) A reputation she retained: Josephus, *c. Ap.* I. 13.
²) The journey is neither chronologically nor geographically significant.
We need not be sceptical of St. Mark's geographical knowledge as many are
(K. NIEDERWIMMER, *Z.N.W.* 57, 1966, 180-1) since he was guided by midrashic, not literal, considerations. The coast must be visited: Zeph. ii 5!
³) *Promise*, 41.
⁴) *Promise*, 45-6; DERRETT, *N.T.S.* 18 (1972), 178 ff., at p. 186.
⁵) Job xxxiv 21; LXX Is. xl 26.
⁶) P.-L. COUCHOUD, *J.T.S.* 34 (1933), 121. GRUNDMANN inclines to support
the identification, allowing she may have been a widow. Keim quoted Volk-
mar as suggesting that the episode was a free composition on the basis of the
Elijah story.
⁷) Ps. xvi (xvii) 6; xvii (xviii) 6, et alibi.
⁸) Sifre on Deut. xi 22; b Ber. 10 b. Pes. 22 b, Mishnah, *ʾĀvot* I.4.
⁹) An unclean spirit, *rūaḥ ṭāmeʾah*, is a spirit of death and tombs: b.
Sanh. 65 b = Soncino Trans. 446.

sated first!' Scholars would excise 'first', even the whole sentence [1]). But 'children' is not a retrodevelopment from 'children' in the next sentence [2]). Matthew omits the phrase perhaps because his hearers took Jewish priority for granted, perhaps because he is not mainly concerned with the Ṣarefat episode (with its emphasis on 'priority'), but with the psalm (to which we come) with its double midrash. St. Mark represents Jesus' ideas in an order approximately as follows: (1) help for gentiles must be authorised or it is impossible; (2) a gentile's cry for help resembles the behaviour of a dog, for gentiles are dogs in scriptural terms [3]); (3) alternately savage and fawning, dogs roam and scavenge [4]); (4) God's 'help' is part of his sustenance, salvation: 'dogs' may have it when brought to God when he is glorified by the children of Israel (Jn. iv 22; Rom. xv 7-9; Gal. iii 23 ff.), who belong to him [5]); (5) in previous dealing between the 'children' and gentiles the 'children' were fed first, so that the children of the gentile could eat afterwards. The Ṣarefat story must be studied in detail [6]).

---

[1]) BULTMANN, KLOSTERMANN, SCHWEIZER, Other views are discussed by Taylor (who thinks 'first' original) at 350. L. GOPPELT, *Christentum und Judentum im ersten und zweiten Jahrhundert* (Gütersloh, 1954), 39-40:-Mt. xv 24; x 5 is correct; Rom i 16, Acts xiii 46 would be anachronistic for Jesus; Mk. vii 27 a is an error, Jesus would not rob the Jews of their due. J. M. ROBINSON, *The Problem of History in Mark* (London, S.C.M., 1957), 64-5, takes the opposite view—the whole episode is only intelligible in the pattern 'first the Jew and then the gentile'.

[2]) Similarly the supposedly harsh saying was supposed by T. R. GLOVER, *Conflict of Religions in the Early Roman Empire* (London, 1909/1918), 127 n. 1, quoted by KLAUSNER and BURKILL, to have been derived from the woman's answer, the true (supposedly) nucleus of the passage.

[3]) Ps. xxii 17 (Targ.); Midr. on Psalms, Ps. 22, para. 26 (gentiles). Is. lvi 11 (Targ.).

[4]) Ps. lix 6-9 (5-8), 15-16 (14-15). Is. lvi 11. The suggestion that 'dog' in such passages has a sodomitical overtone (BURKILL's use of D. W. THOMAS, 'Kelebh', *V.T.* 10, 1960, 41 ff., '"bitch" indeed!') is otiose.

[5]) Exod. iv 22; Deut. xiv 1; Is. i. 2; Hos. xi. 1, Lk. xv. 31; Rom. ix. 4; 1 QM XVII.3; Acts iii 25; Mishnah, *ʾAvot* III.14 (R.ʿAqiba), *Shab.* XIV.4. P. BILLERBECK at STRACK-BILLERBECK, *Kommentar zum Neuen Testament aus Talmud und Midrasch* I (Munich, 1924/1961), 476-8. Cf. Mt. xxiii 15. Rom. ix 6-8. expresses the idea of universal salvation through faith, fitting the Centurion probably better than the Syro-Phoenician woman. Grundmann thinks 'children' means disciples. R. L. LINDSEY's translation of Mark (Jerusalem, N.D.) is the only one to distinguish between 'sons' in Jesus's words and 'children' in the woman's reply (most satisfactory).

[6]) J. GRAY, *I and II Kings* (London, S.C.M., 1963). Recognised as relevant by CRANFIELD, SCHWEIZER and others. The splendid article by L. C. CROCKETT, 'Luke 4.25-27 and Jewish-Gentile relations in Luke-Acts', *J.B.L.* 88 (1969),

1 K. xvii symbolised God's need for Jewish-gentile reciprocity.
Many gentiles, unknown to themselves, know him. The ancient world
was concerned about reciprocity [1]), which could endure, as an
obligation, over generations [2]). The wanderer from mountain to
mountain could receive hospitality from gentiles, and this had a
significance for the church in reference to proselytism (Lk iv 26) [3]).
God ordered the widow (an unlikely person) of Ṣarefat (S. of Sidon
and N. of Tyre) to feed Elijah, who insisted upon being fed first, so
actually as to threaten to deprive her and her children. He cries
after her [4]), and she is rewarded with infinite bread. He dwells (for
seemliness' sake) [5]) on her roof, but she is his landlady; hence when
her son appears to be lifeless [6]) she blames him, and he appeals to
God as if to one in duty bound to look after the widow as she had
looked after him [7]). After Isaac, say the rabbis, the boy is the first
instance of resurrection. The Ṣarefat story is about the power of
charity [8]). Did reciprocity now lean in favour of God, whose
'child' Elijah was, especially since the son who was revived was
Jonah [9]), a notable servant of God? *Non liquet.* Though Jonah,

177-183 establishes the background (reconciliation) and the currency of the
Elijah stories (Sir. xlviii; Ps. Philo, *Bibl. Ant.* xlviii; Rev. xi 6). Asc. Is. ii 14.
It has not been noticed that the principle behind Mt. x 41a is applied in our
incident and in that of the Centurion.

[1]) See DERRETT, *Law in the New Testament* (London, 1970), index, 'reciprocation', also my treatment of the Friend at Midnight in the Daube
(theological) Festschrift, ed. Barrett and others (forthcoming).

[2]) Midr. R. Exod., IV.2 = Sonc. 78. Our passage is referred to.

[3]) W. FAIRWEATHER, *Jesus and the Greeks* (Edinburgh, 1924), 249-275.
W. ELTESTER, ed., *Jesus in Nazareth* (Berlin/N.Y., De Gruyter, 1972).
Jeremias's ideas on the Nazareth episode in *Promise* have not commanded
universal acceptance, but this does not detract from his most acceptable
conclusions.

[4]) 1 K. xvii 11. ἐβόησεν ὀπίσω αὐτῆς.

[5]) See G. FRIEDLANDER, *Pirḳe de Rabbi Eliezer* (N.Y., 1965), ch. 33,
pp. 239-240.

[6]) Whether he actually *died* remains an open question: b. Nidd. 70 b,
Ḥul. 7 b.

[7]) God revived the boy *through* Elijah: Midr. R. Num XIV.1 = Sonc. 561.
Note that the food he ate was hers: the famous discrepancy between the
written and the recited text of 1. K. xvii 15. The Qere, LXX (BL only),
Targum, Syr. have *hiy' wā hū'* (she and he) (preferred by Kittel), but the MT
and Vulg, followed by versions including the *N.E.B.*, have the reverse. He
as guest ate first, but it was for her that the miracle was performed, so that
both readings make sense. Midr. R., S.S. II, 5, para. 3.

[8]) Midr. R. Gen. L. ii = Sonc. 441-2; Midr. R., S.S. II, 5, para. 3. Pirqe
de Rabbi Eliezer, ch. 33.

[9]) E. G. HIRSCH, *Jew. Encycl.* VII (1904), 226. Midr. R. Gen. XLVIII.11 =

despite his Sidonian background, served God, the destitute widow received her son (Heb. xi 35; cf. Lk. vii 13-15) so that God is no more obliged (as it were) than she is. Hence Sidonians can hardly claim that their far-off hospitality to Elijah (a heritable asset) entitles them to help on the principle alleged by Elijah at 1 K. xvii 20. That reciprocity figures in such a question is shown by the 'elders'' speech to Jesus (Lk. vii 4-5): the gentile has done something for our nation, and we collectively (including Jesus) must do something for him.

Now Elijah's gift of a livelihood to the widow and her children [1]), and of life to her son, depended from her faith, tested by the demand to be fed first (1 K. xvii 13). First feed the children of Yahweh [2]) and then the gentiles are to be fed: in exchange for a perishable cake an imperishable sustenance was given. Cakes provided by Yahweh give unfailing strength (1 K. xix 6-8). The Syro-Phoenician woman had no claim on the basis of reciprocity, but the work of Elijah might supply a precedent. Jews certainly thought in terms of authorisation, the right to act and to abstain from action. Jesus could not legitimately help the woman unless reciprocity required, or a precedent supported it. Matthew places here the saying found at x 6 too that Jesus' mission is exclusively to the lost sheep of the house of Israel. Gentiles must have an individual claim before he may use the power God has given him. Elijah had required of the woman such faith as is implied in her feeding a stranger first. When the woman makes the correct reply, Matthew comments directly on her faith.

The words urging her to yield precedence to Jewish suppliants (was he on the way to heal such?) allude to Ps. xvii 14. The psalm is unique in ending with the assertion that the psalmist, protected

---

Sonc. 959-60. The boy was resuscitated as a reward for her hospitality: GINZBERG, *Legends of the Jews* IV, 243-4. Yer. Sukk. 5.55a; *P.R.E.* (cit. sup.); Jerome, introd. to comm. on Jonah. FIELD, *Origen's Hexapla* I, 632 n. 29. GINZBERG, 318. Seder Eliyahu Rabah we Seder Eliyahu Zuṭa' (ed. FRIEDMANN, Vienna, 1900) 18, 97-8 shows the son of the widow as the 'Messiah of the tribe of Joseph'. The statement that Jonah was the Messiah is derived from Elijah's saying he should receive his portion first and afterwards her son should receive his. The Shunammite was the mother of Habakkuk.

[1]) God says there will be enough for all: xvii 14. The LXX had a different text from the MT, in which, for 'son', 'children' was read. Further evidence for this reading is awaited.

[2]) 1 K. xvii 13, 15.

from his enemies (gentiles, sinners?) will be *sated* on waking with God's form (or glory) (the attribute of Moses: Num. xii 8), for in righteousness (or through charity) he will see his face. We learn from Tob. xii 9 that through acts of charity one will be *sated* with life (χορτασθήσονται ζωῆς) [1]). The previous words in the psalm read in modern versions as if more curses on the 'enemy'. 'Men of the world' are referred to, the unregenerate, and a prophecy is made that their belly should be filled with God's hidden things, or treasure, that 'children' (*the* children or *their* children) should *be sated*, and that they should leave their remains, or residue, to their babies.

‏...ישבעו בנים והניחו יתרם לעוליהם:‏

Alternative renderings are possible. 'Thy treasured ones shall fill their belly' is possible, but no surviving version so takes it [2]). *yisbeʿw bāniym*, which means 'children shall be sated', is so taken by Symmachus, the Targum, Midrash on Psalms, and many older translators as by some modern; it can be rendered 'they shall be satisfied with children', as if that were an inferior promise—adopted by some modern translators to an unimpressive result [3]). We may rather take the verse to mean that Israel shall be satisfied (a word of prophetic significance) [4]) and so shall their issue, contrasting with the gentiles, whose overthrow is in the psalmist's mind. There shall even be a residue which passes to the Israelites' issue. *Satisfaction* is shown by there being remnants (cf. Mk vi 43, viii 8, emphasised at 19-21). Divine help will be superabundant, to the children first rather than to the babes and sucklings, the ones that, but for a miracle, would understand little (Mt. xi 25, xxi 16; Lk. x 21) [5]). In the Asian household fully weaned children eat roughly in order of seniority. Thus the words put into Jesus's mouth by Mark reflect

---

[1]) Cod. Sin. (adopted by BROOKE-McLEAN-THACKERAY, 1940). The Midrash on Psalms says (para. 14), quoting Is. xl. 5, that by practising charity *all flesh* should see the glory of God on the authority of this verse.

[2]) *ṣefūnēychā*; cf. Ps. xxxi 20.

[3]) *R.S.V.* and *N.E.B.*, for example. The translation 'their sons are (or shall be) sated' is adopted by J. CALÈS, *Le Livre des Psaumes* I (1936), 209; E. A. LESLIE (*Psalms*, N.Y., 1949), 353: H.-J. KRAUS, *Psalmen* (NEUKIRCHEN-VLUYN, 1966), 128, 133; M. DAHOOD, *Psalms* I (N.Y., 1966), 93; M. BUTTEN-WIESER, *The Psalms* (Chicago, 1938), 480, 484-5. See Symmachus ad loc., and especially Midr. on Ps., Braude I, 217-8.

[4]) See p. 169 n. 1 infra.

[5]) S. LÉGASSE, *Jésus et l'Enfant. 'Enfants'* . . . *dans la Tradition Synoptique* (Paris, Gabalda, 1969).

Jesus's own conception of his function: "Is it not the case that the children, i.e., God's household, must first be *fully* satisfied [1]), before there can be a remnant for others (Is. xlii 5-7)? How can you claim divine mercy when the Jews, to whom the Messiah is sent, have not exhausted his power?" Would it not compromise his mission if he neglected the objects of it, God's 'household'—would this not be disobedience to God? Jesus is not merely testing her faith—he is represented as in a quandary.

Children of the house figure in the Elijah precedent, children of Yahweh in Jesus's opening remark. He continues with a graphic analogy. "It is wrong [2]) to take the children's bread and throw (or merely 'give') it to the little dogs." We have met bread in the Elijah story, the least scrap worth talking about [3]). Truly living is conveyed by 'bread'. The 'demonized' daughter, if saved, will be given this bread. The word κυνάριον is a diminutive, not as a mitigation of the harshness of the saying [4]), nor as an insignificant variant of κύων [5]), but in allusion to Ps. xvii 14: unless the children are fed full they will not 'drop', or 'let fall', bits of bread for the puppies to snap up. The Jewish family collected bits of bread

---

[1]) *sābaʿ*. ψ. xxxvi 19, civ 40, cvi (cf. Hos. iv 10, Mic. vi 14, Jl. ii 18-19, Am. iv 6-8); Exod. xvi 3, 8; Lev. xxvi 5; Ezk. xvi 48. Note the Messianic ψ. cxxxi 11, 15-17. Is. lviii 7-11. Targ. Is. xxxiii 16.

[2]) οὐ καλόν has shades of meaning, so has *loʾ-tov*. Here it recalls 1 Sam. xxvi 16; Neh. v 8; Is. lxv 2; Ezk. xviii 18 (cf. Prov. xxiv 23) rather than Gen. ii 18; Exod. xviii 17; 2 Sam. xvii 7; Prov. xxv27. συμφέρει is not the synonym for καλόν here.

[3]) 1 K. xvii 17 (*v. infra*).

[4]) J. SCHNIEWIND, *Das Evangelium nach Markus*, 6th edn. (Göttingen, 1952), 107-8. Jeremias at *Promise*, 29. Jeremias doubts the original use of a diminutive. In actual fact κυνάριον (which is *synonymous* with κυνίδιον) is a pure diminutive at Plato, *Euthydemus* 298D-E (Loeb edn., p. 474); and fairly clearly at Xenophon, *Cyropaedia* VIII. 4,20 (Loeb edn., ii. 384-6). Theopompus comicus 90 (T. KOCK, *Com. Att. Frag.* I, 1880, 755) is inconclusive, likewise Alcaeus com. 33 (ibid. 763). At Arrian's Epictetus IV.1.111 it is a depreciatory diminutive, 'a paltry dog '(Loeb edn. ii, 282). κυνίδιον is certainly diminutive, 'puppy' at Aristophanes, *Acharneis*, 542 (Loeb edn., 52): Xenophon, *Oeconomicus* XIII.8 (Loeb edn., 472), and Plato (supra). MICHEL at KITTEL, ThWzNT III (1938/1957), 1103-4 (pet dog of any age) appears to have missed the point. When fully grown dogs would scavenge or be fed at their post (if guard dogs), they would not scramble 'under' (i.e. round about) the table. Whether Jews had pet dogs, toy dogs in our sense is not known; and whether Greeks were more friendly to house-dogs than Jews were is also unknown.

[5]) So BURKILL, consistently with Michel (supra). The number of diminutives in our passage is interesting, but is not conclusive of a 'devaluation' of vocabulary in 'popular' Greek.

worth identifying as such [1]) (a frugal people, they retained a superstitious veneration for bread, and remnants had magical potency), and threw out crumbs or pieces not worth collecting. Children would toss scraps, especially if they had wiped their fingers on them, to their favourite puppies. Jesus is *not* thinking of infants, but of the metaphorical 'children' of scriptural jargon. The gentiles are like roaming dogs. The Sidonian and presumably Tyrian peoples were still, in scriptural terms, little better than dogs, as several passages in scripture and rabbinical sources suggest.[2])

The 'Son of David' will think of the psalm, even when speaking to an illiterate gentile. She knew nothing of Jewish scripture. A reference to a psalm would be lost on her. But, technical as the Jewish law is on this as on other subjects, even illiterate Greeks recognised that to take from A the asset of B destined for A and to cause it to be consumed by C, in whom B has a minor or no interest is a species of theft. In Jewish law this was somehow brought within the concept of stealing [3]). It was not necessary for the wrongdoer to keep the object or derive profit from it himself. If he were *entrusted* with the asset we should say it was a breach of trust. In Greek laws the injury inflicted on B would be an offence and both compensation and punishment were thinkable [4]). Even a layman sees that to deprive A of property destined for him by B is an offence, whether or not the offender derives benefit from so doing. The sharp Jewish mind could calcuate the loss in monetary terms to B if his fine bread, the table bread, were given to dogs for whom an inferior bread was certainly a diet (if, as house dogs, they had a diet) [5]). To feed dogs with children's bread would mean a cal-

---

[1]) b. Ber. 52 b = Sonc. 317. Billerbeck IV/2, p. 626 (d).

[2]) BILLERBECK I, 724 ff. 1 En. lxxxix 42-9. Midr. on Psalms iv 8. b. Meg. 7 b. J. BOWMAN, *The Gospel of Mark* (Leiden, 1965) 171-2 refers to the Samaritan Passover Liturgy, but I was unable to verify the reference.

[3]) B. S. JACKSON, *Theft in Early Jewish Law* (Oxford, 1972), 72, 94-99. The law relating to 'sacrilege' expounded there is particularly relevant to our enquiry. Property notionally belonging to God (as in Jesus's metaphor) would be subject to this.

[4]) R. TAUBENSCHLAG, *The Law of Greco-Roman Egypt in the Light of the Papyri* (N.Y., 1944), 343 ff. I am not saying that any Egyptian Greek would start proceedings on facts such as suggested in our metaphor! It is the principle which is of interest.

[5]) It is not true that dogs actually kept by a family are carnivorous. I know of Asian dogs who are fed on coarse bread. Dogs' dough as a particular kind of bread is mentioned at Mishnah, Ḥull. I. 8 (H. DANBY, *The Mishnah*, Oxford, 1933, 84).

culable financial loss to the householder. For householders had inferior diets even for their table servants, who were glad of scraps from the guests (a kind of tipping), a practice about which the thoughtful rabbis had more than one opinion. If gentiles are dogs, and Jews are children, and bread is life, Jesus cannot, *prima facie*, as a master of righteousness, give life to a gentile, until the Israelites are sated and have a surplus, all the Jews having first turned to him for the life-giving gift. Jesus is not, as Lohmeyer and Grundmann say [1]), the householder in our metaphor— God is; and similarly there is no eucharistic overtone to this story in its original shape. Jesus must have thought of the Last Days when, all needs having come to an end, the demands of righteous gentiles could be attended to. Has that time come? Only a real life crisis can supply the solution.

The woman's answer is regarded as persistence, wit, readiness of Syrian repartee (cf. 1 K. xx 32-3) [2]). Sharpwittedness aided her response, but how prompt was it? She reinterprets the same psalm, the same verse! She takes up the Elijah story. She alludes to a maxim Jesus evoked, having a genuine Jewish application. And she utters (without knowing it) a warning. 'Because of that word' Jesus cured her daughter. She provided the authority he needed. As we shall see, she did not declare herself content with a crumb of what was really meant for Israel (Jeremias)—a breach of trust on Jesus's part—but declared that the householder (God) intended to feed both Jews and gentiles!

If we take Ps. xvii 14 to mean children literally, the 'Babes' are smaller creatures. 'Weaned babes' could fancifully apply to puppies. The contrast between the diners and dogs who have no right to be fed from their meal, a contrast obvious to all [3]), was deftly turned, and the puppies become the little creatures to whom

---

[1]) GRUNDMANN, *Markus*, 154-5.

[2]) So TAYLOR. KLOSTERMANN: 'Jesus wird gewonnen . . . durch die Schlagfertigkeit der Frau'. P. CARRINGTON, *According to Mark* (Cambridge, 1960), 156-8. B. W. BACON, *Beginnings of the Gospel Story* (New Haven, 1909), 80, correctly: her answer 'was received by Jesus as an enlargement of his own point of view'. I see no connection with Gen. xxxii 24-32.

[3]) See Midr. R. Levit. IX, para. 3 = Sonc. 108-9: 'a dog has eaten of Jannai's bread (*piystā* = bit of bread)'; the dog then quotes scripture to the host's astonishment! *Could* this have been inspired by our passage? Mt. vii 6 is relevant. Holy things must not be redeemed and then thrown to dogs (which makes sense of the saying at last): b. Shev. 11 b = Sonc. 48 (à propos of the Red Heifer). To throw a noble thing to dogs humiliates: b. B.Q. 85 a.

'left-overs' are promised in the psalm. The crumbs that are let drop (as Matthew puts it) are fragments which no one bothers to collect, and which puppies snatch up: indeed, if they are not kept out they will greedily snatch at the children's food. It was such crumbs that were brought by the crows to Elijah[1]), from the table of the righteous king Jehoshaphat[2]). Elijah was himself fed like a crow or a dog. A 'crumb' is the smallest morsel: and it is that which Elijah begged from the woman of Ṣarefat[3]). A crumb, bit, or scrap: it is all the same[4]). Though she did not realise it, the Syro-Phoenician woman re-quotes scripture, with a common-sense midrash. If her daughter may 'eat', the demon must be expelled; for a table cannot be laid for demons (Is. lxv 11)!

She repeats consciously what must have been a common maxim[5]). There is Hellenic evidence for a similar saying: dogs will clean up every scrap of what diners leave, a model of scavenging[6]). God provides, as the Jews knew, for all creatures, even dogs and crows[7]). The principle at Ps. cxlvii 9, Job xxxviii 41, Ps. Sal. v 8-11, Mt. vi 26, Lk. xii 24 is well attested in rabbinical literature, and is relied upon in the oft-quoted but seldom understood passage at Baba Bathra 8a[8]). A rabbi, masquerading as an ignoramus, seeks, and

---

[1]) Crows: see the discussion at L. GINZBERG, *Legends of the Jews* IV. 196-7, VI. 317. The theory that they were Arab merchants is interesting since it enhances the 'gentile-reciprocity' theme. With 1 K. xvii 4-5 cf. Is. xxxiii 16.

[2]) b. Sanh. 113 a = Sonc. 780; Ḥul. 5a; Midr. R. Num. XXIII. 9 = Sonc. 875; Midr. R. Gen. XXXIII. 5 = Sonc. 265. Tanḥuma (Buber) IV, 165; Ginzberg, 317 n. 7. Elijah was provided with bread and meat (cf. LXX, influenced by Exod. xvi 8, 12, with MT). The meat cannot have been offal. Were Ahab's slaughters orthodox? Could E. have eaten remnants from Ahab's table (tainted with unrighteous gains, cf. Naboth)? Therefore the bread came from Jehoshaphat's table. Crows are a lesson on God's providence: Midr. R. Num. XXIII. 9, Job xxxv 11; Midr. R. Lev. XIX. 1 = Sonc. 235.

[3]) 1 K. xvii 11: *pat leḥem*. LXX ψωμός. Actually crumb at ψ. cxlvii 6. Cf. 1 Sam. xxviii 22, Job xxxi 17; Prov. xvii 1, xxviii 21.

[4]) *pat, piystāʾ, peʿrusāh, pērūriyn* (crumbs) (the last is used by translators of our passage into Hebrew). See the begging incident at b. Ber 31 b = Sonc. 192. JASTROW, *Dict.* 1171. At Yer. Pes. VI, 33 c, 'one must remove crumbs' uses *piysātāʾ* (sic).

[5]) D. SMITH, *Exp. T.* 12 (1901), 319-321. J. MUNCK, *Paulus und die Heilsgeschichte* (Aarhus, 1954), 257.

[6]) Philostratus, *Vita Apollonii Tyan.* I.19 (Loeb. edn., i, 54) (cited by most commentators, ancient and modern): τοῖς κυσί . . . τοῖς σιτουμένοις τὰ ἐκπίπτοντα τῆς δαιτός . . .

[7]) Why dogs and crows? Because of their services to Adam. *Pirqe deʿ R. Eliezer*, ch. 21 (trans., 156-7) (citing Job xxxviii 41 and Ps. cxlvii 9!).

[8]) Midr. R. Lev. XIX. 1 = Sonc. 235 on the Job passage (the DSS targum

obtains a 'crumb' [1]) on the basis that he is to be fed like a dog or a crow. The woman says: though there be no obligation upon you, and I have no claim on the basis of reciprocity (the case is different from Rahab's: Josh. ii 11-18; and from Hiram's servants: 1 K. v 9; and the principle in Ezra iii 7 does not apply), you should feed me by way of charity. The psalm says 'in charity I shall behold your (God's) face'. Refusal of charity would thus be unthinkable. God shows compassion to all creatures, irrespective of race [2]), as Jesus contended in another context [3]).

Further 'the puppies under the table eat of the crumbs' amounts to a lightly veiled warning. Adonibezek, though nothing of a king in himself [4]), had seven kings under his table gathering crumbs, each with his thumbs (or hands) and his big toes (or feet) cut off. They were utterly humiliated. For treating fellow humans thus he himself had his thumbs and toes cut off—retribution from Yahweh [5]). He was a Canaanite, and this (not antiquarianism) is why Matthew describes our woman as a Canaanite. Adonibezek, in his brief appearance in history, saw himself as gathering crumbs from Yahweh's table, because he had forced other gentiles to gather crumbs beneath his. The relevance of Jdg. i to our story was discovered recently [6]), the finder modestly leaving it to others to show how it fits into the midrashic framework of our passage.

---

on Job does not include this verse). b. B.B. 8 a = Sonc. 33-4. Billerbeck, I, 726. Mishnah, *Qidd.* IV. 14 illustrates the proposition that all who are created to serve their Maker are entitled to sustenance without care (covert allusion to Ps. cxlvii 9). The psalm is referred to at b. Ket. 49 b = Sonc. 284 (*a fortiori* parents must feed their children). Ps. Sal. v 11 is especially interesting as it shows kings, people, and beggars equally 'fed' by God. Note that χορτάζω and cognate words properly fit foddering and fattening *animals*! On Job xxxviii 41 see N. H. Tur-Sinai, *The Book of Job* (Jerusalem, 1957), 537-9. In Ps. cxlvii 9 *behemāh* includes dogs according to R. Meir (c. 150): Mishnah, *Kil.* VIII. 6.

[1]) *patiy*: 'my bread', literally 'my morsel'. See above, p. 171 n. 3.

[2]) Deut. x 18 discussed with Gen. xxviii 20 at Midr. R. Gen. LXX. 5 = Sonc. 638, and Midr. R. Num. VIII. 9 = Sonc. 235. The separation from the Canaanites was deep-rooted: Gen. xxiv. 3. Could the second Isaac ignore it ?

[3]) Mt. v 45; Lk. vi 35b-36.

[4]) Yalqūṭ Shimʿoni on Jdg. i 7 (ed B. Landau, Jerusalem, 1960), ii, 704.

[5]) Jdg. i 5-7 *melqeṭiym* = pick or glean (ἦσαν συλλέγοντες τὰ ὑποκάτω [Targ. laḥmāʾ teḥūt] τῆς τραπέζης μου); see Ps. civ (ciii) 28: the action of animals.

[6]) W. Storch, 'Zur Perikope von der Syrophönizierin . . .', *B.Z.*, N.S. 14 (1970), 256-7. For the passage: C. F. Burney, *Book of Judges* (N.Y. 1970), 3-6.

It is worth noting that the woman does not ask for 'absent healing', though this was known in her cultural environment [1]), nor does his use of this method imply any reluctance on Jesus's part to visit her daughter.

THE CENTURION'S 'BOY'

(Mt. viii 5-13; Lk. vii 1-10; Jn. iv 46-54).

The story contrasts with the woman's. Scripture authorised Jesus's charity towards her. The Centurion's profession of faith gives him his title to help. Gentiles can quote scripture (even Satan does: Mt. iv 6). God speaks to gentiles, and may inspire them as well as Jews [2]). The Centurion's story has many other ironies: we have seen how St. Luke thought Jethro reappeared here; and there are other scriptural allusions notably to Naaman (2 K. v).

From the discrepancies between the Matthaean and the Lucan versons we gather that Matthew stands closer to Q, the additions and modifications having been introduced by Luke for motives we can begin to reconstruct. The many textual puzzles may yield to a new interpretation: thus Lk. vii 7a (omitted by Mt. and by D, etc.) may well be Luke's own conception. The query as to whether the sufferer was the centurion's son or servant/slave remains unsolved [3]). We were intended to be in doubt! The intense concern of the Centurion for the boy suggests a deep emotional attachment [4]); if it was a son he might have been illegitimate (were Herodian centurions allowed to marry?); if it was a slave he could have been a 'dolly boy' whom the centurion loved the more deeply for having conquered desire. We do not know. The adolescent or youth was highly disturbed with a complaint thought to be susceptible of spirit healing. Matthew says he was paralysed, Luke that he was near

---

[1]) DITTENBERGER, *Sylloge*, 803, 1 ff. (citedby KLOSTERMANN, GRUNDMANN, and others).

[2]) Josephus, *Bell.* IV. 366, 370; VI. 40, 411. H. GUTTMANN, *Die Darstellung der jüdischen Religion bei Flavius Josephus* (Breslau, 1928), 45-6. Acts x 1-3, 34, 44-7.

[3]) BULTMANN says certainly son, Gaechter servant. T. KEIM, *History of Jesus of Nazara* iii (London, 1877), 219: son (such zeal for a servant was impossible!). H. F. D. SPARKS, *J.T.S.* 42 (1941), 179-80 (certainly son). A. PLUMMER, *Critical and Exegetical Commentary* (Edinburgh, 1900), 196 (servant). H. J. CADBURY in F. J. FOAKES JACKSON and K. LAKE, *Beginnings of Christianity* I/v (London, 433), 365.

[4]) GRUNDMANN suggests that instead of δοῦλος he called him παῖς out of affection: not verifiable, unfortunately.

death. Which really knew what was the matter with him? If the boy was afraid of being sent to be sold, as a result of his master's 'withdrawal' from him, that would account for hysterical symptoms: pure speculation on my part—we were intended to be in doubt.

The Centurion must have met Jesus personally, perhaps after some introduction by respectable Jews (the word *elders* Luke caught up from Exod. xviii 18 Pal. Targ.). Luke makes much of reciprocity. The Centurion was evidently a God-fearer [1]), had a place in public esteem (virtually a προστάτης of the community), and (we may be sure), if the story which St. Luke gathered was correct, he had a seat in the synagogue [2]). He will have heard the Law and the Prophets, will have spoken Aramaic as well as Greek; indeed he may well have been a native Palestinian [3]). He will have obeyed the Noachide Laws, if no more [4]), for which Jethro suggested a competent system of administration (for the laws referred to in Exod xviii were prior to the Decalogue!). Luke's double sending of messengers and afterwards 'friends' does not appeal, because, apart from the awkwardness of the request to come, and the stopping in the road, the Centurion wanted to hear the *word* personally, since even messengers trained to repeat messages exactly will not have been a substitute for personal hearing. Luke has a motive for making out that there remained a distance between the man and Jesus (cf. 2 K. v 10).

Did Jesus volunteer to go and cure the boy? It is plain that if he considered going it was to see the patient. Many, suspecting a refusal [5]), would point the Matthaean words with a question-mark,

---

[1]) Therefore as good as a Jew for most purposes: Philo, *Leg. ad Caium*, 211. J. KLAUSNER, *From Jesus to Paul* (London, 1942 ?), ch. 3. Josephus, *c. Ap.* 10, 123. Acts x 2, xiii 16, 26, xvi 14, xviii 7, xvii 4. Jeremias, *Promise*, 15-16. W. G. BRAUDE, *Jewish Proselyting in the First Five Centuries of the Common Era* (Providence, 1940), 40-1, 137-8.

[2]) M. HENGEL, *Z.N.W.* 57 (1966), 145 (ἐξουσία and δεσποτεία). B. LIFSHITZ, *Donateurs et fondateurs dans les synagogues juives* (Paris, Gabalda, 1967).

[3]) Jos., *Ant.* XIX, 354-365. He was most unlikely to have been a Roman (delegated to supervise customs), and was an officer of Antipas. A. N. SHERWIN-WHITE, *Roman Society and Roman Law in the New Testament* (Oxford, 1963), 123-4, 156; S. BUSS, *Roman Law and History in the New Testament* (London, 1901), 343-4, 347.

[4]) See J. H. GREENSTONE, *J.E.* VII (1904), 648-50. b. Sanh. 56a-b, 57 b. A.Z. 26 a!

[5]) So KLOSTERMANN, BULTMANN (Jesus's scruples were overcome), JEREMIAS, VAN DER LOOS.

'Do you mean that I should go and heal him?' and there would be a consequential difference of tone in the Centurion's reply. This is implausible: the point in the story lies in a willing Jesus being stopped in his tracks [1]). Since the Centurion was a God-fearer, though not a proselyte [2]), there was no reason to hesitate to visit his house even if one had been concerned for ritual purity (Mishnah, 'Āhₐlot), which Jesus was not. Luke explains, as it were, why the Centurion was entitled to sympathetic treatment, as an exception in a life dedicated to service of the Jews; but Q probably did not have this feature, assuming that its hearers would already have known that a centurion who addressed Jesus as 'Lord' [3]) would have been favourably received—perhaps a large assumption? Whatever his reasons for not being a full proselyte (he was too humble?) the point of the story lies in his remaining a gentile (which St. John, if it is indeed the same incident, was content to obscure) [3a]).

The climax is Jesus's approval of the man's faith, greater than he had found in Israel, and Luke may well be right in placing the emphasis so, 'not even in Israel'. Was his faith in Jesus's power of absent healing, or in Jesus personally? [4]) Q has retained a verbatim account of the man's protestation of faith. It appears literally Jewish, and implies that Jesus was God's representative as Moses was. It is not true that for 'under authority' we should read 'in authority' [5]). There is no basis for this [6]). It is because he is under authority that he has his own authority. Because Jesus is 'sent',

---

[1]) So HOOKE (infra).

[2]) As Keim thought. KLAUSNER correctly refutes this. On the Sebomenoi (gentiles favouring Judaism) there are good references at A. D. NOCK, *Essays on Religion and the Ancient World* (Oxford, 1972), I, 51.

[3]) F. J. FOAKES JACKSON and K. LAKE, *op. cit.*, I/i (1920), 413-415. R.N. LONGENECKER, *Christology of Early Jewish Christianity* (London, S.C.M., 1970), 129-130. I. de la Potterie at *Mélanges B. Rigaux* (Gembloux, 1970), 117-146. G. BORNKAMM at W. D. DAVIES and D. DAUBE, ed., *Background of the New Testament and its Eschatology . . . C. H. Dodd* (Cambridge, 1956), 251 (on Mt. xv 22).

[3a]) E. F. SIEGMAN, *C.B.Q.* 30 (1968) 183-98.

[4]) VAN DER LOOS, 539.

[5]) T. H. WEIR, *The Variants in the Gospel Reports* (Paisely,1920): see *Exp. T.* 32 (1921), 284; C. J. CADOUX thereon, ibid., 474; Weir replies at ibid., 33 (1921-2), 280. G. ZUNTZ, *J.T.S.* 46 (1945) 183-190. M. BLACK, *An Aramaic Approach to the Gospels and Acts*, 3rd edn. (Oxford, 1967), 158-9. Jeremias, *Promise*, 30. Manson, *Sayings*, 65.

[6]) FAIRWEATHER (p. 251) understood it correctly. E. V. RIEU's translation is correct: 'for I too am a man who derives his power from above . . .' (marvellous recreation of *double entendre*!). Jeremias, in both studies, is persuasive, but he cannot see Jesus as a subordinate!

'commanded', possessed (if that is correct) ¹) by the power ²) of God he is enabled to effect cures as he does—and is authorised to teach what he teaches. Scholars have noted this ³) in obscure places and it accords with the constitutional proposition which the Centurion makes, and must be accepted.

'But speak with the word, and my boy shall be healed. For I too am a man under authority (or 'power'). I have soldiers under me and I tell one to go and he goes, and another one to come and he comes, and my servant (or 'slave') to do something and he does it'. The implication is that one vested with power (ἐξουσία is equivalent to *potestas*, which implies unlimited, not legally circumscribed, power) can issue orders which will be carried out on the principle *qui facit per alium facit per se*. It was on this principle that the success of the Roman army was built, as the world knew ⁴): devolution of command and strict discipline. Asians admired this, and Antipas must have conducted his administration on the principle of *potestas* ⁵) since his predecessors *se dederant in potestatem*. Not only the soldiery ⁶) but the magistracy in these 'kingdoms' operated on the principle of devolution of 'power' from the emperor, with his *tribunicia potestas* (δημαρχικὴ ἐξουσία) ⁷) and personal authority

---

¹) S. V. McCasland, *By the Finger of God* (N.Y., 1951).

²) The Father's commandment: Jn. v 19-20, 30, 36-7, 43; vi 57; viii 28; x 18, 25, 37; xiv 10, 31; xv 10; xvi 15; xx 21.

³) A. E. Garvie, *Exp. T.* 20 (1909), 377; H. H. Stainsby, *ibid.*, 30 (1919), 328-9; C. J. Cadoux, *ibid.*, 32 (1921), 474. The most powerful refutation of the 'in authority' mare's nest is the splendid article of S. H. Hooke, 'Jesus and the Centurion', *Exp. T.* 69 (1957-8), 79-80.

⁴) Polybius VI. 39, 11. On discipline in the Roman army see G. Webster *Roman Imperial Army* (London, 1969), 31, 262; G. R. Watson, *Roman Soldier* (London, 1969), 117-126. Josephus, surely a first-class witness, testifies to the devolution of command as a factor in the Romans' success: *B.J.* II, 577-80.

⁵) 'Dominion' (subject only to the ultimate responsibility to a superior, if any), rather than 'authority' (which, wrongly, suggests legal restraint). For the word ἐξουσία see F. Preisigke, *Wörterbuch der griechischen Papyrusurkunden* I (Berlin, 1925), 520-1(1) and E. Kiessling, *Wört. der gr. Papyrusurk.* IV/4 (Marburg, 1971), 830-1, ll. 52 ff. A full discussion is at U v. Lübtow, Pauly's *R.E.* XXII, 1040 ff., but the neatest and most perfect account for our purposes is E. Bund, 'Potestas', *Der Kleine Pauly* IV, 1093-4. *Potestas* is slightly wider than *imperium*, according to many. See, for its use, 2 Mac. iii 6; Lk. xxiii 7; Jn. xix 10-11.

⁶) On discipline see above, n. 4. Justinianus, *Digesta* XLIX. 16, 12, 2; ibid., 13.4. I am obliged to Mr. A. N. Sherwin-White for a card dated 7 March 1972 on this subject.

⁷) P. Lond. 1178.9; B.G.U. 1074.1 (both of the 1st cent.); B.G.U. 74.3 (2nd. cent.) and seven further examples are quoted. A title of Caesar.

which the grovelling Agrippa acknowledged in the Petronius episode
(*v. infra*). The Centurion's words imply components of the Jewish
faith (which had no creed as such), and imply it more by conduct
than profession (which is impressive). Jethro said, 'Now I know that
the Lord is greater than all the gods' (Exod. xviii 11). God is one [1]);
he is the source of all power [2]); he is the supreme ruler [3]); his command is a πρόσταγμα [4]); he provides for the universe [5]); it is to him
we must cleave [6]); we must love him and fear him [7]); we must
serve, i.e. be subservient, to him [8]) and therefore to his representatives; we must walk in his ways [9]); he rules Jews and gentiles too
and to him gentiles also must turn[10]). God acts by word alone[11]). Jesus
cures with a word (as at Ps. cvii 18-20)[12]). He does so as God's subordinate. God tells men to go, and they go[13]); to come, and they

---

[1]) The *Shᵉmāᶜ*: Deut. vi 1-6; xi 13-21; Num. xv 37-41. For propositions
regarding the Jewish faith at the period readers will naturally consult
Bonsirven's *Textes Rabbiniques* and G. F. MOORE's *Judaism*. R. A. STEWART's
Rabbinic Theology (Edinburgh and London, 1961) is also helpful.

[2]) Master of the Universe: b. Ber. 4 a. The *Shᵉmāᶜ* implies *malkūt*. S.
SCHECHTER, *Some Aspects of Rabbinic Theology*, (London, 1909) ch. 6.

[3]) J.-B. FREY, 'Dieu et le monde d'après des conceptions juives au temps
de Jésus-Christ', *R.B.*, N.S. 13 (1916), 33-60: a massive collection of references at pp. 47-8. Eccl. xlvi 5; En. i. 4, lxxxiv 2; 2 Macc. xiii 4; 3 Macc. v 35,
vi 2. Mekilta on Exod. xx 2: God like a king whose decrees are worth nothing
unless his sovereignty is accepted by his subjects. Nock, op. cit., I, 74-5 gives
references to the oriental use of *kyrios* and *despotes* in respect of kings or gods.

[4]) Jos., *c. Ap.* II, 231; *Ant.*, II, 291. 1 Clem. 1 5. Hermas, simil. V, 1. 5.

[5]) Philo (Loeb edn., i, p. 136). Josephus (Loeb edn., i, pp. 368-70). K.
KOHLER, *Jewish Theology* (N.Y. 1918).

[6]) Deut. x 20, xi 22.

[7]) Deut. vi 2, 13; x 20. Mt. iv 10; Lk. iv 8 (B. GERHARDSSON, *The Testing
of God's Son*, Lund, 1966, 62 ff.). Obedience is better than sacrifice: 1 Sam.
xv 22; 2 Chron. vii 14, xii 7.

[8]) Exod. xxiii 25; Deut. vi 13, xi 13, xiii 5. In the ancient world subservience and service were essentially connected, the dis-connection (even in
Asia) is quite modern.

[9]) Deut. x 12, xiii 5, xxvi 17, xxviii 9; Lev. xix 2.

[10]) Jer. x 7, xxxii 27 ('. . . is anything too hard for me ?). Is. xlv 22-24.

[11]) Gen. i 3, 9, 11, 14-15, 24, 30; Exod. xx 1; Deut. v 4-5, 22. Frey, supra,
citing Wis. ix 1; Jub. xii 4; Test. Napt. ix 5; cf. Ps. xxxiii 9, cxlviii 5; Jdt.
xvi 14; En. xxxiii 4; Wis. xii 18. See also Exod. xx 19; Deut. viii 3.

[12]) Mt. viii 16. The method, according to St. Matthew (17) was transference
of sickness to the healer, known to students of magical healing.

[13]) Exod. iii 10, iv 19-20, 27, vii 26 (viii 1), xix 10, 14, xxxii 7; Deut. v 13;
Josh. i 2; 2 Sam. vii 4-17; 1 K. xviii 1-2; Is. xxxviii 5; Ezk. iii 24. And not to
go: Num. xxii 12. The 'way of the Lord': Ps. xxxiii 8, c 8, cxviii 1, 3, cxxvii 1;
Prov. xxviii 6, 18, 26. The notion of 'going' = death (Eccles. v 15-16, xii 5;
Ps. xxxix 13; Job xvi 22) is probably absent here.

come [1]). He orders his servants and they obey. [2]). Disobedience leads
to destruction. The Centurion by 'servants' thinks not of demons of
disease (as some have thought)[3]), but angels, since angels are God's,
and so Jesus's, intermediaries and assistants [4]). St. Luke probably
was put in mind of the apostles.   *

   Why was the Centurion apprehensive about Jesus's coming under
his 'roof'? Luke took pains to visualise his position, and produced
an incongruous result. If a holy man enters a house to perform a
service for the owner the question arises whether he will accept
hospitality there. Most spirit-healers would watch what they could
gain (the Naaman story shows what was usually expected). No
hospitality could repay an especially holy healer, nor could one
offer him payment or create a situation whereby the healer would be
under obligation to entertain his former host. Dining was reciprocal,
an aspect of solidarity. An 'untouchable' which both our gentiles
remained [5]), could not presume to inflict upon a Jewish holy man
the humiliation of accepting an obligation or alternatively refusing
his compromising offer of hospitality. Jesus was a special case,
but it was up to him to choose his host, as we know from the
Zacchaeus episode[6]). Moreover, there was the feeling of awe, which
Luke elaborates. The approach of the extremely venerable person
progressively increases awe, and fear supervenes that the house
(in giving shade) would diminish the 'power' of the comer. Jewish
law makes much of the concept of overshadowing ('$\bar{a}h^a lot$) (hence
'roof') in connection with death-pollution (and the boy might be

---

   [1]) Gen. vii 1; Exod. xxiv 1-3, 12-13, xxxiv, 2, 4; Deut. x 1, 3, xxxi 14. Jl.
iii 12. Ps. lxv 2, 5; Is. lx 5; lxvi 23.
   [2]) 1 K. xvii 5, 10; Num. xxxii 20-27. Exod. xxxv 1; Lev. xviii 4-5, 19-31,
xx 8, 22, xxii 31, xxv 18; Num. xv 39-40; Deut. xii 14, 17-19, xxvi 16, xxvii
10, xxxii 45-6, and infinite other examples. Ps. cxlviii 5. Obedience to God
through Elijah: 1 K. xvii 15. Devolution of orders is common: Exod. viii
1-2 (5-6); Num. xxvii 8, 20, 22-3; Deut. xxxi 7-8; Josh. iv 15-18.
   [3]) JEREMIAS (evil spirit). FAIRWEATHER (p. 252). SCHMID and GAECHTER
on the passage. GAECHTER rightly implies that there could not be a silent
contradiction of Mt. xii 25-27. On *expelling* demons cf. Jos., *Ant.* viii 2, 5;
b. Meila 17 b.
   [4]) K. BORNHÄUSER, *Das Wirken des Christus* (Gütersloh, 1921), 71. Mk.
xiii 27; Mt. iv 11; xxiv 31; xxvi 53. Cf. Lk. xvi 22. Is. vi 6-7 may be in point.
J.-B. FREY, 'L'Angéologie juive au Temps de Jésus-Christ', *R. Sc. Phil. et
Théol.* 5 (1911), 75-110. J. BONSIRVEN, *Palestinian Judaism in the Time of
Christ* (N.Y., 1965), ch. 2. Exod. xxiii 23; xxxii 34; Num. xxii 20-23, 32, 35.
   [5]) J. I. HASLER (a writer with Asian experience), *Exp. T.* 45 (1934),
459-461.
   [6]) DERRETT, *Law in the New Testament* (London, 1970), 278-285.

about to die!), but the concept is relevant even outside the pollution of death. A holy man's shadow will itself have 'power' (Acts v 15). Under the roof one supersensorily contacts its limitations (e.g. had it been bought out of 'pure' wealth?) and holy men's reactions are unpredictable. This, rather than fear that the house might be ritually impure, is the reason behind the protestation that he was not ἱκανός.

The Centurion transfers by analogy the concept he is proud to operate in his secular life (that of ἐξουσία, *potestas*) to the spirit world, and catches the spirit of Judaism as Jesus knows it. Even as a mere gentile he knows that kings, supreme holders of *potestas*, are life-givers, or are believed to be by the simple [1]). When St. Luke read the Q account he must have been struck by the irony it contained. The man exercised *potestas*, but here seemed to have been frustrated. The spirit world was full of *potestates* of various kinds [2]). In the secular world his word was law: but here was a servant who could not go! By contrast he asks Jesus to help, and Jesus went; he asked him to stop, and he stopped. By a kind of collegiality he applied to Jesus for *potestas* in the spirit world; and Jesus complied. Was it Jesus's function to comply? That was the *potestas* 'given' to him [3]). The relationship between military officers and the secular power on the one hand and the spiritual power on the other had, before St. Luke wrote, been explored twice—in ancient times, and in A.D. 39-40 in the episode of Petronius and the Images which gives us a documentation of the subject.

Within the Elijah story (2 K i) there is the story of Ahaziah, son of Ahab, a virtual apostate, which explains the power of Elijah vis-à-vis earthly potentates. We read it carefully since Luke recollected it at Acts xx 9. The king orders Elijah to come; he refuses

---

[1]) A. M. Hocart, *Kings and Councillors* (ed. R. Needham) (Chicago and London, 1970). 2 K. v 6-8 is most relevant (A. Finkel, *Pharisees*, 1964, 100)!

[2]) Frey, cited at p. 178 n. 3 supra, at p. 93. G. B. Caird, *Principalities and Powers* (Oxford, 1956). H. Schlier, *Principalities and Powers in the New Testament* (N.Y., 1962). Thus 'power over them' is logical: Mk. iii 15, vi 7, 12. C. K. Barrett, *The Holy Spirit and the Gospel Tradition* (1947), 69 ff., 78-82; Hans Conzelmann, *The Theology of St. Luke* (London, 1960), 181 ff. D. Daube's article on ἐξουσία à propos of Mk. i 22, 27 at *J.T.S.* 39 (1938) 45-59 has impressed lexicographers but is contradicted by A. W. Argyle at *Exp. T.* 80 (1968-9), 343, and discussed by Barrett at 80-1.

[3]) God gives this ἐξουσία: Mt. ix 8! The power can be delegated: Mt. x 1. Delegation there must be: Mk. xi 28, Mt. xxi 23 = Lk. xx 2. So Mt. xxviii 18; also Mk. xiii 34; Jn. xix 11.

twice and would have refused a third time had not God ordered him
to go. Apart from the saints and Nebuchadnezzar this is the most
striking example of prophetic disobedience to a king. The king orders
his captain of fifty (πεντηκόνταρχος) to go, and he goes (to his death),
and the next to go (similarly), and the third; the last too goes but
begs his life to be spared, twice using the plea that he should be
dear (ἐντιμωθήτω, cf. Lk. vii 2, ἔντιμος) to Elijah. Elijah respects his
humility. In the face of the coming of divine power no one can stand,
no one is sufficient (ἱκανός) [1]) and humility is religiously as well as
socially appropriate [2]). The king died because he consulted Baal-
zebub, not Yahweh; Elijah would have cured him had he 'enquired'
of Yahweh. Our Centurion combines the two features of obedience
to his secular superior with humility before the representative of
Yahweh and rejection of evil spirits. The theme of sending intermediaries (two kinds of ἄγγελος) is very prominent in the Ahaziah
story, and this (I submit) is why Luke modified Q as he did. Q told
of a gentile who knew Judaism through his ears as a God-fearer, was
admitted to social intercourse with Jews, *and* knew Judaism with
his heart, since he turned to God and not to heathen deities in a
crisis (cf. Mk. iii 23-24). In his concern for his servant he already
resembled a Jewish master [3]). The story of Ahaziah is a warning to
kings and their officers, promising life to those, who, irrespective of
their submission to secular *potestas*, can preserve themselves by
spiritual submission to a greater *potestas*. Were the soldiers of the
centurion positively affected by the event, more or less as he was?
Just as kings appoint centurions, so the spirit world (he believed)
had its hierarchy, its devolution of 'power', as Jethro recommended
and Moses accepted: for the 'judges' instituted at that time were
both secular and spiritual authorities.

The intellectual position was already established. Caesar exercised the highest *potestas* [4]). All Greek words for 'Lord' applied
to him. When God's commands were likely to be violated by the
commands of Caesar the Jews protested that they would give their
lives 'to a man': more than rhetoric, as Petronius discovered. The
latter, ordered to instal Caesar's statue in the Temple, argued that he
must carry out Caesar's orders or forfeit his life. He actually said,

---

[1]) K. H. RENGSTORF at ThWzNT III, 294 ff.

[2]) Jl. ii 11; Mal. iii 2; Rev. vi 15, 17. The ἄρχων Naaman had great
struggles with humility (2 K. v 9-11, 15) but ended up echoing the words of
Jethro (cf. 2 K. v 15 with Exod. xviii 11).

[3]) Job xxxi 13-15. b. Giṭṭ. 37 b.   [4]) See p. 177 n. 7 supra.

if we are to believe Josephus ¹), that he too was under orders, as the
Jews were under God's orders to the contrary. The rhetorical account given by Philo emphasises the Jews' irony when they spoke
of their Lord and Master. Petronius was expected to think they
meant Caesar, but they meant God ²). Yet Petronius was as know-
ledgeable about Judaism as he was about *potestas*! ³) An irresistible
force approached an immovable object. The quality of Caesar's *imperium* was like that of God: but, implied the Jews, Caesar can kill
the body but he cannot take away the world to come (Lk. xii 4-5:
ἐξουσία again!). Thus everyone who retained acquaintance with a
notorious piece of Jewish history knew that our Centurion (more
perspicacious than Petronius), without deserting his duty as a
soldier, could admit that the God of the Hebrew nation was the
universal master in spiritual matters, and Jesus his appointed
subordinate. Jesus healed by will alone: but he did this through
the power conferred upon him by God ⁴).

I have already drawn attention to the appropriateness of Jethro
in this story, and surmised that St. Luke must have consulted it
when drafting his version of this episode. It is believed that the
Haftarah read out in the synagogue with the 'Jethro' *seder* was Is.
xxxiii 13 ff ⁵). Some words in that *haftarah* are certainly relevant

¹) The whole passage, *Ant.* XVIII, 261-288, is fascinating. The crucial
words are at the parallel passage in *Bell.*, II, 192-202, at 195 (Loeb edn., ii,
399): καὶ ἐμοὶ φυλακτέος ὁ τοὐμοῦ δεσπότου νόμος . . . καὶ γὰρ αὐτός, ὥσπερ
ὑμεῖς, ἐπιτάσσομαι. E. SCHÜRER, *History of the Jewish People in the Time of
Jesus Christ* I/ii (Edinburgh, 1890), 99-105 (the parallel not noticed). It is
of value to understand the emperor's intentions. The *andrias* (as of a king or a
hero) was to be placed in the god's (i.e. Yahweh's) temple as a votive offering,
and not as an insult (the word *andrias* differs from *agalma*, whereas *eikon* is
indifferent). The position is fully documented by A. D. NOCK, 'ΣΥΝΝΑΟΣ
ΘΕΟΣ', *H.S.C.P.* 41 (1930), 1-62, reprinted at *Essays* (supra), I (1972), 202-
51; see especially p. 346 n. 8.
²) Philo, *Leg. ad. Caium*, 218, 233-9. For the vocabulary, e.g. δεσπότης,
δυνάστης see rich references at FREY, *R.B.*, N.S. 13 (1916), 33 ff., at
p. 48 nn. 6-7.
³) Philo, *Leg. ad Caium*, 245. Josephus also shows Petronius as a devotee
of the Temple!
⁴) The text does not support W. Manson's idea that Jesus merely guarant-
eed a cure: *Gospel of Luke* (London, 1930) 76. The famous and rare case of
distant healing by a holy man, b. Ber. 34 b (FIEBIG, *Jüdische Wunderge-
schichte*, 20) (R. Ḥanina b. Dosa) is not a parallel, since he did not purport to
be God's agent, but only suppliant, and Jesus does not operate by mere
prayer (Jn. xi 41-2!!). And Ḥ. was not a notable in other respects: SCHECHTER,
Some Aspects of Rabbinic Theology, 7 .
⁵) See J. MANN, *The Bible as Read and Preached in the Old Synagogue* I
(Cincinnati, 1940), 446-52.

to the theme: 'Hear (or 'they shall hear'), those that are far off, what I have done; and know (or 'they shall know'), those that are near, my might . . . the Lord is our judge, the Lord is our ruler, the Lord is our king: he will save us . . . the sojourner shall not say 'I am ill', the people that dwells in her (Jerusalem) whose inquity has been taken away . . . Draw near, O nations; hearken, O peoples (otherwise 'rulers', 'kingdoms') . . . ' It is not known whether St. Luke intended his gospel to fit into any existing lectionary, but if he did the Torah and Prophets lections would seem to be sufficiently appropriate. But the question must be approached on a comprehensive basis.

CONCLUSION: TEACHING AND FACT

The stories tell upon what footing gentiles might participate in the life-giving force at the Messiah's disposal. The Centurion's boy and the woman's daughter were both cured as a free gift: in neither case did he act by way of reciprocity. The faith (if any) of the two young people was irrelevant. In both cases the Name of God was hallowed amongst the heathen, plainly a command incumbent upon Jesus as upon every Jew. That the conversations took place can hardly be doubted: the intellectual and literary aspects must have had a factual peg from which to hang. The characteristic appearance of a legal debate certifies the inherent Jewishness of each episode, since Jews had a great taste for such debates with gentiles in which the former invariably worsted the latter [1]). It is significant that, in appearance only, the gentiles have the upper hand in these two instances. Gentiles could claim Jesus's attention either on the basis that they accepted his Father as Master of the Universe and him as his delegate, or on the basis that they came to him as objects of charity. In the latter case all allusion to 'Jewish legalism' is irrelevant. The Centurion's secular experience brought him to this act of faith (rather like the Unjust Steward), and he took upon himself the yoke of the Kingdom (as if he were reciting the Sh^{e}ma'). The woman's human need was enough. Whether this was understood by the apostles can be left open, since the problem with which they were faced was different. The relevance of the Syro-

---

[1]) An impressive list is given at Bultmann, op. cit., 42 n. 2. A gentile quotes scripture at Tanḥuma, Terumah 100 quoted by Billerbeck at p. 725 (a story of R. ʿAqiba). The pagans could sometimes be more successful: Yahweh against Serapis in P. Oxy. 1242 (dated in the time of Caracalla according to VON PREMERSTEIN, Philol. Suppl. xvi/2 (1923), 64 ff.).

Phoenician woman to Rom. i 16, ii 9, 10; Acts iii 26, xiii 46 is obvious.

Why did St. Luke omit the story of the woman? [1]) Parts of her tale are scattered elsewhere in his gospel, verbally or by implication (Lk. xi 13; xvi 21). And 1 K. xvii 23 reappears at Lk. ix 42. In the eschatological scheme inaugurated by Jesus there is no difference between Jew and Greek, both being entitled to the same benefits. The notion 'Jew first and then the Greek' [2]) is scripturally accurate [3]) and logically and historically unexceptionable. But once the gentiles come to Jesus because they know he is God's deputy or because they believe he will aid them in charity, they are upon as good a footing as if they were actually born to the expectation of the world to come [4]). St. Luke is (in my view) unlikely to have been offended by the 'first' aspect, or by the humble position of one content with 'crumbs'; for in his story of the Centurion he combined the themes of reciprocity, charity, and (emphatically) humility (Prov. xxii 4) as well as the praise of a gentile who literally fulfilled Zech. viii 20-23.

Could there have been a historical event behind each healing? Could reminiscence have played a part (as the crisp texts suggest)? Or was this merely an assurance that gentiles had nothing better, and they might afterwards look for nothing less? After the Ascension, one might reply, Jewish Christians too were as remote from Jesus as Greeks! Many writers deny the historicity of the healing [5]). Little is known of spiritual healing (for it is chiefly in primitive societies that one now finds the necessary naivity and self-submission). To dismiss the miracles out of hand is unjustified. In the last two decades strides have been made in child and adolescent psychiatry. The old approach to miracles, viz. that the intent

---

[1]) CROCKETT, cit. sup., shows at 179-180 the exploitation of the Elijah and Elisha stories in Lk. and Acts, seemingly rendering the Syrophoenician woman unnecessary.

[2]) Rom. i. 16, ii 11-16, 26-9, iii. 9, xvi 26.

[3]) Is xlii 5-7.

[4]) BRAUDE, *Jewish Proselyting*, 41, refers to b. Shab. 31 a and *Pesiqta Rabbati* ch. 35, para. 3 (trans. BRAUDE, 1968, ii, 674). Note the mention of Jethro there.

[5]) Keim, following Strauss, 'wish uttered in the imperative'. Burkill (originally Mk. vii 27 b was a downright rejection of gentiles). Many regard it as unimportant relative to the teaching about faith being fulfilled in experience through Jesus (Schweizer). Even Lindars speaks of the miraculous element as requiring 'agnostic reserve'.

of the evangelist is best understood if one eschews factual investigation, no longer matches with our information. It is accepted
that acute distress amongst children, especially schizophrenia, is
due to open or hidden disturbance in their guardians, usually their
parents. Acute symptoms, such as eneuresis and encopresis, are
caused by home conditions which yield to psychiatric treatment not
primarily of the child but rather of his family. In some cases, which
appear miraculous to the layman, the psychiatrist can detect that
much of the trouble lies with highly disturbed parents or guardians, whose symptoms are traceable to their own parents [1]), and
in many cases the accurate diagnosis of the origin of the trouble,
combined with effective treatment of the adult, will cure the
child. The release of pressure on the child may have what in retro-
spect can be described as an immediate cure, especially where the
neurosis originates in anxiety. What is remarkable in these New
Testament cases is that the cure of the adult, who may well have
been the real patient, rather than the cure of the child, who was
the ostensible patient, took place so quickly. It is unnecessary
to imagine that Jesus sent messengers or that the children were
already cured by learning that their guardians were on the way to
Jesus, or some telepathic awareness on his part (Cadoux). The
guardians were (if I am right in this guess) cured after what purports to be a discussion. Mark and Q give only an edited summary

---

[1]) N. W. ACKERMAN, *The Psychodynamics of Family Life* (N.Y., 1958),
chs. 14, 15, 19, 21. A. H. BOWLEY, *Problems of Family Life*, 2nd edn. (London, 1948); *The Natural Development of the Child* (Edinburgh and London,
1957), 137-9, 142-3; D. W. WINNICOTT, *The Child and the Outside World*
(London, 1959), 98 ff.; E. H. ERIKSON, *Childhood and Society* (N.Y., 1956),
ch. 5; E. J. ANTHONY, 'Effects of training under stress in children', in J. M.
TANNER, ed., *Stress and Psychiatric Disorder* (Oxford, Blackwell, 1960), 34-
46; R. D. LAING, *The Divided Self* (London, 1959), ch. 11; *The Politics of the
Family and other Essays* (London, 1971), esp. pp. 36-8. C. G. JUNG, *Structure
and Dynamics of the Psyche (Works*, vol. 8) (London, 1960), 304: the psychological *after-effects* of parents can lead to a systematised cult, e.g. ancestor-
worship. Laing's ideas (above) relate especially to schizophrenics, who, in the
ancient world, must have been classic 'demonized' cases. Laing has abandoned the concept of 'schizophrenia' as a specific condition. His ideas arouse
scepticism amongst 'orthodox' psychiatrists, but they command very wide
respect. R. D. LAING and A. ESTERSON, *Sanity, Madness and the Family*[2]
(London, 1970), 12: 'We set out to illustrate by eleven examples that, if we
look at some experience and behaviour without reference to family interaction, they may appear comparatively socially senseless, but that if we look
at the same . . . in their original family context they are liable to make more
sense'. Their evidence impresses.

of what took place, but it seems very short. Modern experts would require several months' therapy to help the adult and so relieve the child; and the modern therapist would need to see the child. But let us look at these conversations more closely. Modern therapy would use suggestion, a kind of hypnosis, free association, and other techniques enabling the hidden past to come to the surface of the mind. What (for example) is this talk (in psychiatric terms) of 'puppies'? How are they related to the woman's relationship to her child? What aggression does her make-up contain? She was divorced, deserted, or a widow, and her child lived in a classic situation for disturbance. The centurion actually initiates a talk about discipline and absolute obedience. He seeks submission to an absolute ideal: his secular experience evidently lacks this quality (as well it might). His servant or slave was in a state of complete disobedience, perhaps as a defensive response. What do we know of a *slave's* mentality; how would their contemporary counterparts to our psychiatrists deal with disturbed ex-dolly-boys, for example? But we do know that both adults were convinced, to the point of utter want of self-consciousness, that a 'man of God' held their answer. The eliciting of this fact could have relieved those adults of the burden they carried, and this could have at once paved the way for the children's cure. I say it is possible: I go no further. Denials of the reality of the events are premature. They would, at those times, have been regarded as miraculous. Gentiles going to a 'man of God' in those two fashions would, of course, be very much more suggestible than Jews, for whom direct access to God in prayer was an everyday experience.

In both stories we find Jesus enacting what is said of God at Ps. cvii 17-20: 'Fools, because of their rebellion and due to their sins, are afflicted. Their soul abhors all food; they draw near to the gates of death. They cry to the Lord in their trouble; he saved them out of their stresses. He *sent his word and healed them,* and delivered them from their destruction.'

FURTHER ANNOTATIONS

p. [163], l. 12. *arton* at *v.* 27 no doubt alludes to the eucharistic crumb which will be given to the gentile 'convert' after her exorcism/baptism on the pattern of Mk. v. 43. A. Farrer, *A Study in St. Mark* (Westminster, 1951), 298-9. J. Jeremias, *Abendmahlsworte Jesu*[4] (Göttingen, 1967), 226.

p. [169], l. 12. On the one hand sacred food must not be allowed to be taken by dogs: (for India) P.V. Kane, *History of Dharmaśāstra* IV (Poona, 1953), 85 n. 203; and on the other hand flesh torn in the field must not be eaten by 'holy man' and must be thrown to the dogs, or to foreigners who are likened to dogs (Neofiti Targum on Exod. xxii.30-31: A. Díez Macho, *Studi e Testi* 231, 1964, 184, §50).

p. [170], n. 5. On low qualities of bread see D. Sperber, *Tarbiz* 36 (1967), 199-201 (citing various sources including b. Qid. 22a).

p. [174], l. 13. The parallel with 2 K. v. 1-14 was seen by A. Finkel, *The Pharisees and the Teacher of Nazareth* (Leiden, 1964), 100, and by Goulder, *Midrash and Lection* (1974), 46, 319-21. The point is that secular authorities could do nothing for this important suppliant, and in his worshipping of the true God whilst for political purposes he adhered to the state religion he suitably anticipated Roman and Greek behaviour in Palestine.

p. [176], n. 3. I admit that *kyrios* can be a respectful form of address, and that at the historical level it is not to be taken to mean more (so Kilpatrick, Moule, and Schweizer). However, as in so many places, the spirit not present to the pagan's *mind* enables him to utter, like a prophet (cf. Mk. xv.39), truths of which he has no real knowledge.

p. [179], l. 5. An allusion to 1 Sam. viii.12 is not unthinkable.

p. [182], n. 4. Ḥanina b. Dosa (on whom see Vermes, *op. cit.*) was a *yogī*, not a miracle-worker, though the distinction is thin. He did not kill the snake by magic, nor revive Zakkai's son by magic: it was by yogic prayer.

This is the point at which to refer to the handling of the Syro-Phoenician woman and the Centurion by R.H. Fuller, *Interpreting the Miracles* (London, 1963), 21-22,48, 59-60. My appreciation of this book has been stated in my preface. But this is an example of the problems raised by the form-critical method. Ḥanina's prayer does not prove that healing-at-a-distance was a Hellenistic wonder-theme, still less that the early church derived the story from unauthentic sources. The form-critical criteria, viz. that we cannot attribute to Jesus anything which could have emerged either from a Hellenistic environment, from rabbinic or quasi-rabbinic Judaism, or from the self-conscious needs of the early church, beg too many questions, especially since the Dead Sea Scrolls were discovered. Fuller says that in the Syro-Phoenician woman's story 'we can see the early church wrestling... with the problem of the gentile mission' and we need not (it seems) look for even a grain of reminiscence. Further, he says that it is often thought that the story of the centurion of Capernaum, as the only (*known*) miracle story in Q, exists *and existed* to urge gentiles to have faith in Jesus as authorised by God; i.e. Christological reflection outstripped the historical Jesus's concern that those people should be healed who have faith in God's saving activity. Without for a moment questioning Fuller's formula of faith as an 'energetic grasping which can call forth the act of God' (p. 73), I draw attention to the systematic reconstruction which tends to delimit Jesus's activity according to a single theological theory.

On the other hand Fuller's approach reminds us of something which I did not sufficiently emphasise in this article, viz. that Jesus's authority (*exousia*), brought into the foreground by the Cleansing of the Temple, is a major theme in St. Mark, and flowers in St. John. The recognition that this emanated from the Creator *as such* and did not relate only to the House of Israel was a major discovery and I do not think it emerged only in the 'early church'—it could well have been Jesus's own, exactly as the Syro-Phoenician story suggests.

RELIGIOUS HAIR

Translators of the Bible are aware that anthropological information greatly assists in the recovery of the original meaning of the books of the Old Testament. A corresponding awakening awaits translators of the New. A very striking discovery (Daube 1971) conclusively proves that St Paul, writing to the church at Corinth on the highly technical subject of the marital status of converts to Christianity (which was then still a sect of Judaism), used somewhat recondite allusions to Jewish law, and used them by analogy, without explanation. This discovery. reveals, as a byproduct, that no translator had understood the passage (1 Cor. 7:12-16). Translators, products of schools teaching Greek with an exclusively classical (i.e. Western) bias, were unable to understand Paul's argument, and the result was the universally recognised 'Pauline Privilege', which, as an unexplained anomaly and departure from Christ's teaching regarding marriage, now happily turns out to be a mare's nest. Not long ago I was able to show (Derrett 1970:471) that the epistle to the Romans was written on the assumption that its readers would have had the Jewish institution of the levirate marriage in mind[1]: and once it was admitted that St Paul wrote for Jewish readers to understand, and expound to their non-Jewish proselytes, a whole string of apologies for Paul became unnecessary. In this note I offer an explanation for a passage, worn threadbare by uncomprehending theological and pastoral debate. A typical critic[2] roundly accuses Paul of absurdity. It is far better to believe that Paul was an Asian (in both senses, a native of Asia and culturally steeped in the Jewish, an Asian culture), and that amongst his correspondents he knew there were leading Jewish personalities who were in touch with Jewish law and lore. If this is accepted, the problem vanishes; but it will take a little space to explain the point since even the most literal translation of the passage (1 Cor. 11: 2–16) cannot convey the meaning adequately. It will be seen that any existing translation fails to do justice to it, and a paraphrase is required. A recent theological study by a scholar renowned for original ideas concerning New Testament history (Jaubert 1972) is valuable for purposes of comparison—but it is innocent of anthropology and law.

But first, who were the Corinthians? It is useful to copy what is said by Kümmel (1966: 200), and to add a little to him: 'Paul taught first of all in the synagogue, then, after the conflict with the Jews, in the house of the proselyte, Titus Justus (Acts 18: 4 sqq.). . . . After Paul's activity of a year and a half in Corinth (Acts 18: 11), there existed a flourishing congregation. It consisted of Gentile Christians (1 Cor. 12: 2), predominantly from the lower classes (1: 26 sqq.), but there was also a Jewish-Christian element (Acts 18: 4; 1 Cor. 7: 18), and an admixture of those of higher social and economic status (1 Cor. 11: 21 sqq.; Acts 18: 8; Rom. 16: 23). After Paul, Apollos, an eloquent, theologically trained Jewish Christian from Alexandria, whom Aquila and Priscilla had won to Christianity (Acts 18: 24 sqq.;

1 Cor. 3: 5 sqq.) worked there for a while in a similar manner.' I should add that whereas 1 Cor. 12: 2 makes it clear that the 'Corinthians' contained men who were (how long back?) Gentiles, the wording of 1 Cor. 7: 18, which refers to men being circumcised prior to their 'conversion', proves that Jews figured in the church to which Paul wrote. But no evidence is so telling as Daube's discovery (1971), which proves that Paul made no conscious concession to the intellectual foreignness of the Gentile proselyte element amongst his correspondents.

To our problem: the text of 1 Cor. 11: 2–16 reads nonsensically; it appears to say that if a woman given to prophecy and prayer is not willing to cover her head while praying or prophesying she had better get her head shaved, and if she would shrink from that she had better keep her head covered. There is something about her husband's power over her head, and about the angels. The last allusion has been laughed at from the time Biblical criticism commenced, if not sooner. The cultural information we need is slender enough, but it has not been provided. First, men and women kept the head covered in prayer (we must leave aside the practice during mourning, as it is irrelevant),[3] until (as is evident) the church broke away from the synagogue, and, on doctrinal grounds, took up the custom (which the Greeks would welcome) of praying bareheaded: that is to say, the males did. *
The theological reason was evidently that instead of approaching God as a servant/ slave (covering the head, like removing the upper-garment or shoes in other cultures, signifying respect) the Christian, mystically united with Christ at baptism, was a son of God and therefore able to ask from him (for that is what prayer meant) without signs of slavish inferiority. Greek women were usually covered in social life (as sculpture confirms), except in their, or their relations', homes.[4] Hebrew women not only kept their hair tied, but covered it securely when in the open, *
were certainly covered when in a public place, and would not be uncovered in a synagogue. In Corinth some women had begun to pray and 'prophesy' in men's company at times of public worship without a head-covering, as an overt sign *
of their sexual liberation and equality: since in Christ there is no male or female (Gal. 3: 28) any more than there is free man or slave. St Paul objects to this vigorously, and almost incoherently. He ends up by saying, 'However, if you insist on arguing, let me tell you, there is no such custom among us, or in any of the congregations of God's people.' It does not follow that the arguments he uses prior to this were insufficient, either for him, or for them.

The real reason why Eastern women's hair is covered is, as Paul himself indicates, its universal acceptance as a sign of sexual attractiveness. It was not merely that the *
head needed to be covered out of respect: it was because of the long tresses that it needed to be covered. It is certain that if a Hebrew woman untied her hair and uncovered it in public she was regarded as 'shameless', and had no reputation whatever: this is said in so many words in the Mishnah.[5] The person injured when a married woman uncovered her hair in public was her husband, who was put to shame. He had a right to his wife's hair being covered in public. Men did not wear long hair (in spite of the unfounded tradition that the apostles wore long hair) and long hair was effeminate and shameful. For that very reason to vow to wear your hair long was a vow of significance! The Nazirite wore his hair long and there was much ceremony at his cutting it off. When women wanted to vow something valuable they sacrificed the sign of their sexuality, and shaved their heads or cut

the hair close. Josephus incidentally tells us that this was the custom.[6] There is no
reason to connect it with the Nazirite vow (which was exclusively masculine), but
a psychological connexion is more than likely. Like most vows, this vow of
disfigurement must have given the votary a sense of importance and prestige:
one can see that this was the main reason for this, the Nazirites', and other vows
taken while the Temple still stood. A woman (perhaps a widow) who had had her
head shaven or shorn *could* appear with her head uncovered in public, and no
doubt she often did so with pride.

The western idea that shaving a woman's head is a punishment for social misbehaviour has no relation to 1 Cor. 11: 2–16. We should render the passage as
follows:–' . . . I want you to understand that Christ is every man's head; while the
husband is his wife's head, and God is Christ's head. If a man prays or prophesies
with his head *covered* he treats his head with dishonour. Whereas if a woman prays
or prophesies with her head *un*covered she dishonours her head [i.e. her husband!].
For it is exactly the same if she had had her head shaved [without his consent, for
all a wife's vows can be annulled by her husband][7]. If a wife makes a practice of
being bareheaded she may indeed have herself cropped. If a woman feels it is
shameful for her to be cropped or shaven she must keep her head covered. Indeed
a man is under no obligation to keep his head covered: he is the image and glory
[or visible representation, pride] of God. But a wife is her husband's glory. Man
was not derived out of Woman, but Woman out of Man. Man was not created for
the sake of Woman, but Woman for the sake of Man [Gen. 2: 18]. On this basis
a woman is obliged to possess upon her head a (sign of) authority[8] for the sake of
the angels [who, as God's messengers, would report her as shameless and lacking
in awareness of the Creator's intention, and, though they are themselves sexless,
are entitled to the same respect as any superior person]. Further, in the Lord there
is no woman without man, nor man without woman [they are mutually essential];
just as Woman proceeded from Man, so a man (or a husband) is required for (every)
woman. All came from God.[9] Judge the matter in your own setting (or for yourselves). Is it fitting that a woman should pray to God bareheaded? Does not Nature
herself teach us: if a man wears his hair long it dishonours him; if a woman wears
her hair long it is her glory? Her hair is given her as a sort of veil. However, if
you insist on arguing. . .'

The ancient world was capable of subtle thinking, but it had a need (education
not being systematic or general) for concrete propositions rather than general-
isations and abstractions. St Paul would have said to us, I suppose, 'The fact that
a married couple are converted to our religion does not mean that both sexes
throw off the ancient conventions, and proprieties. The husband is entitled to his
wife's modesty in public even if their thoughts are directed towards God. For the
husband's rights are not forfeited simply because their spiritual status has been
changed by their conversion.' It was not that Christian husbands, whether Jewish
or Gentile, had a right to sexual jealousy of angels (if not of fellow-worshippers);
but they had a right to their wives' behaving as married women do. The alternative,
if the husbands agree, is the shaven head of the female votary: but that does not
seem to be what the Corinthian ladies have in mind. And if ever there was a place
where proprieties had to be observed and suspicions averted it was Corinth, upon
which the Temple of Aphrodite looked down.[10]

NOTES

1 Derrett 1970: ch. 18. The discovery is commented by L. L. Vallauri in *Studia et documenta historiae et iuris* **37**, 440–3 (1971).

2 C. S. C. Williams in Peake 1962: 960 ('Scandal of unveiled woman', 'to argue that if she is uncovered, she might as well be shaven, is absurd'). C. H. Dodd speaks of a 'tangle of prejudice' (Sneath 1927: 321).

3 Impurity by reason of death is irrelevant; but grief was dramatised with the wearing of sackcloth and *putting ashes on the head*. Head-squalidness was an overt sign of desperate woe, just as a well-oiled and combed head was a sign of joy. It is conceivable that women with dust and ashes on their heads did not cover the head with their garments. Jaubert (1972: 424–5) draws attention to Bab. Talmud, Sanh. 58b and Ned. 30b.　　　　　　　*

4 It is usually believed that the veiling of women was a practice adopted from Judaism (Schlatter 1955: 75), but this appears to be untrue.　　　　　　　*

5 Baba Qamma VIII.6; Danby 1933: 343. A woman's hair is a sexual incitement: Bab. Talmud, Ber. 24a.　　　　　　　*

6 *Bell. Jud.* ii, §§ 313–14.

7 Mishnah, Ned. X; Danby 1933: 277–8. So in India (it is common sense): *Visnu-dharma-sutra* XXV. 15.　　　　　　　*

8 Note that the Greek *exousia* is the equivalent of the Latin *potestas*, and in Jewish customary law as well as Roman law the wife was certainly in her husband's *potestas* until he divorced her or died. For a different approach see Hooker 1963–1964.

9 Therefore, even unmarried or widowed women must also keep to the convention in this respect. .

10 In the twelfth century B.C. concubines were veiled only when they became wives; wives and widows must veil in public; daughters must veil themselves; harlots who veiled were liable to fifty lashes; one who failed to report a veiled harlot was liable to flogging and enslavement: Middle Assyrian Laws §§40, 41 (trans. T. J. Meek in Pritchard 1950: 183).

REFERENCES

Danby, H. 1933. *The Mishnah.* London: Oxford Univ. Press.

Daube, D. 1971. Pauline contributions to a pluralistic culture. In *Jesus and man's hope* (eds) D. G. Miller & D. Y. Hadidian. Pittsburgh: Pittsburgh Theological Seminary.

Derrett, J. D. M. 1970. *Law in the New Testament.* London: Darton, Longman & Todd.

Hooker, M. 1963–4. Authority on her head: an examination of 1 Cor. 11:10. *New Test. Stud.* 10, 410–16.

Jaubert, Annie 1972. La voile des femmes (1 Cor. xi. 2–16). *New Testament Studies.* **18**, 419–30

Kümmel, W. G. 1966. *Introduction to the New Testament.* London: S. C. M. Press.

Peake, A. S. 1962. *Peake's commentary on the Bible* (eds) M. Black & H. H. Rowley. London: Nelson.

Pritchard J. B. (ed.) 1950. *Ancient Near Eastern texts relating to the Old Testament.* Princeton: Univ. Press.

Schlatter, A. 1955. *The Church in the New Testament period.* London: S. P. C. K.

Sneath, E. H. (ed.) 1927. *Evolution of ethics.* New Haven: Yale Univ. Press.

FURTHER ANNOTATIONS

Tit. This article could have been entitled 'St. Paul's style of scriptural exegesis in a social context', but the snappy anthropological title was quite rightly given to it by the editor because hair is unquestionably as much an anthropological as a psychological topic. The sacrificing of hair at the Temple in Jerusalem is paralleled by the head-shaving and hair-disposal at Kālighāt (Calcutta) in India, and Tirupati (Andhra Pradesh, ibid.). For the anthropological background it is essential to see C. Berg, *The Unconscious Significance of Hair* (London, 1951); E.R. Leach, 'Magical Hair', *J.R. Anth. Inst.* 88 (1958), 147-64; also P. Hershman, 'Hair, sex, and dirt', *Man* 9/2 (1974), 274-98.

p. [100], l. 27. For the pun on *môrâ* see above, p. xii n. 1. The suggestion of a pun was put forward by Fitzmyer (below) but he chose another word.

p. [100], l. 29. The topic is handled by J.C. Hurd, *Origins of 1 Cor.* (London, 1965), 182-6, 228, 281-2. J.A. Fitzmyer, *Essays on the Semitic Background of the New Testament* (London, 1971), ch. 9, is good with a rich bibliography. He draws attention to C. Spicq, *R.B.* 68 (1939), 557-62; S. Lösch, *T.Q.* 127 (1947), 230-51, R. de Vaux, *R.B.* 44 (1936), 397-412, and A. Jeremias (see n. 10 below), *Der Schleier vom Sumer bis heute* (Leipzig, 1931). Fitzmyer suggests that there was a pun on the root ŠLṬ, but I am unable to verify the particulars. He draws attention to Qumran angelology at 1 QM 7.4-6, 1 Q Sa 2.3-11 and 4 Q Db. Absence of a veil might, he suggests, be a bodily defect such as would offend angels concerned with the holiness of the Host.

p. [100], l. 38. G. Theissen, 'Soziale Schichtung in der korinthischen Gemeinde', *Z.N.W.* 65 (1974), 232-72.

p. [101], l. 18. Romans bared the head out of respect (Plutarch, *Crassus*) But the Jews thought a covered head was a symbol of servitude (Targ. Pal.. Gen. xl.18-19) or a sign of shame (Mishnah, Soṭ. IX.15), and that may be why Moses stood uncovered before God: Exod. xxxiv.34.

p. [101], l. 25. A betrothed girl must veil herself before her husband: Gen. xxiv.65. A married woman's uncovered head might be a ground for divorce (j. Giṭṭ. 9,50d). The behaviour of Tamar is peculiar and requires separate consideration (Gen. xxxviii.14, 18). Proselytes were, according to Jewish ideas, a 'new creation', and this enabled women's status to be reviewed.

p. [101], l. 29. They will not have been imitating the Sôṭâ (Num. v. 18), whose typically loosened hair and uncovered head suggests shame, but it is quite possible that they followed the precedent of the women accepted and approved by Christ as at Jn. xi.2, xii.3 and Lk. vii.37-9.

p. [101], l. 37. The hair containing a vitalizing force (or śrī-) and a consecrated person's shaving it after a long period may be seen in this light. J. Gonda, *Numen* 3 (1956), 56; J.C. Heesterman, *The Ancient Indian Royal Consecration* (The Hague, 1957), 215, quoting *Jaiminiya-brāhmaṇa* II.204. The Hindu law generally presumes against the shaving of the head and recent Vedic graduates were not to shave the head. The exceptions are listed narrowly. Aptly P.V. Kane, *History of Dharmaśāstra*, II, 590-1, much exercised about the penitential head-shaving of Hindu widows until quite recently, discusses all the authorities.

p. [102], l. 2. On the contrary, though in practice female Nazirites were little heard of, the biblical texts specifically provide for them (Num. vi.2) and it is admitted that vows not to shave or cut the hair, and other abstentions, existed independently of biblical Naziritism.

p. [102], l. 12. Shakespeare, *Measure for M.* Act IV, sc. 2, ll. 3-5.

p. [102], l. 32. A destitute woman, appealing to a respectable man, could veil herself in her hair: b. Ket. 66b.

p. [103], n. 3. b. Sanh. 58b (bareheadedness means not being married, for Jews and heathens alike).

p. [103], n. 4. S. Carlebach, 'Haarverhüllung des jüd. Weibes', in *D. Hoffmann Fest.* (Berlin, 1914), 454-9, attempts to show (as against A. Rosenzweig, *Kleidung u. Schmuck im bibl. u. talmud. Schrifttum* [Berlin, 1905]) that covering the head was a Jewish religious rule and did not originate from non-Jewish influences. Women must keep their head covered: E. Shereshevsky, *J.Q.R.* 65 (1974), 108-9. The exactly equivalent Hindu custom is more usefully adapted to our purpose since widows used to be shaved. 1 Cor. xi.5 is actually quoted by W. Ward, *View... of the Hindoos* (Serampore, 1818), i,91 n.

p. [103], n. 5. M. Grünbaum, *Neue Beiträge* (Leiden, 1893), 221. F. Delitzsch, *Jewish Artisan Life* (New York, 1883), 42. Mishnah, Naz. IV.7.

p. [103], n. 7. *Kāla-Mādhava*, 257-8. G. Jhā, *Manu-smṛti : Notes* II (Calcutta, 1924), 405, *ad v.* cliii. P.V. Kane, *History of Dharmaśāstra* IV, 603 (tonsuring the head with the husband's permission).

MARCO VII 15-23:
IL VERO SIGNIFICATO DI « PURIFICARE »

Mc. VII 19 c. è una questione controversa assai nota. Si
ritiene che Marco abbia introdotto [1] a questo punto parole che
dànno a Gesù l'apparenza di un legislatore, cosa che si può
mettere in dubbio da un punto di vista storico [2]. È lecito dubitare del potere che Gesù poteva avere di scartare le leggi
dietetiche ebraiche in base a considerazioni storiche; c'è anche
motivo di sospettare della sua volontà effettiva di farlo. Se ef-
fettivamente Gesù scartò le leggi dietetiche, l'episodio del sogno
di Pietro (Atti X 10-16) sarebbe stato inutile, la parte correlativa
del Decreto Apostolico (Atti XV 20) sarebbe stata perversa e
tutte le dispute intorno al ' cibo degli idoli ' nella prima ai
Corinzi sarebbero oziose. Gli Apostoli non conoscevano nessun
pronunciamento di Gesù sulla « indifferenza » dei cibi e delle
bevande in sé e per sé (i passi Rom. XIV 2 e Col. II 20-23
riguardano l'ascesi) e risulta perciò assai poco plausibile l'interpretazione convenzionale di Mc. VII 19 che si trova in tutte le
nostre traduzioni. La questione ruota su una lettera soltanto,
un omega. Se l'omega di καθαρίζων fosse un omicron e se la
parola *brōmata* potesse avere un diverso significato, tutti i pro-
blemi che la frase ci pone sarebbero superati.
    Osserviamo il passo nel suo complesso.

15 Οὐδέν ἐστιν ἔξωθεν τοῦ ἀνθρώπου εἰσπορευόμενον εἰς
αὐτὸν ὃ δύναται κοινῶσαι αὐτόν· ἀλλὰ τὰ ἐκ τοῦ ἀνθρώπου
ἐκπορευόμενά ἐστιν τὰ κοινοῦντα τὸν ἄνθρωπον. 17 Καὶ ὅτε
εἰσῆλθεν εἰς οἶκον ἀπὸ τοῦ ὄχλου, ἐπηρώτων αὐτὸν οἱ μαθηταὶ
αὐτοῦ τὴν παραβολήν. 18 Καὶ λέγει αὐτοῖς, Οὕτως καὶ ὑμεῖς
ἀσύνετοί ἐστε; οὐ νοεῖτε ὅτι πᾶν τὸ ἔξωθεν εἰσπορευόμενον εἰς
τὸν ἄνθρωπον οὐ δύναται αὐτὸν κοινῶσαι, 19 ὅτι οὐκ εἰσπορεύεται
αὐτοῦ εἰς τὴν καρδίαν ἀλλ' εἰς τὴν κοιλίαν, καὶ εἰς τὸν ἀφεδρῶνα
ἐκπορεύεται καθαρίζων (lege καθαρίζον) πάντα τὰ βρώματα;
20 ἔλεγεν δὲ ὅτι τὸ ἐκ τοῦ ἀνθρώπου ἐκπορευόμενον ἐκεῖνο
κοινοῖ τὸν ἄνθρωπον· 21 ἔσωθεν γὰρ ἐκ τῆς καρδίας τῶν ἀνθρώπων
οἱ διαλογισμοὶ οἱ κακοὶ ἐκπορεύονται... 23 πάντα ταῦτα τὰ πονηρὰ
ἔσωθεν ἐκπορεύεται καὶ κοινοῖ τὸν ἄνθρωπον.

Vediamo che cosa succede se si tenta una nuova ipotesi.
Se si ritiene che il testo corretto suoni καθαρίζον, come riportano
taluni manoscritti, il soggetto del participio sarà τὸ ἔξωθεν
εἰσπορευόμενον. Βρώματα non significherà in questo caso « cibo » (escludendo le bevande!), bensì « materia putrefatta »,
« sporcizia », accezioni ben documentate nel greco di vari periodi[3]. Nella frase non ci sono interruzioni. Le parole non sono
tra virgolette e non costituiscono un corumento dell'Evangelista.
La traduzione è:

« Certamente voi sapete che niente che entri nell'uomo
da *fuori* è capace di ' contaminarlo ' perché non entra nella
sua mente (alla lettera: nel suo cuore) ma soltanto (nel) suo
ventre e passa nello scolo purgandolo così di tutta la sporcizia? Ed egli disse: « Ciò che esce *fuori* d'un uomo è ciò che
lo ' contamina ', perché da dentro, dalla mente dell'uomo, procedono i pensieri iniqui... Tutti quei peccati procedono dal di
dentro e lo ' contaminano ' ».

Questa è un *midrash* elaborato su un detto di Gesù che può
essere autentico, cioè: « Ciò che entra dentro non può contaminare, ma ciò che esce da un uomo può! ». Per capire occorre rammentare alcuni fatti[4].

1. Lo stato normale degli uomini è comune, profano, cioè
ritualmente inadatto alla presenza divina e pertanto ' contaminato '.

2. Una persona ritualmente purificata non è più qualificata per la preghiera se ' contaminata '.

3. Coloro che sono uniti nel culto formano una comunità
santa. Cibi contaminanti e impedimenti simili fanno venir meno
la schiettezza e la qualificazione della compagnia. La comunità
rimane qualificata per il culto grazie anche all'astensione dal
cibo impuro (cfr. Deut. XIV 21).

4. Se la mera astensione da certi cibi e bevande fosse equi-

valente alla ‘ santità ’ si giungerebbe a includere di diritto
gente insincera, mentre persone sincere ma negligenti in fatto
di dieta rimarrebbero escluse (così Ass. *Mos.* VII 9-10). Perciò
il detto di Gesù ha una rilevanza sociale ed è inclusa appunto
in una parte del Vangelo di Marco riguardante i Gentili (cfr.
Flavio Giuseppe, *B. J.* VII 264).

5. L'idea di una santità interiore contrastante con una contaminazione esteriore e viceversa (cfr. specie Mt. XXIII 25-26;
Lc. XI 39-41) è familiare nel Giudaismo [5], come anche l'idea
affine che la sostanza contaminante, impura, non trasmette ugual-
mente l'impurità all'esterno e all'interno dell'uomo [6]. Inoltre
la facoltà che hanno gli oggetti impuri, di far sì che chi ne
mangia renda impuri altri oggetti, era materia di discussione [7].
C'era una messe di spunti per la predicazione, coi quali si met-
teva a contrasto con la sostanziale disubbidienza alla Legge la
« santità » superficiale.

6. In particolare agli Ebrei era familiare l'equazione morale « peccato » = impurità cioè una squalifica rituale metaforica,
la « contaminazione » [8].

Che i peccati si potessero « lavare » è un pensiero antico,
sviluppato nel processo storico del pensiero. La folla avrebbe
ben potuto però esitare a scartare una preferenza per ciò che
viene facilmente notato, i segni esteriori della « purezza » e
della « santità ».

7. Tutte le società asiatiche sanno che le escrezioni che il
corpo emette attraverso orifizi (in contrasto con ciò che pro-
viene dal corpo altrimenti) [9] è contaminante. Contaminano chi
le espelle e spesso anche colui sul quale incidentalmente o de-
liberatamente vadano a cadere [10].

Ciò che passa nel corpo può squalificare come membri d'una
comunità di preghiera, ma la persona stessa è resa ‘ intocca-
bile ’, ‘ contaminata ’ da certe escrezioni. La donna mestruante
ne è l'esempio tipico e più drammatico. Come la contaminazione
metaforica proveniva da atti iniqui, secondo la tradizione pro-
fetica del Giudaismo [11], così il non essere lavati, cioè la mancanza di penitenza, rendeva il colpevole moralmente contaminato.
Ciò che esce dall'uomo nelle sue escrezioni lo contamina fino a
che non si purifichi (non può pregare Iddio finché le sue mani
ed i suoi piedi non sono ritualmente puliti); ciò che da un uomo
procede quanto a delitti e peccati lo lascia contaminato fino al
pentimento (cui si deve aggiungere, nei casi congrui, la resti-
tuzione).

La tesi di Gesù è che a parte le leggi dietetiche, che hanno qui rilevanza soltanto per la loro funzione simbolica, ciò che
contamina l'uomo è la sua intenzione prava (διαλογισμός; cfr.

Test. Benj VIII 3). Quando questa si è esternata in azioni egli ne resta contaminato e la sua purità rituale va perduta. Cibi e bevande proibiti che entrano dalla bocca incidentalmente o deliberamente si limitano a transitare per il dotto digerente; il loro effetto, quando c'è, dura soltanto per il tempo che vi rimangono. Certi dotti ebrei arriverebbero a dubitare perfino se chi mangia è contaminato una volta che il cibo abbia varcato la gola [12].

Resta, l'interrogativo come si poté commettere l'errore di leggere- ίζων per -ίζον.

La soluzione è semplice. A parte il desiderio dei Gentili che Gesù avesse abrogato le leggi dietetiche, le parole di Marco esigono in ambito greco un commento. Il verbo καθαίρω / καθαρίζω si usa in greco costantemente nel senso rituale di « purificare ritualmente ». La costruzione, come in questo caso, col doppio accusativo, per cui si purifica qualcuno da qualcosa, è testimoniata, ma non è comune [13]. Quando si sia letta la parola *brōmata* come « cibi », invece che come « materia corrotta » la parola consueta καθαρίζω = « purifico » diventa inintelligibile, dato che non si può certo rendere puri dei cibi espellendone il residuo impuro per uno scolo. Così a qualcuno venne l'idea brillante che -ίζον fosse un errore per -ίζων e alterò il testo in conformità. Certo questo fu il tema di parecchie discussioni e poté essere perfino il risultato di un dibattito pubblico solenne. Tutti sapevano che *o* ed *ω* erano pronunciati, in quasi tutto il mondo di lingua greca, in modo identico [14]. I frammenti dei Vangeli sembra che abbiano avuto una loro vita orale a parte quella scritta: era facile sospettare che si fosse trascritta la vocale sbagliata. Erano ben note certe confusioni [15] e si riteneva che questa fosse semplicemente una in più. Così la non necessaria « correzione » entrò nel migliore dei manoscritti e di lì nei testi stampati, salvo – ed è interessante notarlo – in un Testamento greco assai diffuso, stampato in Grecia!

E adesso possiamo capire la perizia letteraria di Gesù. Esistono due paradossi. Ciò che entra dentro all'uomo non contamina lui ma il suo canale digerente fino a quando abbandona lo stomaco! Ciò che esce *fuori* dell'uomo non lo contamina, come si pensa, con la sua escrezione, bensì con i segni palesi della prava intenzione. Evitare i cibi contaminanti doveva servire a mantenere pura l'intenzione. L'idea della contaminazione causa l'escrezione era in rapporto con la ri-purificazione prima di entrare con la preghiera alla presenza di Dio. Ogni contaminazione perciò riguarda la condizione spirituale, cioè la presenza o l'assenza del peccato. Se ciò è vero per l'Ebreo lo è altrettanto per il Gentile. La manipolazione redazionale del testo al fine di incoraggiare il Gentile cristiano a riconciliarsi col giudaismo quale veniva predicato dalla Chiesa primitiva, era, a quel che sembra, interamente giustificata.

¹ W. Brandt *Jüdische Reinheitslehre* (Giessen 1910), 57 n. 1. V. Taylor *Gosp. acc. to St. Mark* (Londra 1963), 345 n. (commento dell'Evangelista). Per M. Black *vide infra*, n. 3. C. S. Rodd, *Exp. T.* 79 (1967/8), 169 (estensione esegetica).

² V. Taylor, 343 n. W. D. Davies, *Christian Origins and Judaism* (Londra 1962), 44. Fra i testi ai quali Gesù contraddirebbe se il significato fosse quello che di solito si crede, ci sarebbe Lev. XVII 15-16. E. Trocmé, *Jesus and His Contemporaries* (Londra 1973), 40 (la libertà di Gesù ' si estendeva fino alla lettera della Legge '). Il nostro problema è trattato da C. E. Carlston, *The Things That Defile (Mc. VII 14) and the Law in Matthew and Mark* in "N.T.S." 15 (1968), 75-96 (si riteneva che Gesù non soltanto accantonasse le tradizioni degli scribi ma anche la forza vincolante della Legge mosaica stessa).

³ P. Chantraine, *Dict Etim. de la Langue Grecque* (Paris 1968), 200. H. Frisk, *gr. etym. Wört.* I (1960), 275. Liddell-Scott-Jones, *Gk.-Eng. Lexicon*, 9 lo preferisce per Mc. VII 19. βρῶμα = marciume (Epist. Jer. 10 LXX); Diosc. (*ca.* A.D. 60), 1, 141, 146, 2.69. βεβρωμένοι = ammuffito; βεβρωμένα = verminoso (Diosc. 3, 9); βρῶμος = puzzo (Giob. VI 7; Sap. XI 19; Gioele II 20 LXX; Diosc., Galeno) ἄβρωμος = senza fetore; βρωμώδης = marcio; βρῶσις = ruggine. Greco mod. βρομιχὸ, « sporco ». N. Bachtin, *Introduction to the Study of Modern Greek* (Cambridge 1935), 76 (la traduzione che dà il Pallis di Mc. VII 19 in greco volgare comporta βρῶματα = fetore, impurità). C'è un equivalente ebraico: essere digerito dalle viscere è *nit'akēl* (Mishnah, Ber. VIII 7). Sulla corruzione negli escrementi cfr. Aristot. Meteor. 381b 6-13. Che si sia sulla pista giusta è attestato dalla vecchia traduzione sirica: βρῶμα = *'ukhla* (« escremento »): così N. Black, *An Aramaic Approach to the Gospels and Acts* ³ (Oxford 1967), 217-8.

⁴ W. H. Gispen, *The Distinction between Clean and Unclean,* in * « O.T.S. » 5 (1948), 190-6; S. Stein, *The Dietary Laws in Rabbinical and Patristic Literature,* « Stud. Patr. » 2 (1927), 141 ss. W. Paschen *Rein und Unrein* (München 1970). J. Neusner, *The Idea of Purity in Ancient Judaism* (Leiden 1973). L. Grunfeld, *The Jewish Dietary Laws* (London 1972). A. Finkel, *The Pharisees and the Teacher of Nazareth* (Leiden-Köln 1964), 42-57. Le impuntature ebraiche sui cibi erano notorie: Epitteto, Dis. I 11, 12-13; 22, 4. Giuseppe Flavio, Ant. XII 120; ibid III 320-1; B. J. II 591-3; Vita, 14, 74-6.

⁵ Filone, Fug. inv. 153. Una persona impura può rendere impuro * l'esterno d'una tazza e lasciare puro l'interno, ma se questo è impuro, l'intero lo è: Bab. Tal., Ber. 52 b.

⁶ *Nebelah* nello stomaco rende impuri fino al tramonto e incapaci * di entrare nel Tempio (Mishnah, Tah. I 1), ma *nebelah* nella vagina (!) non rende impura la donna (Nidd. 42 b)!

⁷ Cfr. Mishnah, Tah. I 1. *Nebelah* in bocca può non contaminare fin tanto che non s'inghiotta: Nidd. 42 b. Che il cibo impuro contamini colui

che mangia non era una decisione biblica, bensì rabbinica: Shab. 13 b, Mishnah, Zav. V 9, 12.

⁸ Lev. XVI 16. Peccato = impurità: Is. VI 5-7, 59, 3; Zac. XIII 1 (vedi le idee rituali e morali connesse in Is. 58, 6). Prov. XXX 12. Sir. XXXIV 25-26. Gio. XIII 10-11; 1 Tess. 2, 3; 4, 7; 2 Cor. VI 16-17; 2 Tim. II 20-22 (?); Apoc. XXI 27. Cfr. Ass. Mos. VII 9-10. Filone, Spec. Leg. III 89, 134-6, 209; Quod Deus 7; Plant. N. 107. Mishnah, De. II. 2-3. Bab. Tal., Pes. 57 a. A Büchler, *Studies in Sin and Atonement* (London 1928), specie §§ 3, 4 (pp. 288-92, 306-7).

⁹ Il sangue e l'acqua dal fianco del Cristo (cfr. la roccia percossa da Mosé in Num. 20, 11 Targ.) si deve comprendere su questo sfondo.

¹⁰ Mishnah, yoma III 2; Maksh VI 6. Giuseppe c. Ap. II 203; B. J. II 149; Tal. Bab. Hag. 20 a, 23 a. Si deve distinguere fra la contaminazione che contamina la persona da cui emana, la contaminazione che contamina un terzo, e la contaminazione che si limita a rendere suscettibile d'essere contaminata una qualche cosa (così Mishnah, Marksh., VI 5-7). La legge ebraica non dichiarava impure nel senso dell'impurità dei cibi le feci nell'intestino crasso o cieco, dentro o fuori del corpo (cfr. Giud. XIV 14): all'atto dell'escrezione si era resi impuri e ci si doveva purificare, ma le feci stesse (igiene a parte) non erano impure neanche se provenienti da cibo o bevanda proibiti.

¹¹ Cfr. nota 8.

¹² Tal. Bab., Hull. 71 a (Rabbah). Midr. R. Num. XIX 1. Cfr. Zav. V 9. I Greci non capivano come il cibo impuro cessasse di essere impuro una volta digerito con lo stomaco (se lo si può vomitare è ancora impuro): Mishnah, Miq. X 8. Il mondo del pensiero greco qui appare inconciliabile.

¹³ L.S.J. ref. ad Omero *Il.* 16, 667; Esch., fr. 45; Erod. I 43.

¹⁴ Blass-Debrunner-Funk, *Gk. Grammar of the N. T.* (Cambridge-Chicago 1961), §§ 22, 28; A. H. Forster, *A.T.R.* 5 (1922), 108-15; L. R. Palmer, *Grammar of the Post-Ptolemaic Papyri I/1* (Oxford-London 1945), 1, 2; M. David e B. A. Van Groningen, *Papyrological Primer*² (Leiden 1965), 17. Fr. F. T. Gignac (Fordham University) scrive (8 dicembre 1972): «... in una selezione di 318 papiri del I secolo trovai 109 casi di o scritto per errore in luogo di ω e 67 di ω in luogo di o». Egli mi ha fornito abbondanti esempi di -ov in luogo di -ων, e prosegue: «Lo scambio fra o e ω è tra i più comuni nei papiri. Non si discute che entrambe rappresentino lo stesso suono nel I secolo». Quanto all'esegesi, Fr. Cignac preferisce il « commento dell'Evangelista » a Mc. VII 19 c, il che renderebbe superflua la ricerca.

¹⁵ Esempi nella nota precedente. Il prof. E. G. Turner attrae la mia attenzione al «Bull. Soc. Pap.» 8 (1971), 52, 11. 17-18: καϑῆκων per καϑῆκον. Cfr. gli esempi tratti dal Nuovo Testamento in B. M. Metzger, *The Text of the New Testament* (Oxford 1964), 190, dove Rom. V 1; Lc. XVI 25 sono citati opportunamente. *Adde*: Lc. XXII 61; Act. VII 16; I Cor. IV 2.

FURTHER ANNOTATIONS

The burden of this article is that if Jesus actually set aside the dietary laws Peter's dream (Acts x.10-16) would have been unnecessary, the relevant portion of the Apostolic Decree (Acts xv.20) would have been perverse, and all the debates regarding 'idol-meat' in 1 Cor. quite otiose. In fact the problem disappears if we read, for *katharizōn* with an omega, *katharizon* with an omicron. The theory then becomes clear. In a modern-sounding analysis of the sin/pollution concept, common to Jews and Hindus, Jesus confines the polluting effect of forbidden foods to the digestive organs: the personality is not affected, for the polluted condition is only temporary. There are rabbinical passages supporting this outlook. Basically, diet does not pollute the individual (only at rabbinical, not biblical law, did diet defile the eater himself): but the individual's *inside* produces pollution due to sinful thoughts/plans, and this can be a lasting contamination.

In our passage *brōmata* means 'filth'. Greeks, failing to understand how 'foods' could be purified by excretion, assumed that there was a false reading and changed *-izon* to *-izōn*. The words sounded exactly alike, so the ancient conjecture was understandable. It is possible that the original saying of Jesus read "What goes in cannot render 'unholy', but what goes out of a man way well do so!" He will have utilised the superstition, common to Judaism and Hinduism, that excretion renders the person impure (the same fluids, etc., coming out otherwise than through the orifices do not have this effect!). The saying is thus brilliant. Mark is dealing with gentiles, and the whole has a social significance, since in these ancient societies 'purity' has relevance to worship, including corporate worship. One cannot worship if one's person, and one's company, is/are impure. The saying is a successful blend of rationalistic and archaic superstitious elements.

Judaism was conversant with the idea that wicked acts defile. A polluted person, e.g. a menstruant, cannot enter company for purposes of prayer. The metaphor was already prepared for in the culture. The correct text is in fact printed in an edition from Greece.

p. [129], n. 4. I have not seen A. Rosenfeld, *Sources for the Dietary Laws* (1975).
p. [129], n. 5. It is remarkable that Menander (540K, Loeb edn., 486) seems to have anticipated Christ: *kai pan to lumainomenon estin endothen*.
p. [129], n. 6. Note the rule found in Manu XI. 153 that the eater of forbidden food remains impure until it has been digested. This corresponds closely to Jesus's notion.
p. [130], n. 8. My contention that Hindu and Jewish ideas are mutually illuminating is supported by material in R. V. De Smet, 'Sin and its removal in India', *Indian Antiquary*, 3rd series, 1 (1964), 163-174. P. Spratt, *Hindu Culture and Personality* (Bombay, 1966), 224.
p. [130], n. 150. An excellent example of desperate doubt on the reading, as between omega and omicron, is 1 Cor. xv.49. All the 'best' authorities read *phoresōmen*, but, though much less well attested, the reading *phoresomen* is adopted by the Textus Receptus, Souter, the B.F.B.S. edition of 1958, the American Greek New Testament[2] (1968) (where it bears the 'C' order of probability) and Tasker's edition of the text used for the New English Bible. Westcott and Hort and Nestle, meanwhile, printed the subjunctive form, attested by so many high-quality witnesses. The truth seems to be that those witnesses or their efficient sources 'corrected' the omicron to an omega,

thinking it to be a mistake, exactly as in our present situation. A very famous fluctuation between omega and omicron is to be seen at Matt. xii.6, where pious scribes changed *meizon* (a greater thing) to *meizōn* (One greater), which latter no modern text now prints, thinking it to be an earlier scribal error.

No doubt some variations from omega to omicron are due to Atticism (for Rom.vi.2, Jas.iv.5 see G.D. Kilpatrick, *Fest. Josef Schmid*, Regensburg, 1963, 133), but that is another matter.

Finally, J. Neusner, in his fascinating study at *N.T.S.* 22 (1976), 486ff., at 494, shows that Jesus utilised a dispute that was then going on between the Houses of Shammai and Hillel on the subject of the uncleanness of the outside (including the handles) and the inside of cups, in order to make a homily with a strictly *moral* intention. 'The Pharisees' interest in purity laws was therefore made into a polemic against them. They do not understand the true meaning of the law, therefore debate among themselves "outer/inner" of *utensils*, while the law really refers to *people* and their moral character.' There is another possibility, when we take our present pericope into account. Granted that his contemporaries amongst the Pharisees were involved in questions regarding ritual purity, so that the basic presuppositions were notorious, Jesus takes the line: 'Granted that you admit so much of the sacred law, the whole point of these images is to teach personal freedom from contamination'. The question about the coincidence of righteousness and charity (which would be bound to interest St. Luke) must be held over for the present.

THE DISPOSAL OF VIRGINS

I

Theologians are unable to translate conclusively a passage in St Paul's writings (1 Cor. 7: 36–38), and what follows is a new commentary upon it. A few verses earlier there is another passage (7: 29–30) which is easy to translate, but which can hardly be understood without help. We shall need the Greek text of the former, but not the latter. The former is described as 'one of the most difficult and controversial in the New Testament' (Hurd 1965: 171), because of the serious ambiguity in the three verses taken collectively, and an alleged non-congruence between all the parts. A critical study by a Jew (Belkin 1935: 49–52) who later evinced deep knowledge of the intellectual ambience, fails for want of philological precision (Kümmel 1954: 292). The better-known commentaries (surveyed by Hurd) are those of Barrett (1968), Conzelmann (1969), and Moffatt (1938). A less-used commentary (Morris 1958: 120–2) tackles the passage with perfect balance, but does not contain its own authentication.

Methodologically, it is questioned whether Jewish information is relevant to the solution of problems arising in the Corinthian church (Davies 1955: 50, 292; Barrett 1968: 184). But we now have examples (Derrett 1973) where Jewish knowledge makes a welcome clarification: all such techniques must be tested by their results. It is to Jewish information that we turn for the elucidation of the text which follows.

36 Εἰ δέ τις ἀσχημονεῖν ἐπὶ τὴν παρθένον αὐτοῦ νομίζει ἐὰν ᾖ ὑπέρακμος, καὶ οὕτως ὀφείλει γίνεσθαι, ὃ θέλει ποιείτω· οὐχ ἁμαρτάνει· γαμείτωσαν. 37 ὃς δὲ ἕστηκεν ἐν τῇ καρδίᾳ αὐτοῦ ἑδραῖος, μὴ ἔχων ἀνάγκην, ἐξουσίαν δὲ ἔχει περὶ τοῦ ἰδίου θελήματος, καὶ τοῦτο κέκρικεν ἐν τῇ ἰδίᾳ καρδίᾳ, τηρεῖν τὴν ἑαυτοῦ παρθένον, καλῶς ποιήσει· 38 ὥστε καὶ ὁ γαμίζων τὴν ἑαυτοῦ παρθένον καλῶς ποιεῖ, καὶ ὁ μὴ γαμίζων κρεῖσσον ποιήσει.

Two main categories of attempt at translation are now available (reproduced from Hurd 1965: 171–2):

If any one thinks that he is behaving dishonourably towards his virgin daughter, if she is past the flower of her age, and if it ought to be, let him do what he will, he does not sin; let them marry. But whosoever is firmly established in his heart being under no necessity but having his will under control, and has determined this in his heart, to keep her as his virgin daughter, he will do well. So that he who gives his own virgin daughter in marriage does well; and he who does not give her in marriage will do better.

If anyone thinks that he is behaving shamefully towards his virgin, if his passions are strong, and if it has to be, let him do what he will, he does not sin; let them marry. But whosoever is firmly established in his heart, being under no necessity but having his desire under control, and has determined this in his heart, to keep his virgin, he will do well. So that he who marries his virgin does well; and he who does not marry will do better.

The traditional interpretation has always been that Paul deals with a parent's or guardian's situation (Kugelman 1948). The present age is coming to an end, and in such a critical period sexual union distracts from devotion (1 Cor. 7: 26–7, 29, 34) whilst *not* being sinful (if within marriage) (1 Cor. 7: 28; 1 Tim. 4: 3, 5: 14). Protestant critics however propounded the now popular view that the predicament was that of spouses who had taken a vow of celibacy. It was supposed, contrary to what Paul says of marriage at 1 Cor. 7: 2–5, 34c, that they lived together in continence; but some husbands had found this unbearable, and asked what they should do. The present article provides a revised translation, showing that the 'he' in the first line of the translation above is the father or legal guardian of the unmarried girl, and that the 'them' of 'let them marry' refers most probably to the male fiancés.

If we admit that St Paul speaks in terms of institutions known to Jewish law (and not undocumented institutions, such as the 'spiritual marriage' or the much later practice of *virgines subintroductae* (Cross 1966: 1300)), it is soon apparent that Greek is inadequate. The category terms fail to coincide with those of Jewish law. The latter vocabulary requires three words relating to marriage: '*ērūsîn* (engagement, betrothal), *qidūšîn* ('hallowing', betrothal viewed as the act of the male party to the marriage), and *nisū'în* ('transfer', 'home-taking', implying consummation of the marriage). In view of the paucity of Greek terms, as much use as possible had to be made of the genuine Greek distinction between 'to give in marriage' and 'to marry'. The latter (*gameō*) is used of the male spouse, and when male and female (not a virgin) are thought of as marrying *gameō* is used (1 Cor. 7: 9), for the male predominates; further when a girl enters into marriage (as at 1 Cor. 7: 28) *gameō* can be used even of her; the former (*gamizō*) is used exclusively of the female's marriage-guardian (normally her father), and the *passive* of that verb is used to describe a girl's marrying: she is 'given in marriage'. Thus a man (of any age) 'marries'; a girl, and especially a virgin, is 'given in marriage'. It was socially unacceptable, even amongst the Greeks, for a woman to initiate her own marriage, only a male was supposed to do that.

Furthermore, Greek did not distinguish, as does the Jewish vocabulary, between three classes of virgins: the *qetanâ*, or female infant, the *na'arâ* (young girl, maiden), and *bogéret* (abstract: *bagrūt*), the girl ripe for marriage (called a 'ripe fig', see below). The Greek *parthenos* had to serve for all three, significantly for the last two. Greek had no vocabulary to express situations of interest to us. We must distinguish a *bogéret* who had not undergone *qidūšîn*—a financial and social problem for her relations, in particular her father; a *na'arâ* who had not undergone *qidūšîn*, a cause for, as yet, less concern; and finally a *bogéret* who had undergone *qidūšîn* but not *nisū'în*, a girl in a dilemma in which she could count on society's lively sympathy—a dilemma which automatically compromised her father or guardian, i.e. if there were undue delay (such as more than a year) in her fiancé's fetching her. Greek *vocabulary* was poor here.

The Greek of 1 Cor. 7: 36–38 must be examined still more carefully. A successful translation must make the sense, the grammar, and the context agree. *Aschēmonein* implies shameful, indecent behaviour (cf. *euschēmon* immediately before, 1 Cor. 7: 35), but also meant 'to incur shame' (as at Deut. 25: 3 lxx) which is more nearly appropriate here. *Hyperakmos* is very like *parakmasē* in the Ben Sirach passage to be quoted below. It is not used of male persons, but of a girl reaching, and thus passing, the peak of maturity; as a metaphor it means 'truly mature', 'mature and a bit more'.[1] *Opheilei* implies debt, a requirement, not compulsion. *Thelēma* means 'will' (as in the Lord's Prayer), *not* especially sexual desire. *Exousia* means authority (the Latin *potestas*), appropriate to a father in relation to a daughter. *Parthenos* can mean an unpenetrated female, but its traditional meaning (if the context does not exclude it) is 'girl ready for marriage'. Here it suggests virgin daughter, and there are two classical Greek examples where it means exactly that.[2] The suggestion that it means widow here is grotesque (Ford 1964), the inscriptions mentioning the deceased as *parthenos* mean that she was unmarried (Léon 1960: 230), and Ford's notions in this context are improbable (Barrett 1968: 184). *Tērō* does not mean to 'keep' in the sense of maintain, but to guard and to watch, which is what guardians of virgins must do. The gospel examples of *gamizō* (see above) are unambiguous,[3] the passages cited in all major dictionaries are quite clear,[4] no example of any other meaning has come to light, and an attempt to urge that it could mean the reverse, viz. 'to marry', fails to convince (Hurd 1965: 175; Kugelman 1948: 67). The discovery that *gamizō* does not (so far) appear in papyri (Kümmel 1954: 287) is less impressive when we reflect that the many papyri dealing with matrimonial topics were concerned with a coming marriage, the betrothal being a thing of the past, and thus they hardly had an occasion to speak of 'giving in marriage'.

Ben Sirach (Ecclesiasticus) 42: 9–11 is very much to the point. The precious surviving fragments of the Hebrew (Vattioni 1968: 227) only serve to show that the Greek is a paraphrase but we have no difficulty in visualising the meaning from a literal translation of the long-known Greek version:

> To her father a daughter is a secret anxiety,
> worrying about her banishes sleep;
> when she is a young girl, lest she pass maturity (*parakmasē*);
> when she has been home-taken, for fear she may be hated;
> whilst she is a virgin, lest she be defiled,
> and become pregnant in her father's compound;
> whilst she dwells with a husband, for fear she may go astray,
> and, after being home-taken, lest she may turn out barren.
> Keep close watch over a headstrong daughter,
> lest she make you an object of joy to your enemies,
> the talk of the town and contemptible to the people,
> and shame you before the whole multitude.

The phrases 'pass maturity', 'home-taken', and, especially 'shame' are variously helpful to us.

Our disputed text may be better translated as follows:

> In all cases where he (the father or guardian) is under the impression that he incurs shame because of his *na'arâ* when she has crossed into the stage of *bagrūt*, and what you allude to is due to happen (i.e. consummation is the normal sequel), he may carry out what he intends (i.e. arrange for her to be home-taken). He is not sinning (in so doing). They (i.e. the prospective sons-in-law) should certainly marry them.[5] But, otherwise, in any case where he is fixed in his mind, immovable, not subject to any pressure (i.e. neither bound by any contract nor pressed to arrange *nisū'în*) and (still) has unfettered authority and absolute discretion, and has actually come to an independent decision, viz. to guard his *bogéret* (i.e. prevent males having access to her), he will be acting properly (in so doing). The result is that anyone who arranges his *bogéret's qidūšîn* and *nisū'în* does act properly, but anyone who abstains from arranging it acts more commendably.

Irrespective of *law* it can never be a norm that the male head of the family should select an alternative which involves him (and so them) in shame and corresponding loss of honour. This is a consideration in its own right.[6]

II

In view of the abundant (inaccurate) theological speculation on our passage some notes must be added to justify the translation offered. *Qidūšin* gave the girl the status of a married woman for very many purposes, but her fiancé had not taken possession of his 'acquisition', and so married her in a socially acceptable sense, until he penetrated her, whereupon she would have ceased to be a virgin even if they were continent thereafter. The story of Palti and Michal[7] proves that the rabbis regarded continence within marriage as altogether anomalous. Thus speculation about 'spiritual marriage' offends against common sense as well as cultural tradition. After Belkin (1935) several theologians (Chadwick 1954/5; Kümmel 1954; Barrett 1968: 184; Conzelmann 1969: 160–1) propound the theory that here we have genuine betrothals, and that the choice lay before the fiancé whether or not to home-take the girl, and whether or not to penetrate her and so consummate the union. The vocabulary (as we have seen) is violated by this, and it also presupposes a provision of Jewish law, to the effect that a fiancée whom her fiancé delayed to take home could be maintained at the latter's expense: the references do not support this extraordinary proposition.

The anxiety about virgins belongs very much to the ancient world. Girls could be betrothed by penetration alone, so that *nisū'in* merely completed what was a fact. The Mishnah says, 'A girl three years old and one day may be betrothed by intercourse . . .' (Mishnah, Nid. V. 4; Danby 1933: 750). This is how Maimonides (A.D. 1180) puts it: 'If she is three years and one day old she may be betrothed by an act of intercourse, with the consent of her father. If she is less than that, and her father has her betrothed by an act of intercourse, she is not betrothed' (Maimonides 1972: 18). *'Ērūsin* was effected, normally, not by this barbarous method, but by the male party's handing to the girl's father a sum, a nominal payment, to acquire the girl. The major real financial aspect, to which the father must apply his mind, is the *ketubah*, the settlement by which the intending husband's family, in his name, bind themselves to protect the woman's future by a payment on the husband's death, or his divorcing her otherwise than for her fault. A father might betroth his daughter very early because he wanted to 'book' a boy in a particular family as his son-in-law. Such practices survive in India with the same motives. Fathers were until recently greatly agitated by their daughters' reaching puberty unmarried.[8]

Pious Jews in Paul's day gave their daughters in marriage at puberty or a little before. The Qumran sect, according to a great authority, required their male members not to marry until they were twenty (instead of the usual seventeen) and to marry girls who could distinguish between good and evil, which (as a reform) seems to insist on their actually having attained puberty. Dupont-Sommer translates (1968: 120): 'Et voici la règle pour toutes les milices de la Congrégation, concernant chaque indigène en Israël . . . Puis, à l'âge de vingt an[s, il sera soumis] [au]recensement . . . Et il ne [s'approchera] d'une femme pour la connaître sexuellement qu'à condition d'avoir vin[g]t ans accomplis quand [elle] connaîtra [le bien] et le mal: et, dans ces conditions, elle sera admise à prendre à témoin contre lui les ordonnances de la Loi et à prendre place dans l'auditoire des ordonnances et parmi la foule qui s'y trouve' (CR appendix I. 6–13). Other scholars (Black 1961: 28–30; Lohse 1964: 47, 282 n. 6; Isaksson 1965: 47; Vermes 1965: 119) translate as if the *husband* must be able to distinguish, etc., as well as being twenty—as if persons of twenty could not distinguish between good and evil in a society where without question legal competence attaches to a boy who has 'put forth two hairs' and is thus presumed to have reached puberty! Josephus, a contemporary, speaking of the Essenes (whom many identify with the Qumran sect), tells[9] how they would not marry a girl before she had menstruated three times, thus proving that she could produce issue. Rabbi 'Aqîba (who died about 135), perhaps the most celebrated orthodox Jewish teacher, said (in a mood reminiscent of Luke 9: 57–62), 'Let him who has a marriageable daughter [i.e. a *bogéret*] go home and give her in marriage' (i.e. even 'Aqîba's course-teaching was, temporarily, inferior to so urgent a duty). The Jerusalemites had a saying that when a daughter reached puberty one should go so far as to emancipate a slave and betroth her to him (Bab. Talm., Pes. 113a). It is wicked (in terms of Lev. 19: 29) to delay marrying off one's *bogéret*, lest she become a harlot.

Now Jewish law ends the father's *potestas* before the girl reaches thirteen (Mishnah, Qid. II. 1; Danby 1933: 323). She must be on the marriage market when most interest is shown in her (when she is just mature). If her betrothal is not effected by then she must make the best terms she can, appointing, if necessary, a stranger as her agent. In ancient India the girl had a right to choose her own bridegroom three years after puberty (Manu IX. 90–93: 'the father loses his dominion over her in consequence of his "preventing" her menses'), but other sources say after three menstrual periods. Menstruation perhaps is at the root of such practices. There was a keen sense of dishonour if what should be the really prestige-worthy matrimonial union (Thieme 1963) turns out to have been with a girl who had been penetrated, and a girl who has been menstruating is as if she were occupied by some power. In Hindu eyes the short period of pre-matrimonial menstruation is one in which the girl is possessed by certain deities (including Fire), and these yield her to the bridegroom only as a result of Vedic marriage ceremonies. So in Jewish law the act of acquisition is specifically called her 'hallowing': she is hallowed, 'set apart' for her eventual husband by the betrothal. Her menstruation passes to her husband's home subject to procedures diminishing the taboo aspect as she enables the husband to perform the commandment to increase and multiply. The value and virtue of a mentally as well as physically mature bride were unknown. To complain, as some theologians have done, that Paul does not show a fitting respect for the virgins' feelings is anachronistic. *

The concept of financial anticipation in betrothals is handled by Goody and Tambiah (1973). In first-century Jewish society the actual endowment of the bride provided the consideration moving the father to permit his daughter to be home-taken. But on the other hand, as we have seen, any delay raised fears. Philo, discussing seduction, emphasises the parent's or guardian's rights in the matter.[10] If the father did not invite the fiancé to perform the home-taking, or, worse still, the latter (fearing the world would soon end) refused the invitation, the social disgrace would fall upon the father; keeping an unmarried virgin at home might even imply that he connived at her immorality. On this basis every daughter had a right to be betrothed and to be home-taken by her fiancé.

The timetable was strict. The details in Maimonides, who purports to rely entirely on ancient sources, seem to be the result of harmonisation, for he utilises a presumption seemingly not overtly stated in them.[11] In post-Mishnaic times, irrespective of whether she could be proved to have menstruated, if, after she was twelve years and one day old, she had 'put forth' two pubic hairs (Bab. Talm., Ket. 29a) she ceased to be a qeṭanâ and became a na'arâ. The na'arût (status of 'maiden') began after the completion of the twelfth year and a day (Yev. 12b, Ket. 39a, Nid. 45a). In other words the father must hurry up and not wait until her maturity was beyond doubt. At this period of the law she became a bogéret six months after she became a na'arâ. From being a ripening fig she became[12] a 'fully ripe fig': such things 'go off', become 'over-ripe' and are more or less useless. In short the father had roughly six months to arrange her marriage on the best terms he could find. In the first century a less schematic statement would be conceivable. Negotiations must start before she reaches puberty, since immediately thereupon she can appoint someone else (possibly no one of the family's choice) to arrange her marriage as she wishes.

All students of 1 Corinthians must consider what were the questions already put to Paul by them. In this case we can safely suppose the following: 'Only men of this world (i.e. non-Christians) marry and give in marriage, and those that are worthy of attaining to the World to Come and the Resurrection of the Dead neither marry nor are given in marriage (Luke 20: 34–35).[13] What of a father's responsibility towards his daughter who is ripe for marriage? There are two problems: (i) that of those whose betrothal is already effected, and (ii) those who are yet to be betrothed. If the father waits they become mistresses of their own fates, in either event. If their fiancés want them, while they are out of their fathers' power, difficulties could arise, should they repudiate their betrothal. If the fiancés neglect them we fear they will engage themselves clandestinely and even become (in the eyes of Jewish law) adulteresses. We have raised questions about the Apostolic Decree and the implications of porneia.[14] Surely this is to be avoided at any cost?'

We have seen Paul's common-sense answer.

III

It is possible now to make better sense of 1 Cor. 7: 29–30, which is translated as follows in the Revised Standard Version: 'I mean, brethren, the appointed time has grown very short; from now on let those who have wives live as though they had none, and those who mourn as though they were not mourning, and those who rejoice as though they were not rejoicing, and those who buy as though they had no goods, and those who deal with the world as though they had no dealings with it. For the form of this world is passing away.' A na'arâ is acquired (Heb. niqnet) with the token payment in betrothal procedure: Mishnah, Qid. I. 1 (Danby 1933: 321). Paul, discussing marriage in general, says that it is better (because of the shortening of time) to avoid it even if this disrupts natural expectations: 'that those that have wives may be as if they had none, [that is to say] those that weep (scil. the brides on leaving, or their female relatives in real or simulated grief at their departure?) as if they did not weep, those that rejoice (i.e. the bridegrooms and their families?) as though they did not rejoice, and those that *buy* (i.e. those that put up the cash) as if they had acquired no right.' Even fiancés should disregard their rights, if possible, and sublimate their anticipation, in order, as Paul says at *v.* 32ff., to devote themselves to pleasing the Lord. He has designed his poetic sentence so that it can cover even conscientiously-alerted couples who have been married off under parental authority: they can go through with marriage, yet still pretend that it is not marriage as understood by the World. The 'real' rejoicing will be when the 'real' Bridegroom is with them (Mat. 9: 15, Jn. 3: 29, Rev. 18: 23). When the Time, the Day, comes the mere fact of acquisition produces no joy: so Paul adapts to the topic of marriage the exhortation of Ezek. 7: 12 ('the buyer has no reason to be glad and the seller none to mourn').[15]

NOTES

[1] Soranus I. 22.3: *hyperakmois pro tēs diakorēseōs* (sexually mature *prior* to being deflowered— of a special menstrual condition). Epiphanius, *haer.* 61.6 (Migne, P.G. 41. 1045B) says *parthenoi hyperakmazousai* ('over-ripe virgins', so to speak) naturally fall into *porneia* (unchastity, fornication). *To hyperakmon* is used of a male who is, not passionate, but 'past it' at Sophronius, *orat.* 7 (Migne, P.G. 87. 3329A). Metaphorical uses: Myro Priensensis, *Mess.* II (C. Müller, F. H. G. IV. 461); Pap. Soc.I t. 666 (vol. 4, 1920), line 18 (of wine); Eusthathius, *Comm. ad Homeri Odysseam*, §.1915.20 (*hyperakma*=excessively). The word *hyperēmeros* ('past the time', 'overdue') is quite different, so also *hyperetēs* ('over-age for service', etc.), *hypergērōs* ('exceedingly old').

[2] Sophocles, *Oed. Tyr.* 1462; Anaxandrides 68 (T. Kock, Com. Att. Frag. ii, 162) quoted by Aristotle, *Rhet.* III. 10.7. What was known to Aristotle cannot be called obscure.

[3] Mat. 22: 30, Mk. 12: 25, Luke 17: 27, 20: 35.

[4] Apollonius, *De synt.* 280.11 (ed. I. Bekker, 1817); Methodius, *Conviv. decem virg.* XIII (Migne, P.G. 18.81C).

[5] For the slip into the plural where a class of cases is being considered see 1 Tim. 5: 4.

[6] Peristiany, 1965, esp. at pp. 49, 144, 146, 227, 246. The different areas and cultures covered by the volume add weight, for our purposes, to the general propositions illustrated.

[7] 1 Sam. 25: 44, 2 Sam. 3: 14–16. To render the episode righteous it was necessary to suppose Palti/Paltiel and Michal wife of David lived in total continence.

[8] Gautama 18: 21, Baudhāyana 4, 1: 11; Vasiṣṭha 17: 70. On the sin of seeing the menstrual blood of an unmarried daughter see Prāyaścittakāṇḍa of Hemādri, Caturvarga-cintāmaṇi (Sampath 1972; Gupta 1972). (Kauṭilya 4.12:8–9.)

[9] *Bell. Jud.* ii. §. 161.

[10] *De spec. leg.* III. 67 (Loeb edn., vol. 7).

[11] Maimonides, 1972: 8–9.

[12] Mishnah, Nid. V. 7. Danby 1933: 751. It will be recollected that the Annunciation to the Virgin Mary was made by the angel Gabriel. Gabriel is in charge of ripening fruits according to Bab. Talm., Sanh. 95b.

[13] Luke poses the problem specifically with the reason that those who are equal to the angels are immortal. Luke 20: 34–36 is a development or expansion of Mk. 12: 25=Mat. 22: 30, having an untraced apostolic authority, such as may lie behind Justin Martyr (?), *De resurr.* 3 (Holl, *Texte und Untersuchungen* 20.2, p. 40).

[14] Simon 1970: 453–4.

[15] Moses Isserles on Karo's *Shulchan 'Arûch, Yoreh De'ah* 402.11 and Eliezer b. Nathan, *Eben ha-'Ezer* 61.1 documents (1565) the spouses' fasting as an atonement on the wedding day: if the custom goes back to ancient times, Paul's imagery would be marvellous.

REFERENCES

Barrett, C. K. 1968. *A commentary on the First Epistle to the Corinthians.* London: A. & C. Black.
Belkin, S. 1935. The problem of Paul's background. *J. Bibl. Lit.* **54**, 41–60.
Black, M. 1961. *The Scrolls and Christian origins.* London: Nelson.
Chadwick, H. 1954/5. All things to all men (1 Cor. ix. 22). *New Test. Stud.* **1**, 261–75.
Conzelmann, H. 1969. *Der erste Brief an die Korinther.* Göttingen: Vanderhoeck & Ruprecht.
Cross, F. M. 1958. *Ancient library of Qumrân.* London: Duckworth.

Cross, F. M. 1966. *Oxford Dictionary of the Christian Church*. London: Oxford Univ. Press.
Danby, H. 1933. *The Mishnah*. London: Oxford Univ. Press.
Davies, W. D. 1955. *Paul and Rabbinic Judaism*. London: S.P.C.K.
Derrett, J. D. M. 1973. Religious hair. *Man* (N.S.) **8**, 101–3.
Dupont-Sommer, A. 1968. *Les écrits Esséniens découverts près de la Mer Morte*. Paris: Payot.
Ford, J. M. 1964. Levirate marriage in St. Paul (1 Cor. vii). *New Test. Stud.* **10**, 361–5.
―――― 1967. *A trilogy on wisdom and celibacy*. Notre Dame, Indiana: Univ. of Notre Dame Press.
Frey, J.-B. 1930. La signification des termes Monandros et Univira. *Rech. Sci. relig.* **20**, 48–60.
Goody, J. & S. J. Tambiah 1973. *Bridewealth and dowry*. Cambridge: Univ. Press.
Gupta, G. R. 1972. Religiosity, economy and patterns of Hindu marriage in India. *Int. J. Sociol. Fam.* **2**, 1–11.
Hurd, J. C. 1965. *The origin of 1 Corinthians*. London: S.P.C.K.
Isaksson, A. 1965. *Marriage and ministry in the New Temple*. Lund: Gleerup.
Kugelman, R. 1948. 1 Cor. 7: 36–8. *Cathl. bibl. Q.* **10**, 63–71.
Kümmel, W. G. 1954. Verlobung und Heirat bei Paulus (1 Cor. 7: 36–8). In *Neutestamentliche Studien für Rudolf Bultmann*. Berlin: A. Töpelmann.
Léon, H. J. 1960. *The Jews of ancient Rome*. Philadelphia: Jewish Publication Society of America.
Lohse, E. 1964. *Die Texte aus Qumran*. Munich: Kösel-Verlag.
Maimonides, Moses. 1972. *Book of women: Code of Maimonides Book IV* (trans.) I. Klein. New Haven, London: Yale Univ. Press.
Moffatt, J. 1938. *The First Epistle of Paul to the Corinthians*. London: Hodder & Stoughton.
Morris, L. 1958. *First Epistle of Paul to the Corinthians*. London: Tyndale Press.
O'Rourke, J. J. 1958. Hypothesis regarding 1 Cor. 7: 36–8. *Cathl. bibl. Q.* **20**, 292–8.
Peristiany, J. G. (ed.). 1965. *Honour and shame: the values of Mediterranean society*. London: Weidenfeld & Nicolson.
Sampath, B. N. 1969. Marriageable age, consent, and soundness of mind in Indian matrimonial law. *Banaras Law J.* **5**, 28–52.
―――― 1972. Child marriage: revision of marriageable age and its effective implementation. *Lawasia* **3**, 386–402.
Simon, M. 1970. The Apostolic Decree and its setting in the ancient church. *Bull. John Rylands Lib.* **52**, 437–60.
Thieme, P. 1963. 'Jungfrauengatte.' *Z. vergleich. Sprachforsch.* (N.S.) **78**/3–4, 161–248.
Vattioni, F. 1968. *Ecclesiastico*. Napoli: Instituto Orientale.
Vermes, G. 1965. *The Dead Sea Scrolls in English*. Harmondsworth: Penguin.

FURTHER ANNOTATION

p. [24], l. 4. A reconsideration of Paul's attitude to marriage is K. Niederwimmer, 'Zur analyse der asketischen Motivation in 1 Kor. 7', *T.L.Z.* 99 (1974), 241-8. Our problem is dealt with with new bibliographical particulars at nn. 13-16. The conclusion is that Paul did not integrate marriage, or did not regard it as integrated, but conceded it, or treated it as a concession. He was a forerunner of the church's general conception in later times, not because he favoured sexual asceticism (which suited him personally) but because he drew limits to an ascetic radicalism which had developed around him and in opposition to him.

This fits well enough with my explanation: there is a sense in which marriage may, as it were temporarily, be suffered in the Christian antechamber to the World to Come. A practical man must know intuitively that a logically perfect asceticism would achieve as much harm as it did good.

p. [24], l. 27. Josephus's vocabulary and Ben Sirach's show that the Jews needed the concept of home-taking, *nisû'în*, to indicate that marriage was complete: *Ant.* xvii.349, 352. Note the LXX vocabulary at Jdg. xii.8-9 (Ibzan, the marriage-arranger of all time).

p. [24], l. 30. The three standpoints are clearly shown in one classical line: Euripides, *Medeia*, 289.

p. [24], l. 31. B.J. Bamberger, 'Qetanah, Na'arah, Bogeret', *H.U.C.A.* 32 (1960), 281ff., G.I. Wenham, 'Betulah "a girl of marriageable age"', *V.T.* 23 (1972), 326-48.

p. [25], l. 10. J.-B. Frey, 'La signification des termes Monandros et Univira', *R.S.R.* 20 (1930), 48-60. B. Kötting, '"Univira" in Inschriften', *Studia I.H. Waszink*.

p. [25], l. 21. Kümmel (1954), 287. For a typical marriage papyrus see Heinemann, *Bildung*, 289.

p. [27], l. 32. R.B. Pandey, in *Proceedings of the (3rd) Indian History Congress* (Calcutta, 1939), 130. H. Chatterjee Śāstri, *Studies in the Social Background of the Forms of Marriage in Ancient India* I (Calcutta, 1972), 41.

ANANIAS, SAPPHIRA, AND THE RIGHT OF PROPERTY

THE task of the biblical exegete is a little less difficult when he tackles lengthy passages having a literary unity, especially any which preserve an account or a piece of teaching which is technical, and of which one can obtain a clear impression only when one has fathomed the technicalities. In this sense legal material, such as we find in the parable of the Unjust Steward, or mixed legal and other cultural material such as we find in the parable of the Great Supper or the Wedding Feast, offers an advantage. If we can understand the background and fully visualise the material relied upon by the original author, encapsulated, as it were, in the details of the story, we cannot err far from a reliable interpretation.

Just such a passage is the extraordinary story of Ananias and Sapphira (Acts v, 1-11), of which it is commonly said that no satisfactory explanation has ever been forthcoming.[1] Its very opaqueness preserves it intact for the eventual enlightenment of a researcher who has the equipment to explain it. It is doubly worth our while to make the attempt, because it deals with the important and perpetual subject of property; and because in that same connection it has been regarded, by clergy and laity alike, as a stumbling-block to the believer. The behaviour of St Peter seems most un-Christian (cf. Matt. xviii, 17). The story seems to have grown in the telling. Its dramatic air seems, at first sight, to depend on the apparently implausible features of the tale itself: the climax at the words, 'Behold, the feet of those who have buried your husband are at the door and shall carry you out', is almost too artistic to permit us to grasp how odd the situation must have been if it occurred as depicted. Or was it odd, or even absurd? The purpose of this paper is to show that it was not. A most important piece of information is contained in the story, which will convey a lesson such as I need not elaborate.

The tale must be read as a sequel to Acts iv, 32-36, to which I turn in a translation of my own (which differs only minutely from others which the reader will have available to him):

> And the company of the believers had a single heart and soul. Not one of them spoke of any of his possessions as belonging exclusively to himself, but everything was common to all of them. And it was with great force that the apostles rendered testimony of the resurrection of the Lord Jesus. And abundant grace was upon all of them.[2] For there was no needy person amongst them, because their practice was that any of them that happened to own landed property or houses would sell them and bring the sale proceeds and lay them before the feet of the apostles, and distribution was then made to each one according to his need. Joseph, surnamed by the apostles Barnabas (which we should translate 'Son of Consolation'),[3] a Levite, native of Cyprus, owned a field, sold it, brought the amount, and laid it at the feet of the apostles.

The story continues immediately with the tale of Ananias and his wife, partly by way of contrast with the faithful behaviour of others illustrated by that of Joseph. What the author is saying is this: the unity formed within the earliest Church was demonstrated by their treating their assets as if they were common. It might not be *propter hoc* — but it was certainly in association with that fact that two further facts were found, first, that the central part of the Christian message was preached most successfully; and next, that the Church itself did not suffer from poverty as might have been expected from the non-productive occupation of the apostles, the emotionally disorientated condition of others, and the numbers of destitute people whom the disciples had drawn to them. The preaching, I submit, was, in the eyes of the author of our text, the more successful for the fact that the hearers of the gospel were satisfied, by the behaviour of the apostles and their associates, that the gospel was authentic.

People's conduct with regard to money shows how their minds work and what their real motives are (Matt. vi, 21). The heart and the purse are seldom far apart (ibid.). If people treat property as common between them, and do not think of attempting to profit from each other, it is clear that they are united. The integrity of the Church was proved to outsiders by their attitude with regard to property. But that was not enough. They might have been united with a different purpose. In fact Asian preachers usually profit from the superstition of their audiences, or their snobbism: and to find that the apostles were not profiting out of their privileged position must have been powerful evidence that this community was not only something new, but also something genuine. That the earliest Church believed that its members, and especially the apostles, should not obtain perquisites from the common funds is proved by the otherwise inexplicably elaborate argument of St Paul in I Cor. ix, 7-18, in which he proves that preachers are entitled to payment but claims that he abstains in order to obtain a higher reward. For the Church was putting into effect Jesus's own teaching that his disciples should rely on God's providence, leaving to him the question of their survival (Ps. xxxvii, 3, 25; Matt. vi, 24-33), and that those who wanted to be 'perfect' should sell their assets and give the proceeds to the poor (Matt. xix, 21). During the transitional stage before the Lord's second coming the first Church postponed thought for the future and lived on its members' capital. During that period the apostles' ministry was effective. Those who do not place earthly survival high amongst their objects will have an objectivity, and, on that account, an authority which cannot be rivalled by those who have pecuniary motives or social ambitions.

The Church did *not* have a rule that property should be legally pooled, should cease to be the legal asset of the proselyte. The virtue   *
of their new life was that they voluntarily merged their assets as they became needed, and when they obtained cash for their immoveables they placed it at the feet of the apostles (not into their hands), in order that the apostles should acquire it not as a personal gift but as trustees by way of a dedication. The analogy was of gifts to God by way of placing upon the altar (cf. Matt. v, 23-24), or *casting* into the Treasury (Mark xii, 41-44), To a Jewish community alive to juridical propositions that difference was significant, and St Peter, in his conversation with Ananias, is depicted as drawing attention to the fact.

It is not hard to see what Ananias and Sapphira were up to. They felt the approach of a call to contribute to the common fund. Though the act of sale would be Ananias's, he could dispose of the sale-proceeds only at the risk of prejudicing his wife's right to what is nowadays called her *ketubah*, the sum of money which was   *
a charge on his assets,[4] and which he must pay her if he divorced her unilaterally, or his heirs must pay her when he died. Sapphira's case could be put like this: 'If you wish, in your enthusiasm for our new sect, to part with your immovable property, our only remaining security, and beggar yourself, taking a chance whether the Almighty will find a continuous succession of landowners as pious as yourself

from now until the Lord's coming, whenever that may be, the responsibility is yours, and I cannot stop you. But my *ketubah* you have no right to prejudice. What I suggest is that I release my right to it on condition (which we can keep to ourselves) that you keep back a proportion of the price, on which both of us may rely if the Church's present system runs out of impetus, as it might well do, sooner or later.' It will not have occurred to her that the kind of peculation she recommended and the role she was playing bore some resemblances to the episode of Eve and the apple. In any case, hopes of keeping a sale-price secret are vain in the East. But whether St Peter knew of the arrangement by hearsay or from the expression on the man's face we shall never know (it is not clear whether the author has 2 Kings v, 26-27 in mind).

It was courteous of him to allege that Satan (and not Sapphira herself) had tempted Ananias to deceive or cheat the Holy Spirit. The man had up to that point been a faithful member of the Church, and it was his faith which had led to his selling his land. Had the title to the land been already vested in the Church (as, e.g. by way of a condition for membership), the position would have been different, and it would have been difficult for him to find a buyer, impossible to find one who would have paid anything near the market value. If that had actually taken place, the Church, as a body of men, would have been cheated, and he would have been punished, submitted to penance, or, if he failed to perform this, excommunicated (cf. Matt. xviii, 17). But, as St Peter says, with the juridical interest characteristic of him, the land was entirely Ananias's until he sold it, and when he sold it the money obtained from the purchaser was legally his (subject to his wife's rights to her *ketubah* as long as she lived). Consequently when he purported to dedicate, as it were, to sacrifice his property as soon as it came to his hand in cash, he was attempting to cheat God because, contrary to the spirit of the Church, the body of Christ, he had not intended to 'sell and give to the poor', and had reserved a portion for himself as if God's providence were not available to him. All proprietary dealings with God came into special categories of their own, which have an essential bearing on this case.

The Church, in which the Holy Spirit was working, was, even as a charitable organization, analogous to the Temple. The rules of Jewish law relating to the conduct of priests relative to the property of the Temple were relevant to the behaviour of the Christians in regard to assets dedicated, vowed to the Church. By an actual or implied vow when he joined the community Ananias had undertaken that when he voluntarily sold his lands he would do so for the community's benefit and not his own. Breach of this vow was a sin. But there was more to it than that. The Church regarded its property as an extension of the property of the Sacred Treasury, and applied to itself the law of tithe which the Jews at large observed in favour of the priests. So far as 'sacrilege' or 'trespass' is concerned, in Jewish law there was a system by which the offender could put an end to his guilt by an appropriate offering.[5] Unintentional trespass on property of the Temple must have been common. The priests, on the other hand, were subject to multiple rules regarding their office in the Temple, some of which could hardly be applied by a court, and the relevant offences could not, according to the Pharisees at least, be expiated by bringing sacrifices. The same applied to non-priests misapplying tithe destined solely for the priests' sustenance. These offences and a few others in vaguely analogous contexts (in which the biblical text did not specify how the offence was to be punished)[6] were not penalised by any human sanction, did not figure in any tariff of penalties, spiritual or temporal, but were punished by the specifically divine punishments, one of which was called 'excision' ('he shall be cut off . . . '),[7] and the other 'death at the hands of Heaven'.[8] No one could prove whether a premature or sudden death was indeed due to sin or to some other cause,[9] and there was no precise learning on what sort of death, or death in what circumstances, could be recognised as the divine punishment. But the existence of these two kinds of punishment, with which man did not presume to interfere, is notorious in Jewish law and beyond dispute.[10] That the early Church believed in divine punishment, and especially for 'tempting', or putting to the test, the Spirit of God, is clear from what St Paul says at I Cor. x, 1-10.

Thus St Peter will have feared for Ananias, whose seeming prudence will have incurred the divine wrath, because, in providing for his and his wife's security, he had been the first to tarnish the integrity of the community, he had introduced corruption (like Eve) and had thus prejudiced the success of the apostles' preaching. With a member who had an eye to the main chance the Church was contaminated. After the death of the unfortunate couple, who had thus been 'cast off', the integrity of the Church was restored and the work of the ministry went on unimpeded.

The death of Ananias need not have been miraculous. To a man imbued with faith the news that he had offended against the Holy Spirit (instead of the apostles) might well have caused a heart failure. The news that her husband had been detected and had

died immediately might well cause a heart failure in his wife. There
were peculiar circumstances to which we shall come presently; but
excitement of a not dissimilar nature occurred to cause a woman's
death once at Devizes in Wiltshire, as recorded in a contemporary
inscription to be seen in the market-place there.[11] What puzzles
modern critical readers is the possibility that the husband might
have been buried immediately without his wife's knowledge.

The death of a pious member of the community would normally
be an event of social significance. Many would accompany the bier
to the tomb, and much expense would attend the preparations for
burial (cf. Mark v, 38-40; Matt. xxvi, 12). Dramatic weeping and
wailing would be expected, and demonstrative grief from friends,
relatives, especially female relatives, and other mourners would be
normal for a regular period of time. But when a man had been
struck down by the hand of Heaven (as Joshua specifically says was
the case with Achan: Josh. vii, 25), his corpse must surely be
consigned rapidly and silently to the grave. No one should mourn
him. The suicide, the rebel against society,[12] the excommunicate,
the apostate, and the criminal condemned to death by the Jewish
court would be buried (if the rulers permitted burial) in haste and
without ceremonial, and no one might (or need) observe the usual
lengthy and troublesome rituals of mourning for him.[13] How much
less would one mourn for one who has sinned against God and has
been struck down in the moment of consciousness of his guilt!
Sapphira's heart would have failed realising that her husband was
not mourned. No one had rent his robe. Their heads were *uncovered*.
The feet of the 'young men' as they approached the door could be
heard *wearing sandals*.[14] She herself would not be permitted to tear
her garments. Small wonder she collapsed! The 'young men' had
wrapped up her husband's body unceremoniously in his robes and
buried him without a burial procession, with no elder or respectable
member of the community accompanying them. No condolences
were due to Sapphira, and none were given her. St Peter's extraordinary announcement fitted an extraordinary event. Naturally the
side of her husband was the obvious place for her corpse, without
ceremony and without memorial.

The author of the passage says that there arose a great fear amongst
all the Church and on all the people to whom news of the event
came. This is much more likely to have been awe, fear of God,
than fear of the possible consequences of cheating the apostles or
the Church. The death of Ananias himself could have been accounted
for (especially by the irreverent) as an accident — like the death at

Devizes I mentioned above. The death of his wife three hours or so afterwards put the affair in a different light. They had conspired to deceive. They were the first so to treat the Church. Their intentions were certainly hostile to the Church's fundamental principle. They died in such circumstances as to show that God would visit with his peculiar punishment members of the Church who violated its founder's laws. Sapphira's death was a manifest validation by God, or certification, of the Church's function, authority and message. 'Death at the hands of Heaven' reappeared as a clear authentication   ✱ of the new Israel, and its covenant. No doubt this awe, this fear of God, had its part to play in the signs and wonders which are described immediately afterwards.

The Church did not gloat over the sudden deaths of the unfortunate couple. St Peter obtained, seemingly, an admission from both of them, and they thus confessed their guilt within the meaning of Josh. vii, 19, and the Jewish law relating to confessions by condemned sinners.[15] Since they confessed their guilt (Ananias's silence at verse 5 amounts to an admission, and Sapphira's answer at verse 8 must be taken as a confession — not a trap by St Peter) they lost their lives on earth with the prospect, however, of sharing in the world to come. Those who die at the hand of Heaven are not deprived necessarily of their share of the next world: even the men of Sodom could, according to Jesus, face the last judgement with a chance of acquittal (cf. Matt. x, 15; xi, 24).[16] Misfortune atones for guilt, and a premature death is an atonement, according to Jewish notions. With their tragic ends and ignominious burials (much more shameful   ✱ to first-century Jews than to us) Ananias and Sapphira atoned for their sin, and retained their right to share with their fellow members of the earliest ecclesia in the eternal life which, in other respects, it would seem they had merited. To this proposition St Paul would assent, it seems, as is indicated by his hypothetical sentence on a sinner at I Cor. v, 4-5.

[1] A. E. Harvey, *Companion to the New Testament* (Oxford and Cambridge, 1970), p. 417. A famous, but poor study is that of P. H. Menoud in *Mélanges Goguel* (Paris 1950), pp. 146-54. An excellent exegesis is that of O. Dibelius, *Die werdende Kirche*, 5th ed. (Hamburg 1951), pp. 62-65. See also E. Haenchen, *Die Apostelgeschichte* (Göttingen 1961), pp. 192-8, and J. Schmitt in *Les Manuscrits de la Mer Morte. Colloque de Strasbourg 25-27 Mai 1955* (Paris 1957), pp. 93-109, esp. 100-07.

[2] The *New English Bible* and the *Jerusalem Bible* take the word *charis* to imply that the church's stock was high with the public, that they were highly esteemed. But it would seem preferable to take, with earlier translators, the next sentence as an explanation; and it can hardly be right that the result of the absence of poverty was prestige: rather they were specially blessed, as evidenced by their want of poverty. *Charis* (according to J.-P. Vernant), cordial liberality, spinning a web of reciprocal obligations, is a typically 'loaded' Greek term (see Arist., *Nic Eth.* 1133 a 2).

[3] The well-known problem about the Aramaic original of this name (Strack-Billerbeck, *Kommentar zum Neuen Testament*, II, 1924, ad loc.) does not concern us.

[4] Mishnah, tractate *Ketuboth* (Danby's *Mishnah*, Oxford 1933, pp. 245ff.). The right could be availed of in a legal (but immoral) trick, illustrated in the Jerusalemite Talmud (j. Sot. fol. 20a), trans. M. Schwab (1885), vii, 262-3.

[5] Mishnah, tractate *Meilah* (Danby, op. cit., pp. 573ff.). Note that for misappropriating *heqdesh* (assets of the Temple) Jewish law does not prescribe two-, four-, or five-fold restitution (which applies to assets of men). Philo says he should die at the hands of Heaven: *Leg. All.* iii, §§ 33-34!

[6] E.g., Lev. xxii, 9.

[7] Num. xv, 31. Mishnah, *Kerithoth* (Danby, op. cit., pp. 562ff.).

[8] Bab. Talmud, *Sanh.* 83a-84a. Maimonides, *Hilcot Sanhedrin*, XIX, 2-3 (*The Code of Maimonides*, Book XIV, trans. A. M. Hershman, Yale Judaica Ser. no. 3 [New Haven and London, 1949], pp. 53-54) lists the offences.

[9] Luke, xiii, 4. An unusual death implies the hand of Heaven: Num. xvi, 28-29.

[10] H. E. Goldin, *Hebrew Criminal Law and Procedure* (New York 1952), pp. 40-43. The fourteenth of the *Fourteen Principles of Maimonides*, in C. B. Chavel, *The Commandments* (London and New York 1967), II, p. 417.

[11] The incident occurred in 1753, and is mentioned by G. W. Wade in his sensible account of our passage at his *New Testament History* (London 1922), p. 500.

[12] See Josephus, *Bell. Jud.* IV, v, 3, 98-99, and elsewhere.

[13] The list of persons for whom no mourning ritual is permitted is set out fully in the most useful *Shemahot*, available with translation and notes, *The Tractate 'Mourning'*, trans. D. Zlotnick, Yale Judaica Ser. no. 17 (New Haven and London 1966), ch. 2.

[14] Mourners keep the head covered, with certain exceptions which do not concern us. The procession to and from the graveyard would normally be barefooted. On these customs, and modifications in the Diaspora (which do not concern us), see Zlotnick, op. cit. The biblical 'authority' is Ezk. xxiv, 23. 'Feet' as a metonymy for 'omen' is evidenced in Hebrew, and remains extremely common in Persian of all periods.

[15] Zlotnick, op. cit., pp. 34-35. Mishnah, *Sanhedrin* VI, 2 (Danby, op. cit., p. 390).

[16] For the principle that death at the hands of Heaven leaves the opportunity of sharing in the world to come see Maimonides, ubi cit., referred to by Goldin, ubi cit., and the *Tractate 'Mourning'* (cit. sup.), II, 7, with reference to Achan. G. W. H. Lampe is quite correct (*Peake's Commentary on the Bible*, ad loc.) in connecting Acts v, 2, with the story of Achan in Josh. vii. For rabbinical discussions of the ultimate fate of the men of Sodom and others punished by God see J. D. M. Derrett, *Law in the New Testament* (London 1970), pp. 88-89.

FURTHER ANNOTATIONS

p. [225], l. 14. The parallel with Lev. x.1-6 which is so striking (see below) has been ignored because the first church's knowledge of, and use of scripture have been under-evaluated.

p [225], l. 18. The episode is barely mentioned by Martin Hengel in his valuable chapter, 'The "love communism" of the primitive community', in his *Property and Riches in the Early Church* (London, 1974), 31.

p. [226], l. 41. The classical sources on Simon Magus (e.g. DB IV, 520-7) with K. Beyschlag, *Simon Magus* (Tübingen, 1974).

p. [227], l. 22. In this there was a plain difference from the Qumran community: Hengel, *op. cit.*, 32. J. Hadot in J. Préaux, ed., *Problèmes d'histoire du Christianisme* III (Brussels, 1973). To lie about one's wealth, however, was an anti-social act in Qumran too: 1 QS VI. 24f.

p. [227], l. 36. Sapphira certainly was entitled to her *ketubah*: Mishnah, 'Arakhin VI.1-2 (trans. Danby, 548-9)!

p. [228], l. 40. We must now turn to Lev. x.1-6. The sons of Aaron offered strange fire before the Lord which he had not commanded them. Fire came forth before the Lord and devoured them, and they died before the Lord. Moses ordered them to be carried out, and they were carried out of the camp in their *chitōns*. The immediate relatives of the dead were then ordered *not* to perform any of the traditional acts of mourning. Lest God be wroth with all the congregation. The entire house of Israel must mourn the Lord's 'burning', i.e. his reaction to the 'strange fire'. The Palestinian Targum says that the burial party took the dead out in their garments *with hooks of iron*. The same Targum says that the dead men's lives were burnt without their bodies' being destroyed. On the basis that the church is the new temple, taking the place of the abode of the *shekinah*, the innovation of Ananias and Sapphira could be likened to that of the unwise sons of Aaron. There is no need to imagine that this was thought up afterwards: the sudden deaths would remind Peter and others of the incident in Lev. x, on which s. Laughlin, *JBL* 95 (1976), 559.

p. [230], l. 17. According to the precept of Lev. x.6. See Philo, *Spec. Leg.* II.27.

p. [230], l. 30. S. *ad* [228], l. 40. S. also E. F. de Ward, *JJS*, 23-4 (1972-3).

p. [231], l. 9. One must remember that after the Temple was destroyed and the Day of Atonement and the scapegoat came to an end interest in the question which acts will atone for one who is guilty of transgressions leading to *karet* or 'death at the hands of heaven' (b. Yoma 19b) slackened. Views in orthodox Judaism are represented at Mishnah, Shev. I.6; Mekilta, Baḥod. VII (Lauterbach, ii, 250); b. Yoma 86a. Some think (J. C. Hurd, *Origins of 1 Cor.*, London, 1965, 135 n. 4) that the sickness and death at 1 Cor. xi.30 were instances of death at the hands of heaven.

p. [231], l. 26. An unaccompanied funeral is an atonement: j. Sanh. VI.9, fol. 23c; j. Ḥag. II.2, fol. 77a. Montefiore and Loewe, *Rabbinical Anthology*, 216.

p. [232], n. 4. See above, pp. 122-3.

p. [232], n. 14. Add 2 K. vi.32 and Is. lii.7.

INDEX OF SCRIPTURAL REFERENCES

(in the order of the Jerusalem Bible)

I. OLD TESTAMENT

Genesis

i.3, 9, 11, 14-15	160	xvi.25	95	xxii.9	200
i.24, 30	160	xvii.2-7	70	xxii.31	161
ii.18	172	xviii.11	160, 163	xxiv.22	38
v.1	66	xviii.13-27	144	xxv.18	161
vii.1	161	xviii.18	157	xxvi.5	151
ix.12, 15-17	68	xix.10	160	xxvi.9, 11-12	68
xiv.22	9	xix.17	139	xxvi.42	68
xv.1	49, 68, 70	xx.1	160		
xv.13-21	68	xx.19	160	Numbers	
xv.18ff.	64	xxi.1	39	iv.9, 16	139
xvi.4-14	68	xxiii.3	45	v.18	174
xviii.25	59	xxiii.20	94	vi.2	174
xxii.4	102	xxiii.23	161	xii.8	150
xxiv.3	155	xxiii.25	160	xiv.2, 27-37, 43-45	70
xxiv.65	174	xxiv.1-3	161	xv.31	200
xxvii.24	84	xxiv.11	140	xv.37-41	160
xxviii.20	155	xxiv.12-13	161	xv.39-40	30, 161
xxx.18	65	xxvii.20-21	139	xvi.28-29	200
xxxi.7	57	xxx.7	139	xvi.41-49	70
xxxi.40	54	xxxii.7	160	xx.5	81
xxxi.41-2	57	xxxii.12	45	xx.11	181
xxxii.24-32	153	xxxii.13	139	xxii.2	160
xxxvii.27	89	xxxii.34	161	xxii.20-23	161
xxxviii.14, 18	174	xxxiii.19	54	xxii.32, 35	161
xxxviii.24	29	xxxiv.2, 4	161	xxvii.8	161
xlii.18	102	xxxv.1	161	xxvii.20, 22-23	161
		xxxv.13-15	139	xxviii.9f.	94
		xxxix.37-38	139	xxxii.20-27	161

Exodus

ii.5	89	Leviticus		Deuteronomy	
ii.24	35	x.1-6	201	i.6	68
ii.25	68	xvi.16	181	i.17	45
iii.10	160	xviii.4-5	161	ii.4, 18	89
iv.19-20	160	xviii.19-31	161	ii.4-7, 26-30	98
iv.22	147	xix.2	45, 160	v	68
iv.27	160	xix.13	56, 75	v.4-5	160
vii.26	160	xix.15	45	v.13	160
viii.1-2	161	xix.17	39	v.22	160
xvi.2	70	xix.18	59	vi.1-6	160
xvi.3	151	xx.8	161	vi.2	160
xvi.7-12	70	xx.14	29	vi.10-12	81
xvi.8	151, 154	xx.22	161	vi.11-15	82
xvi.20	27	xxi.9	29	vi.13	160

INDEX OF NAMES AND TOPICS

(including references to Midrash Rabbah, Mishnah, and 'Test. XII Patr.', but not to the Talmuds)